# OXFORD SHAKESPEARE CONCORDANCES

OXFORD SHAKESPEARE CONCORDANCES

# TWELFTH NIGHT

A CONCORDANCE TO THE TEXT
OF THE FIRST FOLIO

OXFORD
AT THE CLARENDON PRESS
1969

*Oxford University Press, Ely House, London W. 1*

GLASGOW   NEW YORK   TORONTO   MELBOURNE   WELLINGTON
CAPE TOWN   SALISBURY   IBADAN   NAIROBI   LUSAKA   ADDIS ABABA
BOMBAY   CALCUTTA   MADRAS   KARACHI   LAHORE   DACCA
KUALA LUMPUR   SINGAPORE   HONG KONG   TOKYO   JOHANNESBURG

FILMSET BY COMPUTAPRINT LIMITED
AND PRINTED IN GREAT BRITAIN
AT THE UNIVERSITY PRESS, OXFORD
BY VIVIAN RIDLER
PRINTER TO THE UNIVERSITY

# GENERAL INTRODUCTION

In this series of Oxford Shakespeare Concordances, a separate
volume is devoted to each of the plays. The text for each concordance
is the one chosen as copy-text by Dr. Alice Walker for the Oxford
Old Spelling Shakespeare now in preparation.

Each concordance takes account of every word in the text, and re-
presents their occurrence by frequency counts, line numbers, and
reference lines, or a selection of these according to the interest of the
particular word. The number of words which have frequency counts
only has been kept as low as possible. The introduction to each
volume records the facsimile copy of the text from which the concordance was prepared, a table of Folio through line numbers and
Globe edition act and scene numbers, a list of the misprints corrected in the text, and an account of the order of printing, and the
proof-reading, abstracted from Professor Charlton Hinman's *The
Printing and Proof-Reading of the First Folio of Shakespeare* (Oxford,
1963).

The following notes on the main features of the concordances may
be helpful.[1]

## A. *The Text*

The most obvious misprints have been corrected, on conservative
principles, and have been listed for each play in the introduction to
the corresponding concordance. Wrong-fount letters have been
silently corrected.

Obvious irregularities on the part of the original compositor—
for example the anomalous absence of full stops after speech prefixes—have been normalized and noted. Colons, semicolons, exclama-
tion and interrogation marks after italicized words have been
modernized to roman fount after current practice, since this aspect of

---

[1] An account of the principles and methods by which the concordances were
edited appears in *Studies in Bibliography*, vol. 22, 1969.

compositorial practice would not normally be studied from a concordance. The spacing of words in the original printed texts, particu-
larly in 'justified' lines, is extremely variable; spacing has been
normalized on the basis of the compositor's practice as revealed in
the particular column or page.

For ease of reference, the contractions *S.*, *L.*, *M.*, and forms such
as *Mist.* and tildes, have been expanded when the compositor's own
preferred practice is clear, and the expansion has been noted in the
text. For M$^r$, the superior character has been lowered silently.
Superior characters like the circumflex in *baâ* and those in ẙ, ẙ, ẙ, and
ẘ, have been ignored. The reader should find little difficulty in dis-
tinguishing the original form of the pronominal contractions when
they are encountered in the text. They are listed under Y and W
respectively.

### B. *Arrangement of entries*

The words in the text are arranged alphabetically, with numerals
and & and &c listed at the end. Words starting with I and J, and U
and V, will be found together under I and V respectively. The reader
should note that the use of U for the medial V (and I for J) leads in
some cases to an unfamiliar order of entry. For example, ADUISED is
listed before ADULTERY. The reader will usually find the word he
wants if he starts his inquiry at the modern spelling, for when the old
spelling differs considerably from the modern spelling, a reference
such as 'ENFORCE *see* inforce' will direct the reader to the entry in the
concordance.

In hyphenated compounds where the hyphen is the second or third
character of the heading-word (as in A-BOORD), the hyphenated form
may be listed some distance from other occurrences of the same word
in un-hyphenated form. In significant cases, references are given to
alert the user.

Under the heading-word, the line numbers or lines of context are
in the order of the text. The heading-word is followed by a frequency
count of the words in short and long (that is, marked with an
asterisk) lines, and the reference lines. When a word has been treated
as one to have a frequency count only, or a list of the line numbers

and count, any further count which follows will refer to the reference lines listed under the same heading. Where there are two counts but no reference lines (as with AN), the first count refers to the speech prefix.

## C. *Special Forms*

(*a*) The following words have not been given context lines and line references but are dealt with only by the counting of their frequency:

A AM AND ARE AT BE BY HE I IN IS IT OF ON SHE THE THEY TO WAS WE WITH YOU

These forms occur so often in most texts that the reader can locate them more easily by examining the text of the play than he could by referring to an extensive listing in the concordance.

Homographs of these words (for example I = *ay*) have been listed in full and are given separate counts under the same heading-word.

(*b*) A larger number of words, consisting mainly of variant spellings, have been given line references as well as frequency counts.

These words are: ACTUS AN AR ART ATT AU BEE BEEING BEEN BEENE BEING BENE BIN BUT CAN CANST CE COULD COULDST DE DECIMA DES DID DIDD DIDDEST DIDDST DO DOE DOES DOEST DOETH DONE DOO DOOE DOOES DOOEST DOOING DOON DOONE DOOS DOOST DOOTH DOS DOST DOTH DU E EN EST ET ETC FINIS FOR FROM HA HAD HADST HAH HAS HAST HATH HAUE HEE HEEL HEELE HEL HELL HER HIM HIR HIS IE IF IL ILL ILLE INTO LA LE LES MA MAIE MAIEST MAIST MAY ME MEE MIGHT MIGHTEST MIGHTST MINE MOI MOY MY NE NO NOE NON NONA NOR NOT O OCTAUA OFF OH OR OU OUR OUT PRIMA PRIMUS QUARTA QUARTUS QUE QUINTA QUINTUS SCAENA SCENA SCOENA SECUNDA SECUNDUS SEPTIMA SEPTIMUS SEXTA SHAL SHALL SHALT SHEE SHOLD SHOLDE SHOLDST SHOULD SHOULDE SHOULDST SIR SO SOE TE TERTIA TERTIUS THAT THEE THEIR THEIRE THEM THEN THER THERE THESE THEYR THIS THOSE THOU THY TIS TU VN VNE VOS VOSTRE VOUS VS WAST WEE WER WERE WERT WHAT WHEN WHER WHERE WHICH WHO WHOM WHOME WHY WIL WILL WILT WILTE WOLD WOLDE WOLDST WOULD WOULDE WOULDEST WOULDST YE YEE YF YOUE YOUR YT & &c 1 2 3 4.

Homographs of words on this list (e.g. *bee* = n.) have been listed in full, and also have separate counts.

(*c*) All speech prefixes, other than *All.*, *Both.*, and those which represent the names of actors, have been treated as count-only words. In some cases, however, where a speech prefix corresponds to a form already on the count-only list (e.g. *Is.*), a full entry has been given. In some other cases, when two counts are given for the same heading-word for no apparent reason, the count which does not correspond to the following full references or to the list of line references is that of the speech prefix form (for example AN in *The Tempest*).

(*d*) Hyphenated compounds such as *all-building-law* have been listed under the full form, and also under each main constituent after the first. In this example there are entries under ALL-BUILDING-LAW, BUILDING, and LAW. When, however, one of the constituents of the compound is a word on the count- or location-only list ((*a*) or (*b*) above), it is dealt with in whichever of these two lists applies. References such as 'AT *see also* bemock't-at-stabs' are given to assist the reader in such cases.

Simple or non-hyphenated compounds such as *o'th'King* have been listed only under the constituent parts—in this example under OTH and KING.

(*e*) 'Justified' lines where the spellings *may* have been affected by the compositor's need to fit the text to his measure are distinguished by an asterisk at the beginning of the reference line. If only location is being given, the asterisk occurs before the line reference. If only frequency counts are being given, the number *after* the asterisk records the frequency of forms occurring in 'justified' lines. Lines which do not extend to the full width of the compositor's measure have not been distinguished as 'justified' lines, even though in many cases the shorter line may have affected the spelling.

## D. *Line Numbers*

The lines in each text have been numbered from the first *Actus Primus* or stage direction and thereafter in normal reading order, including all stage directions and act and scene divisions. Each typographical line has been counted as a unit when it contains matter for inclusion in the concordance. Catchwords are not included in the count. The only general exception is that turn-overs are regarded as belonging to their base-lines; where a turn-over occurs on a line by itself, it has been reckoned as part of the base-line, and the line containing only the turn-over has not been counted as a separate line. Turn-overs may readily be distinguished by vertical stroke and single bracket after the last word of the base-line; for example *brought with* | (*child,*.

When two or more lines have been joined in order to provide a fuller context, the line-endings are indicated by a vertical stroke |, and the line reference applies to that part of the line before the vertical stroke. For the true line-numbers of words in the following part of the context line, the stated line-number should be increased by one each time a vertical stroke occurs, save when the next word is a turn-over.

The numbering of the quarto texts has been fitted to that of the corresponding Folio texts; lines in the Quarto which do not occur in the Folio are prefixed by +. The line references are similarly specified. The line references of these concordances therefore provide a consistent permanent numbering of each typographical line of text, based on the First Folio.

## PROGRAM CHANGES

Preparation of concordances to the first few texts, and the especial complexity of *Wiv.*, have enabled some improvements to be made to the main concordance program. For texts other than *Tmp.*, *TGV*, *MM*, and *Err.*, the concordances have been prepared with the improved program.

Speech-prefixes now have separate entries under the appropriate heading-word and follow any other entry under the same heading-word. Entries under AN in *Wiv.*, AND and TO in *TN*, and AD in *AYL* offer examples. This alteration provides a clearer record of the total number of occurrences of words which occur both as speech-prefixes and also as forms on the 'count only' or 'locations only' lists.

Another modification supplies a more precise reference to the location of words such as BEENE for which line numbers but no full lines are given. When a 'location only' word is encountered to the right of the 'end-of-line' bar (which shows that lines of text have been joined together in order to provide a sufficient context), the line number is now adjusted to supply the exact reference. In the concordances to the texts listed above, users will find that in some instances the particular occurrence of a 'location only' word which they wish to consult in the text is to be found in the line after the one specified in the concordance; this depends on whether lines have been joined in the computer-readable version of the text from which the concordance was made. It is not expected that readers will be seriously inconvenienced by this. Should a concordance to the First Folio be published, it will, of course, incorporate all improvements.

# TWELFTH NIGHT

The copy for the concordance to *TN* was the Lee facsimile of the First Folio (Oxford, 1902) which shows, according to Professor Charlton Hinman's *Printing and Proof-Reading* (Oxford, 1963. V. 1, p. 263) the corrected states of Z1, Z3ᵛ, and Z5; none of the variants is significant for the text. He gives the following order of printing (v. 2, p. 515) for this part of the Folio:

By By [Here a jump back to quire Y, but no delay is in evidence.]  By By
b1:6ᵛ                                                              Y3ᵛ:4

By By   By By   By By   By By   By By   By By   By By   By By
Y3:4ᵛ   Y2ᵛ:5  Y2:5ᵛ   Y1:6ᵛ   Y1ᵛ:6   Z3ᵛ:4   Z3:4ᵛ   Z2ᵛ:5

By By   By      By By [Here a jump to quire c.]
Z2:5ᵛ   Z1:[6ᵛ] Z1ᵛ:6

## TABLE OF LINE AND ACT/SCENE NUMBERS

| Page | Col. | Comp. | F line nos. | Globe act/scene nos. |
|------|------|-------|-------------|----------------------|
| Y2 | a | B | 1–48 | 1.1.1–1.1.41 |
|    | b | B | 49–93 | 1.2.42 |
| Y2ᵛ | a | B | 94–154 | 1.3.40 |
|    | b | B | 155–220 | 1.3.118 |
| Y3 | a | B | 221–80 | 1.4.29 |
|    | b | B | 281–342 | 1.5.56 |
| Y3ᵛ | a | B | 343–409 | 1.5.123 |
|    | b | B | 410–75 | 1.5.193 |
| Y4 | a | B | 476–541 | 1.5.268 |
|    | b | B | 542–607 | 1.5.328 |
| Y4ᵛ | a | B | 608–64 | 2.2.7 |
|    | b | B | 665–725 | 2.3.26 |
| Y5 | a | B | 726–91 | 2.3.99 |
|    | b | B | 792–857 | 2.3.179 |
| Y5ᵛ | a | B | 858–917 | 2.4.30 |
|    | b | B | 918–81 | 2.4.96 |
| Y6 | a | B | 982–1043 | 2.5.31 |
|    | b | B | 1044–109 | 2.5.106 |
| Y6ᵛ | a | B | 1110–75 | 2.5.186 |
|    | b | B | 1176–235 | 3.1.26 |
| Z1 | a | B | 1236–301 | 3.1.99 |
|    | b | B | 1302–67 | 3.1.163 |
| Z1ᵛ | a | B | 1368–426 | 3.2.51 |
|    | b | B | 1427–84 | 3.3.17 |

| Page | Col. | Comp. | F line nos. | Globe act/scene nos. |
|------|------|-------|-------------|----------------------|
| Z2 | a | B | 1485–543 | 3.4.22 |
|    | b | B | 1544–606 | 3.4.92 |
| Z2ᵛ | a | B | 1607–72 | 3.4.165 |
|     | b | B | 1673–737 | 3.4.238 |
| Z3 | a | B | 1738–803 | 3.4.314 |
|    | h | B | 1804–69 | 3.4.385 |
| Z3ᵛ | a | B | 1870–930 | 4.1.4 |
|     | b | B | 1931–90 | 4.2.7 |
| Z4 | a | B | 1991–2056 | 4.2.77 |
|    | b | B | 2057–117 | 4.3.3 |
| Z4ᵛ | a | B | 2118–75 | 5.1.13 |
|     | b | B | 2176–240 | 5.1.91 |
| Z5 | a | B | 2241–306 | 5.1.149 |
|    | b | B | 2307–70 | 5.1.214 |
| Z5ᵛ | a | B | 2371–436 | 5.1.277 |
|     | b | B | 2437–502 | 5.1.340 |
| Z6 | a | B | 2503–43 | 5.1.380 |
|    | b | B | 2544–80 (Finis) | 5.1.417 |

Misprints, etc. corrected in the text are:

| Page | Line | Misprint | Page | Line | Misprint |
|------|------|----------|------|------|----------|
| Y2 | 64 | sttong | | 1312 | y'are |
|    | 78 | *Vio,* | | 1314 | your |
| Y2ᵛ | 211 | wlll | | 1349 | your |
|     | 212 | we | | 1353 | you'l |
|     | 217 | Connt | Z1ᵛ | 1474 | rrauell, |
|     | 217 | her, | Z2 | 1498 | Th∧offence |
|     | 220 | swear∧t. | | 1537 | metry |
| Y3 | 263 | rhe | | 1576 | ler |
| Y3ᵛ | 383 | guitlesse, | | 1583 | look∧d |
|     | 475 | I / (I | | 1586 | *exit* |
| Y4 | 548 | *Vio,* | Z2ᵛ | 1690 | Yon |
| Y4ᵛ | 629 | Heanens | | 1690 | fot't: |
|     | 725 | *Quenbus:* | Z3 | 1836 | *EnterOfficers.* |
| Y5 | 775 | *To,* | | 1844 | 2∧*Off.* |
|    | 829 | Malnolio, | | 1856 | 2∧*Off.* |
| Y6 | 1015 | *exeunt* | Z3ᵛ | 1896 | ttue, |
|    | 1102 | het | Z4 | 2104 | goue. |
| Y6ᵛ | 1112 | alter∧d: | Z4ᵛ | 2203 | yet |
|     | 1159 | thce | Z5 | 2341 | homc. |
|     | 1164 | tht | | 2344 | incardinatc. |
|     | 1166 | pollticke | | 2350 | you |
|     | 1212 | *secnndus* | | 2363 | panyn: |
|     | 1223 | Chureh | Z5ᵛ | 2438 | ftom |
| Z1 | 1271 | *exit* | | 2492 | your |
|    | 1307 | seruice■ | Z6 | 2544 | Lotd |

*December, 1968*        T. H. H.

# TWELFTH NIGHT

A = 194*205, 1*4
*a nights: your Cosin, my Lady, takes great exceptions | to your ill
houres.                                                                     123
*To. Approach Sir *Andrew*: not to bee a bedde after                       701
*a hungrie, to challenge him the field, and then to breake                 823
*Fab*. What dish a poyson has she drest him?                              1123
*that suffers vnder probation: *A*. should follow, but *O*. | does.       1138
ABANDOND = 1
If she be so abandon'd to her sorrow                                       269
ABATEMENT = 1
But falles into abatement, and low price                                    17
ABEDDE *see* bedde
ABHORRES = 1*1
*in yellow stockings, and 'tis a colour she abhorres, and                 1203
That heart which now abhorres, to like his loue. *Exeunt*                 1380
ABIDE *see* bide
ABILITY = 1
Out of my leane and low ability | Ile lend you something: my hauing is
not much,                                                                 1861
ABIURD = 1
(They say) she hath abiur'd the sight | And company of men.                 90
ABOUE = 3*3
*To. Shee'l none o'th Count, she'l not match aboue hir                     218
*One draught aboue heate, makes him a foole, the second | maddes
him, and a third drownes him.                                             426
What is your Parentage? | *Vio*. Aboue my fortunes, yet my state is well:   572
*Ol*. What is your Parentage? | Aboue my fortunes, yet my state is well;   585
*I am aboue thee, but be not affraid of greatnesse: Some                  1150
If I do feigne, you witnesses aboue | Punish my life, for tainting of my
loue.                                                                     2294
ABOUT = 4*6
*dam'd colour'd stocke. Shall we sit about some Reuels?                     243
*Oliuiaes* Father tooke much delight in. He is about the | house.           896
*Vio*. About your yeeres my Lord.                                          916
o'fauour with my Lady, about a Beare-baiting heere.                       1024
*Mal*. Calling my Officers about me, in my branch'd                       1063
*Clo*. Foolery sir, does walke about the Orbe like the                    1251
*set 'em downe, go about it. Let there bee gaulle e-|nough                 1427
*in thy inke, though thou write with a Goose-pen, | no matter: about it.  1428

ABOUT *cont.*
*were best to haue some guard about you, if hee                    1532
*starke naked: for meddle you must that's certain, or for- | sweare to
weare iron about you.                                              1769
ABSENCE = 1
of thy excuse: my Lady will hang thee for thy absence.            299
ABSENT = *1
*Ma*. Yet you will be hang'd for being so long absent,            311
ABUSD = 1*2
*man thus abus'd, I am no more madde then you are,                2033
*Mall*. Foole, there was neuer man so notoriouslie a- | bus'd:    2072
*Ol*. He hath bene most notoriously abus'd.                       2549
ABUSE = 1
A Ring in chace of you. So did I abuse | My selfe, my seruant, and I
feare me you:                                                     1327
ABUSED = *1
*friends I am abused: so that conclusions to be as kisses, if     2173
ACCENT = *1
*accent sharpely twang'd off, giues manhoode more                1697
ACCESSE = 1
Be not deni'de accesse, stand at her doores,                      265
ACCIDENT = 1
Yet doth this accident and flood of Fortune,                      2125
ACCOMPLISHD = *1
*Most excellent accomplish'd Lady, the heauens raine O- | dours on you. 1298
ACCORDING = 1
According to my birth, what do you say?                           2146
ACCOST = 4*2
*Tob*. Accost Sir *Andrew*, accost.                               165
*Ma*. Good Mistris accost, I desire better acquaintance | *Ma*. My name
is *Mary* sir.                                                    168
*And*. Good mistris *Mary*, accost.                               170
*To*, You mistake knight: Accost, is front her, boord | her, woe her,
assayle her.                                                      171
company. Is that the meaning of Accost? | *Ma*. Far you well
Gentlemen.                                                        174
ACCOSTED = *1
*you should then haue accosted her, and with some excel- | lent   1401
ACCOUNTED = *1
*me, was yet of many accounted beautiful: but thogh               635
ACQUAINTANCE = 2*2
I saw him hold acquaintance with the waues, | So long as I could see. 66
*Ma*. Good Mistris accost, I desire better acquaintance | *Ma*. My name
is *Mary* sir.                                                    168
*Toby*, I will wash off grosse acquaintance, I will be point      1167
Taught him to face me out of his acquaintance,                    2240
ACQUIT = 1
*Vio*. I will acquit you.                                         1733
ACROSSE *see* a-crosse
ACHIEUES *see* atcheeues
ACT = 1
It shall become thee well to act my woes:                         276
ACTE = 2
That they may fairely note this acte of mine. *Exeunt*. | *Finis Actus
Quartus*.                                                         2150
He finished indeed his mortall acte                               2413

ACTING = 1
And acting this in an obedient hope,                                    2510
ACTION = 1*1
*with him: Ile haue an action of Battery against him, if                1950
Hath my Maides garments: he vpon some Action                            2442
ACTIONS = 1
Thy tongue, thy face, thy limbes, actions, and spirit,                  588
ACTUS *l.*1  610 611 1212 1213 1917 2151 2152 = 8
ADDE = 1*1
*Ma. They that adde moreour, hee's drunke nightly | in your company.    152
His life I gaue him, and did thereto adde                               2232
ADDICTED = *1
*being addicted to a melancholly, as shee is, that it                   1206
ADDRESSE = 1
Therefore good youth, addresse thy gate vnto her,                       264
ADDS = *1
*selfe. She adds moreouer, that you should put your Lord                664
ADHERES = *1
*degree, but Fellow. Why euery thing adheres togither,                  1600
ADIEU = 2
And so adieu good Madam, neuer more,                                    1377
Adieu good man diuell. *Exit*                                           2112
ADMIRABLE = 2
*Clo.* Beshrew me, the knights in admirable fooling.                    779
*An.* O twill be admirable.                                             863
ADMIRE = *1
*To. Wonder not, nor admire not in thy minde why I doe call*            1672
ADMIT = 2
Because she will admit no kinde of suite, | No, not the Dukes.          97
As it is spoke, she neuer will admit me.                                270
ADMITTED = 1
*Val.* So please my Lord, I might not be admitted,                      30
ADORATIONS = 1
*Ol.* How does he loue me? | *Vio.* With adorations, fertill teares,    547
ADORD = 1
*An.* I was ador'd once too.                                            873
ADORE = 1*2
But come what may, I do adore thee so,                                  654
*Mal. I may command where I adore, but silence like a Lu-|cresse knife:* 1115
*Mal. I may command, where I adore*: Why shee may                       1125
ADORES = *1
*To.* She's a beagle true bred, and one that adores me: | what o'that?  871
ADUANCD = 1*1
*Cesario*, you are like to be much aduanc'd, he hath known              252
Cocke of him, how he iets vnder his aduanc'd plumes.                    1048
ADUANTAGE = *1
*Lady: it shall aduantage thee more, then euer the bea-|ring of Letter
did.                                                                    2096
ADUERSE = 1
Into the danger of this aduerse Towne,                                  2236
ADUISE = 1
*Clo.* Aduise you what you say: the Minister is heere.                  2079
ADUISES = *1
*thus aduises thee, that sighes for thee. Remember who                 1158
AEGYPTIANS = 1
*but ignorance, in which thou art more puzel'd then the | Aegyptians in
their fogge.                                                            2029

3

AFFAIRES = *1
*in his affaires, vnlesse it bee to report your Lords taking | of this:
recciue it so. 667
AFFAYRE = 1
For this affayre: some foure or fiue attend him, 287
AFFAYRES = 1
Take, and giue backe affayres, and their dispatch, 2132
AFFECT = *1
*told me she did affect me, and I haue heard her self come 1041
AFFECTION = 1
Or thy affection cannot hold the bent: 926
AFFECTIOND = *1
*constantly but a time-pleaser, an affection'd Asse, that 841
AFFECTIONS = 1
Hath kill'd the flocke of all affections else 42
AFFIRMATIUES = *1
*your foure negatiues make your two affirmatiues, why 2174
AFFRAID = 1*2
*I am aboue thee, but be not affraid of greatnesse: Some 1150
Be not affraid good youth, I will not haue you, 1347
*I am affraid this great lubber the World will proue a 1931
AFRAID = 1
Mal. Be not afraid of greatnesse: 'twas well writ. 1561
AFTER = 10*5
Assure your selfe, after our ship did split, 59
*o'my Coz: for he's in the third degree of drinke: hee's | drown'd: go
looke after him. 429
Ol. Run after that same peeuish Messenger 598
*To. Approach Sir Andrew: not to bee a bedde after 701
*To be vp after midnight, and to go to bed then is early: 707
*so that to go to bed after midnight, is to goe to bed be- | times. 708
*Mal. And then to haue the humor of state: and after 1068
After the last enchantment you did heare, 1326
Ol. I haue sent after him, he sayes hee'l come: 1522
*be look'd too: Fellow? not Maluolio, nor after my 1599
till he take leaue, and presently after him. 1715
And. Slid Ile after him againe, and beate him. 1912
*that giue fooles money, get themselues a good re- | port, after
foureteene yeares purchase. 1939
It is as fat and fulsome to mine eare | As howling after Musicke. 2264
Ol. Where goes Cesario? | Vio. After him I loue, 2290
AGAIN = *1
*And. Now sir, haue I met you again: ther's for you. 1942
AGAINE = 10*3
*flower; The Lady bad take away the foole, therefore I | say againe,
take her away. 344
Vnlesse (perchance) you come to me againe, 577
drowne her remembrance againe with more. 640
*thing more, that you be neuer so hardie to come againe 666
*To. To anger him wee'l haue the Beare againe, and 1025
I bad you neuer speake againe of him; 1320
Ol. Yet come againe: for thou perhaps mayst moue 1379
And I beseech you come againe to morrow. 1727
Ol. Well, come againe to morrow: far-thee-well, 1734
*Vio. I will returne againe into the house, and desire 1759
And. Slid Ile after him againe, and beate him. 1912
Clo. I am gone sir, and anon sir, | Ile be with you againe: 2105

AGAINE *cont.*
*\*Fab.* This is to giue a dogge, and in recompence desire | my dogge
againe.     2158
AGAINST *see also* 'gainst = 6\*2
*\*speake with you. What is to be said to him Ladie, hee's | fortified
against any deniall.     439
*\*Fab.* I know the knight is incenst against you, euen to     1778
*Vio.* I do assure you tis against my will.     1828
*\*with him: Ile haue an action of Battery against him, if     1950
Against thy peace. Go with me to my house,     1971
So much against the mettle of your sex,     2488
Set this deuice against *Maluolio* heere,     2531
We had conceiu'd against him. *Maria* writ     2533
AGE = 1\*1
And dallies with the innocence of loue, | Like the old age.     937
*\*Clo.* You haue said sir: To see this age: A sentence is     1225
AGEN = 3\*2
That straine agen, it had a dying fall:     8
*To.* And thou let part so Sir *Andrew*, would thou | mightst neuer draw
sword agen.     176
*\*draw sword agen: Faire Lady, doe you thinke you haue | fooles in
hand?     179
*Ol.* Why then me thinkes 'tis time to smile agen:     1341
*\*Clo.* Marry sir, lullaby to your bountie till I come a- | gen.     2195
AGO = 4
For but a month ago I went from hence,     81
He might haue tooke his answer long ago.     556
We made each other, but so late ago.     2379
*A great while ago the world begon*, | *hey ho, &c.*     2576
AGONE = \*1
*\*Clo.* O he's drunke sir *Toby* an houre agone: his eyes | were set at eight
i'th morning.     2361
AGUEFACE = 1
*\*parish top. What wench? *Castiliano vulgo*: for here coms | Sir *Andrew
Agueface*.     158
AGUE-CHEEKE = 2\*1
*To.* Who, Sir *Andrew Ague-cheeke*? | *Ma.* I he.     135
*\*and so looke to thy selfe. Thy friend as thou vsest him, & thy | sworne
enemie*, Andrew Ague-cheeke.     1686
*\*set vpon *Ague-cheeke* a notable report of valor, and driue     1708
AH = 3
*Mal.* To be Count *Maluolio*. | *To.* Ah Rogue.     1051
*Mal.* Ah ha, does she so? | *\*To.* Go too, go too: peace, peace, wee must
deale     1617
cries ah ha, to the diuell:     2110
AHUNGRIE *see* hungrie
AIDE *see* ayde
AIRE *see also* ayre = 1
And make the babling Gossip of the aire,     567
AIRES *see* ayres
ALAS = 12\*2
*\*Vio.* Alas, I tooke great paines to studie it, and 'tis | Poeticall.     489
breach of the sea, was my sister drown'd. | *Ant.* Alas the day.     632
Alas, O frailtie is the cause, not wee,     688
As I am woman (now alas the day)     695
*Vio.* And so they are: alas, that they are so:     929
Alas, their loue may be call'd appetite,     985

ALAS *cont.*
*Clo.* Alas why is she so? | *Mal.* Foole, I say.                                    2062
*Clo.* Alas sir, how fell you besides your fiue witts?                            2071
*\*Clo.* Alas sir be patient. What say you sir, I am shent | for speaking to
you.                                                                              2088
*Ol.* Alas, it is the basenesse of thy feare,                                    2306
and yet alas, now I remember me,                                                  2446
*Ol.* Alas *Maluolio*, this is not my writing,                                   2515
*Ol.* Alas poore Foole, how haue they baffel'd thee?                             2540
*But when I came alas to wine,* | *with hey ho, &c.*                             2568
ALBEIT = 1
Albeit the quality of the time, and quarrell                                     1499
ALE = 2
*is no Whip-stocke. My Lady has a white hand, and the | Mermidons
are no bottle-ale houses.                                                         728
Shall be no more Cakes and Ale?                                                   812
ALEHOUSE = *1
*like Tinkers at this time of night? Do yee make an Ale- | house                 788
ALIUE = 1
Lady, you are the cruell'st shee aliue,                                           533
ALL = 35*14
With eye-offending brine: all this to season                                      36
Hath kill'd the flocke of all affections else                                     42
These soueraigne thrones, are all supply'd and fill'd                             44
*\*Ma.* I, but hee'l haue but a yeare in all these ducates:                       140
without booke, & hath all the good gifts of nature.                              144
Thou knowst no lesse, but all: I haue vnclasp'd                                  262
*Du.* Be clamorous, and leape all ciuill bounds,                                 271
And all is semblatiue a womans part.                                             285
All if you will: for I my selfe am best                                          288
me faith say I. Well, it's all one. *Exit*                                       423
*Vio.* Excellently done, if God did all.                                         528
*Ant.* The gentlenesse of all the gods go with thee:                             651
*\*An.* Excellent: Why this is the best fooling, when | all is done. Now a
song.                                                                             730
*with excellencies, that it is his grounds of faith, that all                    844
For such as I am, all true Louers are,                                           902
Vnstaid and skittish in all motions else,                                        903
*\*My shrowd of white, stuck all with Ew, O prepare it.*                         946
*Du.* Let all the rest giue place: Once more *Cesario*,                          966
But mine is all as hungry as the Sea,                                            988
*Vio.* I am all the daughters of my Fathers house,                             1010
And all the brothers too: and yet I know not.                                  1011
*\*Mar.* Get ye all three into the box tree: *Maluolio*'s                        1032
*\*Mal.* 'Tis but Fortune, all is fortune. *Maria* once                          1040
*Fab.* This winnes him, Liuer and all.                                          1109
*\*Fab.* Sowter will cry vpon't for all this, though it bee | as ranke as a
Fox.                                                                            1132
*\*And.* Odours, pregnant, and vouchsafed: Ile get 'em | all three already.     1303
And baited it with all th'vnmuzled thoughts                                     1333
I loue thee so, that maugre all thy pride,                                      1367
*\*To.* Neuer trust me then: and by all meanes stirre on                        1438
And not all loue to see you (though so much                                     1472
Sonnet is: Please one, and please all.                                         1545
*\*To.* Which way is hee in the name of sanctity. If all                        1607
*\*Mal.* Go hang your selues all: you are ydle shallowe                          1645
*a firago: I had a passe with him, rapier, scabberd, and all:                   1793

6

ALL *cont.*
  Are all the people mad? 1944
  *Clo.* Nay I am for all waters. 2048
  *darkenesse, send Ministers to me, Asses, and doe all they 2077
  So farre exceed all instance, all discourse, 2126
  *saying is, the third payes for all: the triplex sir, is a good 2188
  All his in dedication. For his sake, 2234
  More by all mores, then ere I shall loue wife. 2293
  And all the Ceremonie of this compact | Seal'd in my function, by my
    testimony: 2322
  *To.* That's all one, has hurt me, and there's th'end on't: 2359
  All the occurrence of my fortune since 2423
  *Vio.* And all those sayings, will I ouer sweare, 2435
  And all those swearings keepe as true in soule, 2436
  *all one: By the Lord Foole, I am not mad: but do you re-|member, 2544
  *But that's all one, our Play is done,* 2578
ALLAY = *1
  *the gift of a Coward, to allay the gust he hath in quarrel-|ling, 147
ALLIANCE = 1
  One day shall crowne th'alliance on't, so please you, 2484
ALLOW = 1*2
  That will allow me very worth his seruice. 111
  *thou shalt hold th'opinion of *Pythagoras*, ere I will allow 2043
  *Ladyship will haue it as it ought to bee, you must allow | *Vox.* 2462
ALLOWD = *2
  *in an allow'd foole, though he do nothing but rayle; 386
  *it in. I heard you were sawcy at my gates, & allowd your 492
ALLYD = *1
  *she's nothing ally'd to your disorders. If you can 795
ALMOST = 1*3
  *Ma.* He hath indeed, almost naturall: for besides that 145
  *when tis almost an Apple: Tis with him in standing wa-|ter, 453
  *Clo.* His eyes do shew his dayes are almost done. | *Mal.* Is't euen so? 801
  *Vio.* By my troth Ile tell thee, I am almost sicke for 1259
ALONE = 5*5
  That it alone, is high fantasticall. 19
  *Vio.* It alone concernes your eare: I bring no ouer-|ture 503
  *Ol.* Giue vs the place alone, 512
  *that I may beare my euils alone. It were a bad recom-|pence 618
  *much out of quiet. For Monsieur Maluolio, let me alone 829
  Shall mistris be of it, saue I alone. 1376
  *gently with him: Let me alone. How do you *Maluolio?* 1619
  you not see you moue him? Let me alone with him. 1632
  *And.* Nay let me alone for swearing. *Exit* 1700
  *An.* Nay let him alone, Ile go another way to worke 1949
ALONG = *1
  *with her, and bring her along with you, it may awake my | bounty
  further. 2193
ALOOFE = 1
  *Du.* Stand you a-while aloofe. *Cesario,* 261
ALOUD = 1
  *To.* Oh peace, and the spirit of humors intimate rea-|ding aloud to
  him. 1099
ALPHABETICALL = *1
  *in this, and the end: What should that Alphabeticall po-|sition 1128
ALREADY = 2*3
  you but three dayes, and already you are no stranger. 253

ALREADY *cont.*

| | |
|---|---|
| *Looke you now, he's out of his gard already: vnles you | 378 |
| *drown'd already sir with salt water, though I seeme to | 639 |
| *And. Odours, pregnant, and vouchsafed: Ile get 'em \| all three already. | 1303 |
| *My Neece is already in the beleefe that he's mad: we may | 1658 |

ALSO = 1

| | |
|---|---|
| Who shortly also dide: for whose deere loue | 89 |

ALTARS = 1

| | |
|---|---|
| To whose ingrate, and vnauspicious Altars | 2269 |

ALTER = *1

| | |
|---|---|
| *touch Fortunes fingers. Farewell, Shee that would alter | 1163 |

ALTERD = 1*1

| | |
|---|---|
| *beene pleas'd, would we had so ended. But you sir, al-\|ter'd | 630 |
| The numbers alter'd: No man must know, | 1112 |

ALTHOUGH = *1

| | |
|---|---|
| *Lyes, as will lye in thy sheete of paper, although the | 1425 |

ALTOGETHER = 1

| | |
|---|---|
| *strangest minde i'th world: I delight in Maskes and Re-\|uels | |
| sometimes altogether. | 222 |

ALWAYES = *1

| | |
|---|---|
| *and their intent euerie where, for that's it, that alwayes | 964 |

AM = 38*49

AMAZD = 2

| | |
|---|---|
| Then what befals my selfe: you stand amaz'd, \| But be of comfort. | 1854 |
| *Du.* Be not amaz'd, right noble is his blood: | 2430 |

AMEN = 1

| | |
|---|---|
| *Who I sir, not I sir. God buy you good sir Topas: Mar-\|ry Amen. I | |
| will sir, I will. | 2085 |

AMEND = 1*1

| | |
|---|---|
| *wil amend: for giue the dry foole drink, then is the foole | 336 |
| *To.* What, what? \| *Mal.* You must amend your drunkennesse. \| *To.* Out | |
| scab. | 1087 |

AMENDS = *1

| | |
|---|---|
| *that transgresses, is but patcht with sinne, and sin that a-\|mends, | 340 |

AMISSE = *1

| | |
|---|---|
| *thou'st him some thrice, it shall not be amisse, and as ma-\|ny | 1424 |

AMONG = *1

| | |
|---|---|
| *'tis thought among the prudent, he would quickely \| haue the gift of a | |
| graue. | 148 |

AMPLE = 1

| | |
|---|---|
| Shall not behold her face at ample view: | 33 |

AN *l.*108 *120 *188 *198 209 227 *377 *386 *453 593 *629 *706 *720
*788 *841 861 918 1046 *1074 1082 1393 *1407 *1439 1517 1621 1651
1835 1885 *1938 *1950 *1959 *1993 *2170 *2171 2244 *2361 *2369 2388
2510 = 17*22

AN = 25*18

ANATOMY = 1

| | |
|---|---|
| foote of a flea, Ile eate the rest of th'anatomy. | 1442 |

AND *see also* &. = 287*204, 7*11

| | |
|---|---|
| *these boots too: and they be not, let them hang them-\|selues in their | |
| owne straps. | 130 |
| *To.* And thou let part so Sir *Andrew*, would thou \| mightst neuer draw | |
| sword agen. | 176 |
| *And.* And you part so mistris, I would I might neuer | 178 |
| *An.* And I thought that, I'de forsweare it. Ile ride \| home to morrow sir | |
| *Toby.* | 202 |
| *To.* Let him be the diuell and he will, I care not: giue | 422 |

AND *cont.*
What is decreed, must be: and be this so. | *Finis, Actus primus.*                                      609
*\*And.* And you loue me, let's doo't: I am dogge at a | Catch.                                         761
*To. Shall I bid him go.* | *Clo. What and if you do?*                                                 806
*And in sad cypresse let me be laide.*                                                                 943
*An.* And we do not, it is pittie of our liues.                                                       1028
*\*Fa.* I, and you had any eye behinde you, you might                                                 1143
*\*Vio.* Nay, and thou passe vpon me, Ile no more with | thee. Hold
there's expences for thee.                                                                            1255
*\*Mar.* La you, and you speake ill of the diuell, how                                                1623
*\*An.* Plague on't, and I thought he had beene valiant,                                              1801
*And.* And I do not. | *Fab.* Come, let's see the euent.                                              1914
*Ol.* How now, art thou mad? | *\*Clo.* No Madam, I do but reade
madnesse: and your                                                                                    2460
*\*and some haue greatnesse throwne vpon them. I                                                      2542
*Clowne sings.* | *When that I was and a little tine boy,*                                            2559
AND = 23\*23
*ANDREW see also An., And.* = 19\*6
*To.* Who, Sir *Andrew Ague-cheeke?* | *Ma.* I he.                                                     135
*\*parish top.* What wench? *Castiliano vulgo*: for here coms | Sir *Andrew
Agueface.*                                                                                             158
*Enter Sir Andrew.*                                                                                    160
*And.* Sir *Toby Belch.* How now sir *Toby Belch?* | *To.* Sweet sir *Andrew.*                         161
*Tob.* Accost Sir *Andrew,* accost.                                                                    165
*To.* And thou let part so Sir *Andrew,* would thou | mightst neuer draw
sword agen.                                                                                            176
*Enter Sir Toby, and Sir Andrew.*                                                                      700
*\*To.* Approach Sir *Andrew*: not to bee a bedde after                                                701
*Enter Sir Toby, Sir Andrew, and Fabian.*                                                            1017
*\*we will foole him blacke and blew, shall we not sir *An-|drew?*                                    1026
*And.* That's mee I warrant you. | *Mal.* One sir *Andrew.*                                           1094
*Enter Sir Toby and Andrew.*                                                                          1281
*Enter Sir Toby, Sir Andrew, and Fabian.*                                                            1382
*\*Fab.* You must needes yeelde your reason, Sir *An-|drew?*                                          1385
*Fab.* There is no way but this sir *Andrew.*                                                         1419
*To.* Wee'l call thee at the Cubiculo: Go. | *Exit Sir Andrew.*                                       1431
*\*cannot hale them together. For *Andrew,* if he were open'd                                         1440
*Enter Sir Andrew.*                                                                                   1663
*\*and so looke to thy selfe. Thy friend as thou vsest him, & thy | sworne
enemie,* Andrew Ague-cheeke.                                                                          1686
*\*To.* Go sir *Andrew*: scout mee for him at the corner                                              1693
*Enter Toby and Andrew.*                                                                              1791
*\*To.* Come sir *Andrew,* there's no remedie, the Gen-|tleman                                        1821
*Enter Andrew, Toby, and Fabian.*                                                                     1941
*Enter Sir Andrew.*                                                                                   2335
*Ol.* Who has done this sir *Andrew?*                                                                 2342
ANDT = \*2
*\*Clo.* Wit, and't be thy will, put me into good fooling:                                             326
*\*And.* And't be any way, it must be with Valour, for                                               1410
ANGER = 1\*1
*\*To.* To anger him wee'l haue the Beare againe, and                                                 1025
In the contempt and anger of his lip,                                                                1362
ANIE = \*1
*\*fatall opposite that you could possibly haue found in anie                                         1785
ANNE = \*1
*\*Clo.* Yes by S.(aint) Anne, and Ginger shall bee hotte y'th | mouth
too.                                                                                                   813

9

ANON = 4
*To*. Ile be with you anon.                                                              1838
*Clo*. I am gone sir, and anon sir, | Ile be with you againe:                            2105
*you say sir, let your bounty take a nappe, I will awake it | anon. *Exit*                2198
But more of that anon. Take him aside.                                                   2255
ANOTHER = 7*2
*Clo*. Truely sir, and pleasure will be paide one time, or | another.                    957
*To*. And aske no other dowry with her, but such ano- |ther iest.                       1187
But would you vndertake another suite                                                   1321
kill one another by the looke, like Cockatrices.                                        1712
*An*. Nay let him alone, Ile go another way to worke                                     1949
*Clo*. She loues another. Who calles, ha?                                               2064
*Clo*. Good M.(aster) *Fabian*, grant me another request. | *Fab*. Any
thing.                                                                                  2155
you could make it another. | *Du*. O you giue me ill counsell.                         2181
*Du*. Well, I will be so much a sinner to be a double-| dealer: there's
another.                                                                               2185
ANSWER = 6*6
But from her handmaid do returne this answer:                                            31
*Ma*. A good lenton answer: I can tell thee where y                                     304
*Clo*. I must catechize you for it Madona, Good my | Mouse of vertue
answer mee.                                                                             354
*Ol*. Speake to me, I shall answer for her: your will.                                  464
*Vio*. To answer by the method, in the first of his hart.                              519
He might haue tooke his answer long ago.                                               556
*Vio*. I will answer you with gate and entrance, but we | are preuented.              1295
*the youth to an answer. I thinke Oxen and waine-ropes                                1439
*Seb*. My kinde *Anthonio*, | I can no other answer make, but thankes,               1480
*might answer him: therefore on, or strippe your sword                               1768
*that it is ineuitable: and on the answer, he payes you as                           1795
But there's no remedie, I shall answer it:                                           1850
ANSWERD = 4
*Du*. It cannot be so answer'd.                                                         975
You tel her so: Must she not then be answer'd? | *Du*. There is no
womans sides                                                                           980
That were I tane heere, it would scarse be answer'd.                                  1496
It might haue since bene answer'd in repaying                                         1501
ANSWERE = 1
Yes Nightingales answere Dawes.                                                       1558
ANT = 20*5
ANTHONIO = 9*1
*Enter Sebastian and Anthonio*.                                                       1466
*Seb*. My kinde *Anthonio*, | I can no other answer make, but thankes,               1480
*2.Off*. *Anthonio*, I arrest thee at the suit of Count *Orsino*                     1844
Yet 'tis not madnesse. Where's *Anthonio* then,                                      2118
*Enter Anthonio and Officers*.                                                        2200
Cride fame and honor on him: What's the matter? | 1.*Offi*. *Orsino*, this
is that *Anthonio*                                                                    2210
*Anthonio* neuer yet was Theefe, or Pyrate,                                           2226
*Seb*. *Anthonio*: O my deere *Anthonio*,                                            2382
*Ant*. *Sebastian* are you? | *Seb*. Fear'st thou that *Anthonio*?                   2385
ANTICKE = 1
That old and Anticke song we heard last night;                                        887
*ANTONIO see also An., Ant.* = 3*1
*Enter Antonio & Sebastian*.                                                          612
*then *Antonio*, my name is *Sebastian* (which I call'd *Rodo-* |*rigo* )            626
*Seb*. O good *Antonio*, forgiue me your trouble.                                    642

10

ANTONIO *cont.*
 Enter *Antonio.*      1827
ANY = 12*17
 *\*And.* As any man in Illyria, whatsoeuer he be, vnder      225
 *\*And.* And I thinke I haue the backe-tricke, simply as | strong as any
  man in Illyria.      231
 *\*sir Toby* would leaue drinking, thou wert as witty a piece | of *Eues*
  flesh, as any in Illyria.      321
 *\*mend* him: any thing that's mended, is but patch'd: vertu      339
 *\*speake* with you. What is to be said to him Ladie, hee's | fortified
  against any deniall.      439
 *\*would,* are as secret as maiden-head: to your eares, Di- | uinity; to any
  others, prophanation.      510
 *\*Ol.* Haue you any Commission from your Lord, to      523
  for your loue, to lay any of them on you.      619
 *\*Catches* without any mitigation or remorse of voice?      790
 *\*To.* Out o'tune sir, ye lye: Art any more then a Stew- | ard?      810
 *\*at* any thing more then contempt, you would not giue      818
 *\*Mar.* The diu'll a Puritane that hee is, or any thing      840
 *\*respect,* then any one else that followes her. What | should I thinke
  on't?      1044
 *\*euident* to any formall capacitie. There is no obstruction      1127
 *\*Fa.* I, and you had any eye behinde you, you might      1143
 *\*And.* And't be any way, it must be with Valour, for      1410
 *\*Vio.* You mistake sir I am sure, no man hath any quar- | rell      1745
  any image of offence done to any man.      1747
 *\*you* hold your life at any price, betake you to your gard:      1749
  Nor know I you by voyce, or any feature:      1872
  Or any taint of vice, whose strong corruption | Inhabites our fraile
  blood.      1875
 *\*To.* I dare lay any money, twill be nothing yet. *Exit*      1916
 *\*there* be any law in Illyria: though I stroke him first, yet      1951
  make the triall of it in any constant question.      2034
 *\*that* I cannot pursue with any safety this sport the vppe- | shot.      2055
 *\*paper,* I tell thee I am as well in my wittes, as any man in | Illyria.      2091
  To any other trust, but that I am mad,      2129
  *Clo.* Good M.(aster) *Fabian,* grant me another request. | *Fab.* Any
  thing.      2155
ANYONE *see* one
ANYS = 1
 *To.* He's as tall a man as any's in Illyria.      137
ANYTHING *see* thing
APPEARD = *1
 *\*Vio.* The rudenesse that hath appear'd in mee, haue I      508
APPEARE = *4
 *\*slough,* and appeare fresh. Be opposite with a kinsman,      1155
 *\*it appeare in thy smiling, thy smiles become thee well. There- | fore*      1179
 *\*Mar.* Why appeare you with this ridiculous bold- | nesse before my
  Lady.      1559
 *\*appeare* stubborne to him: for she incites me to that in      1590
APPEARES = *1
 *\*then* a Hare, his dishonesty appeares, in leauing his frend      1907
APPETITE = 2*1
  The appetite may sicken, and so dye.      7
 *\*with* a distemper'd appetite. To be generous, guiltlesse,      383
  Alas, their loue may be call'd appetite,      985

APPLE = 1*1
*when tis almost an Apple: Tis with him in standing wa-|ter,                              453
An apple cleft in two, is not more twin                                                   2388
APPLYES = *1
*great man, and now applyes it to a foole. Vent my fol-|ly:                               1930
APPREHEND = 1
In priuate brabble did we apprehend him.                                                  2216
APPREHENDED = 1
Where being apprehended, his false cunning                                                2238
APPROACH = 1*3
Ol. Let him approach: Call in my Gentlewoman.                                             457
*approach rather to wonder at you, then to heare you. If                                  493
*To. Approach Sir Andrew: not to bee a bedde after                                        701
*his first approach before my Lady: hee will come to her                                 1202
APPROACHES = 1
Toby approaches; curtsies there to me. | To. Shall this fellow liue?                     1077
APPROBATION = *1
*approbation, then euer proofe it selfe would haue earn'd | him. Away.                   1698
APROUE = *1
*Mal. I thinke nobly of the soule, and no way aproue | his opinion.                      2040
APT = 4*2
I know thy constellation is right apt                                                     286
*Clo. Apt in good faith, very apt: well go thy way, if                                    320
O world, how apt the poore are to be proud?                                              1342
Vio. And I most iocund, apt, and willinglie,                                             2288
Du. Madam, I am most apt t'embrace your offer:                                           2486
APTLY = *1
*the Gentleman (as I know his youth will aptly receiue it)                               1709
AQUA = 1
Ma. Nay but say true, do's it worke vpon him? | To. Like Aqua vite
with a Midwife.                                                                          1199
ARBITREMENT = *1
*a mortall arbitrement, but nothing of the circumstance | more.                         1779
ARE see also y'are = 52*32
ARGUMENT = 1*1
*Fab. This was a great argument of loue in her toward | you.                             1391
Might well haue giuen vs bloody argument:                                                1500
ARGUMENTS = 1*2
*surly with seruants: Let thy tongue tang arguments of                                   1156
The rather by these arguments of feare | Set forth in your pursuite.                     1478
*langer with arguments of state, put thy selfe into the                                  1593
ARIUD = *1
*Vio. Euen now sir, on a moderate pace, I haue since a-|riu'd but
hither.                                                                                  660
ARREST = *1
*2.Off. Anthonio, I arrest thee at the suit of Count Orsino                              1844
ART see also th'art l.13 224 282 587 684 *810 *811 909 *1154 *1160 1218
    *1239 1244 *1574 1670 1921 1934 *1987 *2029 2073 2309 2460 = 16*8, 1
As full of labour as a Wise-mans Art:                                                    1278
ARTS = 1
*dancing, and beare-bayting: O had I but followed the | Arts.                            207
AS = 70*77
'Tis not so sweet now, as it was before.                                                 12
Receiueth as the Sea. Nought enters there,                                               15
I saw him hold acquaintance with the waues, | So long as I could see.                    66
Vio. Who gouernes heere? | Cap. A noble Duke in nature, as in name.                      74
And then 'twas fresh in murmure (as you know                                             82

AS *cont.*

| | |
|---|---|
| For such disguise as haply shall become | 106 |
| Thou shalt present me as an Eunuch to him, | 108 |
| *To.* He's as tall a man as any's in Illyria. | 137 |
| *to her as long as there is a passage in my throat, & drinke | 155 |
| *And.* As any man in Illyria, whatsoeuer he be, vnder | 225 |
| *And.* And I thinke I haue the backe-tricke, simply as \| strong as any | |
| man in Illyria. | 231 |
| *as make water but in a Sinke-a-pace: What dooest thou | 238 |
| As it is spoke, she neuer will admit me. | 270 |
| Is as the maidens organ, shrill, and sound, | 284 |
| And thou shalt liue as freely as thy Lord, \| To call his fortunes thine. | 290 |
| *not open my lippes so wide as a brissle may enter, in way | 298 |
| *or to be turn'd away: is not that as good as a hanging to \| you? | 312 |
| *sir *Toby* would leaue drinking, thou wert as witty a piece \| of *Eues* | |
| flesh, as any in Illyria. | 321 |
| *As there is no true Cuckold but calamity, so beauties a | 343 |
| *Non facit monachum*: that's as much to say, as I weare not | 348 |
| *Clo.* Thou hast spoke for vs (Madona) as if thy eldest | 406 |
| *for a boy: as a squash is before tis a pescod, or a Codling | 452 |
| in my hand: my words are as full of peace, as matter. | 505 |
| *would, are as secret as maiden-head: to your eares, Di- \|uinity; to any | |
| others, prophanation. | 510 |
| *and euery particle and vtensile labell'd to my will: As, | 538 |
| I am the man, if it be so, as tis, | 682 |
| For such as we are made, if such we bee: | 689 |
| What will become of this? As I am man, | 693 |
| As I am woman (now alas the day) | 695 |
| *To.* A false conclusion: I hate it as an vnfill'd Canne. | 706 |
| *sweet a breath to sing, as the foole has. Insooth thou wast | 722 |
| *An.* A mellifluous voyce, as I am true knight. | 754 |
| *bad me tell you, that though she harbors you as her kins- \|man, | 794 |
| *An.* 'Twere as good a deede as to drink when a mans | 822 |
| *The best perswaded of himselfe: so cram'd (as he thinkes) | 843 |
| For such as I am, all true Louers are, | 902 |
| For women are as Roses, whose faire flowre | 927 |
| Tell her I hold as giddily as Fortune: | 971 |
| Say that some Lady, as perhappes there is, | 977 |
| Hath for your loue as great a pang of heart | 978 |
| As you haue for *Oliuia*: you cannot loue her: | 979 |
| As loue doth giue my heart: no womans heart | 983 |
| But mine is all as hungry as the Sea, | 988 |
| And can digest as much, make no compare | 989 |
| In faith they are as true of heart, as we. | 995 |
| As it might be perhaps, were I a woman \| I should your Lordship. | 997 |
| *place, as I would they should doe theirs: to aske for my \| kinsman | |
| *Toby.* | 1070 |
| *Fab.* Sowter will cry vpon't for all this, though it bee \| as ranke as a | |
| Fox. | 1132 |
| *Mal. M, O, A, I.* This simulation is not as the former: | 1146 |
| *being addicted to a melancholly, as shee is, that it | 1206 |
| *as like husbands, as Pilchers are to Herrings, the Hus- \|bands | 1247 |
| *Foole should be as oft with your Master, as with my Mi- \|stris: | 1253 |
| As full of labour as a Wise-mans Art: | 1278 |
| *Ol.* I would you were, as I would haue you be. \| *Vio.* Would it be better | |
| Madam, then I am? | 1358 |
| *And.* As plaine as I see you now. | 1390 |

AS *cont.*

*policie I hate: I had as liefe be a Brownist, as a Politi-|cian.          1411
*thou'st him some thrice, it shall not be amisse, and as ma-|ny           1424
*Lyes, as will lye in thy sheete of paper, although the                   1425
*and you finde so much blood in his Liuer, as will clog the               1441
*Indies: you haue not seene such a thing as tis: I can hard-|ly           1459
As might haue drawne one to a longer voyage)                              1473
But were my worth, as is my conscience firme,                             1484
I am as madde as hee, | If sad and merry madnesse equall bee.             1536
If it please the eye of one, it is with me as the very true               1544
*manner how: as a sad face, a reuerend carriage, a slow                   1595
*Fa. If this were plaid vpon a stage now, I could con-|demne it as an
improbable fiction.                                                       1649
*and so looke to thy selfe. Thy friend as thou vsest him, & thy | sworne
enemie, Andrew Ague-cheeke.                                               1686
*of the Orchard like a bum-Baylie: so soone as euer thou                  1694
*seest him, draw, and as thou draw'st, sweare horrible: for               1695
*the Gentleman (as I know his youth will aptly receiue it)                1709
*but thy intercepter full of despight, bloody as the Hun-|ter,            1741
*vndertake that with me, which with as much safetie you                   1767
*Vio. This is as vnciuill as strange. I beseech you doe                   1771
*me this courteous office, as to know of the Knight what                  1772
*by his forme, as you are like to finde him in the proofe of              1783
*that it is ineuitable: and on the answer, he payes you as                1795
*surely, as your feete hits the ground they step on. They                1796
marry Ile ride your horse as well as I ride you.                          1807
*Fa. He is as horribly conceited of him: and pants, &                     1811
lookes pale, as if a Beare were at his heeles.                            1812
*me, as he is a Gentleman and a Soldiour, he will not hurt | you. Come
on, too't.                                                                1824
*be as good as my word. Hee will beare you easily, and | raines well.     1841
As to vpbraid you with those kindnesses                                   1869
*goes as fairely, as to say, a carefull man, & a great | scholler. The
Competitors enter.                                                        1994
*Clo. Bonos dies sir Toby: for as the old hermit of Prage                 1998
Mal. As hell sir Topas.                                                   2021
*Clo. Why it hath bay Windowes transparant as bari-|cadoes,               2022
*as lustrous as Ebony: and yet complainest thou of ob-|struction?         2024
*Mal. I say this house is as darke as Ignorance, thogh                    2031
*Ignorance were as darke as hell; and I say there was ne-|uer             2032
*Mal. Good foole, as euer thou wilt deserue well at                       2065
*as I am a Gentleman, I will liue to bee thankefull to thee | for't.      2067
I am as well in my wits (foole) as thou art.                             2073
*Clo. But as well: then you are mad indeede, if you be                    2074
*paper, I tell thee I am as well in my wittes, as any man in | Illyria.   2091
As I perceiue she do's: there's something in't                           2134
Fab. Now as thou lou'st me, let me see his Letter.                        2154
*friends I am abused: so that conclusions to be as kisses, if             2173
*my desire of hauing is the sinne of couetousnesse: but as                2197
As blacke as Vulcan, in the smoake of warre:                             2204
It is as fat and fulsome to mine eare | As howling after Musicke.         2264
Be that thou know'st thou art, and then thou art | As great as that thou
fear'st.                                                                  2309
Were you a woman, as the rest goes euen,                                  2405
If this be so, as yet the glasse seemes true,                            2431
And all those swearings keepe as true in soule,                          2436
As doth that Orbed Continent, the fire, | That seuers day from night.     2437

AS *cont.*

How does he sirrah? | *Cl.* Truely Madam, he holds *Belzebub* at the
staues end as      2451
*well as a man in his case may do: has heere writ a letter to      2453
*you, I should haue giuen't you to day morning. But as a      2454
*Ladyship will haue it as it ought to bee, you must allow | *Vox.*      2462
*yet haue I the benefit of my senses as well as your Ladie-|ship.      2472
*me as you please. I leaue my duty a little vnthought of,      2476
To thinke me as well a sister, as a wife,      2483

ASIDE = 1

But more of that anon. Take him aside.      2255

ASKE = 3*2

*place, as I would they should doe theirs: to aske for my | kinsman
*Toby.*      1070
*To.* And aske no other dowry with her, but such ano-|ther iest.      1187
What shall you aske of me that Ile deny,      1728
Makes me to aske you for my purse. It greeues mee      1852
*heere in necessity, and denying him: and for his coward-|ship aske
*Fabian.*      1908

ASKING = 1

That honour (sau'd) may vpon asking giue.      1729

ASLEEPE = *1

*with you. I told him you were asleepe, he seems to haue      437

ASMUCH = 1

And I (poore monster) fond asmuch on him:      691

ASPECT = 1

Then in a Nuntio's of more graue aspect.      278

ASSAYLANT = *1

*be yare in thy preparation, for thy assaylant is quick, skil-|full, and
deadly.      1743

ASSAYLE = 1

*To,* You mistake knight: Accost, is front her, boord | her, woe her,
assayle her.      171

ASSE = 4*4

*And.* Why I thinke so: I am not such an asse, but I      188
*To.* Welcome asse, now let's haue a catch.      719
*constantly but a time-pleaser, an affection'd Asse, that      841
*An.* And your horse now would make him an Asse.      861
*Mar.* Asse, I doubt not.      862
*And.* S'light; will you make an Asse o'me.      1393
*Clo.* Marry sir, they praise me, and make an asse of me,      2170
*now my foes tell me plainly, I am an Asse: so that by my      2171

ASSES = *1

*darkenesse, send Ministers to me, Asses, and doe all they      2077

ASSE-HEAD = *1

*To.* Will you helpe an Asse-head, and a coxcombe, &      2369

ASSUME = 1

If spirits can assume both forme and suite, | You come to fright vs.      2400

ASSURANCE = 1*2

*modest assurance, if you be the Ladie of the house, that | (I      475
*into a desperate assurance, she will none of him. And one      665
Plight me the full assurance of your faith,      2141

ASSURE = 2*2

Assure your selfe, after our ship did split,      59
*and assure thy selfe, there is no loue-Broker in the world,      1416
*To.* You'l finde it otherwise I assure you: therefore, if      1748
*Vio.* I do assure you tis against my will.      1828

AT = 30*29
ATCHEEUE = 1
*Mal.* Some atcheeue greatnesse. | *Ol.* What sayst thou? 1565
ATCHEEUES = *1
*are become great, some atcheeues greatnesse, and some 1151
ATCHIEUE = *1
*Clo.* Why some are borne great, some atchieue great-|nesse, 2541
ATTEMPT = *1
*it, by some laudable attempt, either of valour or | policie. 1408
ATTEND = 3
She will attend it better in thy youth, 277
For this affayre: some foure or fiue attend him, 287
Grace and good disposition attend your Ladyship: 1352
ATTENDANCE = 1
*Duke.* Who saw *Cesario* hoa? | *Vio.* On your attendance my Lord heere. 259
ATTENDANTS = 2
*Enter Duke, Curio, and Attendants.* 257
*Enter Oliuia and attendants.* 2250
ATTENDED = 1
*Ma* I know not (Madam) 'tis a faire young man, and | well attended. 396
ATTENDS = 1*1
attends your Ladyships pleasure. | *Ol.* Ile come to him. 1581
*attends thee at the Orchard end: dismount thy tucke, 1742
ATTESTED = 1
Attested by the holy close of lippes, 2320
ATTIRE = 1
*Enter Valentine, and Viola in mans attire.* 250
ATTRACTS = 1
That nature prankes her in, attracts my soule. 973
ATTYRE = 1
But this my masculine vsurp'd attyre: 2416
AUDIENCE = 1
And tell them, there thy fixed foot shall grow | Till thou haue audience. 266
AUGHT *see* ought
AUGMENTATION = *1
*then is in the new Mappe, with the augmentation of the 1458
AUOIDE = *1
*he cannot by the Duello auoide it: but hee has promised 1823
*AUSSI see* ousie
AUSTERE = 1
familiar smile with an austere regard of controll. 1082
AUTHORITIE = 1
Whereto thy speech serues for authoritie 70
AUTHORS = 1
But when we know the grounds, and authors of it, 2523
AUTHOURS = *1
*proud, I will reade politicke Authours, I will baffle Sir 1166
AWAKE = *3
*onely to exasperate you, to awake your dormouse valour, 1399
*with her, and bring her along with you, it may awake my | bounty
further. 2193
*you say sir, let your bounty take a nappe, I will awake it | anon. *Exit* 2198
AWAY = 16*7
Away before me, to sweet beds of Flowres, 46
*or to be turn'd away: is not that as good as a hanging to | you? 312
and for turning away, let summer beare it out. 315
*Ol.* Take the foole away. 331

AWAY *cont.*
*Clo.* Do you not heare fellowes, take away the Ladie.                    332
*flower; The Lady bad take away the foole, therefore I | say againe,
take her away.                                                           344
*Ol.* Sir, I bad them take away you.                                     346
*Brothers soule, being in heauen. Take away the Foole, | Gentlemen.      363
*for I neuer saw her. I would bee loath to cast away my                   467
*haue saued mee my paines, to haue taken it away your                    663
*The Song. | Come away, come away death,*                                941
*Fye away, fie away breath,*                                             944
*thankefull. And when she went away now, let this Fel-|low              1598
*approbation, then euer proofe it selfe would haue earn'd | him. Away.  1698
Take him away, he knowes I know him well.                               1848
2.*Off.* Come sir away.                                                 1856
1.*Off.* What's that to vs, the time goes by: Away.                     1884
1.*Off.* The man growes mad, away with him: | Come, come sir.           1891
Call forth the holy Father. | *Du.* Come, away.                         2299
*Ol.* Away with him? Who hath made this hauocke | with them?            2365
AWHILE *see* a-while
AYDE = 1
Conceale me what I am, and be my ayde,                                   105
AYE *see also* I = 1
*Ol.* Aye me detested, how am I beguil'd?                               2296
AYRE = 3*1
Me thought she purg'd the ayre of pestilence;                            25
Betweene the elements of ayre, and earth,                               569
*Mar.* Nay pursue him now, least the deuice take ayre, | and taint.    1653
This is the ayre, that is the glorious Sunne,                          2115
AYRES = 1
More then light ayres, and recollected termes                           889
A-CROSSE = *1
*And.* H'as broke my head a-crosse, and has giuen Sir                  2339
A-WHILE = 1
*Du.* Stand you a-while aloofe. *Cesario,*                              261
BABBLE = 1
*thy selfe to sleepe, and leaue thy vaine bibble | babble.             2081
BABLING = 2
And make the babling Gossip of the aire,                                567
Then lying, vainnesse, babling drunkennesse,                           1874
BABYLON = 1
*There dwelt a man in Babylon, Lady, Lady.*                             778
BACKE = 2*2
Where like *Orion* on the Dolphines backe,                               65
*Orsino's* is return'd, I could hardly entreate him backe: he          1580
*his desire. Backe you shall not to the house, vnlesse you             1766
Take, and giue backe affayres, and their dispatch,                     2132
BACKE-TRICKE = *1
*And.* And I thinke I haue the backe-tricke, simply as | strong as any
man in Illyria.                                                         231
BAD = 4*4
*Clo.* Many a good hanging, preuents a bad marriage:                   314
*flower; The Lady bad take away the foole, therefore I | say againe,
take her away.                                                          344
*Ol.* Sir, I bad them take away you.                                   346
*that I may beare my euils alone. It were a bad recom-|pence           618
*Ant.* Pardon me sir, your bad entertainment.                          641
*bad me tell you, that though she harbors you as her kins-|man,        794

BAD *cont.*
I bad you neuer speake againe of him;                                      1320
Bad me come smiling, and crosse-garter'd to you,                           2507
BADE *see* bad
BAFFELD = 1
*Ol.* Alas poore Foole, how haue they baffel'd thee?                       2540
BAFFLE = *1
*proud, I will reade politicke Authours, I will baffle Sir                 1166
BAITED = 1
And baited it with all th'vnmuzled thoughts                                1333
BAITING = 1
o'fauour with my Lady, about a Beare-baiting heere.                        1024
BANGD = *1
*iests, fire-new from the mint, you should haue bangd                      1402
BANISHT = 1
From my remembrance, clearly banisht his.                                  2450
BANKE = 1
That breathes vpon a banke of Violets;                                     10
BAR = *1
*on him: at which time, we wil bring the deuice to the bar                 1661
BARBAROUS = 1
Fit for the Mountaines, and the barbarous Caues,                           1965
BARICADOES = *1
*Clo.* Why it hath bay Windowes transparant as bari-|cadoes,               2022
BARRE = 1
hand to'th Buttry barre, and let it drinke.                                184
BARREFULL = 1
*Vio.* Ile do my best | To woe your Lady: yet a barrefull strife,          292
BARREN = 1*2
I let go your hand, I am barren. *Exit Maria*                              193
*a barren rascall: I saw him put down the other day, with                  376
*Madam, why laugh you at such a barren rascall,                            2545
BASE = 1
Though I confesse, on base and ground enough                               2227
BASENESSE = 1
*Ol.* Alas, it is the basenesse of thy feare,                              2306
BASIS = *1
*To.* Why then build me thy fortunes vpon the basis of                     1413
BATCHELLOR = 1
He was a Batchellor then. | *Cap.* And so is now, or was so very late:     79
BATTERY = *1
*with him: Ile haue an action of Battery against him, if                   1950
BAULKT = *1
*hand, and this was baulkt: the double gilt of this oppor-|tunitie         1404
BAWBLING = 1
A bawbling Vessell was he Captaine of,                                     2205
BAWCOCK = *1
*To.* Why how now my bawcock? how dost y chuck? | *Mal.* Sir.             1635
BAY = *1
*Clo.* Why it hath bay Windowes transparant as bari-|cadoes,               2022
BAYLIE = *1
*of the Orchard like a bum-Baylie: so soone as euer thou                    1694
BAYTING = *1
*dancing, and beare-bayting: O had I but followed the | Arts.             207
BE *see also* shalbe = 92*85
BEAGLE = *1
*To.* She's a beagle true bred, and one that adores me: | what o'that?     871

BEARD = 1*3
*loue, wherein by the colour of his beard, the shape of his                      849
*Clo. Now Ioue in his next commodity of hayre, send | thee a beard.     1257
*like an ysickle on a Dutchmans beard, vnlesse you do re-|deeme         1407
*Mar. Nay, I prethee put on this gown, & this beard,                         1986
BEARE = 4*4
and for turning away, let summer beare it out.                               315
*that I may beare my euils alone. It were a bad recom-|pence                 618
Betweene that loue a woman can beare me, | And that I owe Oliuia.     990
*To. To anger him wee'l haue the Beare againe, and                          1025
*An. Will either of you beare me a challenge to him?                         1420
A Fiend like thee might beare my soule to hell.                              1735
lookes pale, as if a Beare were at his heeles.                               1812
*be as good as my word. Hee will beare you easily, and | raines well.  1841
BEARER = 1
Seb. Ile be your purse-bearer, and leaue you | For an houre.             1516
BEARES = *2
*Fab. And his opposit the youth beares in his visage no | great presage
of cruelty.                                                                  1443
*Vio. With the same hauiour that your passion beares,                     1723
BEARE-BAITING = 1
o'fauour with my Lady, about a Beare-baiting heere.                       1024
BEARE-BAYTING = *1
*dancing, and beare-bayting: O had I but followed the | Arts.          207
BEARING = 1*1
*Lady: it shall aduantage thee more, then euer the bea-|ring of Letter
did.                                                                         2096
With such a smooth, discreet, and stable bearing                         2133
BEATE = 2*1
*An. O, if I thought that, Ide beate him like a dogge.                     835
And. Slight I could so beate the Rogue. | To. Peace I say.               1049
And. Slid Ile after him againe, and beate him.                           1912
BEATING = 1
Can bide the beating of so strong a passion,                             982
BEAUTEOUS = 2
And though that nature, with a beauteous wall                            100
Vertue is beauty, but the beauteous euill                                1889
BEAUTIE = 1*2
*Vio. Most radiant, exquisite, and vnmatchable beau-|tie.               465
*out diuers scedules of my beautie. It shalbe Inuentoried               537
Could be but recompenc'd, though you were crown'd | The non-pareil
of beautie.                                                                  545
BEAUTIES = *2
*As there is no true Cuckold but calamity, so beauties a                 343
*taken great paines to con it. Good Beauties, let mee su-|staine       469
BEAUTIFUL = *1
*me, was yet of many accounted beautiful: but thogh                     635
BEAUTIFULL = 1
Ol. O what a deale of scorne, lookes beautifull?                         1361
BEAUTY = 2
Vio. Tis beauty truly blent, whose red and white,                        531
Vertue is beauty, but the beauteous euill                                1889
BECAUSE = 1*2
Because she will admit no kinde of suite, | No, not the Dukes.       97
*Dost thou thinke because thou art vertuous, there                       811
*And. Ile helpe you sir Toby, because we'll be drest to-|gether.       2367

BECOM = *2
*To. Shall I play my freedome at tray-trip, and becom | thy bondslaue?  1194
*Ol. Euen what it please my Lord, that shal becom him  2272
BECOME = 3*3
For such disguise as haply shall become  106
It shall become thee well to act my woes:  276
What will become of this? As I am man,  693
*are become great, some atcheeues greatnesse, and some  1151
*it appeare in thy smiling, thy smiles become thee well. There- |fore  1179
*in such a gowne. I am not tall enough to become the  1991
BECOMS = 1
An. But it becoms me wel enough, dost not?  212
BED = 5*5
*To be vp after midnight, and to go to bed then is early:  707
*so that to go to bed after midnight, is to goe to bed be- |times.  708
to lye straight in my bed: I know I can do it.  832
*obserue his construction of it: For this night to bed, and  867
*To. Let's to bed knight: Thou hadst neede send for | more money.  874
to go to bed now: Come knight, come knight. Exeunt  882
Ol. Wilt thou go to bed Maluolio?  1552
Mal. To bed? I sweet heart, and Ile come to thee.  1553
Ol. Get him to bed, and let his hurt be look'd too.  2371
BEDDE = *3
*To. Approach Sir Andrew: not to bee a bedde after  701
*Veluet gowne: hauing come from a day bedde, where I | haue left
Oliuia sleeping.  1064
*sheete were bigge enough for the bedde of Ware in Eng- |land,  1426
BEDS = 2
Away before me, to sweet beds of Flowres,  46
But when I came vnto my beds, | with hey ho, &c.  2572
BEE l.114 *129 *466 *467 *515 *667 *671 *672 689 *701 *813 *1042
*1101 *1132 *1165 *1174 *1422 *1427 1537 *1788 *1815 *1992 *2053
*2067 *2462 2491 = 4*22
BEEFE = *1
*am a great eater of beefe, and I beleeue that does harme | to my wit.  199
BEENE see also bene, bin l.*442 *630 *1033 1060 *1396 *1434 *1801
*2356 2374 2424 2425 = 4*7
BEFALL = 1
But iealousie, what might befall your trauell,  1474
BEFALS = 1
Then what befals my selfe: you stand amaz'd, | But be of comfort.  1854
BEFORE = 10*7
'Tis not so sweet now, as it was before.  12
Away before me, to sweet beds of Flowres,  46
To. Why let her except, before excepted.  125
*these gifts a Curtaine before 'em? Are they like to take  234
*for a boy: as a squash is before tis a pescod, or a Codling  452
*that, for some houre before you tooke me from the  631
An. Before me she's a good wench.  870
*see more detraction at your heeles, then Fortunes before | you.  1144
*his first approach before my Lady: hee will come to her  1202
That comes before his eye. This is a practice,  1277
To fall before the Lion, then the Wolfe?  1344
*To. And they haue beene grand Iurie men, since before | Noah was a
Saylor.  1396
*Mar. Why appeare you with this ridiculous bold- |nesse before my
Lady.  1559

BELEEUE *cont.*
*beleeue such impossible passages of grossenesse. Hee's in | yellow
stockings.                                                              1451
**Clo.* Will you make me beleeue, that I am not sent for | you?        1919
*make him beleeue thou art sir *Topas* the Curate, doe it              1987
*Mal.* Beleeue me I am not, I tell thee true.                          2100
**Clo.* Nay, Ile nere beleeue a madman till I see his brains           2101
BELEEUES = 1
That he beleeues himselfe, so do not I:                                1895
BELEEUING = *1
*that meanes to be saued by beleeuing rightly, can euer                1450
BELIKE = 1*1
*Seb.* Belike you slew great number of his people.                     1497
*to taste their valour: belike this is a man of that | quirke.         1762
BELLES = *1
*tripping measure, or the belles of S.(aint) *Bennet* sir, may put | you in
minde, one, two, three.                                                2189
BELONG = 1
*Duke.* Belong you to the Lady *Oliuia*, friends?                      2161
BELOUD = 1*1
That is belou'd. How dost thou like this tune?                         905
**Mal.* To the vnknowne belou'd, *this, and my good Wishes*:           1105
BELYE = 1
For they shall yet belye thy happy yeeres,                             281
BELZEBUB = *1
How does he sirrah? | **Cl.* Truely Madam, he holds *Belzebub* at the
staues end as                                                          2451
BENCH = 1
a bench, but hee'l speake with you.                                     444
BENE *l.*1501 2549 = 2
BENEATH = 1
So farre beneath your soft and tender breeding,                        2489
BENEFIT = *1
*yet haue I the benefit of my senses as well as your Ladie-|ship.      2472
BENNET = *1
*tripping measure, or the belles of S.(aint) *Bennet* sir, may put | you in
minde, one, two, three.                                                2189
BENT = 1
Or thy affection cannot hold the bent:                                 926
BERD = *1
**Mar.* Thou mightst haue done this without thy berd | and gowne, he
sees thee not.                                                         2049
BESEECH = 3*1
*Vio.* Deere Lady. | *Ol.* Giue me leaue, beseech you: I did send,     1324
And I beseech you come againe to morrow.                               1727
**Vio.* This is as vnciuill as strange. I beseech you doe              1771
*Vio.* I beseech you what manner of man is he?                         1781
BESET = 1
Drew to defend him, when he was beset:                                 2237
BESHREW = 2
*Clo.* Beshrew me, the knights in admirable fooling.                   779
Do not denie, beshrew his soule for mee,                               1975
BESIDES = 3*3
**Ma.* He hath indeed, almost naturall: for besides that              145
*Ol.* Go too, y'are a dry foole: Ile no more of you: be-|sides you grow
dis-honest.                                                            333
*speech: for besides that it is excellently well pend, I haue          468

BESIDES *cont.*
*my complection. Besides she vses me with a more ex-|alted                1043
*Mal.* Besides you waste the treasure of your time, | with a foolish
knight.                                                                    1092
*Clo.* Alas sir, how fell you besides your fiue witts?                     2071
BESMEARD = 1
Yet when I saw it last, it was besmear'd                                   2203
BESPAKE = 1
But I bespake you faire, and hurt you not.                                 2351
BESPEAKE = 1
In the South Suburbes at the Elephant | Is best to lodge: I will bespeake
our dyet,                                                                  1508
BEST = 4*4
All if you will: for I my selfe am best                                    288
*Vio.* Ile do my best | To woe your Lady: yet a barrefull strife,          292
Lady: make your excuse wisely, you were best.                             324
*An.* Excellent: Why this is the best fooling, when | all is done. Now a
song.                                                                      730
*The best perswaded of himselfe: so cram'd (as he thinkes)                843
*Ant.* To morrow sir, best first go see your Lodging?                     1487
In the South Suburbes at the Elephant | Is best to lodge: I will bespeake
our dyet,                                                                  1508
*were best to haue some guard about you, if hee                          1532
BESTOW = 1
How shall I feast him? What bestow of him?                                1523
BESTOWD = 1*1
The parts that fortune hath bestow'd vpon her:                            970
*Counts Seruing-man, then euer she bestow'd vpon mee:                     1387
BESTOWE = *1
*selfe: for what is yours to bestowe, is, not yours to re-|serue.         483
BESTOWED = *1
*bestowed that time in the tongues, that I haue in fencing               206
BETAKE = *2
*To.* That defence thou hast, betake the too't: of what                   1739
*you hold your life at any price, betake you to your gard:               1749
BETHINKE = 1
And now I do bethinke me, it was shee                                     2518
BETHOUGHT = *1
*oath sake: marrie hee hath better bethought him of his                  1814
BETIMES = *2
*midnight, is to be vp betimes, and *Deliculo surgere*, thou | know'st.   702
*so that to go to bed after midnight, is to goe to bed be-|times.         708
BETRAY = *1
*to betray him: He does smile his face into more lynes,                   1457
BETROTHD = 1
You are betroth'd both to a maid and man.                                 2429
BETTER = 10*9
*Ma.* Good Mistris accost, I desire better acquaintance | *Ma.* My name
is *Mary* sir.                                                            168
She will attend it better in thy youth,                                   277
*wise man. For what saies *Quinapalus*, Better a witty foole,            329
*him: Infirmity that decaies the wise, doth euer make the | better foole. 368
*better increasing your folly: Sir *Toby* will be sworn that             371
fooles, no better then the fooles Zanies.                                 381
Poore Lady, she were better loue a dreame:                                683
*do I too: he does it with a better grace, but I do it more | naturall.  781
*Vio.* My legges do better vnderstand me sir, then I vn-|derstand        1292

23

BETTER *cont.*
If one should be a prey, how much the better 1343
*Ol.* I would you were, as I would haue you be. | *Vio.* Would it be better
Madam, then I am? 1358
Loue sought, is good: but giuen vnsought is better. 1372
You should finde better dealing: what's to do? 1485
*soules. He may haue mercie vpon mine, but my hope is better*, 1685
*oath sake: marrie hee hath better bethought him of his 1814
no better in your wits then a foole. 2075
*Clo.* Truely sir, the better for my foes, and the worse | for my friends. 2165
*Du.* Iust the contrary: the better for thy friends. 2167
*then the worse for my friends, and the better for my foes. 2175
BETTERS = *1
*the degree of my betters, & yet I will not compare with | an old man. 226
BETWEEN = 1
to see a huswife take thee between her legs, & spin it off. 214
BETWEENE = 4*3
*betweene boy and man. He is verie well-fauour'd, 454
Betweene the elements of ayre, and earth, 569
Betweene that loue a woman can beare me, | And that I owe *Oliuia.* 990
*can be saide? Nothing that can be, can come betweene 1603
*capacity, and breeding: his employment betweene his 1703
Hath newly past, betweene this youth, and me. 2317
Hath beene betweene this Lady, and this Lord. 2424
BEWITCHD = 1
he takes it at heart. Pray God he be not bewitch'd. 1624
BIAS = 1
But Nature to her bias drew in that. 2426
BIBBLE = *1
*thy selfe to sleepe, and leaue thy vaine bibble | babble. 2081
BID = 4*2
*not dry: bid the dishonest man mend himself, if he mend, 337
bid him turne you out of doores, neuer trust me. 774
leaue of her, she is very willing to bid you farewell. 798
*To.* Shall I bid him go. | *Clo.* What and if you do? 806
*To.* Shall I bid him go, and spare not? | *Clo.* O no, no, no, no, you dare
not. 808
*nor I am not sent to you by my Lady, to bid you come 1924
BIDDING = 1
what you meane by bidding me taste my legs. 1293
BIDDY = *1
*To.* I biddy, come with me. What man, tis not for 1637
BIDE = 2*1
*Ol.* Well sir, for want of other idlenesse, Ile bide your | proofe. 356
Can bide the beating of so strong a passion, 982
My loue can giue no place, bide no denay. *Exeunt* 1015
BIGGE = 1*1
So bigge, to hold so much, they lacke retention. 984
*sheete were bigge enough for the bedde of *Ware* in Eng- | land, 1426
BIGGER = *1
*the bigger, I am indeede not her foole, but hir cor- | rupter of words. 1248
BIN *l.* *297 1797 2427 = 2*1
BINDE = 1
Most prouident in perill, binde himselfe, 62
BIRD = 1
*Mal.* That the soule of our grandam, might happily | inhabite a bird. 2037

24

BIRDBOLTS = *1
*and of free disposition, is to take those things for Bird-|bolts,    384
BIRTH = 2
According to my birth, what do you say?    2146
*Vio.* And dide that day when *Viola* from her birth | Had numbred
thirteene yeares.    2410
BITER = 1
Rascally sheepe-biter, come by some notable shame?    1022
BLABS = 1
When my tongue blabs, then let mine eyes not see.    115
BLACKE = 2*2
*On my blacke coffin, let there be strewne:*    949
*we will foole him blacke and blew, shall we not sir An-|drew?    1026
*Mal.* Not blacke in my minde, though yellow in my    1548
As blacke as Vulcan, in the smoake of warre:    2204
BLAME = 1
*Ol.* Blame not this haste of mine: if you meane well    2137
BLANKE = 1
*Du.* And what's her history? | *Vio.* A blanke my Lord: she neuer told
her loue,    999
BLANKES = 1
Would they were blankes, rather then fill'd with me.    1316
BLAZON = 1
Do giue thee fiue-fold blazon: not too fast: soft, soft,    589
BLEMISH = 1
In Nature, there's no blemish but the minde:    1887
BLENT = 1
*Vio.* Tis beauty truly blent, whose red and white,    531
BLESSE = 3
*And.* Blesse you faire Shrew. | *Mar.* And you too sir.    163
then a foolish wit. God blesse thee Lady.    330
*To.* Ioue blesse thee M.(aster) Parson.    1997
BLEW = *1
*we will foole him blacke and blew, shall we not sir An-|drew?    1026
BLINDE = 1
Whom the blinde waues and surges haue deuour'd:    2394
BLOOD = 6*3
*consanguinious? Am I not of her blood: tilly vally. La-|die,    777
*hands, let thy blood and spirit embrace them, and to in-|vre    1153
*and you finde so much blood in his Liuer, as will clog the    1441
This does make some obstruction in the blood:    1542
Or any taint of vice, whose strong corruption | Inhabites our fraile
blood.    1875
*To.* What, what? Nay then I must haue an Ounce or | two of this
malapert blood from you.    1959
and let your flesh and blood obey it.    2184
But had it beene the brother of my blood,    2374
*Du.* Be not amaz'd, right noble is his blood:    2430
BLOODLESSE = *1
*With bloodlesse stroke my heart doth gore, M.O.A.I. doth | sway my
life.*    1117
BLOODY = 3*3
*Ant.* Th'offence is not of such a bloody nature,    1498
Might well haue giuen vs bloody argument:    1500
*but thy intercepter full of despight, bloody as the Hun-|ter,    1741
*Toby* a bloody Coxcombe too: for the loue of God your    2340
*And.* If a bloody coxcombe be a hurt, you haue hurt    2353

BLOODY *cont.*
me: I thinke you set nothing by a bloody Coxecombe.  2354
BLOUDIE = 1
Whom thou in termes so bloudie, and so deere | Hast made thine enemies?  2222
BLOUDY = *1
*his valour. He is indeede sir, the most skilfull, bloudy, &  1784
BLOW = *2
*To. And do's not *Toby* take you a blow o'th lippes, | then?  1083
*Fa. A good note, that keepes you from the blow of y | (Law  1674
BLOWES = 1
*Fa. O peace, now he's deepely in: looke how imagi- | nation blowes him.  1058
BOATE = 1
Hung on our driuing boate: I saw your brother  61
BODIES = *1
*soules and bodies hath he diuorc'd three, and his incense- | ment  1755
BOLDE = *1
*Ma. In the warrs, & that may you be bolde to say in | your foolerie.  307
BOLDLY = *1
*that, yet thus farre I will boldly publish her, shee  637
BOLDNESSE = 1*1
*Mar. Why appeare you with this ridiculous bold- | nesse before my Lady.  1559
What foolish boldnesse brought thee to their mercies,  2221
BOLTES = 1
To. Boltes and shackles. | Fa. Oh peace, peace, peace, now, now.  1072
BOND = 1
*Priest.* A Contract of eternall bond of loue,  2318
BONDS = 1
words are very Rascals, since bonds disgrac'd them. | *Vio.* Thy reason man?  1234
BONDSLAUE = 1
*To. Shall I play my freedome at tray-trip, and becom | thy bondslaue?  1194
BONES = 2
And the free maides that weaue their thred with bones,  935
*My poore corpes, where my bones shall be throwne:*  951
BONOS = *1
*Clo. Bonos dies* sir *Toby*: for as the old hermit of *Prage*  1998
BOOKE = 2*1
without booke, & hath all the good gifts of nature.  144
To thee the booke euen of my secret soule.  263
*cons State without booke, and vtters it by great swarths.  842
BOORD = 1*1
*To,* You mistake knight: Accost, is front her, boord | her, woe her, assayle her.  171
And this is he that did the *Tiger* boord,  2213
BOOTS = *1
*these boots too: and they be not, let them hang them- | selues in their owne straps.  130
BORE = *1
*bore a minde that enuy could not but call faire: Shee is  638
BORNE = 3*3
The like of him. Know'st thou this Countrey? | *Cap.* I Madam well, for I was bred and borne  71
*To. What shall we do else: were we not borne vnder | Taurus?  244
saying was borne, of I feare no colours.  305

26

BORNE *cont.*
*and a sister, both borne in an houre: if the Heauens had    629
*Mal.* Some are borne great. | *Ol.* Ha?    1563
*Clo.* Why some are borne great, some atchieue great-|nesse,    2541
BORROWD = *1
*For youth is bought more oft, then begg'd, or borrow'd.    1524
BOSOME = 5*1
of it. Where lies your Text? | *Vio.* In *Orsinoes* bosome.    516
*Ol.* In his bosome? In what chapter of his bosome?    518
*ye well at once, my bosome is full of kindnesse, and I    647
Enough is shewne, a Cipresse, not a bosome,    1335
I haue one heart, one bosome, and one truth,    1374
BOTCHD = 1
This Ruffian hath botch'd vp, that thou thereby    1973
BOTCHER = *1
*he is no longer dishonest; if hee cannot, let the Botcher    338
BOTH = 8*3
(Courage and hope both teaching him the practise)    63
*Ma.* That if one breake, the other will hold: or if both | breake, your
gaskins fall.    318
*and a sister, both borne in an houre: if the Heauens had    629
*That can sing both high and low.*    742
*impetuositie. This will so fright them both, that they wil    1711
Both day and night did we keepe companie.    2249
If spirits can assume both forme and suite, | You come to fright vs.    2400
*Vio.* If nothing lets to make vs happie both,    2415
You are betroth'd both to a maid and man.    2429
Thou shalt be both the Plaintiffe and the Iudge | Of thine owne cause.    2524
If that the iniuries be iustly weigh'd, | That haue on both sides past.    2538
BOTTLE-ALE = 1
*is no Whip-stocke. My Lady has a white hand, and the | Mermidons
are no bottle-ale houses.    728
BOTTOME = 1
With the most noble bottome of our Fleete,    2208
BOUGHT = *1
*For youth is bought more oft, then begg'd, or borrow'd.    1524
BOUND = 1*4
*An.* Let me yet know of you, whither you are bound.    620
bound to the Count Orsino's Court, farewell. *Exit*    650
*Vio.* I am bound to your Neece sir, I meane she is the | list of my
voyage.    1289
*To.* Come, wee'l haue him in a darke room & bound.    1657
*Vio.* I shall bee much bound to you for't: I am one,    1788
BOUNDS = 1
*Du.* Be clamorous, and leape all ciuill bounds,    271
BOUNTEOUSLY = 1
I prethee (and Ile pay thee bounteously)    104
BOUNTIE = *1
*Clo.* Marry sir, lullaby to your bountie till I come a-|gen.    2195
BOUNTY = 1*1
*with her, and bring her along with you, it may awake my | bounty
further.    2193
*you say sir, let your bounty take a nappe, I will awake it | anon. *Exit*    2198
BOW = 1*1
*To.* O for a stone-bow to hit him in the eye.    1062
*and yet to crush this a little, it would bow to mee, for e-|uery    1147

BOWRES = 1
Loue-thoughts lye rich, when canopy'd with bowres. | *Exeunt*     47
BOWT = *1
*will for his honors sake haue one bowt with you:     1822
BOX = *1
*Mar. Get ye all three into the box tree: *Maluolio*'s     1032
BOY = 9*3
*for a boy: as a squash is before tis a pescod, or a Codling     452
*betweene boy and man. He is verie well-fauour'd,     454
Come hither Boy, if euer thou shalt loue     900
Hath it not boy? | *Vio*. A little, by your fauour.     911
For boy, howeuer we do praise our selues,     920
*Du*. But di'de thy sister of her loue my Boy?     1009
*To*. Did she see the while, old boy, tell me that.     1389
*To*. A very dishonest paltry boy, and more a coward     1906
That most ingratefull boy there by your side,     2229
Come boy with me, my thoughts are ripe in mischiefe:     2285
Boy, thou hast saide to me a thousand times,     2433
*Clowne sings*. | *When that I was and a little tine boy*,     2559
BOYLD = 1
let me be boyl'd to death with Melancholly.     1020
BRABBLE = 1
In priuate brabble did we apprehend him.     2216
BRAG = 1
Then you haue heard him brag to you he will.     1834
BRAINE = 1*2
That liue in her. When Liuer, Braine, and Heart,     43
*motley in my braine: good *Madona*, giue mee leaue to | proue you a
foole.     349
*an ordinary foole, that has no more braine then a stone.     377
BRAINES = 1*1
*drinke to my Neece, till his braines turne o'th toe, like a     157
braines, for heere he comes. *Enter Sir Toby*.     408
BRAINS = *1
*Clo. Nay, Ile nere beleeue a madman till I see his brains     2101
BRALL = *1
*on carpet consideration, but he is a diuell in priuate brall,     1754
BRANCHD = *1
*Mal. Calling my Officers about me, in my branch'd     1063
BRAULE *see also* brall = 1
And let no quarrell, nor no braule to come,     2527
BREACH = 1
breach of the sea, was my sister drown'd. | *Ant*. Alas the day.     632
BREAKE = 2*2
*Ma. That if one breake, the other will hold: or if both | breake, your
gaskins fall.     318
*a hungrie, to challenge him the field, and then to breake     823
*Fab*. Nay patience, or we breake the sinewes of our | plot?     1090
BREAST = *1
*And. By my troth the foole has an excellent breast. I     720
BREATH = 3*2
What thriftlesse sighes shall poore *Oliuia* breath?     696
*sweet a breath to sing, as the foole has. Insooth thou wast     722
*To. A contagious breath.     755
*Fye away, fie away breath*,     944
*pastime tyred out of breath, prompt vs to haue mercy     1660

BREATHD = 1
My soule the faithfull'st offrings haue breath'd out                              2270
BREATHES = 1
That breathes vpon a banke of Violets;                                             10
BRED = 2*1
The like of him. Know'st thou this Countrey? | *Cap*. I Madam well, for
I was bred and borne                                                              71
*To*. She's a beagle true bred, and one that adores me: | what o'that?            871
*Clo* Would not a paire of these haue bred sir?                                   1262
BREED = *1
*Letter being so excellently ignorant, will breed no terror                      1705
BREEDING = 1*1
*capacity, and breeding: his employment betweene his                             1703
So farre beneath your soft and tender breeding,                                  2489
BREEFE = 1*1
*you be not mad, be gone: if you haue reason, be breefe:                         494
*Fa*. Very breefe, and to exceeding good sence-lesse.                            1678
BRESTED = 1
Liue you the Marble-brested Tirant still.                                        2280
BRIEFE = *1
*To*. Go, write it in a martial hand, be curst and briefe:                      1421
BRIMSTONE = 1*1
*To*. Fire and Brimstone. | *Fa*. O peace, peace.                               1066
*to put fire in your Heart, and brimstone in your Liuer:                         1400
BRINE = 1
With eye-offending brine: all this to season                                    36
BRING = 5*6
*Ma*. Now sir, thought is free: I pray you bring your                           183
*Vio*. It alone concernes your eare: I bring no ouer-|ture                       503
*Clo*. I would play Lord *Pandarus* of *Phrygia* sir, to bring | a *Cressida* to
this *Troylus*.                                                                  1264
*To*. Come bring vs, bring vs where he is. | *Exeunt Omnes*.                      1463
*on him: at which time, we wil bring the deuice to the bar                       1661
*To*. To him in thine owne voyce, and bring me word                             2051
*with her, and bring her along with you, it may awake my | bounty
further.                                                                         2193
Ile bring you to a Captaine in this Towne,                                       2420
*Vio*. The Captaine that did bring me first on shore                            2441
*Ol*. See him deliuer'd *Fabian*, bring him hither:                             2481
BRINGS = 1
*and you smile not he's gag'd: and thus the whirlegigge | of time, brings
in his reuenges.                                                                 2546
BRISKE = 1
Of these most briske and giddy-paced times.                                     890
BRISSLE = *1
*not open my lippes so wide as a brissle may enter, in way                       298
BROCKE = 1
*To*. Marrie hang thee brocke.                                                   1114
BROKE = *2
*And*. H'as broke my head a-crosse, and has giuen Sir                           2339
*Du*. My Gentleman *Cesario*? | *And*. Odd's lifelings heere he is: you
broke my head                                                                   2345
BROKER = *1
*and assure thy selfe, there is no loue-Broker in the world,                    1416
BROTHER = 10*2
To pay this debt of loue but to a brother,                                      40
*Vio*. And what should I do in Illyria? | My brother he is in Elizium,          53

BROTHER *cont.*
*\*Vio.* O my poore brother, and so perchance may he be. 57
Hung on our driuing boate: I saw your brother 61
In the protection of his sonne, her brother, 88
*\*death of her brother thus?* I am sure care's an enemie to | life. 120
Proue true imagination, oh proue true, | That I deere brother, be now
tane for you. 1896
*Vio.* He nam'd *Sebastian*: I my brother know 1900
In fauour was my Brother, and he went 1902
But had it beene the brother of my blood, 2374
*Seb.* Do I stand there? I neuer had a brother: 2391
Such a *Sebastian* was my brother too: 2398
BROTHERS = 3*1
A brothers dead loue, which she would keepe fresh 37
*Clo.* Good Madona, why mournst thou? | *Ol.* Good foole, for my
brothers death. 358
*\*Brothers soule, being in heauen. Take away the Foole, | Gentlemen. 363
And all the brothers too: and yet I know not. 1011
BROUGHT = 1*2
*\*knight that you brought in one night here, to be hir woer 134
*\*Fa.* I would exult man: you know he brought me out 1023
What foolish boldnesse brought thee to their mercies, 2221
BROW = 1
*Vio.* My father had a moale vpon his brow. | *Seb.* And so had mine. 2408
BROWNIST = *1
*\*policie I hate: I had as liefe be a Brownist, as a Politi-|cian. 1411
BUDDE = 1
But let concealment like a worme i'th budde 1001
BUILD = *1
*\*To.* Why then build me thy fortunes vpon the basis of 1413
BULKE = 1
For shallow draught and bulke vnprizable, 2206
BULLETS = *1
*\*that you deeme Cannon bullets: There is no slan-|der 385
BUM-BAYLIE = *1
*\*of the Orchard like a bum-Baylie: so soone as euer thou 1694
BURNE = *1
*\*To.* Come, come, Ile go burne some Sacke, tis too late 881
BUSINESSE = *1
*\*put to Sea, that their businesse might be euery thing, 963
BUT *l.*17 31 34 40 81 126 *140 *146 182 *188 189 *198 *207 212 *238 253
262 *317 *339 *340 *341 *343 *372 *386 388 *400 *431 444 *484 *525
543 545 555 570 *622 *630 *635 *638 654 662 *704 *711 *758 *781 *787
803 *838 *841 886 891 972 974 976 986 988 992 1001 1006 1008 1009
*1040 *1110 *1115 *1121 *1137 *1138 *1150 *1178 *1187 1199 *1207
*1226 *1233 *1241 *1248 *1252 *1267 1272 1280 *1295 *1301 1321 1371
1372 1419 *1436 1468 1474 1481 1484 1529 *1531 1543 *1597 *1600
*1633 *1662 1668 1670 *1676 *1685 *1707 1721 1722 *1730 *1741 *1754
*1757 *1779 1799 *1823 1850 1855 1885 1887 1888 1889 *1913 1974
*1993 *2001 2012 *2029 *2074 *2098 2099 2124 2129 2135 *2180 *2196
*2197 2218 2219 2253 2255 *2256 2276 2281 2325 2330 *2344 2351
*2355 2374 2379 2403 2416 2426 *2454 *2461 *2465 *2474 2517 2523
*2543 *2544 2557 2562 2564 2568 2572 2578 = 84*82
BUTTRY = 1
hand to'th Buttry barre, and let it drinke. 184

BUY = *1
*Who I sir, not I sir. God buy you good sir Topas: Mar-|ry Amen. I
will sir, I will.                                                          2085
BY = 44*41, 1*1
*in some commerce with my Ladie, and will by and by | depart.    ,        1691
Come by and by to my Chamber. *Exit*                                      2056
BYRLADY = 1
*Clo.* Byrlady sir, and some dogs will catch well.                        763
BYTH = 1
*Ma.* Sir, I haue not you by'th hand.                                     181
CABINE = 1
*Ol.* Why, what would you? | *Vio.* Make me a willow Cabine at your
gate,                                                                     561
CAKES = 1
Shall be no more Cakes and Ale?                                          812
CALAMITY = *1
*As there is no true Cuckold but calamity, so beauties a                  343
CALL = 11*4
*that you call in question the continuance of his loue. Is               255
And thou shalt liue as freely as thy Lord, | To call his fortunes thine.  290
*Ol.* Let him approach: Call in my Gentlewoman.                           457
And call vpon my soule within the house,                                  563
*bore a minde that enuy could not but call faire: Shee is                638
*Clo.* Hold thy peace, thou Knaue knight. I shall be con-|strain'd in't, to
call thee knaue, Knight.                                                  765
call me knaue. Begin foole: it begins, *Hold thy peace.*                 768
*To.* Send for money knight, if thou hast her not i'th | end, call me Cut. 878
*And.* I knew 'twas I, for many do call mee foole.                       1096
*To.* Wee'l call thee at the Cubiculo: Go. | *Exit Sir Andrew.*          1431
*Ol.* Go call him hither.                                                 1534
*To.* Wonder not, nor admire not in thy minde why I doe call
quickly. Ile call sir *Toby* the whilst.                                 1672
                                                                         1988
*Clo.* Fye, thou dishonest sathan: I call thee by the                    2017
Call forth the holy Father. | *Du.* Come, away.                          2299
CALLD = 4*2
*then *Antonio*, my name is *Sebastian* (which I call'd *Rodo-|rigo*)     626
*my Ladie haue not call'd vp her Steward *Maluolio*, and                  773
Alas, their loue may be call'd appetite,                                  985
Since lowly feigning was call'd complement:                              1311
None can be call'd deform'd, but the vnkinde.                             1888
And since you call'd me Master, for so long:                             2490
CALLES = 2
*Mal.* Gentlewoman, my Lady calles. *Exit.*                              458
*Clo.* She loues another. Who calles, ha?                                2064
CALLING = *1
*Mal.* Calling my Officers about me, in my branch'd                      1063
CALS = 1
*Mal.* Who cals there?                                                   2006
CAME = 6
O, it came ore my eare, like the sweet sound                             9
*Ol.* Whence came you sir? | *Vio.* I can say little more then I haue
studied, & that                                                         472
*Vio.* How can this be? | *Du.* When came he to this Towne?              2245
*But when I came to mans estate, | with hey ho, &c.*                     2564
*But when I came alas to wine, | with hey ho, &c.*                       2568
*But when I came vnto my beds, | with hey ho, &c.*                       2572

31

CAMST = 1
First told me thou wast mad; then cam'st in smiling,　　　　　2519
CAN *l.*109 189 229 230 *304 351 *473 742 *795 832 *852 *853 982 989
990 1015 *1236 *1334 1368 *1417 *1450 *1459 1481 *1603 1751 *1757
1787 1800 1867 1888 2078 2169 *2191 2245 2303 2392 2400 2502
2504 = 26*15
CANARIE = *2
*To. O knight, thou lack'st a cup of Canarie: when did | I see thee so
put downe?　　　　　194
*An. Neuer in your life I thinke, vnlesse you see Ca- | narie　　　196
CANDLE = *1
*my hand, helpe me to a Candle, and pen, inke, and paper:　　　2066
CANDY = 1
That tooke the *Phoenix*, and her fraught from *Candy*,　　　2212
CANNE = *1
*To. A false conclusion: I hate it as an vnfill'd Canne.　　　706
CANNON = *1
*that you deeme Cannon bullets: There is no slan- | der　　　385
CANNOT = 8*7
*he is no longer dishonest; if hee cannot, let the Botcher　　　338
*Ol. Your Lord does know my mind, I cannot loue him　　　550
A gracious person; But yet I cannot loue him:　　　555
I cannot loue him: let him send no more,　　　576
*An. If I cannot recouer your Neece, I am a foule way | out.　　　876
Or thy affection cannot hold the bent:　　　926
*Vio.* But if she cannot loue you sir.　　　974
*Du.* It cannot be so answer'd.　　　975
As you haue for *Oliuia*: you cannot loue her:　　　979
*cannot but turn him into a notable contempt: if you wil | see it follow
me.　　　1207
*cannot hale them together. For *Andrew*, if he were open'd　　　1440
*To.* If this Letter moue him not, his legges cannot: | Ile giu't him.　　　1688
*he cannot by the Duello auoide it: but hee has promised　　　1823
Much more, for what I cannot do for you,　　　1853
*that I cannot pursue with any safety this sport the vppe- | shot.　　　2055
CANOPYD = 1
Loue-thoughts lye rich, when canopy'd with bowres. | *Exeunt*　　　47
CANST *l.*1177 = *1
CANTONS = 1
Write loyall Cantons of contemned loue,　　　564
CAP = 1
Though now you haue no sea-cap on your head:　　　1847
CAP = 10
CAPACITIE = 1*1
That notwithstanding thy capacitie,　　　14
*euident to any formall capacitie. There is no obstruction　　　1127
CAPACITY = *1
*capacity, and breeding: his employment betweene his　　　1703
CAPER = 1*1
*To.* What is thy excellence in a galliard, knight? | *And.* Faith, I can cut
a caper.　　　228
*To.* No sir, it is leggs and thighes: let me see thee ca- | per. Ha, higher:
ha, ha, excellent. *Exeunt*　　　247
CAPILET = 1
Ile giue him my horse, gray Capilet.　　　1804
*CAPTAINE see also Cap.* = 6
*Enter Viola, a Captaine, and Saylors.*　　　50

*CAPTAINE cont.*
  *Vio.* There is a faire behauiour in thee Captaine,          99
  A bawbling Vessell was he Captaine of,           2205
  Ile bring you to a Captaine in this Towne,        2420
  *Vio.* The Captaine that did bring me first on shore   2441
  He hath not told vs of the Captaine yet,         2551
CARE = 2*6
  *To.* Let him be the diuell and he will, I care not: giue    422
  *An.* I, I. I care not for good life.              738
  *Clo.* Not so sir, I do care for something: but in my con-|science  1241
  *sir, I do not care for you: if that be to care for no-|thing  1242
  *Cosine *Toby*, let some of my people haue a speciall care  1584
  *did not I tell you? Sir *Toby*, my Lady prayes you to haue | a care of
  him.                                             1615
  *that had rather go with sir Priest, then sir knight: I care  1789
CAREFULL = *1
  *goes as fairely, as to say, a carefull man, & a great | scholler. The
  Competitors enter.                         1994
CARES = *1
  *death of her brother thus? I am sure care's an enemie to | life.  120
CARPET = *1
  *on carpet consideration, but he is a diuell in priuate brall,  1754
CARRANTO = *1
  *to Church in a Galliard, and come home in a Carranto?  236
CARRIAGE = *1
  *manner how: as a sad face, a reuerend carriage, a slow  1595
CARRY = 1*1
  *Fab.* Carry his water to th'wise woman.         1625
  *carry it thus for our pleasure, and his pennance, til our ve-|ry  1659
CARS = *1
  *Fa.* Though our silence be drawne from vs with cars, | yet peace.  1079
CARST = *1
  *Vio.* I warrant thou art a merry fellow, and car'st for | nothing.  1239
CASE = 1*1
  When time hath sow'd a grizzle on thy case?     2327
  *well as a man in his case may do: has heere writ a letter to  2453
CAST = 1*4
  *for I neuer saw her. I would bee loath to cast away my  467
  *Mal.* Saying, Cosine *Toby*, my Fortunes hauing cast  1085
  *thy selfe to what thou art like to be: cast thy humble  1154
  *the Letter. Cast thy humble slough sayes she: be oppo-|site  1591
  Since you to non-regardance cast my faith,      2277
CASTILIANO = *1
  *parish top. What wench? *Castiliano vulgo*: for here coms | Sir *Andrew*
  *Agueface*.                                    158
CATAYAN = *1
  *To.* My Lady's a *Catayan*, we are politicians, *Maluolio*s  775
CATCH = 6*1
  Euen so quickly may one catch the plague?      591
  *To.* Welcome asse, now let's haue a catch.     719
  *rowze the night-Owle in a Catch, that will drawe three  759
  *And.* And you loue me, let's doo't: I am dogge at a | Catch.  761
  *Clo.* Byrlady sir, and some dogs will catch well.   763
  *An.* Most certaine: Let our Catch be, *Thou Knaue*.  764
  *An.* Good ifaith: Come begin. *Catch sung*     770
CATCHER = 1
  *Fab.* Heere comes my noble gull catcher.     1191

CATCHES = *2
*Catches without any mitigation or remorse of voice? 790
*To. We did keepe time sir in our Catches. Snecke vp. 792
CATECHIZE = *1
*Clo. I must catechize you for it Madona, Good my | Mouse of vertue
answer mee. 354
CATTERWALLING = *1
*Mar. What a catterwalling doe you keepe heere? If 772
CAUES = 1
Fit for the Mountaines, and the barbarous Caues, 1965
CAUGHT = 1
the Trowt, that must be caught with tickling. Exit 1038
CAUSE = 5
Alas, O frailtie is the cause, not wee, 688
my reuenge finde notable cause to worke. 846
For that I woo, thou therefore hast no cause: 1370
You drew your sword vpon me without cause, 2350
Thou shalt be both the Plaintiffe and the Iudge | Of thine owne cause. 2524
CELEBRATION = 1
What time we will our celebration keepe 2145
CEREMONIE = 1
And all the Ceremonie of this compact | Seal'd in my function, by my
testimony: 2322
CERTAIN = *1
*starke naked: for meddle you must that's certain, or for- | sweare to
weare iron about you. 1769
CERTAINE = 1*2
*Vio. Most certaine, if you are she, you do vsurp your 482
An. Most certaine: Let our Catch be, Thou Knaue. 764
*Vio. Nay that's certaine: they that dally nicely with 1228
CESARIO = 15*3
*Cesario, you are like to be much aduanc'd, he hath known 252
Duke. Who saw Cesario hoa? | Vio. On your attendance my Lord heere. 259
Du. Stand you a-while aloofe. Cesario, 261
Now good Cesario, but that peece of song, 886
Marke it Cesario, it is old and plaine; 933
Du. Let all the rest giue place: Once more Cesario, 966
Vio. Cesario is your seruants name, faire Princesse. 1309
Cesario, by the Roses of the Spring, 1365
*speake with her: nor your name is not Master Cesario, 1925
Be not offended, deere Cesario: 1967
Cesario, you do not keepe promise with me. 2258
Ol. What do you say Cesario? Good my Lord. 2261
Ol. Where goes Cesario? | Vio. After him I loue, 2290
Ol. Whether my Lord? Cesario, Husband, stay. 2301
Feare not Cesario, take thy fortunes vp, 2308
*And. The Counts Gentleman, one Cesario: we tooke 2343
Du. My Gentleman Cesario? | *And. Odd's lifelings heere he is: you
broke my head 2345
We will not part from hence. Cesario come 2555
CHACE = 1
A Ring in chace of you. So did I abuse | My selfe, my seruant, and I
feare me you: 1327
CHAINE = *1
*To. Th'art i'th right. Goe sir, rub your Chaine with 815
CHALLENGD = *1
*I'de haue challeng'd him. Let him let the matter slip, and 1803

CHALLENGE = 2*6
*a hungrie, to challenge him the field, and then to breake ........ 823
*To. Doo't knight, Ile write thee a Challenge: or Ile ........ 825
*valour. Challenge me the Counts youth to fight with him ........ 1414
*An. Will either of you beare me a challenge to him? ........ 1420
*An. Heere's the Challenge, reade it: I warrant there's | vinegar and
pepper in't. ........ 1665
I challenge thee for. ........ 1677
*But sir, I will deliuer his Challenge by word of mouth; ........ 1707
*To. I wil meditate the while vpon some horrid message | for a
Challenge. ........ 1716
CHAMBER = 2
And water once a day her Chamber round ........ 35
Come by and by to my Chamber. Exit ........ 2056
CHAMBER-MAID = 1
And. What's that? | To. My Neeces Chamber-maid. ........ 166
CHAMPIAN = *1
*champian discouers not more: This is open, I will bee ........ 1165
CHANCE = 1*1
Cap. True Madam, and to comfort you with chance, ........ 58
*To. I will way-lay thee going home, where if it be thy chance | to kill
me. | Fa. Good. ........ 1679
CHANGEABLE = *1
*Tailor make thy doublet of changeable Taffata, for thy ........ 961
CHANTRY = 1
Into the Chantry by: there before him, ........ 2139
CHAPTER = 1
Ol. In his bosome? In what chapter of his bosome? ........ 518
CHARGE = 2
Ol. Hold Toby, on thy life I charge thee hold. | To. Madam. ........ 1962
O welcome Father: | Father, I charge thee by thy reuerence ........ 2312
CHARGES = *1
*willing to keepe in: therefore it charges me in manners, ........ 624
CHARITY = 1
Of charity, what kinne are you to me? ........ 2395
CHARMD = 1
Fortune forbid my out-side haue not charm'd her: ........ 675
CHARRACTER = 2
With this thy faire and outward charracter. ........ 103
Though I confesse much like the Charracter: ........ 2516
CHAUNT = 1
Do vse to chaunt it: it is silly sooth, ........ 936
CHAWSES = 1
To. Art thou good at these kicke-chawses Knight? ........ 224
CHECKE = 1
And like the Haggard, checke at euery Feather ........ 1276
CHECKES = 1
To. And with what wing the stallion checkes at it? ........ 1124
CHEEKE = 4*1
To. Who, Sir Andrew Ague-cheeke? | Ma. I he. ........ 135
Feede on her damaske cheeke: she pin'd in thought, ........ 1002
*and so looke to thy selfe. Thy friend as thou vsest him, & thy | sworne
enemie, Andrew Ague-cheeke. ........ 1686
*set vpon Ague-cheeke a notable report of valor, and driue ........ 1708
I should my teares let fall vpon your cheeke, ........ 2406
CHERRIE-PIT = *1
*grauity to play at cherrie-pit with sathan. Hang him foul | Colliar. ........ 1638

35

CHEURILL = *1
*but a cheu'rill gloue to a good witte, how quickely the     1226
CHIDE = 1
I will no further chide you.     1469
CHIN = *1
*with lids to them: Item, one necke, one chin, & so forth.     540
CHINNE = *1
*one, though I would not haue it grow on my chinne. Is | thy Lady
within?     1260
CHOOSE = 1*1
*not choose but know who I am. If thou entertainst my loue, let     1178
Mayst smile at this: Thou shalt not choose but goe:     1974
CHRISTIAN = *2
*more wit then a Christian, or an ordinary man ha's: but I     198
*Heathen, a verie Renegatho; for there is no christian     1449
CHUCK = *1
*To. Why how now my bawcock? how dost y chuck? | Mal. Sir.     1635
CHURCH = 3*4
*to Church in a Galliard, and come home in a Carranto?     236
Clo. No sir, I liue by the Church.     1217
*Clo. No such matter sir, I do liue by the Church: For,     1219
*I do liue at my house, and my house dooth stand by the | Church.     1220
*begger dwell neer him: or the Church stands by thy Ta- | bor,     1223
if thy Tabor stand by the Church.     1224
*Schoole i'th Church: I haue dogg'd him like his murthe- | rer.     1455
CHURCHMAN = 1
Vio. Art thou a Churchman?     1218
CHURLISH = 1
Inuites me in this churlish messenger:     680
CIPRESSE = 1
Enough is shewne, a Cipresse, not a bosome,     1335
CIRCUMSTANCE = 1*2
*obstacle, no incredulous or vnsafe circumstance: What     1602
*a mortall arbitrement, but nothing of the circumstance | more.     1779
Do not embrace me, till each circumstance,     2417
CITY = 2
With the memorials, and the things of fame | That do renowne this
City.     1490
Most of our City did. Onely my selfe stood out,     1503
CIUILL = 1*1
Du. Be clamorous, and leape all ciuill bounds,     271
*I speake too loud: Where's Maluolio, he is sad, and ciuill,     1525
CL = *1
CLAD = 1
But am in that dimension grossely clad,     2403
CLAMOROUS = 1
Du. Be clamorous, and leape all ciuill bounds,     271
CLAUSE = 1
Do not extort thy reasons from this clause,     1369
CLEARE = 1
Why you haue giuen me such cleare lights of fauour,     2506
CLEARLY = 1
From my remembrance, clearly banisht his.     2450
CLEERE = 1*2
*to me: my remembrance is very free and cleere from     1746
Let me be cleere of thee.     1922
*and the cleere stores toward the South north, are     2023

CLEFT = 1
An apple cleft in two, is not more twin                                    2388
CLO = 37*61
CLOATHES = *1
*these cloathes are good enough to drinke in, and so bee                   129
CLOCKE = 2
*Clocke strikes.*                                                          1345
The clocke vpbraides me with the waste of time:                           1346
CLODDE-POLE = *1
*in the youth: he will finde it comes from a Clodde-pole.                  1706
CLOG = *1
*and you finde so much blood in his Liuer, as will clog the               1441
CLOSE = 2*1
Doth oft close in pollution: yet of thee                                  101
*this Letter wil make a contemplatiue Ideot of him. Close                 1036
Attested by the holy close of lippes,                                     2320
CLOW = 1*1
*CLOWNE see also Cl., Clo., Clow.* = 11
*Enter Maria, and Clowne.*                                                 296
*Enter Clowne.*                                                           715
*Clowne sings. | O Mistris mine where are you roming?*                    739
*Enter Curio & Clowne.*                                                   931
*Enter Viola and Clowne.*                                                 1214
*Enter Sebastian and Clowne.*                                            1918
*Enter Maria and Clowne.*                                                1985
*Enter Clowne and Fabian.*                                               2153
*Enter Toby and Clowne.*                                                  2352
*Enter Clowne with a Letter, and Fabian.*                                2448
*Clowne sings. | When that I was and a little tine boy,*                 2559
CLOYMENT = 1
That suffer surfet, cloyment, and reuolt,                                 987
CLOYSTRESSE = 1
But like a Cloystresse she will vailed walke,                            34
COATS = 1
in some of your coats for two pence.                                     1947
COCKATRICES = 1
kill one another by the looke, like Cockatrices.                         1712
COCKE = 1
Cocke of him, how he iets vnder his aduanc'd plumes.                     1048
COCKNEY = *1
*Cockney: I prethee now vngird thy strangenes, and tell                  1932
CODLING = *1
*for a boy: as a squash is before tis a pescod, or a Codling             452
COFFER = 1
Hold, there's halfe my Coffer.                                           1864
COFFIN = 1
*On my blacke coffin, let there be strewne:*                             949
COHERE *see* co-here
COLD = 1
*To.* O I, make vp that, he is now at a cold sent.                       1131
COLLIAR = 1
*grauity to play at cherrie-pit with sathan. Hang him foul | Colliar.    1638
COLOUR = 2*2
*loue, wherein by the colour of his beard, the shape of his              849
*Mar.* My purpose is indeed a horse of that colour.                     860
*in yellow stockings, and 'tis a colour she abhorres, and              1203
Still in this fashion, colour, ornament,                                 1903

COLOURD = *1
*dam'd colour'd stocke. Shall we sit about some Reuels? 243
COLOURS = 2
*Clo. Let her hang me: hee that is well hang'de in this | world, needs to
feare no colours. 300
saying was borne, of I feare no colours. 305
COMBINATION = 1
A solemne Combination shall be made | Of our deere soules. Meane
time sweet sister, 2553
COME = 44*27
*Mar. By my troth sir Toby, you must come in earlyer 122
*to Church in a Galliard, and come home in a Carranto? 236
Ol. Cosin, Cosin, how haue you come so earely by | this Lethargie? 417
Ol. Giue me my vaile: come throw it ore my face, 460
Ol. Come to what is important in't: I forgiue you | the praise. 487
Vnlesse (perchance) you come to me againe, 577
If that the youth will come this way to morrow, 603
But come what may, I do adore thee so, 654
*thing more, that you be neuer so hardie to come againe 666
*Mal. Come sir, you peeuishly threw it to her: and 670
*To. Come on, there is sixe pence for you. Let's haue | a song. 732
What's to come, is still vnsure. 750
Then come kisse me sweet and twentie: 752
An. Good ifaith: Come begin. Catch sung 770
*that they come from my Neece, and that shee's in loue | with him. 858
*To. Come, come, Ile go burne some Sacke, tis too late 881
to go to bed now: Come knight, come knight. Exeunt 882
Come, but one verse. 891
Come hither Boy, if euer thou shalt loue 900
Du. O fellow come, the song we had last night: 932
The Song. | Come away, come away death, 941
To. Come thy wayes Signior Fabian. 1018
Fab. Nay Ile come: if I loose a scruple of this sport, 1019
Rascally sheepe-biter, come by some notable shame? 1022
*told me she did affect me, and I haue heard her self come 1041
*Veluet gowne: hauing come from a day bedde, where I | haue left
Oliuia sleeping. 1064
*his first approach before my Lady: hee will come to her 1202
*will conster to them whence you come, who you are, and 1269
*Vio. Madam, I come to whet your gentle thoughts | On his behalfe. 1317
And yet when wit and youth is come to haruest, 1348
Ol. Yet come againe: for thou perhaps mayst moue 1379
To. Come bring vs, bring vs where he is. | Exeunt Omnes. 1463
Ol. I haue sent after him, he sayes hee'l come: 1522
come, for sure the man is tainted in's wits. 1533
*legges: It did come to his hands, and Commaunds shall 1549
Mal. To bed? I sweet heart, and Ile come to thee. 1553
attends my Ladyships pleasure. | Ol. Ile come to him. 1581
*Mal. Oh ho, do you come neere me now: no worse 1587
*can be saide? Nothing that can be, can come betweene 1603
*To. I biddy, come with me. What man, tis not for 1637
*To. Come, wee'l haue him in a darke room & bound. 1657
And I beseech you come againe to morrow. 1727
Ol. Well, come againe to morrow: far-thee-well, 1734
*To. Come sir Andrew, there's no remedie, the Gen-|tleman 1821
*me, as he is a Gentleman and a Soldiour, he will not hurt | you. Come
on, too't. 1824

COME *cont.*

| | |
|---|---|
| *Fab.* O good sir *Toby* hold: heere come the Officers. | 1837 |
| 2.*Off.* Come sir away. | 1856 |
| 2.*Off.* Come sir, I pray you go. | 1878 |
| 1.*Off.* The man growes mad, away with him: \| Come, come sir. | 1891 |
| *\*To.* Come hither Knight, come hither *Fabian*: Weel | 1898 |
| *And.* And I do not. \| *Fab.* Come, let's see the euent. | 1914 |
| *nor I am not sent to you by my Lady, to bid you come | 1924 |
| *To.* Come on sir, hold. | 1948 |
| *\*To.* Come sir, I will not let you go. Come my yong | 1954 |
| *souldier put vp your yron: you are well flesh'd: Come \| on. | 1955 |
| *\*Ol.* Nay come I prethee, would thoud'st be rul'd by me | 1981 |
| Come by and by to my Chamber. *Exit* | 2056 |
| Whiles you are willing it shall come to note, | 2144 |
| *\*Clo.* Marry sir, lullaby to your bountie till I come a-\|gen. | 2195 |
| Come boy with me, my thoughts are ripe in mischiefe: | 2285 |
| Call forth the holy Father. \| *Du.* Come, away. | 2299 |
| If spirits can assume both forme and suite, \| You come to fright vs. | 2400 |
| Bad me come smiling, and crosse-garter'd to you, | 2507 |
| And let no quarrell, nor no braule to come, | 2527 |
| We will not part from hence. *Cesario* come | 2555 |

COMEDIAN = 1

| | |
|---|---|
| *Ol.* Are you a Comedian? \| *\*Vio.* No my profound heart: and yet (by the verie | 477 |

COMES = 11*11

| | |
|---|---|
| *Vio.* I thanke you: heere comes the Count. | 258 |
| *\*Ma.* Peace you rogue, no more o'that: here comes my braines, for heere he comes. *Enter Sir Toby*. | 323 |
| | 408 |
| *him to vnderstand so much, and therefore comes to speake | 436 |
| *a fore knowledge of that too, and therefore comes to | 438 |
| *And.* Heere comes the foole yfaith. | 716 |
| *To.* Heere comes the little villaine: How now my \| Mettle of India? | 1030 |
| *in the name of ieasting, lye thou there: for heere comes | 1037 |
| *Mal.* And then *I.* comes behind. | 1142 |
| *Fab.* Heere comes my noble gull catcher. | 1191 |
| That comes before his eye. This is a practice, | 1277 |
| *\*To.* Looke where the youngest Wren of mine comes. | 1446 |
| *it comes to passe oft, that a terrible oath, with a swagge-\|ring | 1696 |
| *in the youth: he will finde it comes from a Clodde-pole. | 1706 |
| *\*Fab.* Heere he comes with your Neece, giue them way | 1714 |
| *Ant.* I must obey. This comes with seeking you: | 1849 |
| *\*Clo.* Sir *Topas* the Curate, who comes to visit *Maluo-\|lio* the Lunaticke. | 2007 |
| That is deceiueable. But heere the Lady comes. | 2135 |
| *Vio.* Here comes the man sir, that did rescue mee. | 2201 |
| *\*Du.* Heere comes the Countesse, now heauen walkes \| on earth: | 2251 |
| *Heere comes sir *Toby* halting, you shall heare more: but if | 2355 |
| *Seb.* So comes it Lady, you haue beene mistooke: | 2425 |

COMFORT = 2*1

| | |
|---|---|
| *Cap.* True Madam, and to comfort you with chance, | 58 |
| *\*Ol.* God comfort thee: Why dost thou smile so, and \| kisse thy hand so oft? | 1554 |
| Then what befals my selfe: you stand amaz'd, \| But be of comfort. | 1854 |

COMFORTABLE = *1

| | |
|---|---|
| *\*Ol.* A comfortable doctrine, and much may bee saide | 515 |

COMING = 1

| | |
|---|---|
| *O stay and heare, your true loues coming,* | 741 |

COMMAND = 1*3
*Mal. I may command where I adore, but silence like a Lu-|cresse knife: 1115
*Mal. I may command, where I adore: Why shee may 1125
*command me: I serue her, she is my Ladie. Why this is 1126
She could not sway her house, command her followers, 2131
COMMAUNDS = *1
*legges: It did come to his hands, and Commaunds shall 1549
COMMEND = *1
*that my Lady loues me. She did commend my yellow 1170
COMMENDATION = *1
*can more preuaile in mans commendation with woman, | then report
of valour. 1417
COMMENDED = *2
*commended thy yellow stockings, and wish'd to see thee 1159
*Mal. Remember who commended thy yellow stock-|ings. 1569
COMMERCE = *1
*in some commerce with my Ladie, and will by and by | depart. 1691
COMMING = 2*1
*comming downe this walke, he has beene yonder i'the 1033
Where is Maluolio? | Mar. He's comming Madame: 1527
*me what I shall vent to my Lady? Shall I vent to hir that | thou art
comming? 1933
COMMISSION = *2
*But this is from my Commission: I will on with 484
*Ol. Haue you any Commission from your Lord, to 523
COMMIT = 1
What else may hap, to time I will commit, 112
COMMODITY = *1
*Clo. Now Ioue in his next commodity of hayre, send | thee a beard. 1257
COMMON = *1
*him a common recreation, do not thinke I haue witte e-|nough 831
COMPACT = 1
And all the Ceremonie of this compact | Seal'd in my function, by my
testimony: 2322
COMPANIE = 2
When least in companie: prosper well in this, 289
Both day and night did we keepe companie. 2249
COMPANY = 3
(They say) she hath abiur'd the sight | And company of men. 90
*Ma. They that adde moreour, hee's drunke nightly | in your company. 152
company. Is that the meaning of Accost? | Ma. Far you well
Gentlemen. 174
COMPARE = 1*1
*the degree of my betters, & yet I will not compare with | an old man. 226
And can digest as much, make no compare 989
COMPASSE = 1
Cap. That were hard to compasse, 96
COMPETITORS = 1
*goes as fairely, as to say, a carefull man, & a great | scholler. The
Competitors enter. 1994
COMPLAINEST = *1
*as lustrous as Ebony: and yet complainest thou of ob-|struction? 2024
COMPLECTION = 1*2
*forehead, and complection, he shall finde himselfe most 851
Du. What kinde of woman ist? | Vio. Of your complection. 913
*my complection. Besides she vses me with a more ex-|alted 1043

COMPLEMENT = 1
Since lowly feigning was call'd complement: 1311
COMPTIBLE = *1
*no scorne; I am very comptible, euen to the least | sinister vsage. 470
COMPUTENT = *1
*computent iniurie, therefore get you on, and giue him 1765
COMS = *1
*parish top. What wench? *Castiliano vulgo*: for here coms | Sir *Andrew
Agueface*. 158
COMST = *1
*To. Thou comst to the Lady Oliuia, and in my sight she vses* 1675
CON = *1
*taken great paines to con it. Good Beauties, let mee su- | staine 469
CONCEALE = 2
Conceale me what I am, and be my ayde, 105
May liue at peace. He shall conceale it, 2143
CONCEALMENT = 1
But let concealment like a worme i'th budde 1001
CONCEITED = *1
*Fa. He is as horribly conceited of him: and pants, & 1811
CONCEIUD = 1
We had conceiu'd against him. *Maria* writ 2533
CONCERNES = *1
*Vio. It alone concernes your eare: I bring no ouer- | ture 503
CONCERNING = 1
*Clo*. What is the opinion of *Pythagoras* concerning | Wilde-fowle? 2035
CONCLUSION = 1*1
*To. A false conclusion: I hate it as an vnfill'd Canne. 706
But in conclusion put strange speech vpon me, 2218
CONCLUSIONS = *1
*friends I am abused: so that conclusions to be as kisses, if 2173
CONCURRES = *1
*man then sir *Toby* to looke to me. This concurres direct- | ly 1588
CONDEMNE = *1
*Fa*. If this were plaid vpon a stage now, I could con- | demne it as an
improbable fiction. 1649
CONDITION = 1
Taint the condition of this present houre, 2528
CONDUCT = *1
*some conduct of the Lady. I am no fighter, I haue heard 1760
CONFESSE = 3
Though I confesse, on base and ground enough 2227
Though I confesse much like the Charracter: 2516
Most freely I confesse my selfe, and *Toby* 2530
CONFINE = 1*2
*Ma*. I, but you must confine your selfe within the | modest limits of
order. 126
*To. Confine? Ile confine my selfe no finer then I am: 128
CONFIRMD = 1
Confirm'd by mutuall ioynder of your hands, 2319
CONFIRME = 1
That I am *Viola*, which to confirme, 2419
CONFIRMES = *1
*Lord and my Neece, confirmes no lesse. Therefore, this 1704
CONS = *1
*cons State without booke, and vtters it by great swarths. 842

CONSANGUINIOUS = *1
*consanguinious? Am I not of her blood: tilly vally. La-│die,  777
CONSCIENCE = 1*1
*Clo. Not so sir, I do care for something: but in my con-│science  1241
But were my worth, as is my conscience firme,  1484
CONSECRATED = 1
And vnderneath that consecrated roofe,  2140
CONSEQUENTLY = *1
*tricke of singularity: and consequently setts downe the  1594
CONSIDER = *1
*How ist with you? What man, defie the diuell: consider,  1620
CONSIDERATION = *1
*on carpet consideration, but he is a diuell in priuate brall,  1754
CONSIST = *1
*Does not our liues consist of the foure Ele-│ments?  709
CONSISTS = *1
*And. Faith so they say, but I thinke it rather consists │ of eating and
drinking.  711
CONSONANCY = *1
*Mal. M. But then there is no consonancy in the sequell  1137
CONSTANCIE = *1
*minde is a very Opall. I would haue men of such constan-│cie  962
CONSTANT = 3
Saue in the constant image of the creature  904
make the triall of it in any constant question.  2034
Du. Still so cruell? │ Ol. Still so constant Lord.  2266
CONSTANTLY = *1
*constantly but a time-pleaser, an affection'd Asse, that  841
CONSTELLATION = 1
I know thy constellation is right apt  286
CONSTER = *1
*will conster to them whence you come, who you are, and  1269
CONSTITUTION = *1
*the excellent constitution of thy legge, it was form'd vn-│der the starre
of a Galliard.  240
CONSTRAIND = *1
*Clo. Hold thy peace, thou Knaue knight. I shall be con-│strain'd in't, to
call thee knaue, Knight.  765
CONSTRAINED = 1
An. 'Tis not the first time I haue constrained one to  767
CONSTRUCTION = 1*1
*obserue his construction of it: For this night to bed, and  867
Vnder your hard construction must I sit,  1329
CONTAGION = 1
To. To heare by the nose, it is dulcet in contagion.  757
CONTAGIOUS = 2
To. A contagious breath.  755
An. Very sweet, and contagious ifaith.  756
CONTEMNED = 1
Write loyall Cantons of contemned loue,  564
CONTEMPLATION = *1
*Fa. Oh peace: Contemplation makes a rare Turkey  1047
CONTEMPLATIUE = *1
*this Letter wil make a contemplatiue Ideot of him. Close  1036
CONTEMPT = 3*2
Plac'd in contempt: Farwell fayre crueltie. Exit  584
*at any thing more then contempt, you would not giue  818

CONTEMPT *cont.*
  great *P's*. It is in contempt of question her hand. 1103
  *cannot but turn him into a notable contempt: if you wil | see it follow
  me. 1207
  In the contempt and anger of his lip, 1362
CONTENT = 1
  Vpon thee in the Letter: prethee be content, 2521
CONTINENT = 1
  As doth that Orbed Continent, the fire, | That seuers day from night. 2437
CONTINUANCE = *1
  *that you call in question the continuance of his loue. Is 255
CONTINUE = *1
  *Val. If the Duke continue these fauours towards you 251
CONTRACT = 1
  *Priest*. A Contract of eternall bond of loue, 2318
CONTRACTED = 1
  You would haue bin contracted to a Maid, 2427
CONTRARY = 1
  *Du*. Iust the contrary: the better for thy friends. 2167
CONTROLL = 1
  familiar smile with an austere regard of controll. 1082
CONUENIENTLY = *1
  *knauery. If he may bee conueniently deliuer'd, I would 2053
CONUENTS = 1
  When that is knowne, and golden time conuents 2552
CONUEY = *1
  *and light: and conuey what I will set downe to my 2095
COOLE = *1
  *To. Past question, for thou seest it will not coole my | (nature 211
COPIE = 1
  If you will leade these graces to the graue, | And leaue the world no
  copie. 534
CORNER = *1
  *To. Go sir *Andrew*: scout mee for him at the corner 1693
CORPES = 1
  *My poore corpes, where my bones shall be throwne:* 951
CORRUPTER = *1
  *the bigger, I am indeede not her foole, but hir cor-|rupter of words. 1248
CORRUPTION = 1
  Or any taint of vice, whose strong corruption | Inhabites our fraile
  blood. 1875
COSIN = 3*1
  *a nights: your Cosin, my Lady, takes great exceptions | to your ill
  houres. 123
  *Ol. By mine honor halfe drunke. What is he at the | gate Cosin? | To.
  A Gentleman. 410
  *Ol*. Cosin, Cosin, how haue you come so earely by | this Lethargie? 417
COSINE = *3
  *Mal*. Saying, Cosine *Toby*, my Fortunes hauing cast 1085
  *Cosine *Toby*, let some of my people haue a speciall care 1584
  *darkenesse, and giuen your drunken Cosine rule ouer me, 2471
COST = 1
  Heere at my house, and at my proper cost. 2485
COUETOUSNESSE = *1
  *my desire of hauing is the sinne of couetousnesse: but as 2197
COULD *l*.67 545 *636 *638 1049 *1129 1185 1186 1470 1541 *1580 *1649
  *1785 2119 2131 2181 2570 = 11*6

COUNCELL = 1
His councell now might do me golden seruice, 2122
COUNSELL = 1*1
*Clo. Two faults Madona, that drinke & good counsell 335
you could make it another. | Du. O you giue me ill counsell. 2181
COUNT = 10*4
Vio. What's shee? | Cap. A vertuous maid, the daughter of a Count 85
the Count himselfe here hard by, wooes her. 217
*To. Shee'l none o'th Count, she'l not match aboue hir 218
Vio. I thanke you: heere comes the Count. 258
Ol. From the Count Orsino, is it? 394
*from the Count, I am sicke, or not at home. What you | will, to
dismisse it. Exit Maluo. 402
bound to the Count Orsino's Court, farewell. Exit 650
Mal. To be Count Maluolio. | To. Ah Rogue. 1051
Vio. I saw thee late at the Count Orsino's. 1250
Y'are seruant to the Count Orsino youth. 1312
Once in a sea-fight 'gainst the Count his gallies, 1494
*Ser. Madame, the young Gentleman of the Count 1579
*2.Off. Anthonio, I arrest thee at the suit of Count Orsino 1844
I was preseru'd to serue this Noble Count: 2422
COUNTERFEIT = 1
mad indeed, or do you but counterfeit. 2099
COUNTERFETS = 1
To. The knaue counterfets well: a good knaue. | Maluolio within. 2004
COUNTES = 1
The Countes man: he left this Ring behinde him 599
COUNTESSE = *2
*Mal. Were not you eu'n now, with the Countesse O-|liuia? 658
*Du. Heere comes the Countesse, now heauen walkes | on earth: 2251
COUNTREY = 1
The like of him. Know'st thou this Countrey? | Cap. I Madam well, for
I was bred and borne 71
COUNTREYMAN = 1
What Countreyman? What name? What Parentage? | Vio. Of Messaline:
Sebastian was my Fatĥer, 2396
COUNTRY = 1
Vio. What Country (Friends) is this? | Cap. This is Illyria Ladie. 51
COUNTS = *4
*the youth of the Counts was to day with my Lady, she is 828
*Counts Seruing-man, then euer she bestow'd vpon mee: 1387
*valour. Challenge me the Counts youth to fight with him 1414
*And. The Counts Gentleman, one Cesario: we tooke 2343
COUPLET = 1
whisper ore a couplet or two of most sage sawes. 1899
COURAGE = 1
(Courage and hope both teaching him the practise) 63
COURT = 2
bound to the Count Orsino's Court, farewell. Exit 650
I haue many enemies in Orsino's Court, 652
COURTEOUS = *1
*me this courteous office, as to know of the Knight what 1772
COURTIER = *1
*And. That youth's a rare Courtier, raine odours, wel. 1300
COWARD = *6
*the gift of a Coward, to allay the gust he hath in quarrel-|ling, 147
*in Illyria: he's a Coward and a Coystrill that will not 156

COWARD *cont.*
*To.* A very dishonest paltry boy, and more a coward     1906
*Fab.* A Coward, a most deuout Coward, religious in | it.     1910
*him for a Coward, but hee's the verie diuell, incardinate.     2344
COWARDSHIP = *1
*heere in necessity, and denying him: and for his coward-|ship aske
*Fabian.*     1908
COXCOMBE = *3
*Toby* a bloody Coxcombe too: for the loue of God your     2340
*And.* If a bloody coxcombe be a hurt, you haue hurt     2353
*To.* Will you helpe an Asse-head, and a coxcombe, &     2369
COXECOMBE = 1
me: I thinke you set nothing by a bloody Coxecombe.     2354
COYSTRILL = *1
*in Illyria: he's a Coward and a Coystrill that will not     156
COZ = *1
*o'my Coz: for he's in the third degree of drinke: hee's | drown'd: go
looke after him.     429
COZIERS = *1
*of my Ladies house, that ye squeak out your Cozi-|ers     789
CO-HERE = 1
Of place, time, fortune, do co-here and iumpe     2418
CRAFT = 1
Or will not else thy craft so quickely grow,     2328
CRAMD = *1
*The best perswaded of himselfe: so cram'd (as he thinkes)     843
CRAMME = *1
*sonne should be a foole: whose scull, Ioue cramme with     407
CRAUE = *1
*yours; therefore I shall craue of you your leaue,     617
CRAUES = 1
And to do that well, craues a kinde of wit:     1273
CREATURE = 1
Saue in the constant image of the creature     904
CREATURES = 1
Then these two creatures. Which is *Sebastian?* | *Ol.* Most wonderfull.     2389
CREDIT = 1
*Mal.* This is much credit to you.     805
CREDITE = 1
Yet there he was, and there I found this credite,     2120
CREEPE = 1
To creepe in at mine eyes. Well, let it be.     594
CRESSIDA = 1*1
*Clo.* I would play Lord *Pandarus* of *Phrygia* sir, to bring | a *Cressida* to
this *Troylus.*     1264
*begger: *Cressida* was a begger. My Lady is within sir. I     1268
CRIDE = 1
Cride fame and honor on him: What's the matter? | 1.*Offi.* *Orsino*, this
is that *Anthonio*     2210
CRIES = 1
cries ah ha, to the diuell:     2110
CROSSE = 3*3
*euer crosse garter'd: I say remember, goe too, thou art     1160
*strange, stout, in yellow stockings, and crosse Garter'd,     1175
*crosse garter'd, a fashion shee detests: and hee will smile     1204
*To.* And crosse garter'd? | *Mar.* Most villanously: like a Pedant that
keepes a     1453

CROSSE *cont.*
*Mal.* And wish'd to see thee crosse garter'd. | *Ol.* Crosse garter'd?    1572
CROSSEGARTERD = *1
*stockings of late, shee did praise my legge being crosse-|garter'd,    1171
CROSSE-GARTERD = 1
Bad me come smiling, and crosse-garter'd to you,    2507
CROSSE-GARTERING = 1
This crosse-gartering, but what of that?    1543
CROW = *1
*I take these Wisemen, that crow so at these set kinde of    380
CROWND = 1
Could be but recompenc'd, though you were crown'd | The non-pareil
of beautie.    545
CROWNE = 1 *1
*and crowne thee for a finder of madmen: but see, but see.    1662
One day shall crowne th'alliance on't, so please you,    2484
CROWNED = 1
Where he sits crowned in his masters spight.    2284
CROWNER = *1
*Ol. Go thou and seeke the Crowner, and let him sitte    428
CRUELL = 4
And my desires like fell and cruell hounds,    27
*I am slaine by a faire cruell maide:*    945
*Du.* Still so cruell? | *Ol.* Still so constant Lord.    2266
Him will I teare out of that cruell eye,    2283
CRUELLST = 1
Lady, you are the cruell'st shee aliue,    533
CRUELTIE = 2
Plac'd in contempt: Farwell fayre crueltie. *Exit*    584
Get thee to yond same soueraigne crueltie:    967
CRUELTY = 1
*Fab.* And his opposit the youth beares in his visage no | great presage
of cruelty.    1443
CRUMS = 1
crums. A stope of Wine *Maria.*    816
CRUSH = *1
*and yet to crush this a little, it would bow to mee, for e-|uery    1147
CRY = 2 *1
Cry out *Oliuia*: O you should not rest    568
*Fab.* Sowter will cry vpon't for all this, though it bee | as ranke as a
Fox.    1132
*Fa.* And *O* shall end, I hope. | *To.* I, or Ile cudgell him, and make him
cry *O*.    1140
CS = 1 *1
*very *C's*, her *V's*, and her *T's*, and thus makes shee her    1102
*An.* Her *C's*, her *V's*, and her *T's*: why that?    1104
CU = 2
CUB = 1
*Du.* O thou dissembling Cub: what wilt thou be    2326
CUBICULO = 1
*To.* Wee'l call thee at the Cubiculo: Go. | *Exit Sir Andrew.*    1431
CUCKOLD = *1
*As there is no true Cuckold but calamity, so beauties a    343
CUCULLUS = *1
*Clo.* Misprision in the highest degree. Lady, *Cucullus*    347

CUDGELL = 1
*Fa.* And *O* shall end, I hope. | *To.* I, or Ile cudgell him, and make him cry *O.* 1140
CUFFE = *1
*To.* Do, cuffe him soundly, but neuer draw thy sword 1913
CUNNING = 4*1
Natures owne sweet, and cunning hand laid on: 532
She loues me sure, the cunning of her passion 679
To force that on you in a shamefull cunning 1330
*and so cunning in Fence, I'de haue seene him damn'd ere 1802
Where being apprehended, his false cunning 2238
CUP = *1
*To.* O knight, thou lack'st a cup of Canarie: when did | I see thee so put downe? 194
CUR = *2
CURATE = *2
*make him beleeue thou art sir *Topas* the Curate, doe it 1987
*Clo.* Sir *Topas* the Curate, who comes to visit *Maluo-|lio* the Lunaticke. 2007
CURIO *see also Cu., Cur.* = 6
*Enter Orsino Duke of Illyria, Curio, and other | Lords.* 2
*Cu.* Will you go hunt my Lord? | *Du.* What *Curio?* | *Cu.* The Hart. 20
*Enter Duke, Curio, and Attendants.* 257
*Enter Duke, Viola, Curio, and others.* 884
*Enter Curio & Clowne.* 931
*Enter Duke, Viola, Curio, and Lords.* 2160
CURRE = *1
*Fab.* Did not I say he would worke it out, the Curre | is excellent at faults. 1135
CURST = *1
*To.* Go, write it in a martial hand, be curst and briefe: 1421
CURTAIN = *1
*but we will draw the Curtain, and shew you the picture. 525
CURTAINE = *1
*these gifts a Curtaine before 'em? Are they like to take 234
CURTESIE = *2
*when the curtesie of it is so fearefull. Speake your office. 502
*that will vse the diuell himselfe with curtesie: sayst thou | that house is darke? 2019
CURTSIES = 1
*Toby* approaches; curtsies there to me. | *To.* Shall this fellow liue? 1077
CUT = 3
*To.* What is thy excellence in a galliard, knight? | *And.* Faith, I can cut a caper. 228
*To.* And I can cut the Mutton too't. 230
*To.* Send for money knight, if thou hast her not i'th | end, call me Cut. 878
CYPRESSE *see also* Cipresse = 1
*And in sad cypresse let me be laide.* 943
DAD = 1
Like a mad lad, paire thy nayles dad, 2111
DAGGER = 1*1
*To.* Hold sir, or Ile throw your dagger ore the house 1945
Who with dagger of lath, in his rage and his wrath, 2109
DALLIE = *1
*Vio.* Why man? | *Clo.* Why sir, her names a word, and to dallie with 1231
DALLIES = 1
And dallies with the innocence of loue, | Like the old age. 937

DALLY = *1
*Vio. Nay that's certaine: they that dally nicely with     1228
DAMASKE = 1
Feede on her damaske cheeke: she pin'd in thought,     1002
DAMD = *1
*dam'd colour'd stocke. Shall we sit about some Reuels?     243
DAMND = *1
*and so cunning in Fence, I'de haue seene him damn'd ere     1802
DANCE = *1
*But shall we make the Welkin dance indeed? Shall wee     758
DANCING = *1
*dancing, and beare-bayting: O had I but followed the | Arts.     207
DANGER = 4
That danger shall seeme sport, and I will go. Exit.     655
I do not without danger walke these streetes.     1493
Into the danger of this aduerse Towne,     2236
(Not meaning to partake with me in danger)     2239
DARE = 1*1
To. Shall I bid him go, and spare not? | Clo. O no, no, no, no, you dare
not.     808
*To. I dare lay any money, twill be nothing yet. Exit     1916
DARES = 1
Ant. One sir, that for his loue dares yet do more     1833
DARKE = 3*3
*To. Come, wee'l haue him in a darke room & bound.     1657
*that will vse the diuell himselfe with curtesie: sayst thou | that house is
darke?     2019
*Mal. I am not mad sir Topas, I say to you this house is | darke.     2026
*Mal. I say this house is as darke as Ignorance, thogh     2031
*Ignorance were as darke as hell; and I say there was ne- | uer     2032
Kept in a darke house, visited by the Priest,     2512
DARKELY = *1
*Seb. By your patience, no: my starres shine darkely     615
DARKENESSE = 1*3
*Clo. Fare thee well: remaine thou still in darkenesse,     2042
*darkenesse, send Ministers to me, Asses, and doe all they     2077
To keepe in darkenesse, what occasion now     2315
*darkenesse, and giuen your drunken Cosine rule ouer me,     2471
DARKNESSE = 1*1
*sir Topas do not thinke I am mad: they haue layde mee | heere in
hideous darknesse.     2015
*Clo. Madman thou errest: I say there is no darknesse     2028
DARST = 1
If thou dar'st tempt me further, draw thy sword.     1958
DAUGHTER = 2
Vio. What's shee? | Cap. A vertuous maid, the daughter of a Count     85
My Father had a daughter lou'd a man     996
DAUGHTERS = 1
Vio. I am all the daughters of my Fathers house,     1010
DAWES = 1
Yes Nightingales answere Dawes.     1558
DAY = 12*5
And water once a day her Chamber round     35
*a barren rascall: I saw him put down the other day, with     376
breach of the sea, was my sister drown'd. | Ant. Alas the day.     632
As I am woman (now alas the day)     695
To. O the twelfe day of December.     783

DAY *cont.*
*the youth of the Counts was to day with my Lady, she is     828
*Veluet gowne: hauing come from a day bedde, where I | haue left
*Oliuia* sleeping.     1064
*Clo.* Well-a-day, that you were sir.     2093
*Ant.* To day my Lord: and for three months before,     2247
Both day and night did we keepe companie.     2249
*Vio.* And dide that day when *Viola* from her birth | Had numbred
thirteene yeares.     2410
That day that made my sister thirteene yeares.     2414
As doth that Orbed Continent, the fire, | That seuers day from night.     2437
*you, I should haue giuen't you to day morning. But as a     2454
One day shall crowne th'alliance on't, so please you,     2484
*for the raine it raineth euery day.*     2563
*and wee'l striue to please you euery day.*     2579
DAYES = 2
you but three dayes, and already you are no stranger.     253
*Clo.* His eyes do shew his dayes are almost done. | *Mal.* Is't euen so?     801
DAYLIGHT = *1
*seruices with thee, the fortunate vnhappy daylight and     1164
DE *l.*144 = 1
DEAD = 2
A brothers dead loue, which she would keepe fresh     37
And sing them lowd euen in the dead of night:     565
DEADLY = 2
With such a suffring, such a deadly life:     558
*be yare in thy preparation, for thy assaylant is quick, skil- | full, and
deadly.     1743
DEALE = 1*1
*Ol.* O what a deale of scorne, lookes beautifull?     1361
*Mal.* Ah ha, does she so? | *To.* Go too, go too: peace, peace, wee must
deale     1617
DEALER = 1
*Du.* Well, I will be so much a sinner to be a double | dealer: there's
another.     2185
DEALING = 1*1
You should finde better dealing: what's to do?     1485
*Clo.* But that it would be double dealing sir, I would     2180
DEATH = 6*3
*death of her brother thus? I am sure care's an enemie to | life.     120
*Clo.* Good Madona, why mournst thou? | *Ol.* Good foole, for my
brothers death.     358
*Mal.* Yes, and shall do, till the pangs of death shake     367
*The Song.* | *Come away, come away death,*     941
*My part of death no one so true did share it.*     947
let me be boyl'd to death with Melancholly.     1020
*can be none, but by pangs of death and sepulcher: Hob, | nob, is his
word: giu't or take't.     1757
I snatch'd one halfe out of the iawes of death,     1880
Like to th'Egyptian theefe, at point of death     2274
DEATHS = 1
To do you rest, a thousand deaths would dye.     2289
DEBT = 1
To pay this debt of loue but to a brother,     40
DECAIES = *1
*him: Infirmity that decaies the wise, doth euer make the | better foole.     368

DECEIUD = 1
Nor are you therein (by my life) deceiu'd,                                    2428
DECEIUEABLE = 1
That is deceiueable. But heere the Lady comes.                               2135
DECEMBER = 1
To. *O the twelfe day of December.*                                          783
DECREED = 1
What is decreed, must be: and be this so. | *Finis, Actus primus.*           609
DEDICATION = 1
All his in dedication. For his sake,                                         2234
DEEDE = *1
*\*An.* 'Twere as good a deede as to drink when a mans                       822
DEEME = *1
*that you deeme Cannon bullets: There is no slan-|der                        385
DEEPELY = *1
*\*Fa.* O peace, now he's deepely in: looke how imagi-|nation blowes
him.                                                                         1058
DEERE = 14*2
Who shortly also dide: for whose deere loue                                  89
To. *Pur-quoy* my deere knight?                                              204
Surprize her with discourse of my deere faith;                              275
*Vio.* I thinke not so, my Lord. | *Du.* Deere Lad, beleeue it;             279
*\*To.* Farewell deere heart, since I must needs be gone.                   799
*\*To.* What for being a Puritan, thy exquisite reason, | deere knight.     836
*Vio.* Deere Lady. | *Ol.* Giue me leaue, beseech you: I did send,          1324
*To.* Thy reason deere venom, giue thy reason.                              1384
*Fa.* This is a deere Manakin to you Sir *Toby.*                            1433
*\*To.* I haue beene deere to him lad, some two thousand | strong, or so.   1434
For which if I be lapsed in this place | I shall pay deere.                 1504
Proue true imagination, oh proue true, | That I deere brother, be now
tane for you.                                                              1896
Be not offended, deere *Cesario*:                                           1967
Whom thou in termes so bloudie, and so deere | Hast made thine
enemies?                                                                   2222
*Seb. Anthonio:* O my deere *Anthonio,*                                     2382
A solemne Combination shall be made | Of our deere soules. Meane
time sweet sister,                                                         2553
DEERELY = 2
How will this fadge? My master loues her deerely,                          690
And whom, by heauen I sweare, I tender deerely,                            2282
DEERO = *1
*in my presence still smile, deero my sweete, I prethee.* Ioue             1180
DEFENCE = *1
*\*To.* That defence thou hast, betake the too't: of what                   1739
DEFEND = 1*1
*\*Vio.* Pray God defend me: a little thing would make                      1818
Drew to defend him, when he was beset:                                     2237
DEFIE = 1*2
*\*To.* Letcherie, I defie Letchery: there's one at the | gate.             419
*How ist with you? What man, defie the diuell: consider,                    1620
If you offend him, I for him defie you.                                     1831
DEFORMD = 1
None can be call'd deform'd, but the vnkinde.                               1888
DEGREE = 2*5
*degree, neither in estate, yeares, nor wit: I haue heard her               219
*the degree of my betters, & yet I will not compare with | an old man.      226
*\*Clo.* Misprision in the highest degree. Lady, *Cucullus*                 347

DEGREE *cont.*
*o'my Coz: for he's in the third degree of drinke: hee's | drown'd: go
looke after him.                                                                   429
*Ol.* That's a degree to loue.                                                     1338
*degree, but Fellow. Why euery thing adheres togither,                             1600
*Mal.* Foole, Ile requite it in the highest degree: | I prethee be gone.           2103
DEITY = 1
Nor can there be that Deity in my nature                                           2392
DELAY = 2
*Ol.* Who of my people hold him in delay? | *Ma.* Sir *Toby* Madam, your
kinsman.                                                                           398
*In delay there lies no plentie,*                                                  751
DELICULO = *1
*midnight, is to be vp betimes, and *Deliculo surgere,* thou | know'st.            702
DELIGHT = *3
*strangest minde i'th world: I delight in Maskes and Re-|uels
sometimes altogether.                                                              222
*Mal.* I maruell your Ladyship takes delight in such                              375
*Oliuiaes* Father tooke much delight in. He is about the | house.                  896
DELIUER = 1*3
*Ol.* Sure you haue some hiddeous matter to deliuer,                              501
deliuer thy indignation to him by word of mouth.                                   826
*To.* Now will not I deliuer his Letter: for the behaui-|our                       1701
*But sir, I will deliuer his Challenge by word of mouth;                           1707
DELIUERD = 2*1
*knauery. If he may bee conueniently deliuer'd, I would                            2053
When they are deliuer'd. | *Ol.* Open't, and read it.                              2456
*Ol.* See him deliuer'd *Fabian,* bring him hither:                                2481
DELIUERED = 1
And might not be deliuered to the world                                            93
DELIUERS = 1
deliuers the Madman. *By the Lord Madam.*                                          2459
DELIUERT = 1
*Fa.* We shall haue a rare Letter from him; but you'le | not deliuer't.            1436
DEMURE = *1
*a demure trauaile of regard: telling them I knowe my                             1069
DENAY = 1
My loue can giue no place, bide no denay. *Exeunt*                                 1015
DENIALL = 2
*speake with you. What is to be said to him Ladie, hee's | fortified
against any deniall.                                                               439
In your deniall, I would finde no sence,                                           559
DENIDE = 2
Be not deni'de accesse, stand at her doores,                                       265
While one would winke: denide me mine owne purse,                                  2242
DENIE = 2
Do not denie, beshrew his soule for mee,                                           1975
You must not now denie it is your hand,                                            2501
DENY = 3
What shall you aske of me that Ile deny,                                           1728
*Ant.* Will you deny me now,                                                       1865
*Du.* Husband? | *Ol.* I Husband. Can he that deny?                                2302
DENYING = *1
*heere in necessity, and denying him: and for his coward-|ship aske
*Fabian.*                                                                          1908
DEPART = 1*1
*in some commerce with my Ladie, and will by and by | depart.                      1691

DEPART *cont.*
*Seb.* I prethee foolish greeke depart from me, there's      1935
DEPLORE = 1
Will I my Masters teares to you deplore.      1378
DERIUES = *1
*To.* Sir, no: his indignation deriues it selfe out of a ve- | ry      1764
DESERTS = 1
Ist possible that my deserts to you | Can lacke perswasion. Do not
tempt my misery,      1866
DESERUE = *1
*Mal.* Good foole, as euer thou wilt deserue well at      2065
DESIRE = 4*7
*Ma.* Good Mistris accost, I desire better acquaintance | *Ma.* My name
is *Mary* sir.      168
Desire him not to flatter with his Lord,      601
*kill him, whom you haue recouer'd, desire it not. Fare      646
*Mar.* If you desire the spleene, and will laughe your      1447
*Ant.* I could not stay behinde you: my desire      1470
You haue desire to purchase: and your store      1514
*Vio.* I will returne againe into the house, and desire      1759
*his desire. Backe you shall not to the house, vnlesse you      1766
*Clo.* Do not desire to see this Letter.      2157
*Fab.* This is to giue a dogge, and in recompence desire | my dogge
againe.      2158
*my desire of hauing is the sinne of couetousnesse: but as      2197
DESIRES = 2
And my desires like fell and cruell hounds,      27
*Mar.* Madam, there is at the gate, a young Gentle- | man, much desires
to speake with you.      392
DESIROUS = *1
*To.* Will you incounter the house, my Neece is desi- | rous      1287
DESIRST = *2
*made if thou desir'st to be so: If not, let me see thee a ste- | ward      1161
*Mal.* Go too, thou art made, if thou desir'st to be so.      1574
DESPERATE = 2*1
*into a desperate assurance, she will none of him. And one      665
My state is desperate for my maisters loue:      694
Heere in the streets, desperate of shame and state,      2215
DESPIGHT = *1
*but thy intercepter full of despight, bloody as the Hun- | ter,      1741
DETERMINATE = *1
*Seb.* No sooth sir: my determinate voyage is meere      621
DETESTED = 1
*Ol.* Aye me detested, how am I beguil'd?      2296
DETESTS = *1
*crosse garter'd, a fashion shee detests: and hee will smile      1204
DETRACTION = *1
*see more detraction at your heeles, then Fortunes before | you.      1144
DEUICE = 4*2
*To.* Excellent, I smell a deuice. | *An.* I hau't in my nose too.      855
*To.* I could marry this wench for this deuice. | *An.* So could I too.      1185
*To.* His very genius hath taken the infection of the | deuice man.      1651
*Mar.* Nay pursue him now, least the deuice take ayre, | and taint.      1653
*on him: at which time, we wil bring the deuice to the bar      1661
Set this deuice against *Maluolio* heere,      2531
DEUILL *see also* diuell = 1
Are empty trunkes, ore-flourish'd by the deuill.      1890

DEUILLS *see* diuils
DEUISE = *1
  *deuise, the very man. I do not now foole my selfe, to let        1168
DEUOTION = 2
  And to his image, which me thought did promise | Most venerable
  worth, did I deuotion.        1882
  That ere deuotion tender'd. What shall I do?        2271
DEUOURD = 1
  Whom the blinde waues and surges haue deuour'd:        2394
DEUOUT = *1
  *Fab. A Coward, a most deuout Coward, religious in | it.        1910
DEXTERIOUSLY = 1
  *Ol.* Can you do it? | *Clo.* Dexteriously, good Madona.        351
DIALOGUE = 1
  *'tis not that time of Moone with me, to make one in so | skipping a
  dialogue.        495
DIANAS = 1
  That say thou art a man: *Dianas* lip        282
DICKE = 1
  Sot, didst see Dicke Surgeon, sot?        2360
DID *l.*24 59 84 *194 *239 528 557 678 *717 *727 *792 888 947 *1041
  *1135 *1170 *1171 1325 1326 1327 1389 *1398 1471 1495 1503 *1549
  *1615 1882 1883 2098 2121 2201 2207 2213 2216 2217 2231 2232 2235
  2249 *2347 2357 2404 2441 2478 = 32*13
DIDE = 4
  That dide some tweluemonth since, then leauing her        87
  Who shortly also dide: for whose deere loue        89
  *Du.* But di'de thy sister of her loue my Boy?        1009
  *Vio.* And dide that day when *Viola* from her birth | Had numbred
  thirteene yeares.        2410
DIDST = 1
  Sot, didst see Dicke Surgeon, sot?        2360
DIE *see also* dye = 1
  To die, euen when they to perfection grow.        930
DIES = *1
  *Clo. Bonos dies* sir *Toby*: for as the old hermit of *Prage*        1998
DIET *see* dyet
DIEU = 1
  And. *Dieu vou guard Monsieur.* | *Vio. Et vouz ousie vostre seruiture.*        1284
DIGEST = 1
  And can digest as much, make no compare        989
DIMENSION = 2
  And in dimension, and the shape of nature,        554
  But am in that dimension grossely clad,        2403
DIRECT = 1
  Farewell, and take her, but direct thy feete,        2330
DIRECTLY = *1
  *man then sir *Toby* to looke to me. This concurres direct- | ly        1588
DIRTIE = 1
  Prizes not quantitie of dirtie lands,        969
DISCARD = *1
  *Mal.* Go off, I discard you: let me enioy my priuate: | go off.        1612
DISCOUERS = *1
  *champian discouers not more: This is open, I will bee        1165
DISCOURSE = 2
  Surprize her with discourse of my deere faith;        275
  So farre exceed all instance, all discourse,        2126

DISCREET = 1 *1
*nor no rayling, in a knowne discreet man, though hee do | nothing but
reproue. 387
With such a smooth, discreet, and stable bearing 2133
DISGRACD = 1
words are very Rascals, since bonds disgrac'd them. | *Vio.* Thy reason
man? 1234
DISGUISE = 2
For such disguise as haply shall become 106
Disguise, I see thou art a wickednesse, 684
DISH = 1
*Fab.* What dish a poyson has she drest him? 1123
DISHONEST *see also* dis-honest = *4
*not dry: bid the dishonest man mend himself, if he mend, 337
*he is no longer dishonest; if hee cannot, let the Botcher 338
*To.* A very dishonest paltry boy, and more a coward 1906
*Clo.* Fye, thou dishonest sathan: I call thee by the 2017
DISHONESTY = *1
*then a Hare, his dishonesty appeares, in leauing his frend 1907
DISLIKE = 1
*Now you see sir, how your fooling growes old, & peo- | ple dislike it. 404
DISMISSE = 1
*from the Count, I am sicke, or not at home. What you | will, to
dismisse it. *Exit Maluo.* 402
DISMOUNT = *1
*attends thee at the Orchard end: dismount thy tucke, 1742
DISORDERS = *1
*she's nothing ally'd to your disorders. If you can 795
DISPATCH = 1
Take, and giue backe affayres, and their dispatch, 2132
DISPLAID = 1
Being once displaid, doth fall that verie howre. 928
DISPOSD = *1
*An.* I, he do's well enough if he be dispos'd, and so 780
DISPOSITION = 1 *2
*and of free disposition, is to take those things for Bird- | bolts, 384
*vpon her, which will now be so vnsuteable to her dispo- | sition, 1205
Grace and good disposition attend your Ladyship: 1352
DISPOSSESSE = *1
*of thy wits, and feare to kill a Woodcocke, lest thou dis- | possesse 2044
DISPUTES = 1
For though my soule disputes well with my sence, 2123
DISSEMBLE = *1
*Clo.* Well, Ile put it on, and I will dissemble my selfe 1989
DISSEMBLED = *1
*in't, and I would I were the first that euer dissembled in 1990
DISSEMBLING = 1
*Du.* O thou dissembling Cub: what wilt thou be 2326
DISTAFFE = *1
*To.* Excellent, it hangs like flax on a distaffe: & I hope 213
DISTEMPER = *1
*ouer me; the malignancie of my fate, might perhaps di- | stemper 616
DISTEMPERD = *1
*with a distemper'd appetite. To be generous, guiltlesse, 383
DISTINCTION = 1
*your Neece, on a forgotten matter wee can hardly make | distinction of
our hands. 853

54

DISTRACT = 1
They say poore Gentleman, he's much distract. 2447
DISTRACTEDLY = 1
For she did speake in starts distractedly. 678
DISTRACTION = 2
I know not what 'twas, but distraction. 2219
*Du*. This sauours not much of distraction. 2480
DISTRUST = 1
That I am readie to distrust mine eyes, 2127
DIS-HONEST = 1
*Ol*. Go too, y'are a dry foole: Ile no more of you: be-|sides you grow
dis-honest. 333
DIUELL = 4*8
*To*. Let him be the diuell and he will, I care not: giue 422
But if you were the diuell, you are faire: 543
*To*. To the gates of Tartar, thou most excellent diuell | of wit. 1209
*How ist with you? What man, defie the diuell: consider, 1620
*Mar*. La you, and you speake ill of the diuell, how 1623
*on carpet consideration, but he is a diuell in priuate brall, 1754
*To*. Why man hee's a verie diuell, I haue not seen such 1792
*I haue his horse to take vp the quarrell, I haue perswaded | him the
youths a diuell. 1809
*that will vse the diuell himselfe with curtesie: sayst thou | that house is
darke? 2019
cries ah ha, to the diuell: 2110
Adieu good man diuell. *Exit* 2112
*him for a Coward, but hee's the verie diuell, incardinate. 2344
DIUELS = *1
*the diuels of hell be drawne in little, and Legion himselfe | possest
him, yet Ile speake to him. 1608
DIUERS = *1
*out diuers scedules of my beautie. It shalbe Inuentoried 537
DIUINITIE = *1
*We will heare this diuinitie. Now sir, what is your text? | *Vio*. Most
sweet Ladie. 513
DIUINITY = *1
*would, are as secret as maiden-head: to your eares, Di-|uinity; to any
others, prophanation. 510
DIUISION = 2
Ile make diuision of my present with you: 1863
*Ant*. How haue you made diuision of your selfe, 2387
DIULL = *1
*Mar*. The diu'll a Puritane that hee is, or any thing 840
DIUORCD = *1
*soules and bodies hath he diuorc'd three, and his incense-|ment 1755
DIVULGD = 1
In voyces well divulg'd, free, learn'd, and valiant, 553
DO *l.*23 31 53 83 *205 *244 *273 292 *332 351 *367 *386 *387 481 *482
571 589 606 608 654 760 *781 *788 801 807 *830 *831 832 847 *880 920
936 1028 1096 *1110 *1168 *1181 *1219 *1220 *1241 *1242 1273 *1292
1355 1369 *1386 *1407 1485 1491 1493 1506 1519 1556 *1587 *1619
1622 1668 1777 1828 1833 1843 1845 1851 1853 1867 *1894 1895 *1913
1914 *1923 1975 *2015 2099 2116 2122 2146 2157 2202 2258 2261 2271
2273 2286 2289 2294 *2297 2332 2333 2349 2377 2391 2417 2418 *2453
*2461 *2465 *2475 2518 *2544 = 64*37
DOCTRINE = *1
*Ol*. A comfortable doctrine, and much may bee saide 515

DOE *l.*\*179 \*327 \*772 \*1070 \*1461 \*1550 \*1631 \*1672 \*1771 \*1775 \*1987
\*2077 = \*12
DOER = 1
is the doer of this, and he is to be thanked.                                    1605
DOES *l.*\*199 \*242 547 \*550 685 \*709 \*781 1139 \*1251 \*1456 \*1457 1530
\*1531 1542 1617 2058 \*2297 2451 = 8\*11
DOEST *l.*1546 2163 = 2
DOGGD = \*1
*Schoole i'th Church: I haue dogg'd him like his murthe-|rer.          1455
DOGGE = 1\*3
*And*. And you loue me, let's doo't: I am dogge at a | Catch.           761
*An*. O, if I thought that, Ide beate him like a dogge.                 835
*Fab*. This is to giue a dogge, and in recompence desire | my dogge
againe.                                                                2158
DOGS = 1
*Clo*. Byrlady sir, and some dogs will catch well.                     763
DOING = \*1
*I haue lymde her, but it is Ioues doing, and Ioue make me            1597
DOLPHINES = 1
Where like *Orion* on the Dolphines backe,                            65
DONE *l.*527 528 \*645 731 801 \*1626 \*1740 1747 1830 1870 1886 \*2049
2342 2375 2487 2497 2578 = 13\*4
DOOEST *l.*\*238 = \*1
DOORE = \*2
*your doore like a Sheriffes post, and be the supporter to            443
*Ol*. Let the Garden doore be shut, and leaue mee to | my hearing.
Giue me your hand sir.                                                 1305
DOORES = 3
Be not deni'de accesse, stand at her doores,                          265
*Enter Viola and Maluolio, at seuerall doores.*                       657
bid him turne you out of doores, neuer trust me.                      774
DOOT = \*2
*And*. And you loue me, let's doo't: I am dogge at a | Catch.           761
*To*. Doo't knight, Ile write thee a Challenge: or Ile                 825
DOOTH *l.*\*1220 = \*1
DORMOUSE = \*1
*onely to exasperate you, to awake your dormouse valour,              1399
DOS *l.*\*780 \*1083 1199 2134 = 2\*2
DOST *l.*\*235 \*811 905 908 993 \*1215 \*1554 \*1635 2316 = 4\*5, 1
*An*. But it becoms me wel enough, dost not?                          212
DOT = \*1
*for nothing, and that that I did, I was set on to do't by sir | *Toby*.  2347
DOTE = 1
And she (mistaken) seemes to dote on me:                              692
DOTH *l.*101 \*365 \*368 745 928 983 \*1117 \*1121 1507 2125 2437 = 7\*5
DOUBLE = 1\*2
*hand, and this was baulkt: the double gilt of this oppor-|tunitie    1404
*Clo*. But that it would be double dealing sir, I would               2180
*Du*. Well, I will be so much a sinner to be a double | dealer: there's
another.                                                              2185
DOUBLET = \*1
*Tailor make thy doublet of changeable Taffata, for thy              961
DOUBT = 1\*1
*Mar*. Asse, I doubt not.                                             862
*semblance I put on; with the which I doubt not, but to              2474
DOUBTFULL = 1
That my most iealious, and too doubtfull soule                        2142

56

DOUE = 1
To spight a Rauens heart within a Doue.  2287
DOWN = *1
*a barren rascall: I saw him put down the other day, with  376
DOWNE = 1*5
*To. O knight, thou lack'st a cup of Canarie: when did | I see thee so
put downe?  194
*put me downe: mee thinkes sometimes I haue no  197
*comming downe this walke, he has beene yonder i'the  1033
*set 'em downe, go about it. Let there bee gaulle e-|nough  1427
*tricke of singularity: and consequently setts downe the  1594
*and light: and conuey what I will set downe to my  2095
DOWRY = 1*1
*To. And aske no other dowry with her, but such ano-|ther iest.  1187
*of him, I would not haue him miscarrie for the halfe of | my Dowry.
Exit  1585
DRAMME = *1
*that no dramme of a scruple, no scruple of a scruple, no  1601
DRAUGHT = 1*1
*One draught aboue heate, makes him a foole, the second | maddes
him, and a third drownes him.  426
For shallow draught and bulke vnprizable,  2206
DRAW = 2*5
To. And thou let part so Sir *Andrew*, would thou | mightst neuer draw
sword agen.  176
*draw sword agen: Faire Lady, doe you thinke you haue | fooles in
hand?  179
*but we will draw the Curtain, and shew you the picture.  525
*seest him, draw, and as thou draw'st, sweare horrible: for  1695
*of: therefore draw for the supportance of his vowe,  1816
*To. Do, cuffe him soundly, but neuer draw thy sword  1913
If thou dar'st tempt me further, draw thy sword.  1958
DRAWE = *1
*rowze the night-Owle in a Catch, that will drawe three  759
DRAWNE = 1*2
*Fa. Though our silence be drawne from vs with cars, | yet peace.  1079
As might haue drawne one to a longer voyage)  1473
*the diuels of hell be drawne in little, and Legion himselfe | possest
him, yet Ile speake to him.  1608
DRAWST = *1
*seest him, draw, and as thou draw'st, sweare horrible: for  1695
DREAME = 4*1
Poore Lady, she were better loue a dreame:  683
dreame on the euent: Farewell. *Exit*  868
*Tob. Why, thou hast put him in such a dreame, that  1197
Or I am mad, or else this is a dreame:  1978
If it be thus to dreame, still let me sleepe.  1980
DREST = 1*1
Fab. What dish a poyson has she drest him?  1123
*And. Ile helpe you sir *Toby*, because we'll be drest to-|gether.  2367
DREW = 5
Vio. He did me kindnesse sir, drew on my side,  2217
*Orsino's* enemie. A witchcraft drew me hither:  2228
Drew to defend him, when he was beset:  2237
You drew your sword vpon me without cause,  2350
But Nature to her bias drew in that.  2426

DRINK = *2
*wil amend: for giue the dry foole drink, then is the foole 336
*An. 'Twere as good a deede as to drink when a mans 822
DRINKE = 1*8
*these cloathes are good enough to drinke in, and so bee 129
*To. With drinking healths to my Neece: Ile drinke 154
*to her as long as there is a passage in my throat, & drinke 155
*drinke to my Neece, till his braines turne o'th toe, like a 157
hand to'th Buttry barre, and let it drinke. 184
*Clo. Two faults Madona, that drinke & good counsell 335
*o'my Coz: for he's in the third degree of drinke: hee's | drown'd: go
looke after him. 429
*To. Th'art a scholler; let vs therefore eate and drinke 713
*he had not beene in drinke, hee would haue tickel'd you | other gates
then he did. 2356
DRINKING = 1*3
*Ma. That quaffing and drinking will vndoe you: I 132
*To. With drinking healths to my Neece: Ile drinke 154
*sir Toby would leaue drinking, thou wert as witty a piece | of Eues
flesh, as any in Illyria. 321
*And. Faith so they say, but I thinke it rather consists | of eating and
drinking. 711
DRIUE = *1
*set vpon Ague-cheeke a notable report of valor, and driue 1708
DRIUES = *1
*with a kinde of iniunction driues mee to these habites of 1173
DRIUING = 1
Hung on our driuing boate: I saw your brother 61
DROP = *2
To. What wilt thou do? | *Mar. I will drop in his way some obscure
Epistles of 847
*To. He shall thinke by the Letters that thou wilt drop 857
DROPT = *1
*He does obey euery point of the Letter that I dropt, 1456
DROWND = 2*3
*Perchance he is not drown'd: What thinke you saylors? 55
*Clo. Like a drown'd man, a foole, and a madde man: 425
*o'my Coz: for he's in the third degree of drinke: hee's | drown'd: go
looke after him. 429
breach of the sea, was my sister drown'd. | Ant. Alas the day. 632
*drown'd already sir with salt water, though I seeme to 639
DROWNE = 1
drowne her remembrance againe with more. 640
DROWNED = 1
And say, thrice welcome drowned Viola. 2407
DROWNES = 1
*One draught aboue heate, makes him a foole, the second | maddes
him, and a third drownes him. 426
DRUNKE = *3
*Ma. They that adde moreour, hee's drunke nightly | in your company. 152
*Ol. By mine honor halfe drunke. What is he at the | gate Cosin? | To.
A Gentleman. 410
*Clo. O he's drunke sir Toby an houre agone: his eyes | were set at eight
i'th morning. 2361
DRUNKEN = 3*1
Ol. What's a drunken man like, foole? 424

DRUNKEN *cont.*
*To. Then he's a Rogue, and a passy measures pauyn: I | hate a
drunken rogue.                                                              2363
*darkenesse, and giuen your drunken Cosine rule ouer me,                   2471
With tospottes still had drunken heades, | for the raine, &c.              2574
DRUNKENNESSE = 2
To. What, what? | Mal. You must amend your drunkennesse. | To. Out
scab.                                                                      1087
Then lying, vainnesse, babling drunkennesse,                               1874
DRY = 4*2
Ma. It's dry sir.                                                          187
can keepe my hand dry. But what's your iest?                               189
Ma. A dry iest Sir. | And. Are you full of them?                          190
Ol. Go too, y'are a dry foole: Ile no more of you: be-|sides you grow
dis-honest.                                                                333
*wil amend: for giue the dry foole drink, then is the foole               336
*not dry: bid the dishonest man mend himself, if he mend,                 337
DU = 48*6
DUBBD = *1
*To. He is knight dubb'd with vnhatch'd Rapier, and                       1753
DUCATES = 1*1
Ma. What's that to th'purpose? | To. Why he ha's three thousand
ducates a yeare.                                                           138
*Ma. I, but hee'l haue but a yeare in all these ducates:                  140
DUE = 1
There lies your way, due West. | Vio. Then Westward hoe:                  1350
DUELLO = *1
*he cannot by the Duello auoide it: but hee has promised                  1823
DUKE see also Du. = 6*1
Enter Orsino Duke of Illyria, Curio, and other | Lords.                   2
Vio. Who gouernes heere? | Cap. A noble Duke in nature, as in name.       74
The forme of my intent. Ile serue this Duke,                              107
*Val. If the Duke continue these fauours towards you                      251
Enter Duke, Curio, and Attendants.                                        257
Enter Duke, Viola, Curio, and others.                                     884
Enter Duke, Viola, Curio, and Lords.                                      2160
DUKE = 5
DUKES = 1
Because she will admit no kinde of suite, | No, not the Dukes.            97
DULCET = 1
To. To heare by the nose, it is dulcet in contagion.                      757
DUMBENESSE = *1
*the youth into dumbenesse: this was look'd for at your                   1403
DURANCE = 1
Is now in durance, at Maluolio's suite,                                   2443
DUST = *1
*dust, like mistris Mals picture? Why dost thou not goe                   235
DUTCHMANS = *1
*like an ysickle on a Dutchmans beard, vnlesse you do re-|deeme          1407
DUTIE = 2
Vio. My dutie Madam, and most humble seruice.                            1307
Vio. My Lord would speake, my dutie hushes me.                           2262
DUTY = *1
*me as you please. I leaue my duty a little vnthought of,                 2476
DWELL = *1
*begger dwell neer him: or the Church stands by thy Ta-|bor,             1223

DWELT = 1
*There dwelt a man in Babylon, Lady, Lady.* 778
DYE = 3
The appetite may sicken, and so dye. 7
*To.* But I will neuer dye. 803
To do you rest, a thousand deaths would dye. 2289
DYET = 1
In the South Suburbes at the Elephant | Is best to lodge: I will bespeake
our dyet, 1508
DYING = 1
That straine agen, it had a dying fall: 8
EACH = 2
We made each other, but so late ago. 2379
Do not embrace me, till each circumstance, 2417
EARE = 4*1
O, it came ore my eare, like the sweet sound 9
*Vio.* It alone concernes your eare: I bring no ouer- | ture 503
*Vio.* My matter hath no voice Lady, but to your owne | most pregnant
and vouchsafed eare. 1301
It is as fat and fulsome to mine eare | As howling after Musicke. 2264
*reade thus: therefore, perpend my Princesse, and giue | eare. 2466
EARELY = 1
*Ol.* Cosin, Cosin, how haue you come so earely by | this Lethargie? 417
EARES = 1*1
*would, are as secret as maiden-head: to your eares, Di- | uinity; to any
others, prophanation. 510
*Mar.* Go shake your eares. 821
EARLY = *1
*To be vp after midnight, and to go to bed then is early: 707
EARLYER = *1
*Mar.* By my troth sir *Toby*, you must come in earlyer 122
EARND = *1
*approbation, then euer proofe it selfe would haue earn'd | him. Away. 1698
EARTH = 2
Betweene the elements of ayre, and earth, 569
*Du.* Heere comes the Countesse, now heauen walkes | on earth: 2251
EASIE = 1
How easie is it, for the proper false 686
EASILY = *1
*be as good as my word. Hee will beare you easily, and | raines well. 1841
EATE = 1*1
*To.* Th'art a scholler; let vs therefore eate and drinke 713
foote of a flea, Ile eate the rest of th'anatomy. 1442
EATER = *1
*am a great eater of beefe, and I beleeue that does harme | to my wit. 199
EATING = 1
*And.* Faith so they say, but I thinke it rather consists | of eating and
drinking. 711
EBONY = *1
*as lustrous as Ebony: and yet complainest thou of ob- | struction? 2024
ECCHO = 1
*Vio.* It giues a verie eccho to the seate | Where loue is thron'd. 906
EDIFIED = 1
*Clo.* Looke then to be well edified, when the Foole 2458
EGYPTIAN = 1
Like to th'Egyptian theefe, at point of death 2274

EMBRACE *cont.*
*Du.* Madam, I am most apt t'embrace your offer:                    2486
EMPLOYMENT = 1*1
*Mal.* What employment haue we heere?                               1097
*capacity, and breeding: his employment betweene his               1703
EMPTY = 1
Are empty trunkes, ore-flourish'd by the deuill.                   1890
ENCHANTMENT = 1
After the last enchantment you did heare,                          1326
ENCOUNTER *see* incounter
END = 3*5
*Iourneys end in louers meeting,*                                  744
*To.* Send for money knight, if thou hast her not i'th | end, call me Cut.  878
*in this, and the end: What should that Alphabeticall po- | sition  1128
*Fa.* And *O* shall end, I hope. | *To.* I, or Ile cudgell him, and make him
cry *O.*                                                           1140
*attends thee at the Orchard end: dismount thy tucke,              1742
*shew on't, this shall end without the perdition of soules,       1806
*To.* That's all one, has hurt me, and there's th'end on't:        2359
How does he sirrah? | *Cl.* Truely Madam, he holds *Belzebub* at the
staues end as                                                      2451
ENDEAUOUR = *1
*Maluolio, Maluolio,* thy wittes the heauens restore: en- | deauour  2080
ENDED = *1
*beene pleas'd, would we had so ended. But you sir, al- | ter'd     630
ENDS = *1
*Ma.* I Sir, I haue them at my fingers ends: marry now            192
ENDUE *see* indue
ENDURE = 1*1
*Ol.* 'Tis in graine sir, 'twill endure winde and wea- | ther.     529
*Youths a stuffe will not endure.*                                 753
ENEMIE = 3*1
*death of her brother thus? I am sure care's an enemie to | life.   120
Wherein the pregnant enemie does much.                             685
*and so looke to thy selfe. Thy friend as thou vsest him, & thy | sworne
enemie,* Andrew Ague-cheeke.                                       1686
*Orsino's* enemie. A witchcraft drew me hither:                    2228
ENEMIES = 3
I haue many enemies in Orsino's Court,                             652
*Vio.* No not a grize: for tis a vulgar proofe | That verie oft we pitty
enemies.                                                           1339
Whom thou in termes so bloudie, and so deere | Hast made thine
enemies?                                                           2222
ENEMY = 1
he's an enemy to mankinde.                                         1621
ENGLAND = *1
*sheete were bigge enough for the bedde of *Ware* in Eng- | land,   1426
ENIOY = *1
*Mal.* Go off, I discard you: let me enioy my priuate: | go off.   1612
ENLARGE *see* inlarge
ENOUGH = 6*9
Stealing, and giuing Odour. Enough, no more,                       11
*these cloathes are good enough to drinke in, and so bee           129
*An.* But it becoms me wel enough, dost not?                       212
*Mal.* Not yet old enough for a man, nor yong enough               451
*An.* I, he do's well enough if he be dispos'd, and so             780
*him a common recreation, do not thinke I haue witte e- | nough     831

ENOUGH *cont.*
*An.* I haue no exquisite reason for't, but I haue reason | good enough.   838
*Vio.* This fellow is wise enough to play the foole,   1272
Enough is shewne, a Cipresse, not a bosome,   1335
*sheete were bigge enough for the bedde of *Ware* in Eng- | land,   1426
*set 'em downe, go about it. Let there bee gaulle e- | nough   1427
*in such a gowne. I am not tall enough to become the   1991
*function well, nor leane enough to bee thought a good   1992
Though I confesse, on base and ground enough   2227

ENRAGD = 1
From the rude seas enrag'd and foamy mouth   2230

ENTER = 64*1
*Enter Orsino Duke of Illyria, Curio, and other | Lords.*   2
*Enter Valentine.*   29
*Enter Viola, a Captaine, and Saylors.*   50
*Enter Sir Toby, and Maria.*   118
*Enter Sir Andrew.*   160
*Enter Valentine, and Viola in mans attire.*   250
*Enter Duke, Curio, and Attendants.*   257
*Enter Maria, and Clowne.*   296
*not open my lippes so wide as a brissle may enter, in way   298
*Enter Lady Oliuia, with Maluolio.*   325
*Enter Maria.*   391
braines, for heere he comes. *Enter Sir Toby.*   408
*Enter Maluolio.*   433
*Enter Maria.*   459
*Enter Violenta.*   462
*Enter Maluolio.*   596
*Enter Antonio & Sebastian.*   612
*Enter Viola and Maluolio, at seuerall doores.*   657
*Enter Sir Toby, and Sir Andrew.*   700
*Enter Clowne.*   715
*Enter Maria.*   771
*Enter Maluolio.*   785
*Enter Duke, Viola, Curio, and others.*   884
*Enter Curio & Clowne.*   931
*Enter Sir Toby, Sir Andrew, and Fabian.*   1017
*Enter Maria.*   1029
*Enter Maluolio.*   1039
*Enter Maria.*   1189
*Enter Viola and Clowne.*   1214
*Enter Sir Toby and Andrew.*   1281
you should enter, if your trade be to her.   1288
*To.* I meane to go sir, to enter.   1294
*Enter Oliuia, and Gentlewoman.*   1297
*Enter Sir Toby, Sir Andrew, and Fabian.*   1382
*Enter Maria.*   1445
*Enter Sebastian and Anthonio.*   1466
*Enter Oliuia and Maria.*   1521
*Enter Maluolio.*   1535
*Enter Seruant.*   1578
*Enter Toby, Fabian, and Maria.*   1606
*Enter Sir Andrew.*   1663
*Enter Oliuia and Viola.*   1713
*Enter Toby and Fabian.*   1736
*Enter Toby and Andrew.*   1791
*Enter Fabian and Viola.*   1808

ENTER *cont.*
*Enter Antonio.*                                                      1827
*Enter Officers.*                                                     1836
*Enter Sebastian and Clowne.*                                         1918
*Enter Andrew, Toby, and Fabian.*                                     1941
*Enter Oliuia.*                                                       1961
*Enter Maria and Clowne.*                                             1985
*goes as fairely, as to say, a carefull man, & a great | scholler. The
Competitors enter.                                                   1994
*Enter Toby.*                                                         1996
*Enter Sebastian.*                                                    2114
*Enter Oliuia, and Priest.*                                          2136
*Enter Clowne and Fabian.*                                           2153
*Enter Duke, Viola, Curio, and Lords.*                               2160
*Enter Anthonio and Officers.*                                       2200
*Enter Oliuia and attendants.*                                       2250
*Enter Priest.*                                                       2311
*Enter Sir Andrew.*                                                   2335
*Enter Toby and Clowne.*                                             2352
*Enter Sebastian.*                                                    2372
*Enter Clowne with a Letter, and Fabian.*                            2448
*Enter Maluolio.*                                                     2494
ENTERCHANGEMENT = 1
Strengthned by enterchangement of your rings,                        2321
ENTERLUDE = *1
*was one sir, in this Enterlude, one sir *Topas* sir, but that's     2543
ENTERS = 1
Receiueth as the Sea. Nought enters there,                             15
ENTERTAINMENT = 1*1
*learn'd from my entertainment. What I am, and what I                 509
*Ant.* Pardon me sir, your bad entertainment.                        641
ENTERTAINST = *1
*not choose but know who I am. If thou entertainst my loue, let*     1178
ENTRANCE = *1
*Vio.* I will answer you with gate and entrance, but we | are preuented.  1295
ENTREAT = 1
*Ant.* I must entreat of you some of that money.                     1857
ENTREATE = 1*1
*Orsino's* is return'd, I could hardly entreate him backe: he        1580
*Du.* Pursue him, and entreate him to a peace:                       2550
ENUY = 1*1
*bore a minde that enuy could not but call faire: Shee is            638
That very enuy, and the tongue of losse                              2209
ENWRAPS = 1
And though tis wonder that enwraps me thus,                          2117
EPISTLES = *2
*To.* What wilt thou do? | *Mar.* I will drop in his way some obscure
Epistles of                                                          847
*madmans Epistles are no Gospels, so it skilles not much             2455
EQUALL = 1
I am as madde as hee, | If sad and merry madnesse equall bee.        1536
EQUINOCTIAL = *1
*Pigrogromitus*, of the *Vapians* passing the Equinoctial of         724
ERE = 6*2
Of what validity, and pitch so ere,                                   16
Ere since pursue me. How now what newes from her?                     28
Who ere I woe, my selfe would be his wife. *Exeunt.*                 294¹

64

ERE *cont.*
*and so cunning in Fence, I'de haue seene him damn'd ere 1802
*thou shalt hold th'opinion of *Pythagoras*, ere I will allow 2043
That ere deuotion tender'd. What shall I do? 2271
More by all mores, then ere I shall loue wife. 2293
That ere inuention plaid on? Tell me why? 2514
ERREST = *1
*Clo.* Madman thou errest: I say there is no darknesse 2028
ERROR = 1
That this may be some error, but no madnesse, 2124
ESCAPE = 1
Mine owne escape vnfoldeth to my hope, 69
ESTATE = 3*1
Till I had made mine owne occasion mellow | What my estate is. 94
*degree, neither in estate, yeares, nor wit: I haue heard her 219
Of great estate, of fresh and stainlesse youth; 552
But when I came to mans estate, | with hey ho, &c. 2564
ESTIMABLE = *1
*I could not with such estimable wonder ouer-farre be-|leeue 636
ET *l.*1285 = 1
ETCETERA *see* &c.
ETERNALL = 1
*Priest.* A Contract of eternall bond of loue, 2318
EUEN *see also* eu'n = 9*5
Euen in a minute; so full of shapes is fancie, 18
To thee the booke euen of my secret soule. 263
*no scorne; I am very comptible, euen to the least | sinister vsage. 470
And sing them lowd euen in the dead of night: 565
Euen so quickly may one catch the plague? 591
*Vio.* Euen now sir, on a moderate pace, I haue since a-|riu'd but
hither. 660
*Clo.* His eyes do shew his dayes are almost done. | *Mal.* Is't euen so? 801
To die, euen when they to perfection grow. 930
*euen with the swiftnesse of putting on. Ioue, and my 1176
*Fab.* I know the knight is incenst against you, euen to 1778
Yet liuing in my glasse: euen such, and so 1901
*Ol.* Euen what it please my Lord, that shal becom him 2272
Pardon me (sweet one) euen for the vowes 2378
Were you a woman, as the rest goes euen, 2405
EUENT = 2
dreame on the euent: Farewell. *Exit* 868
*And.* And I do not. | *Fab.* Come, let's see the euent. 1914
EUER *see also* ere = 4*9
*him: Infirmity that decaies the wise, doth euer make the | better foole. 368
Come hither Boy, if euer thou shalt loue 900
*euer crosse garter'd: I say remember, goe too, thou art 1160
*Counts Seruing-man, then euer she bestow'd vpon mee: 1387
*that meanes to be saued by beleeuing rightly, can euer 1450
And thankes: and euer oft good turnes, 1482
*of the Orchard like a bum-Baylie: so soone as euer thou 1694
*approbation, then euer proofe it selfe would haue earn'd | him. Away. 1698
*Ol.* Will it be euer thus? Vngracious wretch, 1964
*in't, and I would I were the first that euer dissembled in 1990
*Mal.* Good foole, as euer thou wilt deserue well at 2065
*Lady: it shall aduantage thee more, then euer the bea-|ring of Letter
did. 2096
And hauing sworne truth, euer will be true. 2148

EUERIE = *1
*and their intent euerie where, for that's it, that alwayes 964
EUERY = 6*8
*and euery particle and vtensile labell'd to my will: As, 538
*Euery wise mans sonne doth know.* 745
*put to Sea, that their businesse might be euery thing, 963
*and yet to crush this a little, it would bow to mee, for e- | uery 1147
*imagination iade mee; for euery reason excites to this, 1169
*I thanke thee, I will smile, I wil do euery thing that thou | wilt haue
me. *Exit* 1181
*Sun, it shines euery where. I would be sorry sir, but the 1252
And like the Haggard, checke at euery Feather 1276
By maid-hood, honor, truth, and euery thing, 1366
*He does obey euery point of the Letter that I dropt, 1456
*degree, but Fellow. Why euery thing adheres togither, 1600
Of heere, and euery where. I had a sister, 2393
*for the raine it raineth euery day.* 2563
*and wee'l striue to please you euery day.* 2579
EUERYTHING *see* euery
EUERYWHERE *see* euerie, euery
EUES = 1
*sir *Toby* would leaue drinking, thou wert as witty a piece | of *Eues*
flesh, as any in Illyria. 321
EUIDENT = *1
*euident to any formall capacitie. There is no obstruction 1127
EUILL = 1
Vertue is beauty, but the beauteous euill 1889
EUILS = *1
*that I may beare my euils alone. It were a bad recom- | pence 618
EUN = *1
*Mal.* Were not you eu'n now, with the Countesse O- |*liuia?* 658
EUNUCH = 2
Thou shalt present me as an Eunuch to him, 108
*Cap.* Be you his Eunuch, and your Mute Ile bee, 114
EW = *1
*My shrowd of white, stuck all with Ew, O prepare it.* 946
EXALTED = *1
*my complection. Besides she vses me with a more ex- |alted 1043
EXAMPLE = *1
*Mal.* There is example for't: The Lady of the *Stra-* |*chy,* 1055
EXASPERATE = *1
*onely to exasperate you, to awake your dormouse valour, 1399
EXCEED = 1
So farre exceed all instance, all discourse, 2126
EXCEEDING = 1
*Fa.* Very breefe, and to exceeding good sence-lesse. 1678
EXCELLENCE = 1
*To.* What is thy excellence in a galliard, knight? | *And.* Faith, I can cut
a caper. 228
EXCELLENCIES = *1
*with excellencies, that it is his grounds of faith, that all 844
EXCELLENT = 7*8
*To.* Then hadst thou had an excellent head of haire. 209
*To.* Excellent, it hangs like flax on a distaffe: & I hope 213
*the excellent constitution of thy legge, it was form'd vn- |der the starre
of a Galliard. 240

EXIT *cont.*

| | |
|---|---|
| me faith say I. Well, it's all one. *Exit* | 423 |
| *Mal.* Gentlewoman, my Lady calles. *Exit.* | 458 |
| Plac'd in contempt: Farwell fayre crueltie. *Exit* | 584 |
| Ile giue him reasons for't: hie thee *Maluolio.* \| *Mal.* Madam, I will. *Exit.* | 604 |
| bound to the Count Orsino's Court, farewell. *Exit* | 650 |
| That danger shall seeme sport, and I will go. *Exit.* | 655 |
| \*for, there it lies, in your eye: if not, bee it his that \| findes it. *Exit.* | 672 |
| \*meanes for this vnciuill rule; she shall know of it by this \| hand. *Exit* | 819 |
| dreame on the euent: Farewell. *Exit* | 868 |
| makes a good voyage of nothing. Farewell. *Exit* | 965 |
| the Trowt, that must be caught with tickling. *Exit* | 1038 |
| \*I thanke thee, I will smile, I wil do euery thing that thou \| wilt haue me. *Exit* | 1181 |
| \*what you would are out of my welkin, I might say Ele-\|ment, but the word is ouer-worne. *Exit* | 1270 |
| *To.* Wee'l call thee at the Cubiculo: Go. \| *Exit Sir Andrew.* | 1431 |
| \*of him, I would not haue him miscarrie for the halfe of \| my Dowry. *Exit* | 1585 |
| \*things, I am not of your element, you shall knowe more \| heereafter. *Exit* | 1646 |
| *And.* Nay let me alone for swearing. *Exit* | 1700 |
| \*To. I will doe so. Signiour *Fabian*, stay you by this \| Gentleman, till my returne. *Exit Toby.* | 1775 |
| *Ant.* Leade me on. *Exit* | 1893 |
| \*To. I dare lay any money, twill be nothing yet. *Exit* | 1916 |
| Come by and by to my Chamber. *Exit* | 2056 |
| Adieu good man diuell. *Exit* | 2112 |
| \*you say sir, let your bounty take a nappe, I will awake it \| anon. *Exit* | 2198 |

EXPENCES = 1

| | |
|---|---|
| \*Vio. Nay, and thou passe vpon me, Ile no more with \| thee. Hold there's expences for thee. | 1255 |

EXPOSE = 1

| | |
|---|---|
| Did I expose my selfe (pure for his loue) | 2235 |

EXPRESSE = \*1

| | |
|---|---|
| \*the rather to expresse my selfe: you must know of mee | 625 |

EXPRESSURE = \*1

| | |
|---|---|
| \*legge, the manner of his gate, the expressure of his eye, | 850 |

EXQUISITE = 1\*3

| | |
|---|---|
| \*Vio. Most radiant, exquisite, and vnmatchable beau-\|tie. | 465 |
| \*To. What for being a Puritan, thy exquisite reason, \| deere knight. | 836 |
| \*An. I haue no exquisite reason for't, but I haue reason \| good enough. | 838 |
| *Mal.* Sir *Topas*, sir *Topas.* \| *Tob.* My most exquisite sir *Topas.* | 2046 |

EXTEND = \*1

| | |
|---|---|
| \*Mal. I extend my hand to him thus: quenching my | 1081 |

EXTENT = 1

| | |
|---|---|
| Let thy fayre wisedome, not thy passion sway \| In this vnciuill, and vniust extent | 1969 |

EXTORT = 1\*1

| | |
|---|---|
| \*of modestie, that you will not extort from me, what I am | 623 |
| Do not extort thy reasons from this clause, | 1369 |

EXTRACTING = 1

| | |
|---|---|
| A most extracting frensie of mine owne | 2449 |

EXTRAUAGANCIE = \*1

| | |
|---|---|
| \*extrauagancie. But I perceiue in you so excellent a touch | 622 |

EXULT = *1
    *Fa*. I would exult man: you know he brought me out          1023
EYE = 7*3
    Mine eye too great a flatterer for my minde:          607
    *for, there it lies, in your eye: if not, bee it his that | findes it. *Exit*.    672
    *legge, the manner of his gate, the expressure of his eye,    850
    My life vpon't, yong though thou art, thine eye    909
    *To*. O for a stone-bow to hit him in the eye.    1062
    *Fa*. I, and you had any eye behinde you, you might    1143
    That comes before his eye. This is a practice,    1277
    *Seb*. Why I your purse? | *Ant*. Haply your eye shall light vpon some toy    1512
    If it please the eye of one, it is with me as the very true    1544
    Him will I teare out of that cruell eye,    2283
EYES = 8*3
    O when mine eyes did see *Oliuia* first,    24
    When my tongue blabs, then let mine eyes not see.    115
    *Item two lippes indifferent redde, Item two grey eyes,    539
    To creepe in at mine eyes. Well, let it be.    594
    *least occasion more, mine eyes will tell tales of me: I am    649
    That me thought her eyes had lost her tongue,    677
    *Clo*. His eyes do shew his dayes are almost done. | *Mal*. Is't euen so?    801
    I pray you let vs satisfie our eyes    1489
    That I am readie to distrust mine eyes,    2127
    More then I loue these eyes, more then my life,    2292
    *Clo*. O he's drunke sir *Toby* an houre agone: his eyes | were set at eight
    i'th morning.    2361
EYE-OFFENDING = 1
    With eye-offending brine: all this to season    36
FA = 11*11
FAB = 15*14
*FABIAN see also Fa., Fab.* = 13*2
    *Enter Sir Toby, Sir Andrew, and Fabian.*    1017
    *To*. Come thy wayes Signior *Fabian*.    1018
    *Enter Sir Toby, Sir Andrew, and Fabian.*    1382
    *Enter Toby, Fabian, and Maria.*    1606
    *Enter Toby and Fabian.*    1736
    *To*. I will doe so. Signiour *Fabian*, stay you by this | Gentleman, till
    my returne. *Exit Toby*.    1775
    *Fabian* can scarse hold him yonder.    1800
    *Enter Fabian and Viola.*    1808
    *To*. Come hither Knight, come hither *Fabian*: Weel    1898
    *heere in necessity, and denying him: and for his coward- |ship aske
    *Fabian*.    1908
    *Enter Andrew, Toby, and Fabian.*    1941
    *Enter Clowne and Fabian.*    2153
    *Clo*. Good M.(aster) *Fabian*, grant me another request. | *Fab*. Any
    thing.    2155
    *Enter Clowne with a Letter, and Fabian.*    2448
    *Ol*. See him deliuer'd *Fabian*, bring him hither:    2481
FACD = 1
    a knaue: a thin fac'd knaue, a gull?    2370
FACE = 7*4
    Shall not behold her face at ample view:    33
    *Ol*. Giue me my vaile: come throw it ore my face,    460
    *Vio*. Good Madam, let me see your face.    522
    *negotiate with my face: you are now out of your Text:    524
    Thy tongue, thy face, thy limbes, actions, and spirit,    588

FACE *cont.*

| | |
|---|---|
| *to betray him: He does smile his face into more lynes, | 1457 |
| *manner how: as a sad face, a reuerend carriage, a slow | 1595 |
| can to face me out of my wits. | 2078 |
| *Du.* That face of his I do remember well, | 2202 |
| Taught him to face me out of his acquaintance, | 2240 |
| *Du.* One face, one voice, one habit, and two persons, | 2380 |

FACIT = *1

| | |
|---|---|
| *Non facit monachum*: that's as much to say, as I weare not | 348 |

FADGE = 1

| | |
|---|---|
| How will this fadge? My master loues her deerely, | 690 |

FAIRE = 9*3

| | |
|---|---|
| That he did seeke the loue of faire *Oliuia*. | 84 |
| *Vio.* There is a faire behauiour in thee Captaine, | 99 |
| With this thy faire and outward charracter. | 103 |
| *And.* Blesse you faire Shrew. \| *Mar.* And you too sir. | 163 |
| *draw sword agen: Faire Lady, doe you thinke you haue \| fooles in hand? | 179 |
| *Ma* I know not (Madam) 'tis a faire young man, and \| well attended. | 396 |
| But if you were the diuell, you are faire: | 543 |
| *bore a minde that enuy could not but call faire: Shee is | 638 |
| For women are as Roses, whose faire flowre | 927 |
| *I am slaine by a faire cruell maide:* | 945 |
| *Vio. Cesario* is your seruants name, faire Princesse. | 1309 |
| But I bespake you faire, and hurt you not. | 2351 |

FAIRELY = 1*1

| | |
|---|---|
| *goes as fairely, as to say, a carefull man, & a great \| scholler. The Competitors enter. | 1994 |
| That they may fairely note this acte of mine. *Exeunt.* \| *Finis Actus Quartus*. | 2150 |

FAITH *see also* ifaith, yfaith = 8*4

| | |
|---|---|
| *An.* Faith Ile home to morrow sir *Toby*, your niece wil | 215 |
| *To.* What is thy excellence in a galliard, knight? \| *And.* Faith, I can cut a caper. | 228 |
| Surprize her with discourse of my deere faith; | 275 |
| *Clo.* Apt in good faith, very apt: well go thy way, if | 320 |
| me faith say I. Well, it's all one. *Exit* | 423 |
| *And.* Faith so they say, but I thinke it rather consists \| of eating and drinking. | 711 |
| *with excellencies, that it is his grounds of faith, that all | 844 |
| In faith they are as true of heart, as we. | 995 |
| *And.* No faith, Ile not stay a iot longer: | 1383 |
| Plight me the full assurance of your faith, | 2141 |
| Since you to non-regardance cast my faith, | 2277 |
| Hold little faith, though thou hast too much feare. | 2334 |

FAITHFULLST = 1

| | |
|---|---|
| My soule the faithfull'st offrings haue breath'd out | 2270 |

FALL = 5*1

| | |
|---|---|
| That straine agen, it had a dying fall: | 8 |
| *Ma.* That if one breake, the other will hold: or if both \| breake, your gaskins fall. | 318 |
| Being once displaid, doth fall that verie howre. | 928 |
| *prose: If this fall into thy hand, reuolue.* In my stars | 1149 |
| To fall before the Lion, then the Wolfe? | 1344 |
| I should my teares let fall vpon your cheeke, | 2406 |

FALLES = 1

| | |
|---|---|
| But falles into abatement, and low price | 17 |

FALNE = 1
But wisemens folly falne, quite taint their wit.     1280
FALSE = 2*2
How easie is it, for the proper false     686
*To. A false conclusion: I hate it as an vnfill'd Canne.     706
*and wordes are growne so false, I am loath to proue rea-|son with
them.     1237
Where being apprehended, his false cunning     2238
FAME = 2
With the memorials, and the things of fame | That do renowne this
City.     1490
Cride fame and honor on him: What's the matter? | 1.Offi. Orsino, this
is that *Anthonio*     2210
FAMILIAR = 1
familiar smile with an austere regard of controll.     1082
FANCIE = 2*1
Euen in a minute; so full of shapes is fancie,     18
*thus neere, that should shee fancie, it should bee one of     1042
Let fancie still my sense in Lethe steepe,     1979
FANCIES = 2
Our fancies are more giddie and vnfirme,     921
*Orsino's* Mistris, and his fancies Queene. *Exeunt*     2558
FANGS *see* phangs
FANTASTICALL = 1
That it alone, is high fantasticall.     19
FAR = 1
company. Is that the meaning of Accost? | *Ma.* Far you well
Gentlemen.     174
FARE *see also* far = 2*2
To tell me how he takes it: Fare you well:     578
*kill him, whom you haue recouer'd, desire it not. Fare     646
*Clo. Fare thee well: remaine thou still in darkenesse,     2042
the soule of thy grandam. Fare thee well.     2045
FAREWELL = 5*2
bound to the Count Orsino's Court, farewell. *Exit*     650
leaue of her, she is very willing to bid you farewell.     798
*To. Farewell deere heart, since I must needs be gone.     799
dreame on the euent: Farewell. *Exit*     868
makes a good voyage of nothing. Farewell. *Exit*     965
*touch Fortunes fingers. Farewell, Shee that would alter     1163
Farewell, and take her, but direct thy feete,     2330
FARRE = 2*3
*I could not with such estimable wonder ouer-farre be-|leeue     636
*that, yet thus farre I will boldly publish her, shee     637
*he were, for I am now so farre in offence with my Niece,     2054
So farre exceed all instance, all discourse,     2126
So farre beneath your soft and tender breeding,     2489
FARTHEEWELL = *1
*Tob. Fartheewell, and God haue mercie vpon one of our     1684
FARWELL = 1
Plac'd in contempt: Farwell fayre crueltie. *Exit*     584
FAR-THEE-WELL = 1
*Ol.* Well, come againe to morrow: far-thee-well,     1734
FASHION = 1*1
*crosse garter'd, a fashion shee detests: and hee will smile     1204
Still in this fashion, colour, ornament,     1903

FAST = 1

Do giue thee fiue-fold blazon: not too fast: soft, soft,                              589

FAT = 1

It is as fat and fulsome to mine eare | As howling after Musicke.        2264

FATALL = *1

*fatall opposite that you could possibly haue found in anie              1785

FATE = 1*1

Fate, shew thy force, our selues we do not owe,                              608

*ouer me; the malignancie of my fate, might perhaps di- |stemper       616

FATES = *1

*haue greatnesse thrust vppon em. Thy fates open theyr                  1152

FATHER = 7*3

*Vio. Orsino*: I haue heard my father name him.                              78

*my father was that *Sebastian* of *Messaline*, whom I                  627

*Oliuiaes* Father tooke much delight in. He is about the | house.        896

My Father had a daughter lou'd a man                                          996

*Ol*. Then lead the way good father, & heauens so shine,              2149

Call forth the holy Father. | *Du*. Come, away.                              2299

O welcome Father: | Father, I charge thee by thy reuerence            2312

What Countreyman? What name? What Parentage? | *Vio*. Of *Messaline*:

Sebastian* was my Father,                                                          2396

*Vio*. My father had a moale vpon his brow. | *Seb*. And so had mine.   2408

FATHERS = 1

*Vio*. I am all the daughters of my Fathers house,                        1010

FAULT = 3

There's something in me that reproues my fault:                          1720

But such a head-strong potent fault it is,                                    1721

Haue done offence, I take the fault on me:                                  1830

FAULTS = 1*1

*Clo*. Two faults Madona, that drinke & good counsell              335

*Fab*. Did not I say he would worke it out, the Curre | is excellent at

faults.                                                                                    1135

FAUOUR = 8*2

*Mal*. Mistris Mary, if you priz'd my Ladies fauour                    817

Hath staid vpon some fauour that it loues:                                  910

Hath it not boy? | *Vio*. A little, by your fauour.                          911

o'fauour with my Lady, about a Beare-baiting heere.                    1024

*Fab*. Shee did shew fauour to the youth in your sight,              1398

*strike him: if shee doe, hee'l smile, and take't for a great | fauour.   1461

1.*Off*. No sir, no iot: I know your fauour well:                          1846

In fauour was my Brother, and he went                                      1902

That screwes me from my true place in your fauour:                    2279

Why you haue giuen me such cleare lights of fauour,                    2506

FAUOURD = *1

*betweene boy and man. He is verie well-fauour'd,                    454

FAUOURS = 1*2

*Val*. If the Duke continue these fauours towards you              251

he inconstant sir, in his fauours. *Val*. No beleeue me.              256

*And*. Marry I saw your Neece do more fauours to the              1386

FAYRE = 3

Plac'd in contempt: Farwell fayre crueltie. *Exit*                        584

For the fayre kindnesse you haue shew'd me heere,                    1859

Let thy fayre wisedome, not thy passion sway | In this vnciuill, and

vniust extent                                                                            1969

FEARE = 9*2

*Vio*. You either feare his humour, or my negligence,                254

FEARE *cont.*

*Clo.* Let her hang me: hee that is well hang'de in this | world, needs to
feare no colours. 300
*Ma.* Make that good. | *Clo.* He shall see none to feare. 302
saying was borne, of I feare no colours. 305
*Ol.* I do I know not what, and feare to finde 606
A Ring in chace of you. So did I abuse | My selfe, my seruant, and I
feare me you: 1327
The rather by these arguments of feare | Set forth in your pursuite. 1478
*of thy wits, and feare to kill a Woodcocke, lest thou dis- | possesse 2044
*Ol.* Alas, it is the basenesse of thy feare, 2306
Feare not *Cesario*, take thy fortunes vp, 2308
Hold little faith, though thou hast too much feare. 2334

FEAREFULL = *1
*when the curtesie of it is so fearefull. Speake your office. 502

FEARST = 2
Be that thou know'st thou art, and then thou art | As great as that thou
fear'st. 2309
*Ant. Sebastian* are you? | *Seb.* Fear'st thou that *Anthonio*? 2385

FEAST = 1
How shall I feast him? What bestow of him? 1523

FEATHER = 1
And like the Haggard, checke at euery Feather 1276

FEATURE = 2
Nor know I you by voyce, or any feature: 1872
Thou hast *Sebastian* done good feature, shame. 1886

FEED = *1
*Whiles you beguile the time, and feed your knowledge 1510

FEEDE = 2
*Vio.* I am no feede poast, Lady; keepe your purse, 580
Feede on her damaske cheeke: she pin'd in thought, 1002

FEELE = 1
Me thinkes I feele this youths perfections 592

FEELINGLY = *1
*feelingly personated. I can write very like my Ladie 852

FEELT = 1
This pearle she gaue me, I do feel't, and see't, 2116

FEETE = 1*1
*surely, as your feete hits the ground they step on. They 1796
Farewell, and take her, but direct thy feete, 2330

FEIGNE = 1
If I do feigne, you witnesses aboue | Punish my life, for tainting of my
loue. 2294

FEIGNED = *1
*Ol.* It is the more like to be feigned, I pray you keep 491

FEIGNING = 1
Since lowly feigning was call'd complement: 1311

FELL = 2
And my desires like fell and cruell hounds, 27
*Clo.* Alas sir, how fell you besides your fiue witts? 2071

FELLOW = 9*8
*And.* Ile stay a moneth longer. I am a fellow o'th 221
*Mal.* Madam, yond young fellow sweares hee will 434
*Du.* O fellow come, the song we had last night: 932
*Toby* approaches; curtsies there to me. | *To.* Shall this fellow liue? 1077
*still, the fellow of seruants, and not woorthie to 1162
*Vio.* I warrant thou art a merry fellow, and car'st for | nothing. 1239

FELLOW *cont.*
*Vio.* This fellow is wise enough to play the foole,      1272
   *Good *Maria*, let this fellow be look'd too. Where's my      1583
*thankefull. And when she went away now, let this Fel-|low      1598
*be look'd too: Fellow? not *Maluolio*, nor after my      1599
*degree, but Fellow. Why euery thing adheres togither,      1600
*Youth, whatsoeuer thou art, thou art but a scuruy fellow.*      1670
*Seb.* Go too, go too, thou art a foolish fellow,      1921
*Mal.* Sir *Topas.* | *Clo.* Maintaine no words with him good fellow.      2083
*Duke.* I know thee well: how doest thou my good | Fellow?      2163
But for thee fellow, fellow thy words are madnesse,      2253
FELLOWES = *1
   *Clo.* Do you not heare fellowes, take away the Ladie.      332
FENCE = *1
   *and so cunning in Fence, I'de haue seene him damn'd ere      1802
FENCER = 1
say, he has bin Fencer to the Sophy.      1797
FENCING = *1
   *bestowed that time in the tongues, that I haue in fencing      206
FERTILL = 1
*Ol.* How does he loue me? | *Vio.* With adorations, fertill teares,      547
FERUOUR = 1
And let your feruour like my masters be,      583
FESTE = *1
*Du.* Who was it? | *Cur. Feste* the Iester my Lord, a foole that the
Ladie      894
FETCH = 2*1
   *Ol.* Fetch him off I pray you, he speakes nothing but      400
I will fetch you light, and paper, and inke.      2102
*Ol.* He shall inlarge him: fetch *Maluolio* hither,      2445
FETTER = 1
But rather reason thus, with reason fetter;      1371
FICTION = 1
   *Fa.* If this were plaid vpon a stage now, I could con-|demne it as an
improbable fiction.      1649
FIE *see also* fye = 2*2
   *To.* Fie, that you'l say so: he playes o'th Viol-de-gam-|boys,      142
*madman: Fie on him. Go you *Maluolio*; If it be a suit      401
*Fye away, fie away breath,*      944
*An.* Fie on him Iezabel.      1057
FIELD = *1
   *a hungrie, to challenge him the field, and then to breake      823
FIEND = 1*3
   *Mar.* Lo, how hollow the fiend speakes within him;      1614
*Fa.* No way but gentlenesse, gently, gently: the Fiend      1633
A Fiend like thee might beare my soule to hell.      1735
*Clo.* Out hyperbolicall fiend, how vexest thou this      2011
FIGHT = 1*2
   *valour. Challenge me the Counts youth to fight with him      1414
Once in a sea-fight 'gainst the Count his gallies,      1494
*To.* There's no remedie sir, he will fight with you for's      1813
FIGHTER = *1
   *some conduct of the Lady. I am no fighter, I haue heard      1760
FILED = 1
(More sharpe then filed steele) did spurre me forth,      1471
FILLD = 2
These soueraigne thrones, are all supply'd and fill'd      44

FILLD *cont.*
Would they were blankes, rather then fill'd with me.                  1316
FIND = *1
*Sad true louer neuer find my graue, to weepe there.*                 953
FINDE = 6*6
In your deniall, I would finde no sence,                             559
*Ol.* I do I know not what, and feare to finde                       606
my reuenge finde notable cause to worke.                             846
*forehead, and complection, he shall finde himselfe most             851
*the Foole make a third, where he shall finde the Letter:            866
*And.* Where shall I finde you?                                      1430
*and you finde so much blood in his Liuer, as will clog the          1441
You should finde better dealing: what's to do?                       1485
*in the youth: he will finde it comes from a Clodde-pole.            1706
*To.* You'l finde it otherwise I assure you: therefore, if           1748
*by his forme, as you are like to finde him in the proofe of         1783
I could not finde him at the Elephant,                               2119
FINDER = *1
*and crowne thee for a finder of madmen: but see, but see.          1662
FINDES = 1*1
*for, there it lies, in your eye: if not, bee it his that | findes it. *Exit.*   672
*quarrell, and hee findes that now scarse to bee worth tal-|king     1815
FINDST = *1
*how thou findst him: I would we were well ridde of this             2052
FINE = 1
*Du.* O she that hath a heart of that fine frame                     39
FINER = *1
*To.* Confine? Ile confine my selfe no finer then I am:              128
FINGERS = *2
*Ma.* I Sir, I haue them at my fingers ends: marry now               192
*touch Fortunes fingers. Farewell, Shee that would alter             1163
FINIS *l.*610 1212 2151 2580 = 4
FINISHED = 1
He finished indeed his mortall acte                                  2413
FIRAGO = *1
*a firago: I had a passe with him, rapier, scabberd, and all:        1793
FIRE = 3*1
With groanes that thunder loue, with sighes of fire.                 549
*To.* Fire and Brimstone. | *Fa.* O peace, peace.                    1066
*to put fire in your Heart, and brimstone in your Liuer:             1400
As doth that Orbed Continent, the fire, | That seuers day from night.  2437
FIRE-NEW = *1
*iests, fire-new from the mint, you should haue bangd                1402
FIRME = 1
But were my worth, as is my conscience firme,                        1484
FIRST = 4*6
O when mine eyes did see *Oliuia* first,                             24
*Vio.* To answer by the method, in the first of his hart.            519
*An.* 'Tis not the first time I haue constrained one to              767
*Mal.* M.O.A.I. doth sway my life. Nay but first                     1121
*his first approach before my Lady: hee will come to her             1202
*Ant.* To morrow sir, best first go see your Lodging?                1487
*there be any law in Illyria: though I stroke him first, yet         1951
*in't, and I would I were the first that euer dissembled in          1990
*Vio.* The Captaine that did bring me first on shore                 2441
First told me thou wast mad; then cam'st in smiling,                 2519

FIT = 3*1

| | |
|---|---|
| For folly that he wisely shewes, is fit; | 1279 |
| *Ant*. It doth not fit me: hold sir, here's my purse, | 1507 |
| *Mar*. You may haue verie fit occasion for't: he is now | 1690 |
| Fit for the Mountaines, and the barbarous Caues, | 1965 |

FIUE = 2

| | |
|---|---|
| For this affayre: some foure or fiue attend him, | 287 |
| *Clo*. Alas sir, how fell you besides your fiue witts? | 2071 |

FIUE-FOLD = 1

Do giue thee fiue-fold blazon: not too fast: soft, soft,     589

FIXED = 1

And tell them, there thy fixed foot shall grow | Till thou haue audience.     266

FLAME = 1

*Vio*. If I did loue you in my masters flame,     557

FLATTER = 1

Desire him not to flatter with his Lord,     601

FLATTERER = 1

Mine eye too great a flatterer for my minde:     607

FLAX = *1

*To*. Excellent, it hangs like flax on a distaffe: & I hope     213

FLEA = 1

foote of a flea, Ile eate the rest of th'anatomy.     1442

FLEETE = 1

With the most noble bottome of our Fleete,     2208

FLESH = 2

| | |
|---|---|
| *sir *Toby* would leaue drinking, thou wert as witty a piece | of *Eues* flesh, as any in Illyria. | 321 |
| and let your flesh and blood obey it. | 2184 |

FLESHD = *1

*souldier put vp your yron: you are well flesh'd: Come | on.     1955

FLINT = 1

Loue make his heart of flint, that you shal loue,     582

FLOCKE = 1

Hath kill'd the flocke of all affections else     42

FLOOD = 1

Yet doth this accident and flood of Fortune,     2125

FLOURISHD = 1

Are empty trunkes, ore-flourish'd by the deuill.     1890

FLOWER = 2*1

| | |
|---|---|
| *flower; The Lady bad take away the foole, therefore I | say againe, take her away. | 344 |
| *Not a flower, not a flower sweete* | 948 |

FLOWRE = 1

For women are as Roses, whose faire flowre     927

FLOWRES = 1

Away before me, to sweet beds of Flowres,     46

FLYE = *1

*Vio*. Me thinkes his words do from such passion flye     1894

FOAMY = 1

From the rude seas enrag'd and foamy mouth     2230

FOES = *4

| | |
|---|---|
| *Clo*. Truely sir, the better for my foes, and the worse | for my friends. | 2165 |
| *now my foes tell me plainly, I am an Asse: so that by my | 2171 |
| *foes sir, I profit in the knowledge of my selfe, and by my | 2172 |
| *then the worse for my friends, and the better for my foes. | 2175 |

FOGGE = 1
*but ignorance, in which thou art more puzel'd then the | Aegyptians in
their fogge.                                                                        2029
FOLD = 1
Do giue thee fiue-fold blazon: not too fast: soft, soft,                          589
FOLLOW = 2*2
*that suffers vnder probation: *A.* should follow, but *O.* | does.                1138
*cannot but turn him into a notable contempt: if you wil | see it follow
me.                                                                                 1207
*selues into stitches, follow me; yond gull *Maluolio* is tur- | ned              1448
*Seb.* Ile follow this good man, and go with you,                                 2147
FOLLOWD = 1
How with a sportfull malice it was follow'd,                                       2536
FOLLOWED = *1
*dancing, and beare-bayting: O had I but followed the | Arts.                      207
FOLLOWER = 1
a Gentleman, and follower of my Ladies.                                            2444
FOLLOWERS = 1
She could not sway her house, command her followers,                              2131
FOLLOWES = *3
*respect, then any one else that followes her. What | should I thinke
on't?                                                                              1044
*man must know.* No man must know. What followes?                                  1111
*one of these Letters are in my name. Soft, here fol- | lowes                      1148
FOLLY = 2*5
*better increasing your folly: Sir *Toby* will be sworn that                       371
*Clo.* No indeed sir, the Lady *Oliuia* has no folly, shee                         1245
For folly that he wisely shewes, is fit;                                           1279
But wisemens folly falne, quite taint their wit.                                   1280
*Seb.* I prethee vent thy folly some-where else, thou | know'st not me.            1927
*Clo.* Vent my folly: He has heard that word of some                              1929
*great man, and now applyes it to a foole. Vent my fol- | ly:                      1930
FOND = 1
And I (poore monster) fond asmuch on him:                                          691
FOOD = 1
*Duke.* | If Musicke be the food of Loue, play on,                                 4
FOOLE = 28*30
He's a very foole, and a prodigall.                                                141
*he's a foole, he's a great quarreller: and but that hee hath                      146
*wise man. For what saies *Quinapalus*, Better a witty foole,                      329
*Ol.* Take the foole away.                                                         331
*Ol.* Go too, y'are a dry foole: Ile no more of you: be- | sides you grow
dis-honest.                                                                         333
*wil amend: for giue the dry foole drink, then is the foole                        336
*flower; The Lady bad take away the foole, therefore I | say againe,
take her away.                                                                     344
*motley in my braine: good *Madona*, giue mee leaue to | proue you a
foole.                                                                             349
*Clo.* Good Madona, why mournst thou? | *Ol.* Good foole, for my
brothers death.                                                                    358
*Ol.* I know his soule is in heauen, foole.                                        361
*Clo.* The more foole (Madona) to mourne for your                                  362
*Brothers soule, being in heauen. Take away the Foole, | Gentlemen.               363
*Ol.* What thinke you of this foole *Maluolio*, doth he | not mend?                365
*him: Infirmity that decaies the wise, doth euer make the | better foole.          368
*I am no Fox, but he wil not passe his word for two pence | that you
are no Foole.                                                                      372

FOOLE *cont.*

| | |
|---|---|
| *an ordinary foole, that has no more braine then a stone. | 377 |
| *in an allow'd foole, though he do nothing but rayle; | 386 |
| *sonne should be a foole: whose scull, Ioue cramme with | 407 |
| *Ol*. What's a drunken man like, foole? | 424 |
| *Clo*. Like a drown'd man, a foole, and a madde man: | 425 |
| *One draught aboue heate, makes him a foole, the second \| maddes him, and a third drownes him. | 426 |
| *Clo*. He is but mad yet Madona, and the foole shall \| looke to the madman. | 431 |
| *And*. Heere comes the foole yfaith. | 716 |
| *And*. By my troth the foole has an excellent breast. I | 720 |
| *sweet a breath to sing, as the foole has. Insooth thou wast | 722 |
| call me knaue. Begin foole: it begins, *Hold thy peace*. | 768 |
| promise with him, and make a foole of him. | 824 |
| *the Foole make a third, where he shall finde the Letter: | 866 |
| *Du*. Who was it? \| *Cur*. *Feste* the Iester my Lord, a foole that the Ladie | 894 |
| *we will foole him blacke and blew, shall we not sir *An-\|drew*? | 1026 |
| *And*. I knew 'twas I, for many do call mee foole. | 1096 |
| *deuise, the very man. I do not now foole my selfe, to let | 1168 |
| *Vio*. Art not thou the Lady *Oliuia's* foole? | 1244 |
| *will keepe no foole sir, till she be married, and fooles are | 1246 |
| *the bigger, I am indeede not her foole, but her cor-\|rupter of words. | 1248 |
| *Foole should be as oft with your Master, as with my Mi-\|stris: | 1253 |
| *Vio*. This fellow is wise enough to play the foole, | 1272 |
| I wish it might, for now I am your foole. | 1360 |
| *great man, and now applyes it to a foole. Vent my fol-\|ly: | 1930 |
| *Clo*. Hey Robin, iolly Robin, tell me how thy Lady \| does. \| *Mal*. Foole. | 2057 |
| *Clo*. My Lady is vnkind, *perdie*. \| *Mal*. Foole. | 2060 |
| *Clo*. Alas why is she so? \| *Mal*. Foole, I say. | 2062 |
| *Mal*. Good foole, as euer thou wilt deserue well at | 2065 |
| *Clo*. M.(aster) *Maluolio*? \| *Mal*. I good Foole. | 2069 |
| *Mall*. Foole, there was neuer man so notoriouslie a-\|bus'd: | 2072 |
| I am as well in my wits (foole) as thou art. | 2073 |
| no better in your wits then a foole. | 2075 |
| *Mal*. Foole, foole, foole I say. | 2087 |
| *Mal*. Good foole, helpe me to some light, and some | 2090 |
| *Mal*. By this hand I am: good foole, some inke, pa-\|per, | 2094 |
| *Mal*. Foole, Ile requite it in the highest degree: \| I prethee be gone. | 2103 |
| *Du*. You can foole no more money out of mee at this | 2191 |
| *Clo*. Looke then to be well edified, when the Foole | 2458 |
| *Ol*. Alas poore Foole, how haue they baffel'd thee? | 2540 |
| *all one: By the Lord Foole, I am not mad: but do you re-\|member, | 2544 |

FOOLERIE = 1

| | |
|---|---|
| *Ma*. In the warrs, & that may you be bolde to say in \| your foolerie. | 307 |

FOOLERY = *1

| | |
|---|---|
| *Clo*. Foolery sir, does walke about the Orbe like the | 1251 |

FOOLES = 5*3

| | |
|---|---|
| *draw sword agen: Faire Lady, doe you thinke you haue \| fooles in hand? | 179 |
| those that are fooles, let them vse their talents. | 310 |
| *fooles: and I that am sure I lacke thee, may passe for a | 328 |
| fooles, no better then the fooles Zanies. | 381 |
| *Clo*. Now Mercury indue thee with leasing, for thou \| speak'st well of fooles. | 389 |

FOOLES *cont*.
    *will keepe no foole sir, till she be married, and fooles are    1246
    *that giue fooles money, get themselues a good re- |port, after
fourteene yeares purchase.    1939
FOOLING = 1*4
    *Clo*. Wit, and't be thy will, put me into good fooling:    326
    *Now you see sir, how your fooling growes old, & peo- |ple dislike it.    404
    *in very gracious fooling last night, when thou spok'st of    723
    *An*. Excellent: Why this is the best fooling, when | all is done. Now a
song.    730
    *Clo*. Beshrew me, the knights in admirable fooling.    779
FOOLISH = 5*2
    *heard my Lady talke of it yesterday: and of a foolish    133
    then a foolish wit. God blesse thee Lady.    330
    *Mal*. Besides you waste the treasure of your time, | with a foolish
knight.    1092
    *Seb*. Go too, go too, thou art a foolish fellow,    1921
    *Seb*. I prethee foolish greeke depart from me, there's    1935
    What foolish boldnesse brought thee to their mercies,    2221
    *A foolish thing was but a toy*,    2562
FOORTH = *1
    *tongue, in the habite of some Sir of note, and so foorth.    1596
FOOT = 1
    And tell them, there thy fixed foot shall grow | Till thou haue audience.    266
FOOTE = 2
    *To*. Wilt thou set thy foote o'my necke.    1192
    foote of a flea, Ile eate the rest of th'anatomy.    1442
FOR *l*.68 70 72 81 89 106 109 *143 *145 *158 *211 281 287 288 299 *311
315 *328 *329 *336 *354 *356 359 *362 *370 *372 *384 *389 *406 408
*429 *451 *452 464 *467 *468 *483 *499 579 602 607 619 *631 *643
*672 678 686 689 694 698 726 *727 *732 738 784 *819 *827 *829 *836
*867 *874 *878 902 920 927 954 *961 *964 978 979 1007 *1035 *1037
1062 *1070 *1075 1096 *1132 *1147 *1158 *1169 *1183 1185 *1219
*1239 *1241 *1242 1256 *1259 1279 *1315 1339 1360 1370 1379 *1403
*1410 *1426 *1440 *1449 *1461 1502 1504 1515 1517 *1524 1526 1533
1540 *1585 *1590 *1627 *1637 *1659 *1662 1664 1673 1677 *1693 *1695
1700 *1701 1717 *1725 *1730 *1743 *1750 *1769 *1816 *1822 1831 1833
1835 *1840 1852 1853 1859 1870 1897 1904 *1908 *1919 *1936 *1942
1943 1947 1952 1965 1975 *1998 *2001 *2018 2048 *2054 2089 2123
*2165 2166 2167 *2175 *2179 2183 *2188 2206 2234 2235 *2247 2253
2295 *2336 *2340 *2344 *2347 2378 2487 2490 2556 2563 2567 2571
2575 = 90*97
FORBEARE = *1
    *forbeare hurling things at him, I know my Ladie will    1460
FORBID = 1
    Fortune forbid my out-side haue not charm'd her:    675
FORCE = 2
    Fate, shew thy force, our selues we do not owe,    608
    To force that on you in a shamefull cunning    1330
FORE = *1
    *a fore knowledge of that too, and therefore comes to    438
FOREHEAD = *1
    *forehead, and complection, he shall finde himselfe most    851
FORGIUE = 2
    *Ol*. Come to what is important in't: I forgiue you | the praise.    487
    *Seb*. O good *Antonio*, forgiue me your trouble.    642

FORGOT = 1
*Ol.* Hast thou forgot thy selfe? Is it so long?                2298
FORGOTTEN = *1
  *your Neece, on a forgotten matter wee can hardly make | distinction of
our hands.                                                      853
FORMALL = *1
  *euident to any formall capacitie. There is no obstruction     1127
FORMD = *1
  *the excellent constitution of thy legge, it was form'd vn- | der the starre
of a Galliard.                                                  240
FORME = 2*1
  The forme of my intent. Ile serue this Duke,               107
  *by his forme, as you are like to finde him in the proofe of  1783
  If spirits can assume both forme and suite, | You come to fright vs.  2400
FORMER = *1
  *Mal.* M, O, A, I. This simulation is not as the former:    1146
FORMES = 2
  In womens waxen hearts to set their formes:                687
  And in such formes, which heere were presuppos'd           2520
FORS = *1
  *To.* There's no remedie sir, he will fight with you for's   1813
FORSWEARE = *2
  *An.* And I thought that, I'de forsweare it. Ile ride | home to morrow sir
*Toby.*                                                         202
  *starke naked: for meddle you must that's certain, or for- | sweare to
weare iron about you.                                           1769
FORT = 3*4
  Ile giue him reasons for't: hie thee *Maluolio.* | *Mal.* Madam, I will.
*Exit.*                                                         604
  *An.* I haue no exquisite reason for't, but I haue reason | good enough.  838
  *Mal.* There is example for't: The Lady of the *Stra-|chy,*  1055
*thee so, for I will shew thee no reason for't.*                1673
  *Mar.* You may haue verie fit occasion for't: he is now     1690
  *Vio.* I shall bee much bound to you for't: I am one,       1788
  *as I am a Gentleman, I will liue to bee thankefull to thee | for't.  2067
FORTH = 3*1
  *with lids to them: Item, one necke, one chin, & so forth.  540
  (More sharpe then filed steele) did spurre me forth,       1471
  The rather by these arguments of feare | Set forth in your pursuite.  1478
  Call forth the holy Father. | *Du.* Come, away.            2299
FORTIFIED = 1
  *speake with you. What is to be said to him Ladie, hee's | fortified
against any deniall.                                            439
FORTUNATE = *1
  *seruices with thee, the fortunate vnhappy daylight and    1164
FORTUNE = 6*2
  Fortune forbid my out-side haue not charm'd her:          675
  The parts that fortune hath bestow'd vpon her:             970
  Tell her I hold as giddily as Fortune:                     971
  *Mal.* 'Tis but Fortune, all is fortune. *Maria* once       1040
  Yet doth this accident and flood of Fortune,               2125
  Of place, time, fortune, do co-here and iumpe              2418
  All the occurrence of my fortune since                     2423
FORTUNES = 5*4
  And thou shalt liue as freely as thy Lord, | To call his fortunes thine.  290
  What is your Parentage? | *Vio.* Aboue my fortunes, yet my state is well:  572
  *Ol.* What is your Parentage? | Aboue my fortunes, yet my state is well;  585

FORTUNES *cont.*

| | |
|---|---|
| *Mal.* Saying, Cosine *Toby*, my Fortunes hauing cast | 1085 |
| *see more detraction at your heeles, then Fortunes before \| you. | 1144 |
| *touch Fortunes fingers. Farewell, Shee that would alter | 1163 |
| *To. Why then build me thy fortunes vpon the basis of | 1413 |
| And suites well for a seruant with my fortunes, | 1526 |
| Feare not *Cesario*, take thy fortunes vp, | 2308 |

FORTY = 1*1

| | |
|---|---|
| *had rather then forty shillings I had such a legge, and so | 721 |
| helpe, I had rather then forty pound I were at home. | 2341 |

FOUL = *1

| | |
|---|---|
| *grauity to play at cherrie-pit with sathan. Hang him foul \| Colliar. | 1638 |

FOULE = *1

| | |
|---|---|
| *An. If I cannot recouer your Neece, I am a foule way \| out. | 876 |

FOUND = 1*1

| | |
|---|---|
| *fatall opposite that you could possibly haue found in anie | 1785 |
| Yet there he was, and there I found this credite, | 2120 |

FOUR = *2

| | |
|---|---|
| *and speaks three or four languages word for word | 143 |
| *not be seene, or if she be it's four to one, she'l none of me: | 216 |

FOURE = 1*2

| | |
|---|---|
| For this affayre: some foure or fiue attend him, | 287 |
| *Does not our liues consist of the foure Ele-\|ments? | 709 |
| *your foure negatiues make your two affirmatiues, why | 2174 |

FOURETEENE = 1

| | |
|---|---|
| *that giue fooles money, get themselues a good re-\|port, after | |
| foureteene yeares purchase. | 1939 |

FOWLE = 1

| | |
|---|---|
| *Clo.* What is the opinion of *Pythagoras* concerning \| Wilde-fowle? | 2035 |

FOX = 1*1

| | |
|---|---|
| *I am no Fox, but he wil not passe his word for two pence \| that you | |
| are no Foole. | 372 |
| *Fab. Sowter will cry vpon't for all this, though it bee \| as ranke as a | |
| Fox. | 1132 |

FRAILE = 1

| | |
|---|---|
| Or any taint of vice, whose strong corruption \| Inhabites our fraile | |
| blood. | 1875 |

FRAILTIE = 1

| | |
|---|---|
| Alas, O frailtie is the cause, not wee, | 688 |

FRAME = 1

| | |
|---|---|
| *Du.* O she that hath a heart of that fine frame | 39 |

FRAUGHT = 1

| | |
|---|---|
| That tooke the *Phoenix*, and her fraught from *Candy*, | 2212 |

FREE = 2*4

| | |
|---|---|
| *Ma. Now sir, thought is free: I pray you bring your | 183 |
| *and of free disposition, is to take those things for Bird-\|bolts, | 384 |
| In voyces well divulg'd, free, learn'd, and valiant, | 553 |
| And the free maides that weaue their thred with bones, | 935 |
| *to me: my remembrance is very free and cleere from | 1746 |
| *Seb. I would be free from thee. What wouldst y now? | 1957 |

FREEDOME = *1

| | |
|---|---|
| *To. Shall I play my freedome at tray-trip, and becom \| thy bondslaue? | 1194 |

FREELY = 2

| | |
|---|---|
| And thou shalt liue as freely as thy Lord, \| To call his fortunes thine. | 290 |
| Most freely I confesse my selfe, and *Toby* | 2530 |

FREND = *1

| | |
|---|---|
| *then a Hare, his dishonesty appeares, in leauing his frend | 1907 |

FRENDS = *1
*Du. Giue me some Musick; Now good morow frends.    885
FRENSIE = 1
A most extracting frensie of mine owne    2449
FRESH = 5*1
O spirit of Loue, how quicke and fresh art thou,    13
A brothers dead loue, which she would keepe fresh    37
And then 'twas fresh in murmure (as you know    82
Of great estate, of fresh and stainlesse youth;    552
*slough, and appeare fresh. Be opposite with a kinsman,    1155
Tempests are kinde, and salt waues fresh in loue.    1905
FRIEND = 3*2
*Not a friend, not a friend greet*    950
*Vio. Saue thee Friend and thy Musick: dost thou liue | by thy Tabor?    1215
*and so looke to thy selfe. Thy friend as thou vsest him, & thy | sworne*
*enemie*, Andrew Ague-cheeke.    1686
Rudesbey be gone. I prethee gentle friend,    1968
FRIENDS = 5*2
Vio. What Country (Friends) is this? | Cap. This is Illyria Ladie.    51
Duke. Belong you to the Lady Oliuia, friends?    2161
*Clo. Truely sir, the better for my foes, and the worse | for my friends.    2165
Du. Iust the contrary: the better for thy friends.    2167
*friends I am abused: so that conclusions to be as kisses, if    2173
*then the worse for my friends, and the better for my foes.    2175
*Clo. By my troth sir, no: though it please you to be | one of my
friends.    2177
FRIGHT = 1*1
*impetuositie. This will so fright them both, that they wil    1711
If spirits can assume both forme and suite, | You come to fright vs.    2400
FROM l.28 31 73 81 394 *402 *484 *509 *523 *623 *631 *858 *1064
*1079 1184 1323 1369 *1402 *1436 1502 *1674 *1706 *1746 *1894 *1935
*1957 1960 2212 2230 2279 2404 2410 2438 2450 2491 2502
2555 = 20*17
FRONT = *1
*To, You mistake knight: Accost, is front her, boord | her, woe her,
assayle her.    171
FROWNE = 1*1
*make out for him: I frowne the while, and perchance    1075
To put on yellow stockings, and to frowne    2508
FRUITES = *1
*Mar. If you will then see the fruites of the sport, mark    1201
FRUITLESSE = 1
And heare thou there how many fruitlesse prankes    1972
FULL = 5*4
Euen in a minute; so full of shapes is fancie,    18
Ma. A dry iest Sir. | And. Are you full of them?    190
in my hand: my words are as full of peace, as matter.    505
*ye well at once, my bosome is full of kindnesse, and I    647
As full of labour as a Wise-mans Art:    1278
*it is no matter how wittie, so it bee eloquent, and full of    1422
*me, and the full prospect of my hopes. Well Ioue, not I,    1604
*but thy intercepter full of despight, bloody as the Hun- | ter,    1741
Plight me the full assurance of your faith,    2141
FULSOME = 1
It is as fat and fulsome to mine eare | As howling after Musicke.    2264
FUNCTION = 1*1
*function well, nor leane enough to bee thought a good    1992

FUNCTION *cont.*
   And all the Ceremonie of this compact | Seal'd in my function, by my
   testimony:        2322
FURIE = *1
   *into a most hideous opinion of his rage, skill, furie, and    1710
FURIOUS = 1
   *Fab.* Giue ground if you see him furious.    1820
FURNISH = 1
   *for your opposite hath in him what youth, strength, skill, | and wrath,
   can furnish man withall.    1750
FURTHER = 4*1
   *Trip no further prettie sweeting.*    743
   I will no further chide you.    1469
   If thou dar'st tempt me further, draw thy sword.    1958
   *with her, and bring her along with you, it may awake my | bounty
   further.    2193
   *My Lord, so please you, these things further thought on,    2482
FUSTIAN = 1
   *Fa.* A fustian riddle. | *To.* Excellent Wench, say I.    1119
FYE = 1*1
   *Fye away, fie away breath,*    944
   *Clo.* Fye, thou dishonest sathan: I call thee by the    2017
GABBLE = *1
   *Haue you no wit, manners, nor honestie, but to gabble    787
GAGD = *2
   *laugh and minister occasion to him, he is gag'd. I protest    379
   *and you smile not he's gag'd: and thus the whirlegigge | of time, brings
   in his reuenges.    2546
GAINST = 2
   Once in a sea-fight 'gainst the Count his gallies,    1494
   *Gainst Knaues and Theeues men shut their gate, | for the raine, &c.*    2566
GAIT *see* gate
GALLIARD = 2*1
   *To.* What is thy excellence in a galliard, knight? | *And.* Faith, I can cut
   a caper.    228
   *to Church in a Galliard, and come home in a Carranto?    236
   *the excellent constitution of thy legge, it was form'd vn- | der the starre
   of a Galliard.    240
GALLIES = 1
   Once in a sea-fight 'gainst the Count his gallies,    1494
GAMBOYS = 1
   *To.* Fie, that you'l say so: he playes o'th Viol-de-gam- | boys,    142
GARD = *2
   *Looke you now, he's out of his gard already: vnles you    378
   *you hold your life at any price, betake you to your gard:    1749
GARDEN = *1
   *Ol.* Let the Garden doore be shut, and leaue mee to | my hearing.
   Giue me your hand sir.    1305
GARMENTS = 1
   Hath my Maides garments: he vpon some Action    2442
GARTERD = 4*3
   *euer crosse garter'd: I say remember, goe too, thou art    1160
   *strange, stout, in yellow stockings, and crosse Garter'd,    1175
   *crosse garter'd, a fashion shee detests: and hee will smile    1204
   *To.* And crosse garter'd? | *Mar.* Most villanously: like a Pedant that
   keepes a    1453
   *Mal.* And wish'd to see thee crosse garter'd. | *Ol.* Crosse garter'd?    1572

GARTERD *cont*.
Bad me come smiling, and crosse-garter'd to you,                                              2507
GARTERING = 1
This crosse-gartering, but what of that?                                                      1543
GASKINS = 1
*Ma*. That if one breake, the other will hold: or if both | breake, your
gaskins fall.                                                                                 318
GATE = 5*3
Therefore good youth, addresse thy gate vnto her,                                            264
*Mar*. Madam, there is at the gate, a young Gentle-|man, much desires
to speake with you.                                                                          392
*Ol*. By mine honor halfe drunke. What is he at the | gate Cosin? | *To*.
A Gentleman.                                                                                  410
*To*. Letcherie, I defie Letchery: there's one at the | gate.                                 419
*Ol*. Why, what would you? | *Vio*. Make me a willow Cabine at your
gate,                                                                                        561
*legge, the manner of his gate, the expressure of his eye,                                   850
*Vio*. I will answer you with gate and entrance, but we | are preuented.                      1295
*Gainst Knaues and Theeues men shut their gate*, | *for the raine*, *&c*.                      2566
GATES = 1*2
*it in. I heard you were sawcy at my gates, & allowd your                                     492
*To*. To the gates of Tartar, thou most excellent diuell | of wit.                            1209
*he had not beene in drinke, hee would haue tickel'd you | other gates
then he did.                                                                                  2356
GAUE = 2
This pearle she gaue me, I do feel't, and see't,                                             2116
His life I gaue him, and did thereto adde                                                     2232
GAULLE = *1
*set 'em downe, go about it. Let there bee gaulle e-|nough                                     1427
GECKE = 1
And made the most notorious gecke and gull,                                                   2513
GENEROUS = *1
*with a distemper'd appetite. To be generous, guiltlesse,                                     383
GENIUS = *1
*To*. His very genius hath taken the infection of the | deuice man.                            1651
GENTLE = 2*3
*question's out of my part. Good gentle one, giue mee                                         474
*Vio*. Madam, I come to whet your gentle thoughts | On his behalfe.
Rudesbey be gone. I prethee gentle friend,                                                   1317
                                                                                             1968
*most modest termes, for I am one of those gentle ones,                                       2018
Where lye my maiden weeds: by whose gentle helpe,                                             2421
GENTLEMAN = 13*9
*Mar*. Madam, there is at the gate, a young Gentle-|man, much desires
to speake with you.                                                                          392
*Ol*. By mine honor halfe drunke. What is he at the | gate Cosin? | *To*.
A Gentleman.                                                                                  410
*Ol*. A Gentleman? What Gentleman?                                                            413
*To*. 'Tis a Gentleman heere. A plague o'these pickle | herring: How
now Sot.                                                                                      414
I am a Gentleman.                                                                             574
I am a Gentleman. Ile be sworne thou art,                                                     587
*To*. Saue you Gentleman. | *Vio*. And you sir.                                                1282
*Ser*. Madame, the young Gentleman of the Count                                               1579
*of the yong Gentleman, giues him out to be of good                                           1702
*the Gentleman (as I know his youth will aptly receiue it)                                     1709
*To*. Gentleman, God saue thee.                                                               1737

GENTLEMAN *cont*.
*To*. I will doe so. Signiour *Fabian*, stay you by this | Gentleman, till
my returne. *Exit Toby*.                                                                                    1775
*To*. Come sir *Andrew*, there's no remedie, the Gen- | tleman                                 1821
*me, as he is a Gentleman and a Soldiour, he will not hurt | you. Come
on, too't.                                                                                                        1824
*Ant*. Put vp your sword: if this yong Gentleman                                               1829
*as I am a Gentleman, I will liue to bee thankefull to thee | for't.                        2067
*And*. The Counts Gentleman, one *Cesario*: we tooke                                          2343
*Du*. My Gentleman *Cesario*? | *And*. Odd's lifelings heere he is: you
broke my head                                                                                                   2345
*Du*. How now Gentleman? how ist with you?                                                      2358
a Gentleman, and follower of my Ladies.                                                          2444
They say poore Gentleman, he's much distract.                                                  2447
GENTLEMEN = 2
company. Is that the meaning of Accost? | *Ma*. Far you well
Gentlemen.                                                                                                        174
*Brothers soule, being in heauen. Take away the Foole, | Gentlemen.        363
GENTLENESSE = 1*1
*Ant*. The gentlenesse of all the gods go with thee:                                       651
*Fa*. No way but gentlenesse, gently, gently: the Fiend                                  1633
GENTLEWOMAN = 3
*Ol*. Let him approach: Call in my Gentlewoman.                                             457
*Mal*. Gentlewoman, my Lady calles. *Exit*.                                                     458
*Enter Oliuia, and Gentlewoman*.                                                                     1297
GENTLY = *3
*gently with him: Let me alone. How do you *Maluolio*?                                   1619
*Fa*. No way but gentlenesse, gently, gently: the Fiend                                  1633
GET = 3*5
*Ol*. Get you to your Lord:                                                                             575
Get thee to yond same soueraigne crueltie:                                                    967
*Mar*. Get ye all three into the box tree: *Maluolio*'s                                    1032
*And*. Odours, pregnant, and vouchsafed: Ile get 'em | all three already.   1303
*Mar*. Get him to say his prayers, good sir *Toby*, gette | him to pray.      1640
*computent iniurie, therefore get you on, and giue him                                  1765
*that giue fooles money, get themselues a good re- | port, after
foureteene yeares purchase.                                                                          1939
*Ol*. Get him to bed, and let his hurt be look'd too.                                     2371
GETTE = *1
*Mar*. Get him to say his prayers, good sir *Toby*, gette | him to pray,     1640
GIANT = *1
*Some mollification for your Giant, sweete Ladie;                                          499
GIDDIE = 1
Our fancies are more giddie and vnfirme,                                                       921
GIDDILY = 1
Tell her I hold as giddily as Fortune:                                                              971
GIDDY-PACED = 1
Of these most briske and giddy-paced times.                                                  890
GIFT = 1*1
*the gift of a Coward, to allay the gust he hath in quarrel- | ling,          147
*'tis thought among the prudent, he would quickely | haue the gift of a
graue.                                                                                                            148
GIFTS = 1*1
without booke, & hath all the good gifts of nature.                                        144
*these gifts a Curtaine before 'em? Are they like to take                              234
GILT = *1
*hand, and this was baulkt: the double gilt of this oppor- | tunitie           1404

GIN = 1

*Fa*. Now is the Woodcocke neere the gin.     1098

GINGER = *1

    *\*Clo*. Yes by *S*.(aint) Anne, and Ginger shall bee hotte y'th | mouth
too.     813

GIUE = 23*16

    Giue me excesse of it: that surfetting,     6
    *\*Clo*. Well, God giue them wisedome that haue it: &     309
    *wil amend: for giue the dry foole drink, then is the foole     336
    *motley in my braine: good *Madona*, giue mee leaue to | proue you a
foole.     349
    *\*To*. Let him be the diuell and he will, I care not: giue     422
    *Ol*. Giue me my vaile: come throw it ore my face,     460
    *question's out of my part. Good gentle one, giue mee     474
    *Ol*. Giue vs the place alone,     512
    *\*Ol*. O sir, I will not be so hard-hearted: I will giue     536
    Do giue thee fiue-fold blazon: not too fast: soft, soft,     589
    Ile giue him reasons for't: hie thee *Maluolio*. | *Mal*. Madam, I will.
*Exit*.     604
    *\*An*. There's a testrill of me too: if one knight giue a     734
    *at any thing more then contempt, you would not giue     818
    *\*Du*. Giue me some Musick; Now good morow frends.     885
    *Du*. Giue me now leaue, to leaue thee.     959
    *Du*. Let all the rest giue place: Once more *Cesario*,     966
    As loue doth giue my heart: no womans heart     983
    To her in haste: giue her this Iewell: say,     1014
    My loue can giue no place, bide no denay. *Exeunt*     1015
    me on your Neece, giue me this prerogatiue of speech.     1086
    *\*Fab*. I will not giue my part of this sport for a pensi-|on     1183
    *\*Ol*. Let the Garden doore be shut, and leaue mee to | my hearing.
Giue me your hand sir.     1305
    *Vio*. Deere Lady. | *Ol*. Giue me leaue, beseech you: I did send,     1324
    *To*. Thy reason deere venom, giue thy reason.     1384
    *And*. I, ist? I warrant him: do but read. | *To*. Giue me.     1668
    *\*Fab*. Heere he comes with your Neece, giue them way     1714
    That honour (sau'd) may vpon asking giue.     1729
    *Ol*. How with mine honor may I giue him that, | Which I haue giuen to
you.     1731
    *computent iniurie, therefore get you on, and giue him     1765
    Ile giue him my horse, gray Capilet.     1804
    *Fab*. Giue ground if you see him furious.     1820
    *money for thee, if you tarry longer, I shall giue worse | paiment.     1936
    *that giue fooles money, get themselues a good re-|port, after
foureteene yeares purchase.     1939
    Take, and giue backe affayres, and their dispatch,     2132
    *\*Fab*. This is to giue a dogge, and in recompence desire | my dogge
againe.     2158
    you could make it another. | *Du*. O you giue me ill counsell.     2181
    *Ant*. *Orsino*: Noble sir, | Be pleas'd that I shake off these names you
giue mee:     2224
    *Du*. Giue me thy hand, | And let me see thee in thy womans weedes.     2439
    *reade thus: therefore, perpend my Princesse, and giue | eare.     2466

GIUEN = 4*2

    Loue sought, is good: but giuen vnsought is better.     1372
    Might well haue giuen vs bloody argument:     1500
    *Ol*. How with mine honor may I giue him that, | Which I haue giuen to
you.     1731

GIUEN *cont.*

| | |
|---|---|
| *\*And.* H'as broke my head a-crosse, and has giuen Sir | 2339 |
| \*darkenesse, and giuen your drunken Cosine rule ouer me, | 2471 |
| Why you haue giuen me such cleare lights of fauour, | 2506 |

GIUENT = *1

| | |
|---|---|
| \*you, I should haue giuen't you to day morning. But as a | 2454 |

GIUES = 1 *3

| | |
|---|---|
| *Vio.* It giues a verie eccho to the seate \| Where loue is thron'd. | 906 |
| \*accent sharpely twang'd off, giues manhoode more | 1697 |
| \*of the yong Gentleman, giues him out to be of good | 1702 |
| \*and he giues me the stucke in with such a mortall motion | 1794 |

GIUING = 1

| | |
|---|---|
| Stealing, and giuing Odour. Enough, no more, | 11 |

GIUT = 2

| | |
|---|---|
| *To.* If this Letter moue him not, his legges cannot: \| Ile giu't him. | 1688 |
| \*can be none, but by pangs of death and sepulcher: Hob, \| nob, is his word: giu't or take't. | 1757 |

GLAD = *1

| | |
|---|---|
| *\*To.* Wouldst thou not be glad to haue the niggard- \|ly | 1021 |

GLASSE = 2

| | |
|---|---|
| Yet liuing in my glasse: euen such, and so | 1901 |
| If this be so, as yet the glasse seemes true, | 2431 |

GLORIOUS = 1

| | |
|---|---|
| This is the ayre, that is the glorious Sunne, | 2115 |

GLOUE = *1

| | |
|---|---|
| \*but a cheu'rill gloue to a good witte, how quickely the | 1226 |

GO = 24*19

| | |
|---|---|
| *Cu.* Will you go hunt my Lord? \| *Du.* What *Curio?* \| *Cu.* The Hart. | 20 |
| I let go your hand, I am barren. *Exit Maria* | 193 |
| *\*Clo.* Apt in good faith, very apt: well go thy way, if | 320 |
| *Ol.* Go too, y'are a dry foole: Ile no more of you: be-\|sides you grow dis-honest. | 333 |
| \*madman: Fie on him. Go you *Maluolio;* If it be a suit | 401 |
| *\*Ol.* Go thou and seeke the Crowner, and let him sitte | 428 |
| \*o'my Coz: for he's in the third degree of drinke: hee's \| drown'd: go looke after him. | 429 |
| *\*Ant.* Will you stay no longer: nor will you not that \| I go with you. | 613 |
| *Ant.* The gentlenesse of all the gods go with thee: | 651 |
| That danger shall seeme sport, and I will go. *Exit.* | 655 |
| \*To be vp after midnight, and to go to bed then is early: | 707 |
| \*so that to go to bed after midnight, is to goe to bed be-\|times. | 708 |
| *To.* Shall I bid him go. \| *Clo.* What and if you do? | 806 |
| *To.* Shall I bid him go, and spare not? \| *Clo.* O no, no, no, no, you dare not. | 808 |
| *Mar.* Go shake your eares. | 821 |
| *\*To.* Come, come, Ile go burne some Sacke, tis too late | 881 |
| to go to bed now: Come knight, come knight. *Exeunt* | 882 |
| *To.* I meane to go sir, to enter. | 1294 |
| *\*To.* Go, write it in a martial hand, be curst and briefe: | 1421 |
| \*set 'em downe, go about it. Let there bee gaulle e-\|nough | 1427 |
| *To.* Wee'l call thee at the Cubiculo: Go. \| *Exit Sir Andrew.* | 1431 |
| Shall we go see the reliques of this Towne? | 1486 |
| *\*Ant.* To morrow sir, best first go see your Lodging? | 1487 |
| *Ol.* Go call him hither. | 1534 |
| *Ol.* Wilt thou go to bed *Maluolio?* | 1552 |
| *\*Mal.* Go too, thou art made, if thou desir'st to be so. | 1574 |
| *\*Mal.* Go off, I discard you: let me enioy my priuate: \| go off. | 1612 |

GO *cont.*

| | |
|---|---|
| *Mal.* Ah ha, does she so? \| *\*To.* Go too, go too: peace, peace, wee must deale | 1617 |
| *\*Mal.* Go hang your selues all: you are ydle shallowe | 1645 |
| *\*To.* Go sir *Andrew*: scout mee for him at the corner | 1693 |
| *\*that had rather go with sir Priest, then sir knight: I care | 1789 |
| 2.*Off.* Come sir, I pray you go. | 1878 |
| *Seb.* Go too, go too, thou art a foolish fellow, | 1921 |
| *\*An.* Nay let him alone, Ile go another way to worke | 1949 |
| *Seb.* Let go thy hand. | 1953 |
| *\*To.* Come sir, I will not let you go. Come my yong | 1954 |
| Against thy peace. Go with me to my house, | 1971 |
| Now go with me, and with this holy man | 2138 |
| *Seb.* Ile follow this good man, and go with you, | 2147 |
| *\*I go sir, but I would not haue you to thinke, that | 2196 |

GOD = 7*9

| | |
|---|---|
| *\*Clo.* Well, God giue them wisedome that haue it: & | 309 |
| then a foolish wit. God blesse thee Lady. | 330 |
| *\*Clow.* God send you sir, a speedie Infirmity, for the | 370 |
| *Vio.* Excellently done, if God did all. | 528 |
| *Mar.* For the loue o'God peace. | 784 |
| *\*Clo.* Now the melancholly God protect thee, and the | 960 |
| *\*Ol.* God comfort thee: Why dost thou smile so, and \| kisse thy hand so oft? | 1554 |
| he takes it at heart. Pray God he be not bewitch'd. | 1624 |
| *\*Tob. Fartheewell, and God haue mercie vpon one of our* | 1684 |
| *To.* Gentleman, God saue thee. | 1737 |
| *\*Vio.* Pray God defend me: a little thing would make | 1818 |
| *And.* Pray God he keepe his oath. | 1826 |
| *Ant.* But oh, how vilde an idoll proues this God: | 1885 |
| *\*Who I sir, not I sir. God buy you good sir Topas: Mar-\|ry Amen. I will sir, I will. | 2085 |
| *\*And.* For the loue of God a Surgeon, send one pre-\|sently to sir *Toby*. | 2336 |
| *\*Toby* a bloody Coxcombe too: for the loue of God your | 2340 |

GODLYNESSE = *1

| | |
|---|---|
| *\*Mar.* No I warrant you, he will not heare of godly-\|nesse. | 1643 |

GODS *see also* odd's, s'light = 1

| | |
|---|---|
| *Ant.* The gentlenesse of all the gods go with thee: | 651 |

GOE = 1*5

| | |
|---|---|
| *\*dust, like mistris *Mals* picture? Why dost thou not goe | 235 |
| *\*so that to go to bed after midnight, is to goe to bed be-\|times. | 708 |
| *\*To.* Th'art i'th right. Goe sir, rub your Chaine with | 815 |
| *\*euer crosse garter'd: I say remember, goe too, thou art | 1160 |
| Mayst smile at this: Thou shalt not choose but goe: | 1974 |
| *\*Mal.* Sir *Topas*, sir *Topas*, good sir *Topas* goe to my \| Ladie. | 2009 |

GOES = 4*1

| | |
|---|---|
| Goes on my Masters greefes. | 1724 |
| 1.*Off.* What's that to vs, the time goes by: Away. | 1884 |
| *\*goes as fairely, as to say, a carefull man, & a great \| scholler. The Competitors enter. | 1994 |
| *Ol.* Where goes *Cesario*? \| *Vio.* After him I loue, | 2290 |
| Were you a woman, as the rest goes euen, | 2405 |

GOING = *1

| | |
|---|---|
| *\*To. I will way-lay thee going home, where if it be thy chance \| to kill me. \| Fa. Good.* | 1679 |

GOLD = 1*1

| | |
|---|---|
| *Vio.* For saying so, there's Gold: | 68 |

GOLD *cont.*
*\*Du.* Thou shalt not be the worse for me, there's gold.                                         2179
GOLDEN = 3
How will she loue, when the rich golden shaft                                                      41
His councell now might do me golden seruice,                                                      2122
When that is knowne, and golden time conuents                                                     2552
GONE = 3*2
*\*you be not mad, be gone: if you haue reason, be breefe:                                         494
*\*To.* Farewell deere heart, since I must needs be gone.                                          799
Rudesbey be gone. I prethee gentle friend,                                                       1968
*Mal.* Foole, Ile requite it in the highest degree: | I prethee be gone.                          2103
*Clo.* I am gone sir, and anon sir, | Ile be with you againe:                                     2105
GOOD = 43*38
*\*these cloathes are good enough to drinke in, and so bee                                         129
without booke, & hath all the good gifts of nature.                                               144
*\*Ma.* Good Mistris accost, I desire better acquaintance | *Ma.* My name
is *Mary* sir.                                                                                     168
*And.* Good mistris *Mary*, accost.                                                                170
*To.* Art thou good at these kicke-chawses Knight?                                                 224
Therefore good youth, addresse thy gate vnto her,                                                 264
*Ma.* Make that good. | *Clo.* He shall see none to feare.                                        302
*\*Ma.* A good lenton answer: I can tell thee where y                                              304
*Clo.* Where good mistris *Mary*?                                                                  306
*\*or to be turn'd away: is not that as good as a hanging to | you?                                312
*\*Clo.* Many a good hanging, preuents a bad marriage:                                             314
*\*Clo.* Apt in good faith, very apt: well go thy way, if                                          320
*\*Clo.* Wit, and't be thy will, put me. into good fooling:                                        326
*\*Clo.* Two faults Madona, that drinke & good counsell                                            335
*\*motley in my braine: good *Madona*, giue mee leaue to | proue you a
foole.                                                                                            349
*Ol.* Can you do it? | *Clo.* Dexteriously, good Madona.                                           351
*\*Clo.* I must catechize you for it Madona, Good my | Mouse of vertue
answer mee.                                                                                       354
*Clo.* Good Madona, why mournst thou? | *Ol.* Good foole, for my
brothers death.                                                                                   358
*Clo.* Good Sir *Toby*.                                                                            416
*\*taken great paines to con it. Good Beauties, let mee su- | staine                              469
*\*question's out of my part. Good gentle one, giue mee                                            474
*\*Vio.* No good swabber, I am to hull here a little lon- | ger.                                   498
*Vio.* Good Madam, let me see your face.                                                           522
*Seb.* O good *Antonio*, forgiue me your trouble.                                                  642
She made good view of me, indeed so much,                                                         676
*\*Queubus*: 'twas very good yfaith: I sent thee sixe pence                                        725
*\*Clo.* Would you haue a loue-song, or a song of good | life?                                     735
*An.* I, I. I care not for good life.                                                              738
*An.* Excellent good, ifaith. | *To.* Good, good.                                                 746
*An.* Good ifaith: Come begin. *Catch sung*                                                        770
*Mar.* Nay good Sir *Toby*.                                                                        800
*\*An.* 'Twere as good a deede as to drink when a mans                                             822
*\*An.* I haue no exquisite reason for't, but I haue reason | good enough.                         838
*To.* Good night *Penthisilea*.                                                                    869
*An.* Before me she's a good wench.                                                                870
*\*Du.* Giue me some Musick; Now good morow frends.                                                885
Now good *Cesario*, but that peece of song,                                                        886
makes a good voyage of nothing. Farewell. *Exit*                                                  965
*\*Mal. To the vnknowne belou'd, this, and my good Wishes*:                                        1105
*\*but a cheu'rill gloue to a good witte, how quickely the                                         1226

GOOD *cont*.

Be not affraid good youth, I will not haue you,                                      1347
Grace and good disposition attend your Ladyship:                                      1352
Loue sought, is good: but giuen vnsought is better.                                   1372
And so adieu good Madam, neuer more,                                                  1377
And thankes: and euer oft good turnes,                                               1482
*Good *Maria*, let this fellow be look'd too. Where's my                              1583
*Mar*. Get him to say his prayers, good sir *Toby*, gette | him to pray.              1640
*Fa*. Good, and valiant.                                                              1671
*Fa*. A good note, that keepes you from the blow of y | (Law                          1674
*Fa*. Very breefe, and to exceeding good sence-lesse.                                 1678
*To*. *I will way-lay thee going home, where if it be thy chance | to kill
me. | Fa*. Good.                                                                      1679
*Fa*. Still you keepe o'th windie side of the Law: good.                              1683
*of the yong Gentleman, giues him out to be of good                                  1702
*To*. Ile make the motion: stand heere, make a good                                  1805
*Fab*. O good sir *Toby* hold: heere come the Officers.                               1837
*be as good as my word. Hee will beare you easily, and | raines well.                1841
Thou hast *Sebastian* done good feature, shame.                                       1886
*that giue fooles money, get themselues a good re- | port, after
foureteene yeares purchase.                                                           1939
*function well, nor leane enough to bee thought a good                                1992
*Studient: but to be said an honest man and a good hous- | keeper                     1993
*To*. The knaue counterfets well: a good knaue. | *Maluolio within*.                  2004
*Mal*. Sir *Topas*, sir *Topas*, good sir *Topas* goe to my | Ladie.                  2009
*Mal*. Sir *Topas*, neuer was man thus wronged, good                                  2014
*Mal*. Good foole, as euer thou wilt deserue well at                                  2065
*Clo*. M.(aster) *Maluolio*? | *Mal*. I good Foole.                                   2069
*Mal*. Sir *Topas*. | *Clo*. Maintaine no words with him good fellow.                 2083
*Who I sir, not I sir. God buy you good sir Topas: Mar- | ry Amen. I
will sir, I will.                                                                     2085
*Mal*. Good foole, helpe me to some light, and some                                   2090
*Mal*. By this hand I am: good foole, some inke, pa- | per,                           2094
Adieu good man diuell. *Exit*                                                         2112
*Seb*. Ile follow this good man, and go with you,                                     2147
*Ol*. Then lead the way good father, & heauens so shine,                              2149
*Clo*. Good M.(aster) *Fabian*, grant me another request. | *Fab*. Any
thing.                                                                               2155
*Duke*. I know thee well: how doest thou my good | Fellow?                            2163
*Clo*. *Primo*, *secundo*, *tertio*, is a good play, and the olde                     2187
*saying is, the third payes for all: the triplex sir, is a good                      2188
*Ol*. What do you say *Cesario*? Good my Lord.                                        2261
*Fab*. Good Madam heare me speake,                                                    2526
GOOSE-PEN = *1
*in thy inke, though thou write with a Goose-pen, | no matter: about it.             1428
GORBODACKE = *1
*of King *Gorbodacke*, that that is, is: so I being M.(aster) Parson,                 2000
GORE = *1
*With bloodlesse stroke my heart doth gore, M.O.A.I. doth | sway my
life*.                                                                               1117
GOSPELS = *1
*madmans Epistles are no Gospels, so it skilles not much                             2455
GOSSIP = 1
And make the babling Gossip of the aire,                                              567
GOUERNES = 1
*Vio*. Who gouernes heere? | *Cap*. A noble Duke in nature, as in name.               74

GOWN = *1
*Mar. Nay, I prethee put on this gown, & this beard,    1986
GOWNE = 1*2
*Veluet gowne: hauing come from a day bedde, where I | haue left
Oliuia sleeping.    1064
*in such a gowne. I am not tall enough to become the    1991
*Mar. Thou mightst haue done this without thy berd | and gowne, he
sees thee not.    2049
GRACE = 2*1
*do I too: he does it with a better grace, but I do it more | naturall.    781
Grace and good disposition attend your Ladyship:    1352
Clo. Put your grace in your pocket sir, for this once,    2183
GRACES = 1
If you will leade these graces to the graue, | And leaue the world no
copie.    534
GRACIOUS = 2*1
A gracious person; But yet I cannot loue him:    555
*in very gracious fooling last night, when thou spok'st of    723
Vio. Madam: | Du. Gracious Oliuia.    2259
GRAINE = *1
*Ol. 'Tis in graine sir, 'twill endure winde and wea-|ther.    529
GRAND = *1
*To. And they haue beene grand Iurie men, since before | Noah was a
Saylor.    1396
GRANDAM = 1*1
*Mal. That the soule of our grandam, might happily | inhabite a bird.    2037
the soule of thy grandam. Fare thee well.    2045
GRANT = 2
Clo. Good M.(aster) Fabian, grant me another request. | Fab. Any
thing.    2155
You can say none of this. Well, grant it then,    2504
GRAPPLE = 1
With which such scathfull grapple did he make,    2207
GRATILLITY = *1
*Clo. I did impeticos thy gratillity: for Maluolios nose    727
GRAUE = 4*1
*'tis thought among the prudent, he would quickely | haue the gift of a
graue.    148
Then in a Nuntio's of more graue aspect.    278
If you will leade these graces to the graue, | And leaue the world no
copie.    534
*Sad true louer neuer find my graue, to weepe there.    953
Since when, my watch hath told me, toward my graue    2324
GRAUITY = *1
*grauity to play at cherrie-pit with sathan. Hang him foul | Colliar.    1638
GRAY = 1
Ile giue him my horse, gray Capilet.    1804
GREAT = 11*14
What great ones do, the lesse will prattle of, )    83
*a nights: your Cosin, my Lady, takes great exceptions | to your ill
houres.    123
*he's a foole, he's a great quarreller: and but that hee hath    146
*am a great eater of beefe, and I beleeue that does harme | to my wit.    199
*taken great paines to con it. Good Beauties, let mee su-|staine    469
*Vio. Alas, I tooke great paines to studie it, and 'tis | Poeticall.    489
Of great estate, of fresh and stainlesse youth;    552
Mine eye too great a flatterer for my minde:    607

GREAT *cont.*

| | |
|---|---|
| *cons State without booke, and vtters it by great swarths. | 842 |
| Hath for your loue as great a pang of heart | 978 |
| great *P's*. It is in contempt of question her hand. | 1103 |
| *are become great, some atcheeues greatnesse, and some | 1151 |
| *Clo*. The matter I hope is not great sir, begging, but a | 1267 |
| *Fab*. This was a great argument of loue in her toward \| you. | 1391 |
| *Fab*. And his opposit the youth beares in his visage no \| great presage of cruelty. | 1443 |
| *strike him: if shee doe, hee'l smile, and take't for a great \| fauour. | 1461 |
| *Seb*. Belike you slew great number of his people. | 1497 |
| *Mal*. Some are borne great. \| *Ol*. Ha? | 1563 |
| *great man, and now applyes it to a foole. Vent my fol-\|ly: | 1930 |
| *I am affraid this great lubber the World will proue a | 1931 |
| *goes as fairely, as to say, a carefull man, & a great \| scholler. The Competitors enter. | 1994 |
| Be that thou know'st thou art, and then thou art \| As great as that thou fear'st. | 2309 |
| The Letter, at sir *Tobyes* great importance, | 2534 |
| *Clo*. Why some are borne great, some atchieue great-\|nesse, | 2541 |
| *A great while ago the world begon*, \| *hey ho*, &c. | 2576 |

GREATNESSE = 3*5

| | |
|---|---|
| *I am aboue thee, but be not affraid of greatnesse: Some | 1150 |
| *are become great, some atcheeues greatnesse, and some | 1151 |
| *haue greatnesse thrust vppon em. Thy fates open theyr | 1152 |
| *Mal*. Be not afraid of greatnesse: 'twas well writ. | 1561 |
| *Mal*. Some atcheeue greatnesse. \| *Ol*. What sayst thou? | 1565 |
| *Mal*. And some haue greatnesse thrust vpon them. \| *Ol*. Heauen restore thee. | 1567 |
| *Clo*. Why some are borne great, some atchieue great-\|nesse, | 2541 |
| *and some haue greatnesse throwne vpon them. I | 2542 |

GREEFE = 1

| | |
|---|---|
| Smiling at greefe. Was not this loue indeede? | 1005 |

GREEFES = 1

| | |
|---|---|
| Goes on my Masters greefes. | 1724 |

GREEKE = *1

| | |
|---|---|
| *Seb*. I prethee foolish greeke depart from me, there's | 1935 |

GREENE = 1

| | |
|---|---|
| And with a greene and yellow melancholly, | 1003 |

GREET = 1

| | |
|---|---|
| ' *Not a friend*, *not a friend greet* | 950 |

GREEUES = 1

| | |
|---|---|
| Makes me to aske you for my purse. It greeues mee | 1852 |

GREW = 1

| | |
|---|---|
| And grew a twentie yeeres remoued thing | 2241 |

GREY = *1

| | |
|---|---|
| *Item two lippes indifferent redde, Item two grey eyes, | 539 |

GRIZE = 1

| | |
|---|---|
| *Vio*. No not a grize: for tis a vulgar proofe \| That verie oft we pitty enemies. | 1339 |

GRIZZLE = 1

| | |
|---|---|
| When time hath sow'd a grizzle on thy case? | 2327 |

GROANES = 1

| | |
|---|---|
| With groanes that thunder loue, with sighes of fire. | 549 |

GROSSE = *1

| | |
|---|---|
| *Toby*, I will wash off grosse acquaintance, I will be point | 1167 |

GROSSELY = 1
But am in that dimension grossely clad,                                    2403
GROSSENESSE = *1
*beleeue such impossible passages of grossenesse. Hee's in | yellow
stockings.                                                                  1451
GROUND = 2*1
*surely, as your feete hits the ground they step on. They                  1796
*Fab.* Giue ground if you see him furious.                                 1820
Though I confesse, on base and ground enough                               2227
GROUNDS = 1*1
*with excellencies, that it is his grounds of faith, that all               844
But when we know the grounds, and authors of it,                           2523
GROW = 4*1
And tell them, there thy fixed foot shall grow | Till thou haue audience.   266
*Ol.* Go too, y'are a dry foole: Ile no more of you: be- | sides you grow
dis-honest.                                                                 333
To die, euen when they to perfection grow.                                 930
*one, though I would not haue it grow on my chinne. Is | thy Lady
within?                                                                    1260
Or will not else thy craft so quickely grow,                               2328
GROWES = 1*1
*Now you see sir, how your fooling growes old, & peo- | ple dislike it.     404
1.*Off.* The man growes mad, away with him: | Come, come sir.              1891
GROWNE = *1
*and wordes are growne so false, I am loath to proue rea- | son with
them.                                                                      1237
GUARD *see also* gard = 1*1
And. Dieu vou guard Monsieur. | *Vio. Et vouz ousie vostre seruiture.*     1284
*were best to haue some guard about you, if hee                           1532
GUILT = 1
A murdrous guilt shewes not it selfe more soone,                          1363
GUILTLESSE = *1
*with a distemper'd appetite. To be generous, guiltlesse,                  383
GULL = 3*2
*with him: If I do not gull him into a nayword, and make                    830
*Fab.* Heere comes my noble gull catcher.                                  1191
*selues into stitches, follow me; yond gull *Maluolio* is tur- | ned       1448
a knaue: a thin fac'd knaue, a gull?                                       2370
And made the most notorious gecke and gull,                               2513
GUST = *1
*the gift of a Coward, to allay the gust he hath in quarrel- | ling,        147
HA *l.*249 1564 1617 2064 2110 = 7
HABIT = *1
*Du.* One face, one voice, one habit, and two persons,                    2380
HABITE = *1
*tongue, in the habite of some Sir of note, and so foorth.                1596
HABITES = 1*1
*with a kinde of iniunction driues mee to these habites of                1173
But when in other habites you are seene,                                  2557
HAD *l.*8 94 *205 *207 209 *629 *630 677 *721 932 996 *1143 *1230 1322
*1411 *1789 *1793 *1801 2243 2273 2341 *2356 2374 2391 2393 2408
2409 2411 2533 2574 = 18*14
HADST *l.*209 726 *874 = 2*1
HAGGARD = 1
And like the Haggard, checke at euery Feather                             1276
HAIRE = 2
*To.* Then hadst thou had an excellent head of haire.                      209

HAIRE *cont.*
*An.* Why, would that haue mended my haire? 210
HALE = *1
*cannot hale them together. For *Andrew*, if he were open'd 1440
HALFE = 3*3
*Ol.* By mine honor halfe drunke. What is he at the | gate Cosin? | *To.*
A Gentleman. 410
*Sunne practising behauiour to his own shadow this halfe 1034
*of him, I would not haue him miscarrie for the halfe of | my Dowry.
*Exit* 1585
Hold, there's halfe my Coffer. 1864
I snatch'd one halfe out of the iawes of death, 1880
Which I had recommended to his vse, | Not halfe an houre before. 2243
HALLOW = 1
Hallow your name to the reuerberate hilles, 566
HALTING = *1
*Heere comes sir *Toby* halting, you shall heare more: but if 2355
HAND = 20*9
*Tob.* By this hand they are scoundrels and substra- | ctors 150
*draw sword agen: Faire Lady, doe you thinke you haue | fooles in
hand? 179
*Ma.* Sir, I haue not you by'th hand. 181
*An.* Marry but you shall haue, and heeres my hand. 182
hand to'th Buttry barre, and let it drinke. 184
can keepe my hand dry. But what's your iest? 189
I let go your hand, I am barren. *Exit Maria* 193
in my hand: my words are as full of peace, as matter. 505
Natures owne sweet, and cunning hand laid on: 532
*is no Whip-stocke. My Lady has a white hand, and the | Mermidons
are no bottle-ale houses. 728
*meanes for this vnciuill rule; she shall know of it by this | hand. *Exit* 819
*Mal.* I extend my hand to him thus: quenching my 1081
*Mal.* By my life this is my Ladies hand: these bee her 1101
great *P's.* It is in contempt of question her hand. 1103
*prose: If this fall into thy hand, reuolue.* In my stars 1149
*Ol.* Let the Garden doore be shut, and leaue mee to | my hearing.
Giue me your hand sir. 1305
*hand, and this was baulkt: the double gilt of this oppor- | tunitie 1404
*To.* Go, write it in a martial hand, be curst and briefe: 1421
*be executed. I thinke we doe know the sweet Romane | hand. 1550
*Ol.* God comfort thee: Why dost thou smile so, and | kisse thy hand so
oft? 1554
*Clo.* By my troth thou hast an open hand: these Wise- | men 1938
*Seb.* Let go thy hand. 1953
*my hand, helpe me to a Candle, and pen, inke, and paper: 2066
*Mal.* By this hand I am: good foole, some inke, pa- | per, 2094
*Du.* Giue me thy hand, | And let me see thee in thy womans weedes. 2439
Heere is my hand, you shall from this time bee | Your Masters Mistris. 2491
You must not now denie it is your hand, 2501
Write from it if you can, in hand, or phrase, 2502
But out of question, tis *Marias* hand. 2517
HANDMAID = 1
But from her handmaid do returne this answer: 31
HANDS = 2*2
*your Neece, on a forgotten matter wee can hardly make | distinction of
our hands. 853
*hands, let thy blood and spirit embrace them, and to in- | vre 1153

HANDS *cont.*
  *legges: It did come to his hands, and Commaunds shall        1549
  Confirm'd by mutuall ioynder of your hands,        2319
HANG = 2*5
  *these boots too: and they be not, let them hang them-|selues in their
  owne straps.        130
  of thy excuse: my Lady will hang thee for thy absence.        299
  *Clo. Let her hang me: hee that is well hang'de in this | world, needs to
  feare no colours.        300
  *To*. Marrie hang thee brocke.        1114
  *the North of my Ladies opinion, where you will hang        1406
  *grauity to play at cherrie-pit with sathan. Hang him foul | Colliar.        1638
  *Mal*. Go hang your selues all: you are ydle shallowe        1645
HANGD = *1
  *Ma*. Yet you will be hang'd for being so long absent,        311
HANGDE = *1
  *Clo. Let her hang me: hee that is well hang'de in this | world, needs to
  feare no colours.        300
HANGING = *2
  *or to be turn'd away: is not that as good as a hanging to | you?        312
  *Clo. Many a good hanging, preuents a bad marriage:        314
HANGS = *1
  *To. Excellent, it hangs like flax on a distaffe: & I hope        213
HAP = 1
  What else may hap, to time I will commit,        112
HAPLY = 2
  For such disguise as haply shall become        106
  *Seb*. Why I your purse? | *Ant*. Haply your eye shall light vpon some toy    1512
HAPPIE = 1
  *Vio*. If nothing lets to make vs happie both,        2415
HAPPILY = *1
  *Mal*. That the soule of our grandam, might happily | inhabite a bird.   2037
HAPPY = 2*1
  For they shall yet belye thy happy yeeres,        281
  *her liking. I thanke my starres, I am happy: I will bee        1174
  I shall haue share in this most happy wracke,        2432
HARBORS = *1
  *bad me tell you, that though she harbors you as her kins-|man,      794
HARD = 4
  *Cap*. That were hard to compasse,        96
  the Count himselfe here hard by, wooes her.        217
  It is too hard a knot for me t'vnty.        698
  Vnder your hard construction must I sit,        1329
HARDIE = *1
  *thing more, that you be neuer so hardie to come againe        666
HARDLY = *3
  *your Neece, on a forgotten matter wee can hardly make | distinction of
  our hands.        853
  *Indies: you haue not seene such a thing as tis: I can hard-|ly      1459
  *Orsino's* is return'd, I could hardly entreate him backe: he      1580.
HARD-HEARTED = *1
  *Ol*. O sir, I will not be so hard-hearted: I will giue        536
HARE = *1
  *then a Hare, his dishonesty appeares, in leauing his frend      1907
HARME = *1
  *am a great eater of beefe, and I beleeue that does harme | to my wit.  199

HART = 3*1
   *Cu*. Will you go hunt my Lord? | *Du*. What *Curio*? | *Cu*. The Hart.   20
   That instant was I turn'd into a Hart,   26
   *Vio*. To answer by the method, in the first of his hart.   519
   *Ol*. I haue said too much vnto a hart of stone,   1718
HARTS = *1
   *Clo*. How now my harts: Did you neuer see the Pic-|ture of we three?   717
HARUEST = 1
   And yet when wit and youth is come to haruest,   1348
HAS *l*.139 *198 *377 409 *720 *722 *728 *1033 1123 *1245 1375 1797
   *1823 *1929 *2339 2342 *2453 = 6*11, *3
   *Mal*. Ha's beene told so: and hee sayes hee'l stand at   442
   *And*. H'as broke my head a-crosse, and has giuen Sir   2339
   *To*. That's all one, has hurt me, and there's th'end on't:   2359
HAST *l*.102 *297 *406 *878 *1197 1370 *1739 *1740 1886 *1938 2223
   2298 2334 2433 = 7*7
HASTE = 2
   To her in haste: giue her this Iewell: say,   1014
   *Ol*. Blame not this haste of mine: if you meane well   2137
HATE = 2*2
   *To*. A false conclusion: I hate it as an vnfill'd Canne.   706
   *policie I hate: I had as liefe be a Brownist, as a Politi-|cian.   1411
   I hate ingratitude more in a man,   1873
   *To*. Then he's a Rogue, and a passy measures pauyn: I | hate a
   drunken rogue.   2363
HATH *l*.39 42 90 144 *145 *146 *147 *252 *508 749 910 911 970 978
   *1301 *1651 1726 *1745 *1750 *1755 *1814 1973 *2022 2254 2317 2324
   2327 2365 2377 2424 2442 2522 2535 2549 2551 = 23*12
HAUE *l*.23 78 *140 149 *179 181 182 *192 *197 *206 210 *219 *231 *233
   262 267 *309 327 417 *437 *468 *473 *494 *501 *508 *520 *523 556
   *628 *645 *646 652 *660 *663 675 719 *732 *735 767 *773 *787 *831
   *838 *962 979 *1021 *1025 *1041 1065 *1068 1097 *1152 1182 *1225
   *1260 1262 1332 1347 1358 1374 *1396 *1401 *1402 *1434 *1436 *1455
   *1459 1467 1473 1500 1501 1511 1514 1522 *1532 1567 *1584 *1585
   *1597 *1615 *1657 *1660 *1684 *1685 *1690 *1698 1718 1732 *1760
   *1785 *1792 *1802 *1803 *1809 *1822 1830 1834 1847 1859 1870 *1942
   *1950 *1959 *2015 *2049 *2076 *2196 *2256 2270 2325 *2353 *2356
   2373 2375 2383 2384 2387 2394 2425 2427 2432 *2454 *2462 *2470
   *2472 *2473 2497 2499 2500 2506 2511 2529 2539 2540 *2542 = 57*82
HAUING = 3*3
   *Mal*. Hauing beene three moneths married to her, | sitting in my state.   1060
   *Veluet gowne: hauing come from a day bedde, where I | haue left
   *Oliuia* sleeping.   1064
   *Mal*. Saying, Cosine *Toby*, my Fortunes hauing cast   1085
   Out of my leane and low ability | Ile lend you something: my hauing is
   not much,   1861
   And hauing sworne truth, euer will be true.   2148
   *my desire of hauing is the sinne of couetousnesse: but as   2197
HAUIOUR = *1
   *Vio*. With the same hauiour that your passion beares,   1723
HAUOCKE = 1
   *Ol*. Away with him? Who hath made this hauocke | with them?   2365
HAUT = 1
   *To*. Excellent, I smell a deuice. | *An*. I hau't in my nose too.   855
HAYRE = *1
   *Clo*. Now Ioue in his next commodity of hayre, send | thee a beard.   1257

HE *see also* h'as = 70*66
HEAD = 2*4
   *To.* Then hadst thou had an excellent head of haire.    209
   *would, are as secret as maiden-head: to your eares, Di-|uinity; to any
   others, prophanation.    510
   Though now you haue no sea-cap on your head:    1847
   *And.* H'as broke my head a-crosse, and has giuen Sir    2339
   *Du.* My Gentleman *Cesario*? | *And.* Odd's lifelings heere he is: you
   broke my head    2345
   *To.* Will you helpe an Asse-head, and a coxcombe, &    2369
HEADES = 1
   *With tospottes still had drunken heades, | for the raine, &c.*    2574
HEAD-STRONG = 1
   But such a head-strong potent fault it is,    1721
HEALTHS = *1
   *To.* With drinking healths to my Neece: Ile drinke    154
HEARD = 3*7
   *Vio. Orsino*: I haue heard my father name him.    78
   *heard my Lady talke of it yesterday: and of a foolish    133
   *degree, neither in estate, yeares, nor wit: I haue heard her    219
   *it in. I heard you were sawcy at my gates, & allowd your    492
   *know you haue heard of. He left behinde him, my selfe,    628
   That old and Anticke song we heard last night;    887
   *told me she did affect me, and I haue heard her self come    1041
   *some conduct of the Lady. I am no fighter, I haue heard    1760
   Then you haue heard him brag to you he will.    1834
   *Clo.* Vent my folly: He has heard that word of some    1929
HEARE = 9*5
   *Clo.* Do you not heare fellowes, take away the Ladie.    332
   Wee'l once more heare *Orsinos* Embassie.    461
   *approach rather to wonder at you, then to heare you. If    493
   *We will heare this diuinitie. Now sir, what is your text? | *Vio.* Most
   sweet Ladie.    513
   *O stay and heare, your true loues coming,*    741
   *To.* To heare by the nose, it is dulcet in contagion.    757
   I had rather heare you, to solicit that, | Then Musicke from the
   spheares.    1322
   After the last enchantment you did heare,    1326
   Hides my heart: so let me heare you speake. | *Vio.* I pittie you.    1336
   *Mar.* No I warrant you, he will not heare of godly-|nesse.    1643
   And heare thou there how many fruitlesse prankes    1972
   That sometime sauours nobly) but heare me this:    2276
   *Heere comes sir *Toby* halting, you shall heare more: but if    2355
   *Fab.* Good Madam heare me speake,    2526
HEARING = 1
   *Ol.* Let the Garden doore be shut, and leaue mee to | my hearing.
   Giue me your hand sir.    1305
HEART *see also* hart = 17*7
   *Du.* O she that hath a heart of that fine frame    39
   That liue in her. When Liuer, Braine, and Heart,    43
   *An.* Wherefore (sweet-heart?) What's your Meta-|phor?    185
   *And.* Taurus? That sides and heart.    246
   *Ol.* Are you a Comedian? | *Vio.* No my profound heart: and yet (by
   the verie    477
   *my speech in your praise, and then shew you the heart of | my
   message.    485
   Loue make his heart of flint, that you shal loue,    582

HEART *cont.*

*To.* Farewell deere heart, since I must needs be gone. 799
So swayes she leuell in her husbands heart: 919
Hath for your loue as great a pang of heart 978
As loue doth giue my heart: no womans heart 983
In faith they are as true of heart, as we. 995
*With bloodlesse stroke my heart doth gore, M.O.A.I. doth | sway my life.* 1117
*That tyrannous heart can think? To one of your receiuing 1334
Hides my heart: so let me heare you speake. | *Vio.* I pittie you. 1336
I haue one heart, one bosome, and one truth, 1374
That heart which now abhorres, to like his loue. *Exeunt* 1380
*to put fire in your Heart, and brimstone in your Liuer: 1400
*Mal.* To bed? I sweet heart, and Ile come to thee. 1553
he takes it at heart. Pray God he be not bewitch'd. 1624
He started one poore heart of mine, in thee. 1976
*Du.* Why should I not, (had I the heart to do it) 2273
To spight a Rauens heart within a Doue. 2287
HEARTED = *1

*Ol.* O sir, I will not be so hard-hearted: I will giue 536
HEARTS *see also* harts = 1
In womens waxen hearts to set their formes: 687
HEATE = 1*1
The Element it selfe, till seuen yeares heate, 32
*One draught aboue heate, makes him a foole, the second | maddes him, and a third drownes him. 426
HEATHEN = *1
*Heathen, a verie Renegatho; for there is no christian 1449
HEAUEN = 4*2
*Ol.* I know his soule is in heauen, foole. 361
*Brothers soule, being in heauen. Take away the Foole, | Gentlemen. 363
*Du.* Too old by heauen: Let still the woman take 917
*Mal.* And some haue greatnesse thrust vpon them. | *Ol.* Heauen restore thee. 1567
*Du.* Heere comes the Countesse, now heauen walkes | on earth: 2251
And whom, by heauen I sweare, I tender deerely, 2282
HEAUENS = 1*4
*and a sister, both borne in an houre: if the Heauens had 629
*Most excellent accomplish'd Lady, the heauens raine O- | dours on you. 1298
*Ant.* Oh heauens themselues. 1877
*Maluolio, Maluolio,* thy wittes the heauens restore: en- | deauour 2080
*Ol.* Then lead the way good father, & heauens so shine, 2149
HEE *l.* *146 *300 *338 *387 *434 *442 *840 *1202 *1204 *1532 1536 *1607 *1814 *1815 *1823 *1841 *2356 = 1*16
HEEL *l.* *140 *442 444 *448 *1461 1522 = 2*4
HEELES = 1*1
*see more detraction at your heeles, then Fortunes before | you. 1144
lookes pale, as if a Beare were at his heeles. 1812
HEERE = 26*14
*Vio.* Who gouernes heere? | *Cap.* A noble Duke in nature, as in name. 74
*Vio.* I thanke you: heere comes the Count. 258
*Duke.* Who saw *Cesario* hoa? | *Vio.* On your attendance my Lord heere. 259
braines, for heere he comes. *Enter Sir Toby.* 408
*To.* 'Tis a Gentleman heere. A plague o'these pickle | herring: How now Sot. 414
*Mal.* Heere Madam, at your seruice. 597
*And.* Heere comes the foole yfaith. 716

HEERE *cont*.
*Mar*. What a catterwalling doe you keepe heere? If       772
*Cur*. He is not heere (so please your Lordshippe) that | should sing it?   892
o'fauour with my Lady, about a Beare-baiting heere.       1024
*To*. Heere comes the little villaine: How now my | Mettle of India?   1030
*in the name of ieasting, lye thou there: for heere comes      1037
*Mal*. What employment haue we heere?       1097
*starres be praised. Heere is yet a postscript. *Thou canst*     1177
*Fab*. Heere comes my noble gull catcher.       1191
That were I tane heere, it would scarse be answer'd.     1496
*Fab*. Heere he is, heere he is: how ist with you sir?     1610
*Fab*. Heere he comes with your Neece, giue them way    1714
*Ol*. Heere, weare this Iewell for me, tis my picture:     1725
*To*. Ile make the motion: stand heere, make a good     1805
*Fab*. O good sir *Toby* hold: heere come the Officers.     1837
For the fayre kindnesse you haue shew'd me heere,     1859
*Ant*. Let me speake a little. This youth that you see | (heere,   1879
*heere in necessity, and denying him: and for his coward- |ship aske
*Fabian*.       1908
*sir *Topas* do not thinke I am mad: they haue layde mee | heere in
hideous darknesse.       2015
*Mal*. They haue heere propertied me: keepe mee in     2076
*Clo*. Aduise you what you say: the Minister is heere.     2079
That is deceiueable. But heere the Lady comes.     2135
Heere in the streets, desperate of shame and state,     2215
*Du*. Heere comes the Countesse, now heauen walkes | on earth:  2251
Heere to vnfold, though lately we intended       2314
*Du*. My Gentleman *Cesario*? | *And*. Odd's lifelings heere he is: you
broke my head       2345
*Heere comes sir *Toby* halting, you shall heare more: but if   2355
Of heere, and euery where. I had a sister,       2393
*well as a man in his case may do: has heere writ a letter to   2453
Heere at my house, and at my proper cost.       2485
Heere is my hand, you shall from this time bee | Your Masters Mistris.  2491
And in such formes, which heere were presuppos'd     2520
Set this deuice against *Maluolio* heere,       2531
HEEREAFTER = 2
*Clo*. *What is loue, tis not heereafter,*       748
*things, I am not of your element, you shall knowe more | heereafter.
*Exit*       1646
HEERES = 2*1
*An*. Marry but you shall haue, and heeres my hand.     182
*To*. Heere's an ouer-weening rogue.       1046
*An*. Heere's the Challenge, reade it: I warrant there's | vinegar and
pepper in't.       1665
HEES = *6
*Ma*. They that adde moreour, hee's drunke nightly | in your company.  152
*o'my Coz: for he's in the third degree of drinke: hee's | drown'd: go
looke after him.       429
*speake with you. What is to be said to him Ladie, hee's | fortified
against any deniall.       439
*beleeue such impossible passages of grossenesse. Hee's in | yellow
stockings.       1451
*To*. Why man hee's a verie diuell, I haue not seen such   1792
*him for a Coward, but hee's the verie diuell, incardinate.   2344
HELD = *1
*Clo*. Well held out yfaith: No, I do not know you,     1923

HELL = 3*2
 *Clo.* I thinke his soule is in hell, Madona.     360
 *the diuels of hell be drawne in little, and Legion himselfe | possest
him, yet Ile speake to him.     1608
 A Fiend like thee might beare my soule to hell.     1735
 *Mal.* As hell sir *Topas.*     2021
 *Ignorance were as darke as hell; and I say there was ne- | uer  2032
HELP = *1
 *Clo.* I will help you too't. But tel me true, are you not  2098
HELPE = 2*4
 *my hand, helpe me to a Candle, and pen, inke, and paper:  2066
 *Mal.* Good foole, helpe me to some light, and some  2090
 helpe, I had rather then forty pound I were at home.  2341
 *And.* Ile helpe you sir *Toby,* because we'll be drest to- | gether.  2367
 *To.* Will you helpe an Asse-head, and a coxcombe, &  2369
 Where lye my maiden weeds: by whose gentle helpe,  2421
HENCE = 2
 For but a month ago I went from hence,  81
 We will not part from hence. *Cesario* come  2555
HENCEFORTH = 1
 Where thou, and I (henceforth) may neuer meet.  2331
HER *see also* hir *l.*28 31 33 35 38 43 45 87 88 *120 125 *155 *171 172
 *173 214 217 *219 264 265 269 *273 275 *300 345 464 *467 *637 640
 *670 *671 *674 675 677 679 681 690 *773 *777 *794 798 *878 918 919
 968 970 971 973 979 980 999 1000 1002 1009 1014 *1041 *1044 1060
 *1101 *1102 1103 1104 *1106 *1107 *1126 *1172 *1174 *1187 *1202
 *1205 *1232 *1248 1288 *1391 *1401 *1597 *1925 2131 2162 *2193 2212
 2304 2330 2410 2426 2535 = 58*39
HERE = 3*6
 *knight that you brought in one night here, to be hir woer  134
 *parish top. What wench? *Castiliano vulgo*: for here coms | Sir *Andrew*
*Agueface.*  158
 the Count himselfe here hard by, wooes her.  217
 *Ma.* Peace you rogue, no more o'that: here comes my  323
 *Ma.* Will you hoyst sayle sir, here lies your way.  497
 *Vio.* No good swabber, I am to hull here a little lon- | ger.  498
 *one of these Letters are in my name. Soft, here fol- | lowes  1148
 *throw: if you will let your Lady know I am here to speake  2192
 *Vio.* Here comes the man sir, that did rescue mee.  2201
HERES = 1
 *Ant.* It doth not fit me: hold sir, here's my purse,  1507
HERESIE = *1
 *Ol.* O, I haue read it: it is heresie. Haue you no more | to say?  520
HERMIT = *1
 *Clo. Bonos dies* sir *Toby*: for as the old hermit of *Prage*  1998
HERRING = 1
 *To.* 'Tis a Gentleman heere. A plague o'these pickle | herring: How
now Sot.  414
HERRINGS = *1
 *as like husbands, as Pilchers are to Herrings, the Hus- | bands  1247
HERSELFE *see* selfe
HES = 5*10
 *To.* He's as tall a man as any's in Illyria.  137
 He's a very foole, and a prodigall.  141
 *he's a foole, he's a great quarreller: and but that hee hath  146
 *in Illyria: he's a Coward and a Coystrill that will not  156
 *Looke you now, he's out of his gard already: vnles you  378

HES *cont.*
  \*o'my Coz: for he's in the third degree of drinke: hee's | drown'd: go
looke after him.        429
  \*Fa. O peace, now he's deepely in: looke how imagi-|nation blowes
him.        1058
  Where is *Maluolio*? | *Mar.* He's comming Madame:        1527
he's an enemy to mankinde.        1621
  \*My Neece is already in the beleefe that he's mad: we may        1658
  \*Clo. O he's drunke sir *Toby* an houre agone: his eyes | were set at eight
i'th morning.        2361
  \*To. Then he's a Rogue, and a passy measures pauyn: I | hate a
drunken rogue.        2363
  They say poore Gentleman, he's much distract.        2447
  \*and you smile not he's gag'd: and thus the whirlegigge | of time, brings
in his reuenges.        2546
HEY = 5\*1
  \*Clo. Hey Robin, iolly Robin, tell me how thy Lady | does. | *Mal.*
Foole.        2057
  *with hey, ho, the winde and the raine:*        2561
  *But when I came to mans estate, | with hey ho, &c.*        2564
  *But when I came alas to wine, | with hey ho, &c.*        2568
  *But when I came vnto my beds, | with hey ho, &c.*        2572
  *A great while ago the world begon, | hey ho, &c.*        2576
HID = \*2
  \*To. Wherefore are these things hid? Wherefore haue        233
  \*Then loue that would seeme hid: Loues night, is noone.        1364
HIDDEOUS = \*1
  \*Ol. Sure you haue some hiddeous matter to deliuer,        501
HIDE = 1\*1
  \*meane? Is it a world to hide vertues in? I did thinke by        239
  Nor wit, nor reason, can my passion hide:        1368
HIDEOUS = 1\*1
  \*into a most hideous opinion of his rage, skill, furie, and        1710
  \*sir *Topas* do not thinke I am mad: they haue layde mee | heere in
hideous darknesse.        2015
HIDES = 1
  Hides my heart: so let me heare you speake. | *Vio.* I pittie you.        1336
HIE = 1
  Ile giue him reasons for't: hie thee *Maluolio.* | *Mal.* Madam, I will.
*Exit.*        604
HIGH = 2
  That it alone, is high fantasticall.        19
  *That can sing both high and low.*        742
HIGHER = 1
  \*To. No sir, it is leggs and thighes: let me see thee ca-|per. Ha, higher:
ha, ha, excellent. *Exeunt*        247
HIGHEST = 1\*1
  \*Clo. Misprision in the highest degree. Lady, *Cucullus*        347
  *Mal.* Foole, Ile requite it in the highest degree: | I prethee be gone.        2103
HILLES = 1
  Hallow your name to the reuerberate hilles,        566
HIM *l.*63 66 71 78 108 110 151 287 \*339 \*368 \*376 \*379 398 \*400 \*401
  \*422 \*426 427 \*428 430 \*435 \*436 \*437 \*439 441 \*453 456 457 \*550 551
  555 576 599 600 601 602 604 \*628 \*646 \*665 691 774 806 808 \*823 824
  826 \*830 \*831 \*833 \*835 \*845 859 861 \*865 898 918 \*1025 \*1026 \*1035
  \*1036 1048 1053 1057 1060 1062 \*1075 \*1081 1101 1109 1123 1141
  \*1197 1198 1199 \*1207 \*1223 \*1315 1320 \*1414 \*1415 \*1420 \*1423

HIM *cont.*

*1424 *1434 *1436 *1455 *1457 *1460 *1461 1522 1523 1534 *1580 1582
*1585 *1589 *1590 1609 *1614 1616 *1619 *1627 1632 *1638 *1640 1641
*1653 1655 *1657 *1661 1668 *1686 1688 1689 *1693 *1695 1699 *1702
1715 1731 *1740 *1750 *1765 *1768 *1773 *1782 *1783 *1786 1787
*1793 1798 1800 *1802 *1803 1804 1810 *1811 *1814 1820 1831 1834
1848 1881 1891 1904 *1908 1912 *1913 *1949 *1950 *1951 *1987 2002
*2051 *2052 2084 2119 2139 2210 2216 2232 2237 2240 2255 *2272 2283
2291 *2344 2365 2371 2445 2481 2487 2533 2550 = 106*92

HIMSELF = *1

| | |
|---|---|
| *not dry: bid the dishonest man mend himself, if he mend, | 337 |

HIMSELFE = 3*4

| | |
|---|---|
| Most prouident in perill, binde himselfe, | 62 |
| the Count himselfe here hard by, wooes her. | 217 |
| *The best perswaded of himselfe: so cram'd (as he thinkes) | 843 |
| *forehead, and complection, he shall finde himselfe most | 851 |
| *the diuels of hell be drawne in little, and Legion himselfe \| possest him, yet Ile speake to him. | 1608 |
| That he beleeues himselfe, so do not I: | 1895 |
| *that will vse the diuell himselfe with curtesie: sayst thou \| that house is darke? | 2019 |

HIR *l.*\*134 *218 *1248 *1933 = *4

HIS *see also* for's, in's *l.*76 88 111 114 *157 *254 *255 256 291 294 360 361
*372 *378 *455 518 *519 556 582 601 *667 *672 801 *844 *848 *849
*850 *867 *1034 1048 *1202 *1257 1277 1313 *1315 1318 1362 1380
*1441 *1443 *1455 *1457 1494 1497 *1549 1625 *1640 *1651 *1659 1688
*1701 *1703 *1707 *1709 *1710 *1755 1758 *1764 *1766 *1783 *1784
*1809 1812 *1814 *1816 *1822 1826 1833 1882 *1894 *1907 *1908 1975
2039 2041 *2101 2109 2122 2154 2202 2214 2232 2234 2235 2238 2240
2243 2284 *2361 2371 2399 2408 2413 2430 2450 *2453 *2465 2547
2558 = 56*52

HISTORY = 1

| | |
|---|---|
| *Du.* And what's her history? \| *Vio.* A blanke my Lord: she neuer told her loue, | 999 |

HIT = 1

| | |
|---|---|
| *To.* O for a stone-bow to hit him in the eye. | 1062 |

HITHER = 7*2

| | |
|---|---|
| Were you sent hither to praise me? | 541 |
| *Vio.* Euen now sir, on a moderate pace, I haue since a-\|riu'd but hither. | 660 |
| Come hither Boy, if euer thou shalt loue | 900 |
| *Ol.* Go call him hither. | 1534 |
| *To.* Come hither Knight, come hither *Fabian*: Weel | 1898 |
| *Orsino's* enemie. A witchcraft drew me hither: | 2228 |
| *Ol.* He shall inlarge him: fetch *Maluolio* hither, | 2445 |
| *Ol.* See him deliuer'd *Fabian*, bring him hither: | 2481 |

HITS = *1

| | |
|---|---|
| *surely, as your feete hits the ground they step on. They | 1796 |

HO = 7*1

| | |
|---|---|
| How now *Maluolio*? \| *Mal.* Sweet Lady, ho, ho. | 1538 |
| *Mal.* Oh ho, do you come neere me now: no worse | 1587 |
| with hey, ho, the winde and the raine: | 2561 |
| But when I came to mans estate, \| with hey ho, &c. | 2564 |
| But when I came alas to wine, \| with hey ho, &c. | 2568 |
| But when I came vnto my beds, \| with hey ho, &c. | 2572 |
| A great while ago the world begon, \| hey ho, &c. | 2576 |

HOA = 3
 *Duke*. Who saw *Cesario* hoa? | *Vio*. On your attendance my Lord heere.  259
 What hoa, *Maluolio*.  595
 *To*. To him sir *Topas*. | *Clow*. What hoa, I say, Peace in this prison.  2002
HOB = *1
 *can be none, but by pangs of death and sepulcher: Hob, | nob, is his
 word: giu't or take't.  1757
HOE = 1
 There lies your way, due West. | *Vio*. Then Westward hoe:  1350
HOLD = 17*7
 I saw him hold acquaintance with the waues, | So long as I could see.  66
 *Ma*. That if one breake, the other will hold: or if both | breake, your
 gaskins fall.  318
 *Ol*. Who of my people hold him in delay? | *Ma*. Sir *Toby* Madam, your
 kinsman.  398
 *of warre, no taxation of homage; I hold the Olyffe  504
 Nor hold him vp with hopes, I am not for him:  602
 *Clo. Hold thy peace*, *thou Knaue* knight. I shall be con-|strain'd in't, to
 call thee knaue, Knight.  765
 call me knaue. Begin foole: it begins, *Hold thy peace*.  768
 *Clo*. I shall neuer begin if I hold my peace.  769
 Or thy affection cannot hold the bent:  926
 Tell her I hold as giddily as Fortune:  971
 So bigge, to hold so much, they lacke retention.  984
 *Vio*. Nay, and thou passe vpon me, Ile no more with | thee. Hold
 there's expences for thee.  1255
 *Ant*. It doth not fit me: hold sir, here's my purse,  1507
 *To*. Prethee hold thy peace, this is not the way: Doe  1631
 *you hold your life at any price, betake you to your gard:  1749
 *Fabian* can scarse hold him yonder.  1800
 *Fab*. O good sir *Toby* hold: heere come the Officers.  1837
 Hold, there's halfe my Coffer.  1864
 *To*. Hold sir, or Ile throw your dagger ore the house  1945
 *To*. Come on sir, hold.  1948
 *Ol*. Hold *Toby*, on thy life I charge thee hold. | *To*. Madam.  1962
 *thou shalt hold th'opinion of *Pythagoras*, ere I will allow  2043
 Hold little faith, though thou hast too much feare.  2334
HOLDS = *1
 How does he sirrah? | *Cl*. Truely Madam, he holds *Belzebub* at the
 staues end as  2451
HOLLOW = *1
 *Mar*. Lo, how hollow the fiend speakes within him;  1614
HOLY = 3
 Now go with me, and with this holy man  2138
 Call forth the holy Father. | *Du*. Come, away.  2299
 Attested by the holy close of lippes,  2320
HOMAGE = *1
 *of warre, no taxation of homage; I hold the Olyffe  504
HOME = 2*4
 *An*. And I thought that, I'de forsweare it. Ile ride | home to morrow sir
 *Toby*.  202
 *An*. Faith Ile home to morrow sir *Toby*, your niece wil  215
 *to Church in a Galliard, and come home in a Carranto?  236
 *from the Count, I am sicke, or not at home. What you | will, to
 dismisse it. *Exit Maluo*.  402
 *To. I will way-lay thee going home, where if it be thy chance | to kill
 me*. | *Fa*. Good.  1679

HOME *cont*.

helpe, I had rather then forty pound I were at home.    2341
HONEST = 1*1

   *Ol.* Go too, y'are a dry foole: Ile no more of you: be-|sides you grow
dis-honest.    333
   *Studient: but to be said an honest man and a good hous-|keeper    1993
HONESTIE = *1

   *Haue you no wit, manners, nor honestie, but to gabble    787
HONOR = 5*1

   *Ol.* By mine honor halfe drunke. What is he at the | gate Cosin? | *To.*
A Gentleman.    410
Haue you not set mine Honor at the stake,    1332
By maid-hood, honor, truth, and euery thing,    1366
   *Ol.* How with mine honor may I giue him that, | Which I haue giuen to
you.    1731
Cride fame and honor on him: What's the matter? | 1.*Offi. Orsino*, this
is that *Anthonio*    2210
And tell me in the modestie of honor,    2505
HONORABLE = *1

   *Vio.* The honorable Ladie of the house, which is she?    463
HONORS = *1

   *will for his honors sake haue one bowt with you:    1822
HONOUR = 2

And laid mine honour too vnchary on't:    1719
That honour (sau'd) may vpon asking giue.    1729
HOOD = 1

By maid-hood, honor, truth, and euery thing,    1366
HOPE = 7*3

   (Courage and hope both teaching him the practise)    63
Mine owne escape vnfoldeth to my hope,    69
   *To.* Excellent, it hangs like flax on a distaffe: & I hope    213
   *Fa.* And *O* shall end, I hope. | *To.* I, or Ile cudgell him, and make him
cry *O.*    1140
   *Clo.* The matter I hope is not great sir; begging, but a    1267
   *An.* I hope sir, you are, and I am yours.    1286
   *soules. He may haue mercie vpon mine, but my hope is better,*    1685
Did I redeeme: a wracke past hope he was:    2231
And acting this in an obedient hope,    2510
Which I haue wondred at. In hope it shall not,    2529
HOPES = 1*1

Nor hold him vp with hopes, I am not for him:    602
   *me, and the full prospect of my hopes. Well Ioue, not I,    1604
HORRIBLE = *1

   *seest him, draw, and as thou draw'st, sweare horrible: for    1695
HORRIBLY = *1

   *Fa.* He is as horribly conceited of him: and pants, &    1811
HORRID = *1

   *To.* I wil meditate the while vpon some horrid message | for a
Challenge.    1716
HORSE = 4*1

   *Mar.* My purpose is indeed a horse of that colour.    860
   *An.* And your horse now would make him an Asse.    861
Ile giue him my horse, gray Capilet.    1804
marry Ile ride your horse as well as I ride you.    1807
   *I haue his horse to take vp the quarrell, I haue perswaded | him the
youths a diuell.    1809

HOTTE = *1
   *Clo.* Yes by S.(aint) Anne, and Ginger shall bee hotte y'th | mouth
too.                                                813

HOUNDS = 1
   And my desires like fell and cruell hounds,               27

HOURE = 3*4
   *and a sister, both borne in an houre: if the Heauens had    629
   *that, for some houre before you tooke me from the       631
   *houre: obserue him for the loue of Mockerie: for I know  1035
   *Seb.* Ile be your purse-bearer, and leaue you | For an houre.  1516
   Which I had recommended to his vse, | Not halfe an houre before.  2243
   *Clo.* O he's drunke sir *Toby* an houre agone: his eyes | were set at eight
i'th morning.                                        2361
   Taint the condition of this present houre,              2528

HOURES = 4
   Not three houres trauaile from this very place.         73
   *a nights: your Cosin, my Lady, takes great exceptions | to your ill
houres.                                           123
   I haue trauail'd but two houres.                   2325
   How haue the houres rack'd, and tortur'd me, | Since I haue lost thee?  2383

HOUSE = 10*13
   *Vio.* The honorable Ladie of the house, which is she?    463
   *I pray you tell me if this bee the Lady of the house,    466
   *modest assurance, if you be the Ladie of the house, that | (I  475
   *phangs of malice, I sweare) I am not that I play. Are you | the Ladie
of the house?                                     479
   And call vpon my soule within the house,            563
   *of my Ladies house, that ye squeak out your Cozi- |ers   789
   *to the house: if not, and it would please you to take    797
   *Oliuiaes* Father tooke much delight in. He is about the | house.  896
   *Vio.* I am all the daughters of my Fathers house,    1010
   *I do liue at my house, and my house dooth stand by the | Church.  1220
   *To.* Will you incounter the house, my Neece is desi- |rous  1287
   *Mar.* The house will be the quieter.              1656
   *Vio.* I will returne againe into the house, and desire    1759
   *his desire. Backe you shall not to the house, vnlesse you  1766
   *To.* Hold sir, or Ile throw your dagger ore the house    1945
   Against thy peace. Go with me to my house,         1971
   *that will vse the diuell himselfe with curtesie: sayst thou | that house is
darke?                                         2019
   *Mal.* I am not mad sir *Topas*, I say to you this house is | darke.  2026
   *Mal.* I say this house is as darke as Ignorance, thogh    2031
   She could not sway her house, command her followers,    2131
   Heere at my house, and at my proper cost.           2485
   Kept in a darke house, visited by the Priest,          2512

HOUSES = 1
   *is no Whip-stocke. My Lady has a white hand, and the | Mermidons
are no bottle-ale houses.                              728

HOUSEWIFE *see* huswife
HOUSKEEPER = *1
   *Studient: but to be said an honest man and a good hous- |keeper  1993

HOW = 43*16
   O spirit of Loue, how quicke and fresh art thou,     13
   Ere since pursue me. How now what newes from her?    28
   How will she loue, when the rich golden shaft        41
   *And.* Sir *Toby Belch*. How now sir *Toby Belch*? | *To.* Sweet sir *Andrew*.  161
   *Ol.* How say you to that *Maluolio*?             374

HOW *cont*.

*Now you see sir, how your fooling growes old, & peo-|ple dislike it. 404

*To*. 'Tis a Gentleman heere. A plague o'these pickle | herring: How now Sot. 414

*Ol*. Cosin, Cosin, how haue you come so earely by | this Lethargie? 417

*Ol*. How does he loue me? | *Vio*. With adorations, fertill teares, 547

To tell me how he takes it: Fare you well: 578

Vnlesse the Master were the man. How now? 590

How easie is it, for the proper false 686

How will this fadge? My master loues her deerely, 690

*Clo*. How now my harts: Did you neuer see the Pic-|ture of we three? 717

*An*. If I do not, neuer trust me, take it how you will. 880

That is belou'd. How dost thou like this tune? 905

*To*. Heere comes the little villaine: How now my | Mettle of India? 1030

Cocke of him, how he iets vnder his aduanc'd plumes. 1048

*Fa*. O peace, now he's deepely in: looke how imagi-|nation blowes him. 1058

*but a cheu'rill gloue to a good witte, how quickely the 1226

O world, how apt the poore are to be proud? 1342

If one should be a prey, how much the better 1343

*it is no matter how wittie, so it bee eloquent, and full of 1422

How shall I feast him? What bestow of him? 1523

How now *Maluolio*? | *Mal*. Sweet Lady, ho, ho. 1538

*Mal*. Why how doest thou man? 1546

*Mar*. How do you *Maluolio*? | *Maluo*. At your request: 1556

*manner how: as a sad face, a reuerend carriage, a slow 1595

*Fab*. Heere he is, heere he is: how ist with you sir? 1610

How ist with you man? 1611

*Mar*. Lo, how hollow the fiend speakes within him; 1614

*gently with him: Let me alone. How do you *Maluolio*? 1619

*How ist with you? What man, defie the diuell: consider, 1620

*Mar*. La you, and you speake ill of the diuell, how 1623

*Mal*. How now mistris? | *Mar*. Oh Lord. 1629

*To*. Why how now my bawcock? how dost y chuck? | *Mal*. Sir. 1635

*Ol*. How with mine honor may I giue him that, | Which I haue giuen to you. 1731

me tell them how much I lacke of a man. 1819

*Ant*. But oh, how vilde an idoll proues this God: 1885

And heare thou there how many fruitlesse prankes 1972

*Seb*. What rellish is in this? How runs the streame? 1977

*Clo*. Out hyperbolicall fiend, how vexest thou this 2011

*how thou findst him: I would we were well ridde of this 2052

*Clo*. Hey Robin, iolly Robin, tell me how thy Lady | does. | *Mal*. Foole. 2057

*Clo*. Alas sir, how fell you besides your fiue witts? 2071

*Duke*. I know thee well: how doest thou my good | Fellow? 2163

*Clo*. No sir, the worse. | *Du*. How can that be? 2168

*Vio*. How can this be? | *Du*. When came he to this Towne? 2245

*Ol*. Aye me detested, how am I beguil'd? 2296

*Du*. How now Gentleman? how ist with you? 2358

How haue the houres rack'd, and tortur'd me, | Since I haue lost thee? 2383

*Ant*. How haue you made diuision of your selfe, 2387

How does he sirrah? | *Cl*. Truely Madam, he holds *Belzebub* at the staues end as 2451

*Ol*. How now, art thou mad? | *Clo*. No Madam, I do but reade madnesse: and your 2460

HOW *cont*.
Du. Is this the Madman? | Ol. I my Lord, this same: How now
Maluolio? 2495
How with a sportfull malice it was follow'd, 2536
Ol. Alas poore Foole, how haue they baffel'd thee? 2540
HOWEUER = 1
For boy, howeuer we do praise our selues, 920
HOWLING = 1
It is as fat and fulsome to mine eare | As howling after Musicke. 2264
HOWRE = 1
Being once displaid, doth fall that verie howre. 928
HOYST = 1
Ma. Will you hoyst sayle sir, here lies your way. 497
HULL = *1
*Vio. No good swabber, I am to hull here a little lon-|ger. 498
HUMBLE = 1*2
*thy selfe to what thou art like to be: cast thy humble 1154
Vio. My dutie Madam, and most humble seruice. 1307
*the Letter. Cast thy humble slough sayes she: be oppo-|site 1591
HUMOR = *1
*Mal. And then to haue the humor of state: and after 1068
HUMORS = *1
*To. Oh peace, and the spirit of humors intimate rea-|ding aloud to
him. 1099
HUMOUR = *1
*Vio. You either feare his humour, or my negligence, 254
HUNG = 1
Hung on our driuing boate: I saw your brother 61
HUNGRIE = *1
*a hungrie, to challenge him the field, and then to breake 823
HUNGRY = 1
But mine is all as hungry as the Sea, 988
HUNT = 1
Cu. Will you go hunt my Lord? | Du. What Curio? | Cu. The Hart. 20
HUNTER = *1
*but thy intercepter full of despight, bloody as the Hun-|ter, 1741
HURLING = *1
*forbeare hurling things at him, I know my Ladie will 1460
HURT = 5*5
*hurt him in eleuen places, my Neece shall take note of it, 1415
he protests he will not hurt you. 1817
*me, as he is a Gentleman and a Soldiour, he will not hurt | you. Come
on, too't. 1824
Vio. Why do you speake to me, I neuer hurt you: 2349
But I bespake you faire, and hurt you not. 2351
*And. If a bloody coxcombe be a hurt, you haue hurt 2353
*To. That's all one, has hurt me, and there's th'end on't: 2359
Ol. Get him to bed, and let his hurt be look'd too. 2371
Seb. I am sorry Madam I haue hurt your kinsman: 2373
HUSBAND = 4
Ol. Whether my Lord? Cesario, Husband, stay. 2301
Du. Husband? | Ol. I Husband. Can he that deny? 2302
Du. Her husband, sirrah? | Vio. No my Lord, not I. 2304
HUSBANDS = 1*2
So swayes she leuell in her husbands heart: 919
*as like husbands, as Pilchers are to Herrings, the Hus-|bands 1247

HUSHES = 1
*Vio.* My Lord would speake, my dutie hushes me.                                          2262
HUSWIFE = 1
  to see a huswife take thee between her legs, & spin it off.                               214
HYPERBOLICALL = *1
  *Clo.* Out hyperbolicall fiend, how vexest thou this                                     2011
I = 288*300, 20*6
  The like of him. Know'st thou this Countrey? | *Cap.* I Madam well, for
  I was bred and borne                                                                      71
  *Ma.* I, but you must confine your selfe within the | modest limits of
  order.                                                                                    126
  *To.* Who, Sir *Andrew Ague-cheeke*? | *Ma.* I he.                                        135
  *Ma.* I, but hee'l haue but a yeare in all these ducates:                                 140
  *Ma.* I Sir, I haue them at my fingers ends: marry now                                    192
  *And.* I, 'tis strong, and it does indifferent well in a                                 242
  *Ol.* I marry, what is he?                                                                421
  *An.* I, I. I care not for good life.                                                     738
  *An.* I, he do's well enough if he be dispos'd, and so                                    780
  *Clo.* Are you ready Sir? | *Duke.* I prethee sing. *Musicke.*                            939
  *Vio.* I but I know. | *Du.* What dost thou knowe?                                        992
  Sir, shall I to this Lady? | *Du.* I that's the Theame,                                  1012
  *To.* O I, make vp that, he is now at a cold sent.                                       1131
  *Fa.* And *O* shall end, I hope. | *To.* I, or Ile cudgell him, and make him
  cry *O*.                                                                                 1140
  *Mal.* And then *I.* comes behind.                                                       1142
  *Fa.* I, and you had any eye behinde you, you might                                      1143
  *Mal.* To bed? I sweet heart, and Ile come to thee.                                      1553
  *To.* I biddy, come with me. What man, tis not for                                       1637
  *And.* I, ist? I warrant him: do but read. | *To.* Giue me.                              1668
  *To.* I but he will not now be pacified,                                                 1799
  *Clo.* M.(aster) *Maluolio*? | *Mal.* I good Foole.                                      2069
  *Clo.* I sir, we are some of her trappings.                                              2162
  *Du.* Husband? | *Ol.* I Husband. Can he that deny?                                      2302
  *Ol.* Did he write this? | *Clo.* I Madame.                                              2478
  *Du.* Is this the Madman? | *Ol.* I my Lord, this same: How now
  *Maluolio*?                                                                              2495
IADE = *1
  *imagination iade mee; for euery reason excites to this,                                 1169
IAWES = 1
  I snatch'd one halfe out of the iawes of death,                                          1880
ICICLE *see* ysickle
IDE = *4
  *An.* And I thought that, I'de forsweare it. Ile ride | home to morrow sir
  *Toby*.                                                                                   202
  *An.* O, if I thought that, Ide beate him like a dogge.                                   835
  *and so cunning in Fence, I'de haue seene him damn'd ere                                 1802
  *I'de haue challeng'd him. Let him let the matter slip, and                              1803
IDEOT = *1
  *this Letter wil make a contemplatiue Ideot of him. Close                               1036
IDLE *see also* ydle = 1
  I thinke is not for idle Markets, sir.                                                   1515
IDLENESSE = *1
  *Ol.* Well sir, for want of other idlenesse, Ile bide your | proofe.                     356
IDOLL = 1
  *Ant.* But oh, how vilde an idoll proues this God:                                       1885
IEALIOUS = 1
  That my most iealious, and too doubtfull soule                                          2142

IEALOUSIE = 2
    But iealousie, what might befall your trauell,      1474
    Kill what I loue: (a sauage iealousie,      2275
IEASTING = *1
    *in the name of ieasting, lye thou there: for heere comes      1037
IEMS = 1
    But 'tis that miracle, and Queene of Iems      972
IEST = 3
    can keepe my hand dry. But what's your iest?      189
    *Ma*. A dry iest Sir. | *And*. Are you full of them?      190
    *To*. And aske no other dowry with her, but such ano-|ther iest.      1187
IESTER = *1
    *Du*. Who was it? | *Cur*. Feste the Iester my Lord, a foole that the
    Ladie      894
IESTS = 1*1
    He must obserue their mood on whom he iests, | The quality of persons,
    and the time:      1274
    *iests, fire-new from the mint, you should haue bangd      1402
IETS = 1
    Cocke of him, how he iets vnder his aduanc'd plumes.      1048
IEWELL = 1*2
    To her in haste: giue her this Iewell: say,      1014
    *winde vp my watch, or play with my some rich Iewell:      1076
    *Ol*. Heere, weare this Iewell for me, tis my picture:      1725
IEZABEL = 1
    *An*. Fie on him Iezabel.      1057
IF *l*.5 *216 *251 269 288 *318 *320 *337 *338 *341 *342 *401 *406 *466
    *475 481 *482 *493 *494 528 534 543 557 603 *629 *643 *645 *671 *672
    682 689 *734 769 *772 *780 *795 *797 807 *817 *830 *835 *876 *878
    *880 900 974 1019 1113 *1129 *1149 *1161 *1178 *1201 *1207 *1222
    1224 *1242 1288 1343 1356 *1423 *1440 *1447 *1461 1504 *1532 1537
    1544 *1574 1576 *1607 *1627 *1649 *1679 1688 *1748 1787 1812 1820
    1829 1831 1835 1839 1904 *1936 *1950 1958 1980 *2053 *2074 2130
    2137 *2173 *2192 2263 2294 *2353 *2355 2400 2415 2431 2502
    2538 = 45*60
IFAITH *see also* yfaith = 4*1
    *An*. Excellent good, ifaith. | *To*. Good, good.      746
    *An*. Very sweet, and contagious ifaith.      756
    *An*. Good ifaith: Come begin. *Catch sung*      770
    *Du*. She is not worth thee then. What yeares ifaith?      915
    *An*. Ifaith, or I either?      1196
IGNORANCE = *3
    *but ignorance, in which thou art more puzel'd then the | Aegyptians in
    their fogge.      2029
    *Mal*. I say this house is as darke as Ignorance, thogh      2031
    *Ignorance were as darke as hell; and I say there was ne-|uer      2032
IGNORANT = *1
    *Letter being so excellently ignorant, will breed no terror      1705
IIGGE = *1
    *My verie walke should be a Iigge: I would not so much      237
ILE *l*.104 107 114 *128 *154 *202 *215 *221 292 333 *356 587 600 604 669
    *825 *881 956 1019 1141 1211 *1255 *1259 *1303 1383 1442 1516 1553
    1582 1609 *1627 1689 1728 1798 1804 *1805 1807 1838 *1840 1862 1863
    1912 *1945 *1949 *1950 1988 *1989 *2101 2103 2106 2147 2286 *2367
    2420 2548 = 35*21

ILL = 2*2

*a nights: your Cosin, my Lady, takes great exceptions | to your ill
houres. 123
*Mal. Of verie ill manner: hee'l speake with you, will | you, or no. 448
*Mar. La you, and you speake ill of the diuell, how 1623
you could make it another. | Du. O you giue me ill counsell. 2181

ILLYRIA = 7*4

Enter Orsino Duke of Illyria, Curio, and other | Lords. 2
Vio. What Country (Friends) is this? | Cap. This is Illyria Ladie. 51
Vio. And what should I do in Illyria? | My brother he is in Elizium, 53
To. He's as tall a man as any's in Illyria. 137
*in Illyria: he's a Coward and a Coystrill that will not 156
*And. As any man in Illyria, whatsoeuer he be, vnder 225
*And. And I thinke I haue the backe-tricke, simply as | strong as any
man in Illyria. 231
*sir Toby would leaue drinking, thou wert as witty a piece | of Eues
flesh, as any in Illyria. 321
*part of Illyria: will you walke towards him, I will make | your peace
with him, if I can. 1786
*there be any law in Illyria: though I stroke him first, yet 1951
*paper, I tell thee I am as well in my wittes, as any man in | Illyria. 2091

IMAGE = 4

Saue in the constant image of the creature 904
when the image of it leaues him, he must run mad. 1198
any image of offence done to any man. 1747
And to his image, which me thought did promise | Most venerable
worth, did I deuotion. 1882

IMAGINATION = 1*2

*Fa. O peace, now he's deepely in: looke how imagi- |nation blowes
him. 1058
*imagination iade mee; for euery reason excites to this, 1169
Proue true imagination, oh proue true, | That I deere brother, be now
tane for you. 1896

IMITATE = 1

For him I imitate: Oh if it proue, 1904

IMPETICOS = *1

*Clo. I did impeticos thy gratillity: for Maluolios nose 727

IMPETUOSITIE = *1

*impetuositie. This will so fright them both, that they wil 1711

IMPLACABLE = *1

*at this moment is so implacable, that satisfaction 1756

IMPORTANCE = 1

The Letter, at sir Tobyes great importance, 2534

IMPORTANT = 1

Ol. Come to what is important in't: I forgiue you | the praise. 487

IMPOSSIBLE = *1

*beleeue such impossible passages of grossenesse. Hee's in | yellow
stockings. 1451

IMPRESSURE = *1

*Her very Phrases: By your leaue wax. Soft, and the im- |pressure 1106

IMPRISOND = 1

Why haue you suffer'd me to be imprison'd, 2511

IMPROBABLE = 1

*Fa. If this were plaid vpon a stage now, I could con- |demne it as an
improbable fiction. 1649

IN see also ifaith, i'th, i'the, i'thy, yfaith, y'th = 138*120

110

INCARDINATE = *1
   *him for a Coward, but hee's the verie diuell, incardinate.    2344
INCENSEMENT = *1
   *soules and bodies hath he diuorc'd three, and his incense-|ment    1755
INCENST = *1
   *Fab. I know the knight is incenst against you, euen to    1778
INCITES = *1
   *appeare stubborne to him: for she incites me to that in    1590
INCONSTANT = 1
   he inconstant sir, in his fauours. *Val.* No beleeue me.    256
INCOUNTER = *1
   *To. Will you incounter the house, my Neece is desi-|rous    1287
INCREASING = *1
   *better increasing your folly: Sir *Toby* will be sworn that    371
INCREDULOUS = *1
   *obstacle, no incredulous or vnsafe circumstance: What    1602
INDEED = 6*3
   *Ma. He hath indeed, almost naturall: for besides that    145
   She made good view of me, indeed so much,    676
   *But shall we make the Welkin dance indeed? Shall wee    758
   *Mar.* My purpose is indeed a horse of that colour.    860
   We men may say more, sweare more, but indeed    1006
   *Clo. No indeed sir, the Lady *Oliuia* has no folly, shee    1245
   mad indeed, or do you but counterfeit.    2099
   *Seb.* A spirit I am indeed,    2402
   He finished indeed his mortall acte    2413
INDEEDE = 3*4
   Smiling at greefe. Was not this loue indeede?    1005
   *that word, might make my sister wanton: But indeede,    1233
   *the bigger, I am indeede not her foole, but hir cor-|rupter of words.    1248
   I did some seruice, of such note indeede,    1495
   *Fa.* Why we shall make him mad indeede.    1655
   *his valour. He is indeede sir, the most skilfull, bloudy, &    1784
   *Clo. But as well: then you are mad indeede, if you be    2074
INDIA = 1
   *To.* Heere comes the little villaine: How now my | Mettle of India?    1030
INDIES = *1
   *Indies: you haue not seene such a thing as tis: I can hard-|ly    1459
INDIFFERENT = *2
   *And. I, 'tis strong, and it does indifferent well in a    242
   *Item two lippes indifferent redde, Item two grey eyes,    539
INDIGNATION = 1*1
   deliuer thy indignation to him by word of mouth.    826
   *To. Sir, no: his indignation deriues it selfe out of a ve-|ry    1764
INDUCED = *1
   *I haue your owne letter, that induced mee to the    2473
INDUE = *1
   *Clo. Now Mercury indue thee with leasing, for thou | speak'st well of
   fooles.    389
INEUITABLE = *1
   *that it is ineuitable: and on the answer, he payes you as    1795
INFECTION = *1
   *To. His very genius hath taken the infection of the | deuice man.    1651
INFIRMITY = *2
   *him: Infirmity that decaies the wise, doth euer make the | better foole.    368
   *Clow. God send you sir, a speedie Infirmity, for the    370

INGRATE = 1
To whose ingrate, and vnauspicious Altars                    2269
INGRATEFULL = 1
That most ingratefull boy there by your side,                2229
INGRATITUDE = 1
I hate ingratitude more in a man,                            1873
INHABITE = 1
*Mal. That the soule of our grandam, might happily | inhabite a bird.   2037
INHABITES = 1
Or any taint of vice, whose strong corruption | Inhabites our fraile
blood.                                                       1875
INIUNCTION = *1
*with a kinde of iniunction driues mee to these habites of    1173
INIURIE = *1
*computent iniurie, therefore get you on, and giue him        1765
INIURIES = 1
If that the iniuries be iustly weigh'd, | That haue on both sides past.   2538
INIURY = 1
and speake out of my iniury. *The madly vs'd Maluolio.*       2477
INKE = 1*5
*inuention: taunt him with the license of Inke: if thou       1423
*in thy inke, though thou write with a Goose-pen, | no matter: about it.   1428
*that neuer saw pen and inke, very wittily sayd to a Neece    1999
*my hand, helpe me to a Candle, and pen, inke, and paper:     2066
*Mal. By this hand I am: good foole, some inke, pa- | per,    2094
I will fetch you light, and paper, and inke.                 2102
INLARGE = 1
Ol. He shall inlarge him: fetch *Maluolio* hither,           2445
INNOCENCE = 2
And dallies with the innocence of loue, | Like the old age.   937
Vio. By innocence I sweare, and by my youth,                 1373
INS = 1
come, for sure the man is tainted in's wits.                 1533
INSOOTH = *1
*sweet a breath to sing, as the foole has. Insooth thou wast   722
INSTANCE = 1
So farre exceed all instance, all discourse,                 2126
INSTANT = 1
That instant was I turn'd into a Hart,                        26
INSTRUMENT = 1
And that I partly know the instrument                        2278
INT = 5*1
swear't. Tut there's life in't man.                          220
Ol. Come to what is important in't: I forgiue you | the praise.   487
*Clo. Hold thy peace, thou Knaue knight. I shall be con- | strain'd in't, to
call thee knaue, Knight.                                     765
*An. Heere's the Challenge, reade it: I warrant there's | vinegar and
pepper in't.                                                 1665
*in't, and I would I were the first that euer dissembled in   1990
As I perceiue she do's: there's something in't               2134
INTENDED = 1
Heere to vnfold, though lately we intended                   2314
INTENT = 1*1
The forme of my intent. Ile serue this Duke,                 107
*and their intent euerie where, for that's it, that alwayes   964
INTERCEPTER = *1
*but thy intercepter full of despight, bloody as the Hun- | ter,   1741

INTERLUDE *see* enterlude
INTIMATE = *1
    *To*. Oh peace, and the spirit of humors intimate rea- | ding aloud to
    him.                                                1099
INTO *l*.17 26 *326 *665 *830 *1032 *1149 *1157 *1207 *1403 *1405 *1448
   *1457 *1593 *1710 *1759 2139 2236 *2470 = 4*15
INTRIM = 1
    No *intrim*, not a minutes vacancie,                         2248
INUENTION = 2*1
    *inuention: taunt him with the license of Inke: if thou        1423
    Or say, tis not your seale, not your inuention:            2503
    That ere inuention plaid on? Tell me why?              2514
INUENTORIED = *1
    *out diuers scedules of my beautie. It shalbe Inuentoried     537
INUISIBLE = 2
    With an inuisible, and subtle stealth                 593
    sir, I would it would make you inuisible.             1243
INUITES = 1
    Inuites me in this churlish messenger:               680
INVRE = *1
    *hands, let thy blood and spirit embrace them, and to in- | vre   1153
IOCUND = 1
    *Vio*. And I most iocund, apt, and willinglie,           2288
IOLLY = *1
    *Clo*. Hey Robin, iolly Robin, tell me how thy Lady | does. | *Mal*.
    Foole.                                          2057
IOT = 2
    *And*. No faith, Ile not stay a iot longer:           1383
    1.*Off*. No sir, no iot: I know your fauour well:        1846
IOUE = 1*7
    *sonne should be a foole: whose scull, Ioue cramme with    407
    *Mal*. *Ioue knowes I loue, but who, Lips do not mooue, no*   1110
    *euen with the swiftnesse of putting on. Ioue, and my     1176
    *in my presence still smile, deero my sweete, I prethee*. Ioue   1180
    *Clo*. Now Ioue in his next commodity of hayre, send | thee a beard.  1257
    *I haue lymde her, but it is Ioues doing, and Ioue make me   1597
    *me, and the full prospect of my hopes. Well Ioue, not I,   1604
    *To*. Ioue blesse thee M.(aster) Parson.             1997
IOUES = *1
    *I haue lymde her, but it is Ioues doing, and Ioue make me   1597
IOURNEYS = 1
    *Iourneys end in louers meeting*,                744
IOYNDER = 1
    Confirm'd by mutuall ioynder of your hands,        2319
IRON *see also* yron = 1
    *starke naked: for meddle you must that's certain, or for- | sweare to
    weare iron about you.                           1769
IS *see also* any's, beauties, care's, heere's, here's, hee's, he's, husbands, it's,
    Knights, Ladies, Lady's, Maluolio's, mans, names, question's, shee's,
    she's, that's, there's, ther's, 'tis, what's, where's, youth's = 123*118, *2
    *of King *Gorbodacke*, that that is, is: so I being M.(aster) Parson,  2000
    *am M.(aster) Parson; for what is that, but that? and is, but is?  2001
IST = 9*2
    *Looke you sir, such a one I was this present: Ist not well | done?  526
    *Clo*. His eyes do shew his dayes are almost done. | *Mal*. Is't euen so?  801
    *Du*. What kinde of woman ist? | *Vio*. Of your complection.   913
    *Fab*. Heere he is, heere he is: how ist with you sir?     1610

IST *cont*.

How ist with you man?      1611
*How ist with you? What man, defie the diuell: consider,      1620
*To*. Ist possible?      1648
*Fab*. Ist so sawcy?      1667
*And*. I, ist? I warrant him: do but read. | *To*. Giue me.      1668
Ist possible that my deserts to you | Can lacke perswasion. Do not
tempt my misery,      1866
*Du*. How now Gentleman? how ist with you?      2358
IT *see also* and't, deliuer't, doo't, do't, feel't, for't, giuen't, giu't, in't, ist,
on't, open't, saw't, see't, sweare't, take't, too't, vpon't = 108*91
ITEM = *3
*Item two lippes indifferent redde, Item two grey eyes,      539
*with lids to them: Item, one necke, one chin, & so forth.      540
ITH = 3*4
*strangest minde i'th world: I delight in Maskes and Re- | uels
sometimes altogether.      222
*To*. Th'art i'th right. Goe sir, rub your Chaine with      815
*To*. Send for money knight, if thou hast her not i'th | end, call me Cut.      878
But let concealment like a worme i'th budde      1001
I saw't i'th Orchard.      1388
*Schoole i'th Church: I haue dogg'd him like his murthe- | rer.      1455
*Clo*. O he's drunke sir *Toby* an houre agone: his eyes | were set at eight
i'th morning.      2361
ITHE = *1
*comming downe this walke, he has beene yonder i'the      1033
ITHY = 1
*Ol*. Prethee reade i'thy right wits.      2464
ITS = 3*1
*Ma*. It's dry sir.      187
*not be seene, or if she be it's four to one, she'l none of me:      216
me faith say I. Well, it's all one. *Exit*      423
it's no matter for that.      1952
ITSELFE *see* selfe
IUDGE = 1
Thou shalt be both the Plaintiffe and the Iudge | Of thine owne cause.      2524
IUDGEMENT = 1
*Fab*. I will proue it legitimate sir, vpon the Oathes of | iudgement, and
reason.      1394
IUMPE = 1
Of place, time, fortune, do co-here and iumpe      2418
IURIE = *1
*To*. And they haue beene grand Iurie men, since before | *Noah* was a
Saylor.      1396
IUST = 1
*Du*. Iust the contrary: the better for thy friends.      2167
IUSTLY = 1
If that the iniuries be iustly weigh'd, | That haue on both sides past.      2538
KEEP = *1
*Ol*. It is the more like to be feigned, I pray you keep      491
KEEPE = 9*6
A brothers dead loue, which she would keepe fresh      37
can keepe my hand dry. But what's your iest?      189
*Vio*. I am no feede poast, Lady; keepe your purse,      580
*willing to keepe in: therefore it charges me in manners,      624
*Mar*. What a catterwalling doe you keepe heere? If      772
*To*. We did keepe time sir in our Catches. Snecke vp.      792

KEEPE *cont.*

| | |
|---|---|
| *will keepe no foole sir, till she be married, and fooles are | 1246 |
| *Fa. Still you keepe o'th windie side of the Law: good. | 1683 |
| And. Pray God he keepe his oath. | 1826 |
| *Mal. They haue heere propertied me: keepe mee in | 2076 |
| What time we will our celebration keepe | 2145 |
| Both day and night did we keepe companie. | 2249 |
| Cesario, you do not keepe promise with me. | 2258 |
| To keepe in darkenesse, what occasion now | 2315 |
| And all those swearings keepe as true in soule, | 2436 |

KEEPES = *2

| | |
|---|---|
| To. And crosse garter'd? \| *Mar. Most villanously: like a Pedant that keepes a | 1453 |
| *Fa. A good note, that keepes you from the blow of y \| (Law | 1674 |

KEPT = 2

| | |
|---|---|
| Vio. Yes being kept together, and put to vse. | 1263 |
| Kept in a darke house, visited by the Priest, | 2512 |

KICKE-CHAWSES = 1

| | |
|---|---|
| To. Art thou good at these kicke-chawses Knight? | 224 |

KILL = 3*2

| | |
|---|---|
| *kill him, whom you haue recouer'd, desire it not. Fare | 646 |
| *To. I will way-lay thee going home, where if it be thy chance \| to kill me. \| Fa. Good. | 1679 |
| kill one another by the looke, like Cockatrices. | 1712 |
| *of thy wits, and feare to kill a Woodcocke, lest thou dis- \|possesse | 2044 |
| Kill what I loue: (a sauage iealousie, | 2275 |

KILLD = 1

| | |
|---|---|
| Hath kill'd the flocke of all affections else | 42 |

KILST = 1

| | |
|---|---|
| To. Thou kilst me like a rogue and a villaine. | 1682 |

KIN = 1

| | |
|---|---|
| One of thy kin has a most weake Pia-mater. | 409 |

KINDE = 6*4

| | |
|---|---|
| Because she will admit no kinde of suite, \| No, not the Dukes. | 97 |
| *I take these Wisemen, that crow so at these set kinde of | 380 |
| Ol. What kinde o'man is he? \| Mal. Why of mankinde. | 445 |
| *Mar. Marrie sir, sometimes he is a kinde of Puritane. | 834 |
| Du. What kinde of woman ist? \| Vio. Of your complection. | 913 |
| *with a kinde of iniunction driues mee to these habites of | 1173 |
| And to do that well, craues a kinde of wit: | 1273 |
| Seb. My kinde Anthonio, \| I can no other answer make, but thankes, | 1480 |
| *of some kinde of men, that put quarrells purposely on o- \|thers, | 1761 |
| Tempests are kinde, and salt waues fresh in loue. | 1905 |

KINDLY = *1

| | |
|---|---|
| *thee kindly: but thou lyest in thy throat, that is not the matter | 1676 |

KINDNESSE = 2*1

| | |
|---|---|
| *ye well at once, my bosome is full of kindnesse, and I | 647 |
| For the fayre kindnesse you haue shew'd me heere, | 1859 |
| Vio. He did me kindnesse sir, drew on my side, | 2217 |

KINDNESSES = 1

| | |
|---|---|
| As to vpbraid you with those kindnesses | 1869 |

KING = 1*1

| | |
|---|---|
| Her sweete perfections with one selfe king: | 45 |
| *of King Gorbodacke, that that is, is: so I being M.(aster) Parson, | 2000 |

KINGS = *1

| | |
|---|---|
| *Vio. So thou maist say the Kings lyes by a begger, if a | 1222 |

KINNE = 1
Of charity, what kinne are you to me? 2395
KINSMAN = 3*3
*Ol.* Who of my people hold him in delay? | *Ma.* Sir *Toby* Madam, your
kinsman. 398
*bad me tell you, that though she harbors you as her kins-|man, 794
*place, as I would they should doe theirs: to aske for my | kinsman
*Toby.* 1070
*slough, and appeare fresh. Be opposite with a kinsman, 1155
*with a Kinsman, surly with seruants, let thy tongue 1592
*Seb.* I am sorry Madam I haue hurt your kinsman: 2373
KISSE = 2
*Then come kisse me sweet and twentie:* 752
*Ol.* God comfort thee: Why dost thou smile so, and | kisse thy hand so
oft? 1554
KISSES = *1
*friends I am abused: so that conclusions to be as kisses, if 2173
KNAUE = 7*1
*An.* Most certaine: Let our Catch be, *Thou Knaue.* 764
*Clo.* Hold thy peace, thou Knaue* knight. I shall be con-|strain'd in't, to
call thee knaue, Knight. 765
call me knaue. Begin foole: it begins, *Hold thy peace.* 768
*To.* The knaue counterfets well: a good knaue. | *Maluolio within.* 2004
a knaue: a thin fac'd knaue, a gull? 2370
KNAUERY = *1
*knauery. If he may bee conueniently deliuer'd, I would 2053
KNAUES = 1
*Gainst Knaues and Theeues men shut their gate, | for the raine, &c.* 2566
KNEW = 1*1
*And.* I knew 'twas I, for many do call mee foole. 1096
*Which you knew none of yours. What might you think? 1331
KNIFE = 1
*Mal. I may command where I adore, but silence like a Lu-|cresse knife:* 1115
KNIGHT = 9*13
*knight that you brought in one night here, to be hir woer 134
*To,* You mistake knight: Accost, is front her, boord | her, woe her,
assayle her. 171
*To.* O knight, thou lack'st a cup of Canarie: when did | I see thee so
put downe? 194
*To.* *Pur-quoy* my deere knight? 204
*To.* Art thou good at these kicke-chawses Knight? 224
*To.* What is thy excellence in a galliard, knight? | *And.* Faith, I can cut
a caper. 228
*An.* There's a testrill of me too: if one knight giue a 734
*An.* A mellifluous voyce, as I am true knight. 754
*Clo.* Hold thy peace, thou Knaue* knight. I shall be con-|strain'd in't, to
call thee knaue, Knight. 765
*To.* Doo't knight, Ile write thee a Challenge: or Ile 825
*To.* What for being a Puritan, thy exquisite reason, | deere knight. 836
*To.* Let's to bed knight: Thou hadst neede send for | more money. 874
*To.* Send for money knight, if thou hast her not i'th | end, call me Cut. 878
to go to bed now: Come knight, come knight. *Exeunt* 882
*Mal.* Besides you waste the treasure of your time, | with a foolish
knight. 1092
*To.* He is knight dubb'd with vnhatch'd Rapier, and 1753
*me this courteous office, as to know of the Knight what 1772
*Fab.* I know the knight is incenst against you, euen to 1778

KNIGHT *cont.*
| | |
|---|---|
| *that had rather go with sir Priest, then sir knight: I care | 1789 |
| *To. Come hither Knight, come hither *Fabian*: Weel | 1898 |

KNIGHTS = 1
| | |
|---|---|
| *Clo.* Beshrew me, the knights in admirable fooling. | 779 |

KNITTERS = 1
| | |
|---|---|
| The Spinsters and the Knitters in the Sun, | 934 |

KNOT = 1
| | |
|---|---|
| It is too hard a knot for me t'vnty. | 698 |

KNOW = 23*22
| | |
|---|---|
| And then 'twas fresh in murmure (as you know | 82 |
| I know thy constellation is right apt | 286 |
| *Ol.* I know his soule is in heauen, foole. | 361 |
| *Ma* I know not (Madam) 'tis a faire young man, and \| well attended. | 396 |
| *Ol.* Your Lord does know my mind, I cannot loue him | 550 |
| Yet I suppose him vertuous, know him noble, | 551 |
| *Ol.* I do I know not what, and feare to finde | 606 |
| *An.* Let me yet know of you, whither you are bound. | 620 |
| *the rather to expresse my selfe: you must know of mee | 625 |
| *know you haue heard of. He left behinde him, my selfe, | 628 |
| *And.* Nay by my troth I know not: but I know, to \| be vp late, is to be | |
| vp late. | 704 |
| *Euery wise mans sonne doth know.* | 745 |
| *meanes for this vnciuill rule; she shall know of it by this \| hand. *Exit* | 819 |
| to lye straight in my bed: I know I can do it. | 832 |
| *Mar.* Sport royall I warrant you: I know my Phy-\|sicke | 864 |
| *Vio.* I but I know. \| *Du.* What dost thou knowe? | 992 |
| And all the brothers too: and yet I know not. | 1011 |
| *Fa.* I would exult man: you know he brought me out | 1023 |
| *houre: obserue him for the loue of Mockerie: for I know | 1035 |
| *man must know. No man must know. What followes? | 1111 |
| The numbers alter'd: No man must know, | 1112 |
| *not choose but know who I am. If thou entertainst my loue, let* | 1178 |
| *forbeare hurling things at him, I know my Ladie will | 1460 |
| *be executed. I thinke we doe know the sweet Romane \| hand. | 1550 |
| *Mal.* Do you know what you say? | 1622 |
| *the Gentleman (as I know his youth will aptly receiue it) | 1709 |
| *me this courteous office, as to know of the Knight what | 1772 |
| *Vio.* Pray you sir, do you know of this matter? | 1777 |
| *Fab.* I know the knight is incenst against you, euen to | 1778 |
| 1.*Off.* No sir, no iot: I know your fauour well: | 1846 |
| Take him away, he knowes I know him well. | 1848 |
| *Vio.* I know of none, | 1871 |
| Nor know I you by voyce, or any feature: | 1872 |
| *Vio.* He nam'd *Sebastian*: I my brother know | 1900 |
| *Clo.* Well held out yfaith: No, I do not know you, | 1923 |
| *Duke.* I know thee well: how doest thou my good \| Fellow? | 2163 |
| *throw: if you will let your Lady know I am here to speake | 2192 |
| I know not what 'twas, but distraction. | 2219 |
| And that I partly know the instrument | 2278 |
| But this your Minion, whom I know you loue, | 2281 |
| Reueales before 'tis ripe: what thou dost know | 2316 |
| *the world shall know it: Though you haue put mee into | 2470 |
| But when we know the grounds, and authors of it, | 2523 |

KNOWE = 1*3
| | |
|---|---|
| *Vio.* I but I know. \| *Du.* What dost thou knowe? | 992 |
| *a demure trauaile of regard: telling them I knowe my | 1069 |

117

KNOWE *cont.*

| | |
|---|---|
| *things, I am not of your element, you shall knowe more \| heereafter. | |
| *Exit* | 1646 |
| *nature the wrongs are thou hast done him, I knowe not: | 1740 |

KNOWES = 2*1

| | |
|---|---|
| *Mal. *Ioue knowes I loue, but who,* Lips do not mooue, no | 1110 |
| not who knowes so much of my mettle. *Exeunt.* | 1790 |
| Take him away, he knowes I know him well. | 1848 |

KNOWLEDGE = *3

| | |
|---|---|
| *a fore knowledge of that too, and therefore comes to | 438 |
| *Whiles you beguile the time, and feed your knowledge | 1510 |
| *foes sir, I profit in the knowledge of my selfe, and by my | 2172 |

KNOWN = *1

| | |
|---|---|
| *Cesario,* you are like to be much aduanc'd, he hath known | 252 |

KNOWNE = 1*1

| | |
|---|---|
| *nor no rayling, in a knowne discreet man, though hee do \| nothing but | |
| reproue. | 387 |
| When that is knowne, and golden time conuents | 2552 |

KNOWST = 5

| | |
|---|---|
| The like of him. Know'st thou this Countrey? \| *Cap.* I Madam well, for | |
| I was bred and borne | 71 |
| Thou knowst no lesse, but all: I haue vnclasp'd | 262 |
| *midnight, is to be vp betimes, and *Deliculo surgere,* thou \| know'st. | 702 |
| *Seb.* I prethee vent thy folly some-where else, thou \| know'st not me. | 1927 |
| Be that thou know'st thou art, and then thou art \| As great as that thou | |
| fear'st. | 2309 |

LA *l.*\*1623 = *1

LABELLD = *1

| | |
|---|---|
| *and euery particle and vtensile labell'd to my will: As, | 538 |

LABOUR = 1

| | |
|---|---|
| As full of labour as a Wise-mans Art: | 1278 |

LACKE = 3*1

| | |
|---|---|
| *fooles: and I that am sure I lacke thee, may passe for a | 328 |
| So bigge, to hold so much, they lacke retention. | 984 |
| me tell them how much I lacke of a man. | 1819 |
| Ist possible that my deserts to you \| Can lacke perswasion. Do not | |
| tempt my misery, | 1866 |

LACKES = 1

| | |
|---|---|
| My Master, not my selfe, lackes recompence. | 581 |

LACKST = *1

| | |
|---|---|
| *To.* O knight, thou lack'st a cup of Canarie: when did \| I see thee so | |
| put downe? | 194 |

LAD = 2*1

| | |
|---|---|
| *Vio.* I thinke not so, my Lord. \| *Du.* Deere Lad, beleeue it; | 279 |
| *To.* I haue beene deere to him lad, some two thousand \| strong, or so. | 1434 |
| Like a mad lad, paire thy nayles dad, | 2111 |

LADIE = 5*12

| | |
|---|---|
| *Vio.* What Country (Friends) is this? \| *Cap.* This is Illyria Ladie. | 51 |
| *Clo.* Do you not heare fellowes, take away the Ladie. | 332 |
| *speake with you. What is to be said to him Ladie, hee's \| fortified | |
| against any deniall. | 439 |
| *Vio.* The honorable Ladie of the house, which is she? | 463 |
| *modest assurance, if you be the Ladie of the house, that \| (I | 475 |
| *phangs of malice, I sweare) I am not that I play. Are you \| the Ladie | |
| of the house? | 479 |
| *Some mollification for your Giant, sweete Ladie; | 499 |

LADIE *cont.*
*We will heare this diuinitie. Now sir, what is your text? | *Vio*. Most
sweet Ladie. 513
*my Ladie haue not call'd vp her Steward *Maluolio*, and 773
*consanguinious? Am I not of her blood: tilly vally. La- | die, 777
*feelingly personated. I can write very like my Ladie 852
*Du*. Who was it? | *Cur*. *Feste* the Iester my Lord, a foole that the
Ladie 894
*command me: I serue her, she is my Ladie. Why this is 1126
*forbeare hurling things at him, I know my Ladie will 1460
*in some commerce with my Ladie, and will by and by | depart. 1691
*Mal*. Sir *Topas*, sir *Topas*, good sir *Topas* goe to my | Ladie. 2009
*Du*. What to peruersenesse? you vnciuill Ladie 2268
LADIES = 3*4
*of my Ladies house, that ye squeak out your Cozi- | ers 789
*Mal*. Mistris Mary, if you priz'd my Ladies fauour 817
*Mal*. By my life this is my Ladies hand: these bee her 1101
*the North of my Ladies opinion, where you will hang 1406
man? Talkest thou nothing but of Ladies? | *Tob*. Well said M.(aster)
Parson. 2012
Or else the Ladies mad; yet if 'twere so, 2130
a Gentleman, and follower of my Ladies. 2444
LADIESHIP = *1
*yet haue I the benefit of my senses as well as your Ladie- | ship. 2472
LADY *see also* byrlady = 28*28
*Vio*. O that I seru'd that Lady, 92
*a nights: your Cosin, my Lady, takes great exceptions | to your ill
houres. 123
*heard my Lady talke of it yesterday: and of a foolish 133
*draw sword agen: Faire Lady, doe you thinke you haue | fooles in
hand? 179
*Vio*. Ile do my best | To woe your Lady: yet a barrefull strife, 292
of thy excuse: my Lady will hang thee for thy absence. 299
Lady: make your excuse wisely, you were best. 324
*Enter Lady Oliuia, with Maluolio*. 325
then a foolish wit. God blesse thee Lady. 330
*flower; The Lady bad take away the foole, therefore I | say againe,
take her away. 344
*Clo*. Misprision in the highest degree. Lady, *Cucullus* 347
*Mal*. Gentlewoman, my Lady calles. *Exit*. 458
*I pray you tell me if this bee the Lady of the house, 466
Lady, you are the cruell'st shee aliue, 533
*Vio*. I am no feede poast, Lady; keepe your purse, 580
*Seb*. A Lady sir, though it was said shee much resem- | bled 634
*Vio*. I left no Ring with her: what meanes this Lady? 674
Poore Lady, she were better loue a dreame: 683
*is no Whip-stocke. My Lady has a white hand, and the | Mermidons
are no bottle-ale houses. 728
*There dwelt a man in Babylon, Lady, Lady*. 778
*Mal*. Sir *Toby*, I must be round with you. My Lady 793
*the youth of the Counts was to day with my Lady, she is 828
Say that some Lady, as perhappes there is, 977 ·
Sir, shall I to this Lady? | *Du*. I that's the Theame, 1012
o'fauour with my Lady, about a Beare-baiting heere. 1024
*Mal*. There is example for't: The Lady of the *Stra- | chy*, 1055
*her *Lucrece*, with which she vses to seale: tis my | Lady: To whom
should this be? 1107

LADY *cont.*

| | |
|---|---|
| *that my Lady loues me. She did commend my yellow | 1170 |
| *his first approach before my Lady: hee will come to her | 1202 |
| *Vio.* Art not thou the Lady *Oliuia's* foole? | 1244 |
| *Clo.* No indeed sir, the Lady *Oliuia* has no folly, shee | 1245 |
| *one, though I would not haue it grow on my chinne. Is \| thy Lady | |
| within? | 1260 |
| *begger: *Cressida* was a begger. My Lady is within sir. I | 1268 |
| *Most excellent accomplish'd Lady, the heauens raine O- \|dours on you. | 1298 |
| *Vio.* My matter hath no voice Lady, but to your owne \| most pregnant | |
| and vouchsafed eare. | 1301 |
| *Vio.* Deere Lady. \| *Ol.* Giue me leaue, beseech you: I did send, | 1324 |
| How now *Maluolio*? \| *Mal.* Sweet Lady, ho, ho. | 1538 |
| *Mal.* Sad Lady, I could be sad: | 1541 |
| *Mar.* Why appeare you with this ridiculous bold-\|nesse before my | |
| Lady. | 1559 |
| *did not I tell you? Sir *Toby*, my Lady prayes you to haue \| a care of | |
| him. | 1615 |
| *if I liue. My Lady would not loose him for more then ile \| say. | 1627 |
| *To.* Thou comst to the Lady Oliuia, and in my sight she vses* | 1675 |
| *some conduct of the Lady. I am no fighter, I haue heard | 1760 |
| *nor I am not sent to you by my Lady, to bid you come | 1924 |
| *me what I shall vent to my Lady? Shall I vent to hir that \| thou art | |
| comming? | 1933 |
| *Clo.* This will I tell my Lady straight, I would not be | 1946 |
| *Clo.* Hey Robin, iolly Robin, tell me how thy Lady \| does. \| *Mal.* | |
| Foole. | 2057 |
| *Clo.* My Lady is vnkind, *perdie.* \| *Mal.* Foole. | 2060 |
| *Lady: it shall aduantage thee more, then euer the bea-\|ring of Letter | |
| did. | 2096 |
| That is deceiueable. But heere the Lady comes. | 2135 |
| *Duke.* Belong you to the Lady *Oliuia*, friends? | 2161 |
| *throw: if you will let your Lady know I am here to speak | 2192 |
| Hath beene betweene this Lady, and this Lord. | 2424 |
| *Seb.* So comes it Lady, you haue beene mistooke: | 2425 |
| *Ol.* Haue I *Maluolio*? No. \| *Mal.* Lady you haue, pray you peruse that | |
| Letter. | 2499 |

LADYS = *1

| | |
|---|---|
| *To.* My Lady's a *Catayan*, we are politicians, *Maluolios* | 775 |

LADYSHIP = 1 *3

| | |
|---|---|
| *Mal.* I maruell your Ladyship takes delight in such | 375 |
| Grace and good disposition attend your Ladyship: | 1352 |
| *Mar.* No Madam, he does nothing but smile: your La-\|dyship | 1531 |
| *Ladyship will haue it as it ought to bee, you must allow \| *Vox.* | 2462 |

LADYSHIPS = 1

| | |
|---|---|
| attends your Ladyships pleasure. \| *Ol.* Ile come to him. | 1581 |

LAID = 2

| | |
|---|---|
| Natures owne sweet, and cunning hand laid on: | 532 |
| And laid mine honour too vnchary on't: | 1719 |

LAIDE = 1

| | |
|---|---|
| *And in sad cypresse let me be laide.* | 943 |

LAMBE = 1

| | |
|---|---|
| Ile sacrifice the Lambe that I do loue, | 2286 |

LANDS = 1

| | |
|---|---|
| Prizes not quantitie of dirtie lands, | 969 |

LANGER = *1

| | |
|---|---|
| | . |
| *langer with arguments of state, put thy selfe into the | 1593 |

LANGUAGES = *1
  *and speaks three or four languages word for word 143
LAPSED = 1
  For which if 1 be lapsed in this place | I shall pay deere. 1504
LAST = 4*1
  *in very gracious fooling last night, when thou spok'st of 723
  That old and Anticke song we heard last night; 887
  *Du.* O fellow come, the song we had last night: 932
  After the last enchantment you did heare, 1326
  Yet when I saw it last, it was besmear'd 2203
LASTING = 1
  And lasting, in her sad remembrance. 38
LATE = 5*2
  He was a Batchellor then. | *Cap.* And so is now, or was so very late: 79
  *And.* Nay by my troth I know not: but I know, to | be vp late, is to be
  vp late. 704
  *To.* Come, come, Ile go burne some Sacke, tis too late 881
  *stockings of late, shee did praise my legge being crosse- | garter'd, 1171
  *Vio.* I saw thee late at the Count *Orsino's*. 1250
  We made each other, but so late ago. 2379
LATELY = 1
  Heere to vnfold, though lately we intended 2314
LATH = 1
  Who with dagger of lath, in his rage and his wrath, 2109
LAUDABLE = *1
  *it, by some laudable attempt, either of valour or | policie. 1408
LAUGH = *2
  *laugh and minister occasion to him, he is gag'd. I protest 379
  *Madam, why laugh you at such a barren rascall, 2545
LAUGHE = *1
  *Mar.* If you desire the spleene, and will laughe your 1447
LAUGHTER = 2
  *Present mirth, hath present laughter:* 749
  May rather plucke on laughter then reuenge, 2537
LAW = 1*2
  *Fa.* A good note, that keepes you from the blow of y | (Law 1674
  *Fa.* Still you keepe o'th windie side of the Law: good. 1683
  *there be any law in Illyria: though I stroke him first, yet 1951
LAY = 1*3
  for your loue, to lay any of them on you. 619
  *A thousand thousand sighes to saue, lay me o where* 952
  *To.* I will way-lay thee going home, where if it be thy chance | to kill
  *me.* | *Fa.* Good. 1679
  *To.* I dare lay any money, twill be nothing yet. *Exit* 1916
LAYDE = *1
  *sir *Topas* do not thinke I am mad: they haue layde mee | heere in
  hideous darknesse. 2015
LEAD = 1*1
  *Vio.* I thanke thee: Lead me on. *Exeunt* 116
  *Ol.* Then lead the way good father, & heauens so shine, 2149
LEADE = 2
  If you will leade these graces to the graue, | And leaue the world no
  copie. 534
  *Ant.* Leade me on. *Exit* 1893
LEANE = 1*1
  Out of my leane and low ability | Ile lend you something: my hauing is
  not much, 1861

LEANE *cont.*
*function well, nor leane enough to bee thought a good 1992
LEAPE = 1
*Du.* Be clamorous, and leape all ciuill bounds, 271
LEARND = 1*1
*learn'd from my entertainment. What I am, and what I 509
In voyces well divulg'd, free, learn'd, and valiant, 553
LEASING = *1
**Clo.* Now Mercury indue thee with leasing, for thou | speak'st well of
fooles. 389
LEAST = 2*3
When least in companie: prosper well in this, 289
*no scorne; I am very comptible, euen to the least | sinister vsage. 470
*least occasion more, mine eyes will tell tales of me: I am 649
**Mar.* Nay pursue him now, least the deuice take ayre, | and taint. 1653
Least that it make me so vnsound a man 1868
LEAUE = 8*7
*sir *Toby* would leaue drinking, thou wert as witty a piece | of *Eues*
flesh, as any in Illyria. 321
*motley in my braine: good *Madona*, giue mee leaue to | proue you a
foole. 349
If you will leade these graces to the graue, | And leaue the world no
copie. 534
*yours; therefore I shall craue of you your leaue, 617
leaue of her, she is very willing to bid you farewell. 798
*Du.* Giue me now leaue, to leaue thee. 959
*Her very Phrases: By your leaue wax. Soft, and the im- | pressure 1106
**Ol.* Let the Garden doore be shut, and leaue mee to | my hearing.
Giue me your hand sir. 1305
*Ol.* O by your leaue I pray you. 1319
*Vio.* Deere Lady. | *Ol.* Giue me leaue, beseech you: I did send, 1324
*Seb.* Ile be your purse-bearer, and leaue you | For an houre. 1516
till he take leaue, and presently after him. 1715
*thy selfe to sleepe, and leaue thy vaine bibble | babble. 2081
*me as you please. I leaue my duty a little vnthought of, 2476
LEAUES = 1
when the image of it leaues him, he must run mad. 1198
LEAUING = 1*1
That dide some tweluemonth since, then leauing her 87
*then a Hare, his dishonesty appeares, in leauing his frend 1907
LEFT = 2*2
The Countes man: he left this Ring behinde him 599
*know you haue heard of. He left behinde him, my selfe, 628
**Vio.* I left no Ring with her: what meanes this Lady? 674
*Veluet gowne: hauing come from a day bedde, where I | haue left
*Oliuia* sleeping. 1064
LEGGE = 1*4
*the excellent constitution of thy legge, it was form'd vn- | der the starre
of a Galliard. 240
*had rather then forty shillings I had such a legge, and so 721
*legge, the manner of his gate, the expressure of his eye, 850
*stockings of late, shee did praise my legge being crosse- | garter'd, 1171
When your yong Nephew *Titus* lost his legge; 2214
LEGGES = 2*2
*To.* Taste your legges sir, put them to motion. 1291
**Vio.* My legges do better vnderstand me sir, then I vn- | derstand 1292
*legges: It did come to his hands, and Commaunds shall 1549

LEGGES *cont.*
   *To.* If this Letter moue him not, his legges cannot: | Ile giu't him.     1688
LEGGS = *1
   *\*To.* No sir, it is leggs and thighes: let me see thee ca-|per. Ha, higher:
   ha, ha, excellent. *Exeunt*     247
LEGION = *1
   *the diuels of hell be drawne in little, and Legion himselfe | possest
   him, yet Ile speake to him.     1608
LEGITIMATE = *1
   *\*Fab.* I will proue it legitimate sir, vpon the Oathes of | iudgement, and
   reason.     1394
LEGS = 2
   to see a huswife take thee between her legs, & spin it off.     214
   what you meane by bidding me taste my legs.     1293
LEMON = 1
   for thy Lemon, hadst it?     726
LEND = 1
   Out of my leane and low ability | Ile lend you something: my hauing is
   not much,     1861
LENTON = *1
   *\*Ma.* A good lenton answer: I can tell thee where y     304
LESSE = 4*1
   What great ones do, the lesse will prattle of, )     83
   Thou knowst no lesse, but all: I haue vnclasp'd     262
   *Fa.* Very breefe, and to exceeding good sence-lesse.     1678
   *\*Lord and my Neece, confirmes no lesse. Therefore, this     1704
   I must haue done no lesse with wit and safety.     2375
LEST *see also* least = *1
   *\*of thy wits, and feare to kill a Woodcocke, lest thou dis-|possesse     2044
LET = 39*33
   When my tongue blabs, then let mine eyes not see.     115
   *To.* Why let her except, before excepted.     125
   *these boots too: and they be not, let them hang them-|selues in their
   owne straps.     130
   *To.* And thou let part so Sir *Andrew*, would thou | mightst neuer draw
   sword agen.     176
   hand to'th Buttry barre, and let it drinke.     184
   I let go your hand, I am barren. *Exit Maria*     193
   *\*To.* No sir, it is leggs and thighes: let me see thee ca-|per. Ha, higher:
   ha, ha, excellent. *Exeunt*     247
   *\*Clo.* Let her hang me: hee that is well hang'de in this | world, needs to
   feare no colours.     300
   those that are fooles, let them vse their talents.     310
   and for turning away, let summer beare it out.     315
   *he is no longer dishonest; if hee cannot, let the Botcher     338
   *\*To.* Let him be the diuell and he will, I care not: giue     422
   *\*Ol.* Go thou and seeke the Crowner, and let him sitte     428
   *Ol.* Let him approach: Call in my Gentlewoman.     457
   *taken great paines to con it. Good Beauties, let mee su-|staine     469
   *Vio.* Good Madam, let me see your face.     522
   I cannot loue him: let him send no more,     576
   And let your feruour like my masters be,     583
   To creepe in at mine eyes. Well, let it be.     594
   *\*An.* Let me yet know of you, whither you are bound.     620
   *\*Ant.* If you will not murther me for my loue, let mee | be your seruant.     643
   *\*To.* Th'art a scholler; let vs therefore eate and drinke     713
   *An.* Most certaine: Let our Catch be, *Thou Knaue.*     764

LET *cont.*

| | |
|---|---|
| *much out of quiet. For Monsieur Maluolio, let me alone | 829 |
| *will worke with him, I will plant you two, and let | 865 |
| *Du.* Too old by heauen: Let still the woman take | 917 |
| *Du.* Then let thy Loue be yonger then thy selfe, | 925 |
| *And in sad cypresse let me be laide.* | 943 |
| *On my blacke coffin, let there be strewne:* | 949 |
| *Du.* Let all the rest giue place: Once more *Cesario*, | 966 |
| But let concealment like a worme i'th budde | 1001 |
| let me be boyl'd to death with Melancholly. | 1020 |
| let me see, let me see, let me see. | 1122 |
| *hands, let thy blood and spirit embrace them, and to in-|vre | 1153 |
| *surly with seruants: Let thy tongue tang arguments of | 1156 |
| *made if thou desir'st to be so: If not, let me see thee a ste-|ward | 1161 |
| *deuise, the very man. I do not now foole my selfe, to let | 1168 |
| *not choose but know who I am. If thou entertainst my loue, let* | 1178 |
| *Ol.* Let the Garden doore be shut, and leaue mee to | my hearing. | |
| Giue me your hand sir. | 1305 |
| Hides my heart: so let me heare you speake. | *Vio.* I pittie you. | 1336 |
| *you let time wash off, and you are now sayld into | 1405 |
| *set 'em downe, go about it. Let there bee gaulle e-|nough | 1427 |
| I pray you let vs satisfie our eyes | 1489 |
| *Mal.* If not, let me see thee a seruant still. | 1576 |
| *Good *Maria*, let this fellow be look'd too. Where's my | 1583 |
| *Cosine *Toby*, let some of my people haue a speciall care | 1584 |
| *with a Kinsman, surly with seruants, let thy tongue | 1592 |
| *thankefull. And when she went away now, let this Fel-|low | 1598 |
| *Mal.* Go off, I discard you: let me enioy my priuate: | go off. | 1612 |
| *gently with him: Let me alone. How do you *Maluolio*? | 1619 |
| you not see you moue him? Let me alone with him. | 1632 |
| *And.* Nay let me alone for swearing. *Exit* | 1700 |
| *I'de haue challeng'd him. Let him let the matter slip, and | 1803 |
| *Ant.* Let me speake a little. This youth that you see | (heere, | 1879 |
| Let me be cleere of thee. | 1922 |
| *An.* Nay let him alone, Ile go another way to worke | 1949 |
| *Seb.* Let go thy hand. | 1953 |
| *To.* Come sir, I will not let you go. Come my yong | 1954 |
| Let thy fayre wisedome, not thy passion sway | In this vnciuill, and | |
| vniust extent | 1969 |
| Let fancie still my sense in Lethe steepe, | 1979 |
| If it be thus to dreame, still let me sleepe. | 1980 |
| *Fab.* Now as thou lou'st me, let me see his Letter. | 2154 |
| and let your flesh and blood obey it. | 2184 |
| *throw: if you will let your Lady know I am here to speak | 2192 |
| *you say sir, let your bounty take a nappe, I will awake it | anon. *Exit* | 2198 |
| *Ol.* Get him to bed, and let his hurt be look'd too. | 2371 |
| I should my teares let fall vpon your cheeke, | 2406 |
| *Du.* Giue me thy hand, | And let me see thee in thy womans weedes. | 2439 |
| And let no quarrell, nor no braule to come, | 2527 |

LETCHERIE = *1

| | |
|---|---|
| *To.* Letcherie, I defie Letchery: there's one at the | gate. | 419 |

LETCHERY = *1

| | |
|---|---|
| *To.* Letcherie, I defie Letchery: there's one at the | gate. | 419 |

LETHARGIE = 1

| | |
|---|---|
| *Ol.* Cosin, Cosin, how haue you come so carely by | this Lethargie? | 417 |

LETHE = 1

| | |
|---|---|
| Let fancie still my sense in Lethe steepe, | 1979 |

124

LETS = 3*3

*To.* Welcome asse, now let's haue a catch.     719
*To.* Come on, there is sixe pence for you. Let's haue | a song.     732
*And.* And you loue me, let's doo't: I am dogge at a | Catch.     761
*To.* Let's to bed knight: Thou hadst neede send for | more money.     874
*And.* And I do not. | *Fab.* Come, let's see the euent.     1914
*Vio.* If nothing lets to make vs happie both,     2415
LETTER = 8*10

*the Foole make a third, where he shall finde the Letter:     866
*this Letter wil make a contemplatiue Ideot of him. Close     1036
*Fa.* We shall haue a rare Letter from him; but you'le | not deliuer't.     1436
*He does obey euery point of the Letter that I dropt,     1456
*with the Letter, she sends him on purpose, that I may     1589
*the Letter. Cast thy humble slough sayes she: be oppo- |site     1591
*To.* If this Letter moue him not, his legges cannot: | Ile giu't him.     1688
*To.* Now will not I deliuer his Letter: for the behaui- |our     1701
*Letter being so excellently ignorant, will breed no terror     1705
*Lady: it shall aduantage thee more, then euer the bea- |ring of Letter
did.     2096
*Fab.* Now as thou lou'st me, let me see his Letter.     2154
*Clo.* Do not desire to see this Letter.     2157
*Enter Clowne with a Letter, and Fabian.*     2448
*well as a man in his case may do: has heere writ a letter to     2453
*I haue your owne letter, that induced mee to the     2473
*Ol.* Haue I *Maluolio*? No. | *Mal.* Lady you haue, pray you peruse that
Letter.     2499
Vpon thee in the Letter: prethee be content,     2521
The Letter, at sir *Tobyes* great importance,     2534
LETTERS = *2

*To.* He shall thinke by the Letters that thou wilt drop     857
*one of these Letters are in my name. Soft, here fol- |lowes     1148
LEUELL = 1

So swayes she leuell in her husbands heart:     919
LICENSE = *1

*inuention: taunt him with the license of Inke: if thou     1423
LIDS = *1

*with lids to them: Item, one necke, one chin, & so forth.     540
LIE *see* lye
LIEFE = *1

*policie I hate: I had as liefe be a Brownist, as a Politi- |cian.     1411
LIES *see also* lyes = 4*1

*Ma.* Will you hoyst sayle sir, here lies your way.     497
of it. Where lies your Text? | *Vio.* In *Orsinoes* bosome.     516
*for, there it lies, in your eye: if not, bee it his that | findes it. *Exit.*     672
*In delay there lies no plentie,*     751
There lies your way, due West. | *Vio.* Then Westward hoe:     1350
LIEST *see* lyest
LIFE = 12*4

*death of her brother thus? I am sure care's an enemie to | life.     120
*An.* Neuer in your life I thinke, vnlesse you see Ca- |narie     196
swear't. Tut there's life in't man.     220
With such a suffring, such a deadly life:     558
*Clo.* Would you haue a loue-song, or a song of good | life?     735
*An.* I, I. I care not for good life.     738
My life vpon't, yong though thou art, thine eye     909
*Mal.* By my life this is my Ladies hand: these bee her     1101

LIFE  *cont.*
*\*With bloodlesse stroke my heart doth gore, M.O.A.I. doth | sway my*
*life.* 1117
*\*Mal. M.O.A.I.* doth sway my life. Nay but first 1121
\*you hold your life at any price, betake you to your gard: 1749
*Ol.* Hold *Toby*, on thy life I charge thee hold. | *To.* Madam. 1962
His life I gaue him, and did thereto adde 2232
More then I loue these eyes, more then my life, 2292
If I do feigne, you witnesses aboue | Punish my life, for tainting of my
loue. 2294
Nor are you therein (by my life) deceiu'd, 2428
LIFELINGS = \*1
*Du.* My Gentleman *Cesario*? | *\*And.* Odd's lifelings heere he is: you
broke my head 2345
LIGHT = 3\*2
More then light ayres, and recollected termes 889
*Seb.* Why I your purse? | *Ant.* Haply your eye shall light vpon some toy 1512
*\*Mal.* Good foole, helpe me to some light, and some 2090
\*and light: and conuey what I will set downe to my 2095
I will fetch you light, and paper, and inke. 2102
LIGHTER = 1
Vpon sir *Toby*, and the lighter people: 2509
LIGHTS = 1
Why you haue giuen me such cleare lights of fauour, 2506
LIKE = 23\*20
O, it came ore my eare, like the sweet sound 9
And my desires like fell and cruell hounds, 27
But like a Cloystresse she will vailed walke, 34
Where like *Orion* on the Dolphines backe, 65
The like of him. Know'st thou this Countrey? | *Cap.* I Madam well, for
I was bred and borne 71
\*drinke to my Neece, till his braines turne o'th toe, like a 157
*\*To.* Excellent, it hangs like flax on a distaffe: & I hope 213
\*these gifts a Curtaine before 'em? Are they like to take 234
\*dust, like mistris *Mals* picture? Why dost thou not goe 235
*\*Cesario*, you are like to be much aduanc'd, he hath known 252
*Ol.* What's a drunken man like, foole? 424
*\*Clo.* Like a drown'd man, a foole, and a madde man: 425
\*your doore like a Sheriffes post, and be the supporter to 443
*\*Ol.* It is the more like to be feigned, I pray you keep 491
And let your feruour like my masters be, 583
\*like Tinkers at this time of night? Do yee make an Ale-|house 788
*\*An.* O, if I thought that, Ide beate him like a dogge. 835
\*feelingly personated. I can write very like my Ladie 852
That is belou'd. How dost thou like this tune? 905
And dallies with the innocence of loue, | Like the old age. 937
But let concealment like a worme i'th budde 1001
She sate like Patience on a Monument, 1004
*\*Mal. I may command where I adore, but silence like a Lu-|cresse knife:* 1115
\*thy selfe to what thou art like to be: cast thy humble 1154
*Ma.* Nay but say true, do's it worke vpon him? | *To.* Like Aqua vite
with a Midwife. 1199
\*as like husbands, as Pilchers are to Herrings, the Hus-|bands 1247
*\*Clo.* Foolery sir, does walke about the Orbe like the 1251
And like the Haggard, checke at euery Feather 1276
Your wife is like to reape a proper man: 1349
That heart which now abhorres, to like his loue. *Exeunt* 1380

LIKE *cont.*
   *like an ysickle on a Dutchmans beard, vnlesse you do re- | deeme   1407
*To.* And crosse garter'd? | *Mar.* Most villanously: like a Pedant that
   keepes a   1453
   *Schoole i'th Church: I haue dogg'd him like his murthe- | rer.   1455
*To. Thou kilst me like a rogue and a villaine.*   1682
   *of the Orchard like a bum-Baylie: so soone as euer thou   1694
   kill one another by the looke, like Cockatrices.   1712
   A Fiend like thee might beare my soule to hell.   1735
   *by his forme, as you are like to finde him in the proofe of   1783
   In a trice, like to the old vice, | your neede to sustaine.   2107
   Like a mad lad, paire thy nayles dad,   2111
   Like to th'Egyptian theefe, at point of death   2274
   Thou neuer should'st loue woman like to me.   2434
   Though I confesse much like the Charracter:   2516
LIKING = *1
   *her liking. I thanke my starres, I am happy: I will bee   1174
LIMBES = 1
   Thy tongue, thy face, thy limbes, actions, and spirit,   588
LIMDE *see* lymde
LIMITS = 1
   *Ma.* I, but you must confine your selfe within the | modest limits of
   order.   126
LINES *see* lynes
LION = 1
   To fall before the Lion, then the Wolfe?   1344
LIP = 2
   That say thou art a man: *Dianas* lip   282
   In the contempt and anger of his lip,   1362
LIPPES = 1*3
   *not open my lippes so wide as a brissle may enter, in way   298
   *Item two lippes indifferent redde, Item two grey eyes,   539
   *To.* And do's not *Toby* take you a blow o'th lippes, | then?   1083
   Attested by the holy close of lippes,   2320
LIPS = *1
   *Mal. Ioue knowes I loue, but who, Lips do not mooue, no*   1110
LIST = 1
   *Vio.* I am bound to your Neece sir, I meane she is the | list of my
   voyage.   1289
LITTLE = 5*7
   *Ol.* Whence came you sir? | *Vio.* I can say little more then I haue
   studied, & that   472
   *Vio.* No good swabber, I am to hull here a little lon- | ger.   498
   Hath it not boy? | *Vio.* A little, by your fauour.   911
   Much in our vowes, but little in our loue.   1008
   *To.* Heere comes the little villaine: How now my | Mettle of India?   1030
   *and yet to crush this a little, it would bow to mee, for e- | uery   1147
   *the diuels of hell be drawne in little, and Legion himselfe | possest
   him, yet Ile speake to him.   1608
   *Vio.* Pray God defend me: a little thing would make   1818
   *Ant.* Let me speake a little. This youth that you see | (heere,   1879
   Hold little faith, though thou hast too much feare.   2334
   *me as you please. I leaue my duty a little vnthought of,   2476
   *Clowne sings. | When that I was and a little tine boy,*   2559
LIUD = 1
   To a strong Maste, that liu'd vpon the sea:   64

LIUE = 6*5

| | |
|---|---|
| That liue in her. When Liuer, Braine, and Heart, | 43 |
| And thou shalt liue as freely as thy Lord, \| To call his fortunes thine. | 290 |
| *Toby* approaches; curtsies there to me. \| *To*. Shall this fellow liue? | 1077 |
| *Vio*. Saue thee Friend and thy Musick: dost thou liue \| by thy Tabor? | 1215 |
| *Clo*. No sir, I liue by the Church. | 1217 |
| *Clo*. No such matter sir, I do liue by the Church: For, | 1219 |
| *I do liue at my house, and my house dooth stand by the \| Church. | 1220 |
| *if I liue. My Lady would not loose him for more then ile \| say. | 1627 |
| *as I am a Gentleman, I will liue to bee thankefull to thee \| for't. | 2067 |
| May liue at peace. He shall conceale it, | 2143 |
| Liue you the Marble-brested Tirant still. | 2280 |

LIUELY = 1

| | |
|---|---|
| *Seb*. O that record is liuely in my soule, | 2412 |

LIUER = 3*2

| | |
|---|---|
| That liue in her. When Liuer, Braine, and Heart, | 43 |
| No motion of the Liuer, but the Pallat, | 986 |
| *Fab*. This winnes him, Liuer and all. | 1109 |
| *to put fire in your Heart, and brimstone in your Liuer: | 1400 |
| *and you finde so much blood in his Liuer, as will clog the | 1441 |

LIUES = 1*1

| | |
|---|---|
| *Does not our liues consist of the foure Ele- \| ments? | 709 |
| *An*. And we do not, it is pittie of our liues. | 1028 |

LIUING = 1

| | |
|---|---|
| Yet liuing in my glasse: euen such, and so | 1901 |

LO = *1

| | |
|---|---|
| *Mar*. Lo, how hollow the fiend speakes within him; | 1614 |

LOATH = *2

| | |
|---|---|
| *for I neuer saw her. I would bee loath to cast away my | 467 |
| *and wordes are growne so false, I am loath to proue rea- \| son with them. | 1237 |

LODGE = 1

| | |
|---|---|
| In the South Suburbes at the Elephant \| Is best to lodge: I will bespeake our dyet, | 1508 |

LODGING = *1

| | |
|---|---|
| *Ant*. To morrow sir, best first go see your Lodging? | 1487 |

LONG = 5*2

| | |
|---|---|
| I saw him hold acquaintance with the waues, \| So long as I could see. | 66 |
| *to her as long as there is a passage in my throat, & drinke | 155 |
| *Ma*. Yet you will be hang'd for being so long absent, | 311 |
| He might haue tooke his answer long ago. | 556 |
| *Seb*. I am not weary, and 'tis long to night | 1488 |
| *Ol*. Hast thou forgot thy selfe? Is it so long? | 2298 |
| And since you call'd me Master, for so long: | 2490 |

LONGER = 2*5

| | |
|---|---|
| *And*. Ile stay a moneth longer. I am a fellow o'th | 221 |
| *he is no longer dishonest; if hee cannot, let the Botcher | 338 |
| *Vio*. No good swabber, I am to hull here a little lon- \| ger. | 498 |
| *Ant*. Will you stay no longer: nor will you not that \| I go with you. | 613 |
| *And*. No faith, Ile not stay a iot longer: | 1383 |
| As might haue drawne one to a longer voyage) | 1473 |
| *money for thee, if you tarry longer, I shall giue worse \| paiment. | 1936 |

LONGING = 1

| | |
|---|---|
| More longing, wauering, sooner lost and worne, \| Then womens are. | 922 |

LOOKD = 1*3

| | |
|---|---|
| *the youth into dumbenesse: this was look'd for at your | 1403 |
| *Good *Maria*, let this fellow be look'd too. Where's my | 1583 |

LOOKD *cont.*
| | |
|---|---|
| *be look'd too: Fellow? not *Maluolio*, nor after my | 1599 |
| *Ol.* Get him to bed, and let his hurt be look'd too. | 2371 |

LOOKE = 4 *7
| | |
|---|---|
| *Looke you now, he's out of his gard already: vnles you | 378 |
| *o'my Coz: for he's in the third degree of drinke: hee's &#124; drown'd: go looke after him. | 429 |
| *Clo.* He is but mad yet Madona, and the foole shall &#124; looke to the madman. | 431 |
| *Looke you sir, such a one I was this present: Ist not well &#124; done? | 526 |
| *that looke on him, loue him: and on that vice in him, will | 845 |
| *Fa.* O peace, now he's deepely in: looke how imagi-&#124;nation blowes him. | 1058 |
| *To.* Looke where the youngest Wren of mine comes. | 1446 |
| *man then sir *Toby* to looke to me. This concurres direct-&#124;ly | 1588 |
| *and so looke to thy selfe. Thy friend as thou vsest him, & thy &#124; sworne enemie*, Andrew Ague-cheeke. | 1686 |
| kill one another by the looke, like Cockatrices. | 1712 |
| *Clo.* Looke then to be well edified, when the Foole | 2458 |

LOOKES = 2
| | |
|---|---|
| *Ol.* O what a deale of scorne, lookes beautifull? | 1361 |
| lookes pale, as if a Beare were at his heeles. | 1812 |

LOOSE = 1 *1
| | |
|---|---|
| *Fab.* Nay Ile come: if I loose a scruple of this sport, | 1019 |
| *if I liue. My Lady would not loose him for more then ile &#124; say. | 1627 |

LORD = 24 *13
| | |
|---|---|
| *Cu.* Will you go hunt my Lord? &#124; *Du.* What *Curio*? &#124; *Cu.* The Hart. | 20 |
| *Val.* So please my Lord, I might not be admitted, | 30 |
| *Duke.* Who saw *Cesario* hoa? &#124; *Vio.* On your attendance my Lord heere. | 259 |
| *Vio.* Sure my Noble Lord, | 268 |
| *Vio.* Say I do speake with her (my Lord) what then? &#124; *Du.* O then, vnfold the passion of my loue, | 273 |
| *Vio.* I thinke not so, my Lord. &#124; *Du.* Deere Lad, beleeue it; | 279 |
| And thou shalt liue as freely as thy Lord, &#124; To call his fortunes thine. | 290 |
| *Ol.* Haue you any Commission from your Lord, to | 523 |
| My Lord, and master loues you: O such loue | 544 |
| *Ol.* Your Lord does know my mind, I cannot loue him | 550 |
| *Ol.* Get you to your Lord: | 575 |
| Desire him not to flatter with his Lord, | 601 |
| *selfe. She adds moreouer, that you should put your Lord | 664 |
| *Du.* Who was it? &#124; *Cur. Feste* the Iester my Lord, a foole that the Ladie | 894 |
| *Vio.* About your yeeres my Lord. | 916 |
| *Vio.* I thinke it well my Lord. | 924 |
| *Du.* And what's her history? &#124; *Vio.* A blanke my Lord: she neuer told her loue, | 999 |
| *Clo.* I would play Lord *Pandarus* of *Phrygia* sir, to bring &#124; a *Cressida* to this *Troylus*. | 1264 |
| You'l nothing Madam to my Lord, by me: | 1353 |
| *Mal.* How now mistris? &#124; *Mar.* Oh Lord. | 1629 |
| *Lord and my Neece, confirmes no lesse. Therefore, this | 1704 |
| *Ant.* To day my Lord: and for three months before, | 2247 |
| *Ol.* What would my Lord, but that he may not haue, | 2256 |
| *Ol.* What do you say *Cesario*? Good my Lord. | 2261 |
| *Vio.* My Lord would speake, my dutie hushes me. | 2262 |
| *Ol.* If it be ought to the old tune my Lord, | 2263 |
| *Du.* Still so cruell? &#124; *Ol.* Still so constant Lord. | 2266 |

LORD *cont.*

| | |
|---|---|
| *\*Ol.* Euen what it please my Lord, that shal becom him | 2272 |
| *Ol.* Whether my Lord? *Cesario*, Husband, stay. | 2301 |
| *Du.* Her husband, sirrah? \| *Vio.* No my Lord, not I. | 2304 |
| *Vio.* My Lord, I do protest. \| *Ol.* O do not sweare, | 2332 |
| Hath beene betweene this Lady, and this Lord. | 2424 |
| deliuers the Madman. *By the Lord Madam.* | 2459 |
| *\*Fab. Reads.* By the Lord Madam, you wrong me, and | 2469 |
| \*My Lord, so please you, these things further thought on, | 2482 |
| *Du.* Is this the Madman? \| *Ol.* I my Lord, this same: How now | |
| *Maluolio*? | 2495 |
| \*all one: By the Lord Foole, I am not mad: but do you re-\|member, | 2544 |

LORDS = 3\*1

| | |
|---|---|
| *Enter Orsino Duke of Illyria, Curio, and other* \| *Lords.* | 2 |
| \*in his affaires, vnlesse it bee to report your Lords taking \| of this: | |
| receiue it so. | 667 |
| None of my Lords Ring? Why he sent her none; | 681 |
| *Enter Duke, Viola, Curio, and Lords.* | 2160 |

LORDSHIP = 1

| | |
|---|---|
| As it might be perhaps, were I a woman \| I should your Lordship. | 997 |

LORDSHIPPE = \*1

| | |
|---|---|
| *\*Cur.* He is not heere (so please your Lordshippe) that \| should sing it? | 892 |

LOSE *see* loose

LOSSE = 1

| | |
|---|---|
| That very enuy, and the tongue of losse | 2209 |

LOST = 4

| | |
|---|---|
| That me thought her eyes had lost her tongue, | 677 |
| More longing, wauering, sooner lost and worne, \| Then womens are. | 922 |
| When your yong Nephew *Titus* lost his legge; | 2214 |
| How haue the houres rack'd, and tortur'd me, \| Since I haue lost thee? | 2383 |

LOUD = 1\*1

| | |
|---|---|
| My Father had a daughter lou'd a man | 996 |
| \*I speake too loud: Where's *Maluolio*, he is sad, and ciuill, | 1525 |

LOUE = 61\*17

| | |
|---|---|
| *Duke.* \| If Musicke be the food of Loue, play on, | 4 |
| O spirit of Loue, how quicke and fresh art thou, | 13 |
| A brothers dead loue, which she would keepe fresh | 37 |
| To pay this debt of loue but to a brother, | 40 |
| How will she loue, when the rich golden shaft | 41 |
| That he did seeke the loue of faire *Oliuia*. | 84 |
| Who shortly also dide: for whose deere loue | 89 |
| \*that you call in question the continuance of his loue. Is | 255 |
| \*Vio.* Say I do speake with her (my Lord) what then? \| *Du.* O then, | |
| vnfold the passion of my loue, | 273 |
| *\*Ol.* O you are sicke of selfe-loue *Maluolio*, and taste | 382 |
| My Lord, and master loues you: O such loue | 544 |
| *Ol.* How does he loue me? \| *Vio.* With adorations, fertill teares, | 547 |
| With groanes that thunder loue, with sighes of fire. | 549 |
| *\*Ol.* Your Lord does know my mind, I cannot loue him | 550 |
| A gracious person; But yet I cannot loue him: | 555 |
| *Vio.* If I did loue you in my masters flame, | 557 |
| Write loyall Cantons of contemned loue, | 564 |
| I cannot loue him: let him send no more, | 576 |
| Loue make his heart of flint, that you shal loue, | 582 |
| for your loue, to lay any of them on you. | 619 |
| *\*Ant.* If you will not murther me for my loue, let mee \| be your seruant. | 643 |
| Poore Lady, she were better loue a dreame: | 683 |

LOUE *cont.*

| | |
|---|---|
| My state is desperate for my maisters loue: | 694 |
| *To*. A loue song, a loue song. | 737 |
| *Clo*. *What is loue, tis not heereafter,* | 748 |
| *\*And*. And you loue me, let's doo't: I am dogge at a \| Catch. | 761 |
| *Mar*. For the loue o'God peace. | 784 |
| *that looke on him, loue him: and on that vice in him, will | 845 |
| *loue, wherein by the colour of his beard, the shape of his | 849 |
| *that they come from my Neece, and that shee's in loue \| with him. | 858 |
| Come hither Boy, if euer thou shalt loue | 900 |
| *Vio*. It giues a verie eccho to the seate \| Where loue is thron'd. | 906 |
| *Du*. Then let thy Loue be yonger then thy selfe, | 925 |
| And dallies with the innocence of loue, \| Like the old age. | 937 |
| Tell her my loue, more noble then the world | 968 |
| *Vio*. But if she cannot loue you sir. | 974 |
| Hath for your loue as great a pang of heart | 978 |
| As you haue for *Oliuia*: you cannot loue her: | 979 |
| As loue doth giue my heart: no womans heart | 983 |
| Alas, their loue may be call'd appetite, | 985 |
| Betweene that loue a woman can beare me, \| And that I owe *Oliuia*. | 990 |
| *Vio*. Too well what loue women to men may owe: | 994 |
| *Du*. And what's her history? \| *Vio*. A blanke my Lord: she neuer told her loue, | 999 |
| Smiling at greefe. Was not this loue indeede? | 1005 |
| Much in our vowes, but little in our loue. | 1008 |
| *Du*. But di'de thy sister of her loue my Boy? | 1009 |
| My loue can giue no place, bide no denay. *Exeunt* | 1015 |
| *houre: obserue him for the loue of Mockerie: for I know | 1035 |
| *Mal*. *loue knowes I loue, but who, Lips do not mooue, no* | 1110 |
| *and in this she manifests her selfe to my loue, & | 1172 |
| *not choose but know who I am. If thou entertainst my loue, let* | 1178 |
| *Ol*. That's a degree to loue. | 1338 |
| *Then loue that would seeme hid: Loues night, is noone. | 1364 |
| I loue thee so, that maugre all thy pride, | 1367 |
| Loue sought, is good: but giuen vnsought is better. | 1372 |
| That heart which now abhorres, to like his loue. *Exeunt* | 1380 |
| *Fab*. This was a great argument of loue in her toward \| you. | 1391 |
| And not all loue to see you (though so much | 1472 |
| Vnguided, and vnfriended, often proue \| Rough, and vnhospitable. My willing loue, | 1476 |
| *Vio*. Nothing but this, your true loue for my master. | 1730 |
| *Ant*. One sir, that for his loue dares yet do more | 1833 |
| Releeu'd him with such sanctitie of loue; | 1881 |
| Tempests are kinde, and salt waues fresh in loue. | 1905 |
| My loue without retention, or restraint, | 2233 |
| Did I expose my selfe (pure for his loue) | 2235 |
| Kill what I loue: (a sauage iealousie, | 2275 |
| But this your Minion, whom I know you loue, | 2281 |
| Ile sacrifice the Lambe that I do loue, | 2286 |
| *Ol*. Where goes *Cesario*? \| *Vio*. After him I loue, | 2290 |
| More then I loue these eyes, more then my life, | 2292 |
| More by all mores, then ere I shall loue wife. | 2293 |
| If I do feigne, you witnesses aboue \| Punish my life, for tainting of my loue. | 2294 |
| *Priest*. A Contract of eternall bond of loue, | 2318 |
| *And*. For the loue of God a Surgeon, send one pre-\|sently to sir *Toby*. | 2336 |
| *Toby* a bloody Coxcombe too: for the loue of God your | 2340 |

LOUE *cont.*
    Thou neuer should'st loue woman like to me.    2434
LOUER = *1
    *\*Sad true louer neuer find my graue, to weepe there.*    953
LOUERS = 2
    *Iourneys end in louers meeting,*    744
    For such as I am, all true Louers are,    902
LOUES = 6*2
    My Lord, and master loues you: O such loue    544
    She loues me sure, the cunning of her passion    679
    How will this fadge? My master loues her deerely,    690
    *O stay and heare, your true loues coming,*    741
    Hath staid vpon some fauour that it loues:    910
    *that my Lady loues me. She did commend my yellow    1170
    *Then loue that would seeme hid: Loues night, is noone.    1364
    *Clo.* She loues another. Who calles, ha?    2064
LOUE-BROKER = *1
    *and assure thy selfe, there is no loue-Broker in the world,    1416
LOUE-SONG = *1
    *\*Clo.* Would you haue a loue-song, or a song of good | life?    735
LOUE-THOUGHTS = 1
    Loue-thoughts lye rich, when canopy'd with bowres. | *Exeunt*    47
LOUST = 1
    *Fab.* Now as thou lou'st me, let me see his Letter.    2154
LOW = 3
    But falles into abatement, and low price    17
    *That can sing both high and low.*    742
    Out of my leane and low ability | Ile lend you something: my hauing is
    not much,    1861
LOWD = 1
    And sing them lowd euen in the dead of night:    565
LOWLY = 1
    Since lowly feigning was call'd complement:    1311
LOYALL = 1
    Write loyall Cantons of contemned loue,    564
LUBBER = *1
    *I am affraid this great lubber the World will proue a    1931
LUCRECE = *1
    *her *Lucrece,* with which she vses to seale: tis my | Lady: To whom
    should this be?    1107
LUCRESSE = *1
    *\*Mal. I may command where I adore, but silence like a Lu-|cresse knife:*    1115
LULLABY = *1
    *\*Clo.* Marry sir, lullaby to your bountie till I come a-|gen.    2195
LUNATICKE = 1
    *\*Clo.* Sir *Topas* the Curate, who comes to visit *Maluo-|lio* the
    Lunaticke.    2007
LUSTROUS = *1
    *as lustrous as Ebony: and yet complainest thou of ob-|struction?    2024
LYE = 4*3
    Loue-thoughts lye rich, when canopy'd with bowres. | *Exeunt*    47
    *Clo.* Sir *Toby* there you lye.    804
    *\*To.* Out o'tune sir, ye lye: Art any more then a Stew-|ard?    810
    to lye straight in my bed: I know I can do it.    832
    *in the name of ieasting, lye thou there: for heere comes    1037
    *Lyes, as will lye in thy sheete of paper, although the    1425
    Where lye my maiden weeds: by whose gentle helpe,    2421

LYES = *2
*Vio. So thou maist say the Kings lyes by a begger, if a 1222
*Lyes, as will lye in thy sheete of paper, although the 1425
LYEST = *1
*thee kindly: but thou lyest in thy throat, that is not the matter 1676
LYING = 1
Then lying, vainnesse, babling drunkennesse, 1874
LYMDE = *1
*I haue lymde her, but it is Ioues doing, and Ioue make me 1597
LYNES = *1
*to betray him: He does smile his face into more lynes, 1457
M = 2*1
Mal. M. Maluolio, M. why that begins my name. 1134
*Mal. M. But then there is no consonancy in the sequell 1137
MA = 13*14
MAD = 11*8
*Clo. He is but mad yet Madona, and the foole shall | looke to the
madman. 431
*you be not mad, be gone: if you haue reason, be breefe: 494
*Mal. My masters are you mad? Or what are you? 786
when the image of it leaues him, he must run mad. 1198
Fa. Why we shall make him mad indeede. 1655
*My Neece is already in the beleefe that he's mad: we may 1658
1.Off. The man growes mad, away with him: | Come, come sir. 1891
Are all the people mad? 1944
Or I am mad, or else this is a dreame: 1978
*sir Topas do not thinke I am mad: they haue layde mee | heere in
hideous darknesse. 2015
*Mal. I am not mad sir Topas, I say to you this house is | darke. 2026
*Clo. But as well: then you are mad indeede, if you be 2074
mad indeed, or do you but counterfeit. 2099
Like a mad lad, paire thy nayles dad, 2111
To any other trust, but that I am mad, 2129
Or else the Ladies mad; yet if 'twere so, 2130
Ol. How now, art thou mad? | *Clo. No Madam, I do but reade
madnesse: and your 2460
First told me thou wast mad; then cam'st in smiling, 2519
*all one: By the Lord Foole, I am not mad: but do you re-|member, 2544
MADAM = 20*9
Cap. True Madam, and to comfort you with chance, 58
The like of him. Know'st thou this Countrey? | Cap. I Madam well, for
I was bred and borne 71
*Mar. Madam, there is at the gate, a young Gentle-|man, much desires
to speake with you. 392
*Ma I know not (Madam) 'tis a faire young man, and | well attended. 396
Ol. Who of my people hold him in delay? | Ma. Sir Toby Madam, your
kinsman. 398
*Mal. Madam, yond young fellow sweares hee will 434
Vio. Good Madam, let me see your face. 522
Mal. Heere Madam, at your seruice. 597
Ile giue him reasons for't: hie thee Maluolio. | Mal. Madam, I will.
Exit. 604
Vio. My dutie Madam, and most humble seruice. 1307
Your seruants seruant, is your seruant Madam. 1314
*Vio. Madam, I come to whet your gentle thoughts | On his behalfe. 1317
You'l nothing Madam to my Lord, by me: 1353

MADAM *cont.*

*Ol.* I would you were, as I would haue you be. | *Vio.* Would it be better
Madam, then I am?     1358
And so adieu good Madam, neuer more,     1377
But in very strange manner. He is sure possest Madam.     1529
*\*Mar.* No Madam, he does nothing but smile: your La- | dyship     1531
*Ol.* Hold *Toby*, on thy life I charge thee hold. | *To.* Madam.     1962
*Seb.* Madam, I will. | *Ol.* O say so, and so be. *Exeunt*     1982
*Vio.* Madam: | *Du.* Gracious *Oliuia.*     2259
*Seb.* I am sorry Madam I haue hurt your kinsman:     2373
How does he sirrah? | *\*Cl.* Truely Madam, he holds *Belzebub* at the
staues end as     2451
deliuers the Madman. *By the Lord Madam.*     2459
*Ol.* How now, art thou mad? | *\*Clo.* No Madam, I do but reade
madnesse: and your     2460
*\*Fab. Reads.* By the Lord Madam, you wrong me, and     2469
*Du.* Madam, I am most apt t'embrace your offer:     2486
*Mal.* Madam, you haue done me wrong, | Notorious wrong.     2497
*Fab.* Good Madam heare me speake,     2526
*\*Madam, why laugh you at such a barren rascall,     2545

MADAME = 2*1

Where is *Maluolio*? | *Mar.* He's comming Madame:     1527
*\*Ser.* Madame, the young Gentleman of the Count     1579
*Ol.* Did he write this? | *Clo.* I Madame.     2478

MADDE = 1*2

*\*Clo.* Like a drown'd man, a foole, and a madde man:     425
I am as madde as hee, | If sad and merry madnesse equall bee.     1536
*\*man thus abus'd, I am no more madde then you are,     2033

MADDES = 1

*\*One draught aboue heate, makes him a foole, the second | maddes
him, and a third drownes him.     426

MADE = 11*2

Till I had made mine owne occasion mellow | What my estate is.     94
She made good view of me, indeed so much,     676
For such as we are made, if such we bee:     689
*\*made if thou desir'st to be so: If not, let me see thee a ste- | ward     1161
*\*Mal.* Go too, thou art made, if thou desir'st to be so.     1574
*Ol.* Am I made?     1575
Whom thou in termes so bloudie, and so deere | Hast made thine
enemies?     2222
*Ol.* Away with him? Who hath made this hauocke | with them?     2365
We made each other, but so late ago.     2379
*Ant.* How haue you made diuision of your selfe,     2387
That day that made my sister thirteene yeares.     2414
And made the most notorious gecke and gull,     2513
A solemne Combination shall be made | Of our deere soules. Meane
time sweet sister,     2553

MADLY = 1

and speake out of my iniury. *The madly vs'd Maluolio.*     2477

MADMAN = 3*3

*\*madman: Fie on him. Go you *Maluolio*; If it be a suit     401
*\*Clo.* He is but mad yet Madona, and the foole shall | looke to the
madman.     431
*\*Clo.* Madman thou errest: I say there is no darknesse     2028
*\*Clo.* Nay, Ile nere beleeue a madman till I see his brains     2101
deliuers the Madman. *By the Lord Madam.*     2459

MADMAN *cont.*
  *Du.* Is this the Madman? | *Ol.* I my Lord, this same: How now
  *Maluolio?*                                                           2495
MADMANS = *1
  *madmans Epistles are no Gospels, so it skilles not much             2455
MADMEN = *1
  *and crowne thee for a finder of madmen: but see, but see.          1662
MADNESSE = 5*1
  I am as madde as hee, | If sad and merry madnesse equall bee.       1536
  *Ol.* Why this is verie Midsommer madnesse.                          1577
  Yet 'tis not madnesse. Where's *Anthonio* then,                      2118
  That this may be some error, but no madnesse,                        2124
  But for thee fellow, fellow thy words are madnesse,                  2253
  *Ol.* How now, art thou mad? | *Clo.* No Madam, I do but reade
  madnesse: and your                                                   2460
MADONA = 3*7
  *Clo.* Two faults Madona, that drinke & good counsell                335
  *motley in my braine: good *Madona*, giue mee leaue to | proue you a
  foole.                                                               349
  *Ol.* Can you do it? | *Clo.* Dexteriously, good Madona.             351
  *Clo.* I must catechize you for it Madona, Good my | Mouse of vertue
  answer mee.                                                          354
  *Clo.* Good Madona, why mournst thou? | *Ol.* Good foole, for my
  brothers death.                                                      358
  *Clo.* I thinke his soule is in hell, Madona.                        360
  *Clo.* The more foole (Madona) to mourne for your                    362
  *Clo.* Thou hast spoke for vs (Madona) as if thy eldest              406
  *Clo.* He is but mad yet Madona, and the foole shall | looke to the
  madman.                                                              431
  *Clo.* So I do Madona: but to reade his right wits, is to            2465
MAID = 4
  *Vio.* What's shee? | *Cap.* A vertuous maid, the daughter of a Count  85
  *And.* What's that? | *To.* My Neeces Chamber-maid.                   166
  You would haue bin contracted to a Maid,                            2427
  You are betroth'd both to a maid and man.                           2429
MAIDE = 1
  *I am slaine by a faire cruell maide:*                               945
MAIDEN = 1
  Where lye my maiden weeds: by whose gentle helpe,                   2421
MAIDENS = 1
  Is as the maidens organ, shrill, and sound,                          284
MAIDEN-HEAD = *1
  *would, are as secret as maiden-head: to your eares, Di-|uinity; to any
  others, prophanation.                                                510
MAIDES = 2
  And the free maides that weaue their thred with bones,               935
  Hath my Maides garments: he vpon some Action                        2442
MAID-HOOD = 1
  By maid-hood, honor, truth, and euery thing,                        1366
MAINTAINE = 1
  *Mal.* Sir *Topas.* | *Clo.* Maintaine no words with him good fellow.  2083
MAIST *l.*1222 = *1
MAISTERS = 1
  My state is desperate for my maisters loue:                          694
MAKE = 26*22
  *as make water but in a Sinke-a-pace: What dooest thou               238
  Rather then make vnprofited returne,                                 272

MAKE *cont*.

*Ma*. Make that good. | *Clo*. He shall see none to feare. 302
Lady: make your excuse wisely, you were best. 324
*Ol*. Make your proofe. 353
*him: Infirmity that decaies the wise, doth euer make the | better foole. 368
*'tis not that time of Moone with me, to make one in so | skipping a
dialogue. 495
*Ol*. Why, what would you? | *Vio*. Make me a willow Cabine at your
gate, 561
And make the babling Gossip of the aire, 567
Loue make his heart of flint, that you shal loue, 582
*But shall we make the Welkin dance indeed? Shall wee 758
*like Tinkers at this time of night? Do yee make an Ale- | house 788
promise with him, and make a foole of him. 824
*with him: If I do not gull him into a nayword, and make 830
*your Neece, on a forgotten matter wee can hardly make | distinction of
our hands. 853
*An*. And your horse now would make him an Asse. 861
*the Foole make a third, where he shall finde the Letter: 866
*Tailor make thy doublet of changeable Taffata, for thy 961
And can digest as much, make no compare 989
*this Letter wil make a contemplatiue Ideot of him. Close 1036
*make out for him: I frowne the while, and perchance 1075
*portend, if I could make that resemble something | in me? Softly,
*M.O.A.I*. 1129
*To*. O I, make vp that, he is now at a cold sent. 1131
*Fa*. And *O* shall end, I hope. | *To*. I, or Ile cudgell him, and make him
cry *O*. 1140
*And*. Ile make one too. *Exeunt*. | *Finis Actus secundus* 1211
words, may quickely make them wanton. 1229
*that word, might make my sister wanton: But indeede, 1233
sir, I would it would make you inuisible. 1243
*And*. S'light; will you make an Asse o'me. 1393
But since you make your pleasure of your paines, 1468
*Seb*. My kinde *Anthonio*, | I can no other answer make, but thankes, 1480
This does make some obstruction in the blood: 1542
*I haue lymde her, but it is Ioues doing, and Ioue make me 1597
*Fa*. Why we shall make him mad indeede. 1655
*part of Illyria: will you walke towards him, I will make | your peace
with him, if I can. 1786
*To*. Ile make the motion: stand heere, make a good 1805
*Vio*. Pray God defend me: a little thing would make 1818
Ile make diuision of my present with you: 1863
Least that it make me so vnsound a man 1868
*Clo*. Will you make me beleeue, that I am not sent for | you? 1919
*make him beleeue thou art sir *Topas* the Curate, doe it 1987
make the triall of it in any constant question. 2034
*Clo*. Marry sir, they praise me, and make an asse of me, 2170
*your foure negatiues make your two affirmatiues, why 2174
you could make it another. | *Du*. O you giue me ill counsell. 2181
With which such scathfull grapple did he make, 2207
*Vio*. If nothing lets to make vs happie both, 2415

MAKES = 3*3

*One draught aboue heate, makes him a foole, the second | maddes
him, and a third drownes him. 426
makes a good voyage of nothing. Farewell. *Exit* 965
*Fa*. Oh peace: Contemplation makes a rare Turkey 1047

MAKES *cont.*
   *very *C's*, her *V's*, and her *T's*, and thus makes shee her    1102
   Makes me to aske you for my purse. It greeues mee    1852
   That makes thee strangle thy propriety:    2307
MAL = 43*43
MALAPERT = 1
   *To. What, what? Nay then I must haue an Ounce or | two of this
   malapert blood from you.    1959
MALICE = 1*1
   *phangs of malice, I sweare) I am not that I play. Are you | the Ladie
   of the house?    479
   How with a sportfull malice it was follow'd,    2536
MALIGNANCIE = *1
   *ouer me; the malignancie of my fate, might perhaps di- | stemper    616
MALL = *1
MALS = *1
   *dust, like mistris *Mals* picture? Why dost thou not goe    235
MALUO = 1
   *from the Count, I am sicke, or not at home. What you | will, to
   dismisse it. *Exit Maluo.*    402
MALUO = 1
MALUOLIO *see also Mal., Mall., Maluo.* = 27*12
   *Enter Lady Oliuia, with Maluolio.*    325
   *Ol. What thinke you of this foole *Maluolio*, doth he | not mend?    365
   *Ol.* How say you to that *Maluolio*?    374
   *Ol. O you are sicke of selfe-loue *Maluolio*, and taste    382
   *madman: Fie on him. Go you *Maluolio*; If it be a suit    401
   *Enter Maluolio.*    433
   What hoa, *Maluolio.*    595
   *Enter Maluolio.*    596
   Ile giue him reasons for't: hie thee *Maluolio.* | *Mal.* Madam, I will.
   *Exit.*    604
   *Enter Viola and Maluolio, at seuerall doores.*    657
   *my Ladie haue not call'd vp her Steward *Maluolio*, and    773
   *Enter Maluolio.*    785
   *much out of quiet. For Monsieur Maluolio, let me alone    829
   *Enter Maluolio.*    1039
   *Mal.* To be Count *Maluolio.* | *To.* Ah Rogue.    1051
   If this should be thee *Maluolio*?    1113
   *Mal. M. Maluolio, M.* why that begins my name.    1134
   *selues into stitches, follow me; yond gull *Maluolio* is tur- | ned    1448
   *I speake too loud: Where's *Maluolio*, he is sad, and ciuill,    1525
   Where is *Maluolio*? | *Mar.* He's comming Madame:    1527
   *Enter Maluolio.*    1535
   How now *Maluolio*? | *Mal.* Sweet Lady, ho, ho.    1538
   *Ol.* Wilt thou go to bed *Maluolio*?    1552
   *Mar.* How do you *Maluolio*? | *Maluo.* At your request:    1556
   *Ol.* What meanst thou by that *Maluolio*?    1562
   *be look'd too: Fellow? not *Maluolio*, nor after my    1599
   *gently with him: Let me alone. How do you *Maluolio*?    1619
   *To.* The knaue counterfets well: a good knaue. | *Maluolio within.*    2004
   *Clo. Sir *Topas* the Curate, who comes to visit *Maluo- |lio* the
   Lunaticke.    2007
   *Clo.* M.(aster) *Maluolio*? | *Mal.* I good Foole.    2069
   *Maluolio, Maluolio*, thy wittes the heauens restore: en- | deauour    2080
   *Ol.* He shall inlarge him: fetch *Maluolio* hither,    2445
   and speake out of my iniury. *The madly vs'd Maluolio.*    2477

*MALUOLIO cont.*

| | |
|---|---|
| Enter *Maluolio.* | 2494 |
| *Du.* Is this the Madman? | *Ol.* I my Lord, this same: How now *Maluolio*? | 2495 |
| *Ol.* Haue I *Maluolio*? No. | *Mal.* Lady you haue, pray you peruse that Letter. | 2499 |
| *Ol.* Alas *Maluolio*, this is not my writing, | 2515 |
| Set this deuice against *Maluolio* heere, | 2531 |

MALUOLIOS = 1*3

| | |
|---|---|
| *\*Clo.* I did impeticos thy gratillity: for *Maluolios* nose | 727 |
| *\*To.* My Lady's a *Catayan*, we are politicians, *Maluolio*s | 775 |
| *\*Mar.* Get ye all three into the box tree: *Maluolio*'s | 1032 |
| Is now in durance, at *Maluolio's* suite, | 2443 |

MAN = 36*29

| | |
|---|---|
| *To.* He's as tall a man as any's in Illyria. | 137 |
| *more wit then a Christian, or an ordinary man ha's: but I | 198 |
| swear't. Tut there's life in't man. | 220 |
| *\*And.* As any man in Illyria, whatsoeuer he be, vnder | 225 |
| *the degree of my betters, & yet I will not compare with | an old man. | 226 |
| *\*And.* And I thinke I haue the backe-tricke, simply as | strong as any man in Illyria. | 231 |
| That say thou art a man: *Dianas* lip | 282 |
| *wise man. For what saies *Quinapalus*, Better a witty foole, | 329 |
| *not dry: bid the dishonest man mend himself, if he mend, | 337 |
| *nor no rayling, in a knowne discreet man, though hee do | nothing but reproue. | 387 |
| *\*Ma* I know not (Madam) 'tis a faire young man, and | well attended. | 396 |
| *Ol.* What's a drunken man like, foole? | 424 |
| *\*Clo.* Like a drown'd man, a foole, and a madde man: | 425 |
| *Ol.* What manner of man? | 447 |
| *\*Mal.* Not yet old enough for a man, nor yong enough | 451 |
| *betweene boy and man. He is verie well-fauour'd, | 454 |
| Vnlesse the Master were the man. How now? | 590 |
| The Countes man: he left this Ring behinde him | 599 |
| I am the man, if it be so, as tis, | 682 |
| What will become of this? As I am man, | 693 |
| *There dwelt a man in Babylon, Lady, Lady.* | 778 |
| My Father had a daughter lou'd a man | 996 |
| *\*Fa.* I would exult man: you know he brought me out | 1023 |
| *man must know.* No man must know. What followes? | 1111 |
| The numbers alter'd: No man must know, | 1112 |
| *deuise, the very man. I do not now foole my selfe, to let | 1168 |
| *Vio.* Why man? | *\*Clo.* Why sir, her names a word, and to dallie with words are very Rascals, since bonds disgrac'd them. | *Vio.* Thy reason man? | 1231 |
| | 1234 |
| Your wife is like to reape a proper man: | 1349 |
| *Counts Seruing-man, then euer she bestow'd vpon mee: | 1387 |
| come, for sure the man is tainted in's wits. | 1533 |
| *Mal.* Why how doest thou man? | 1546 |
| *man then sir *Toby* to looke to me. This concurres direct-|ly | 1588 |
| How ist with you man? | 1611 |
| *How ist with you? What man, defie the diuell: consider, | 1620 |
| *\*To.* I biddy, come with me. What man, tis not for | 1637 |
| *\*To.* His very genius hath taken the infection of the | deuice man. | 1651 |
| *\*Vio.* You mistake sir I am sure, no man hath any quar-|rell | 1745 |
| any image of offence done to any man. | 1747 |

MAN *cont.*
*for your opposite hath in him what youth, strength, skill, | and wrath, can furnish man withall.                                                    1750
*to taste their valour: belike this is a man of that | quirke.        1762
*Vio*. I beseech you what manner of man is he?                        1781
*To*. Why man hee's a verie diuell, I haue not seen such             1792
me tell them how much I lacke of a man.                               1819
1.*Off*. This is the man, do thy Office.                             1843
Least that it make me so vnsound a man                               1868
I hate ingratitude more in a man,                                    1873
1.*Off*. The man growes mad, away with him: | Come, come sir.        1891
*great man, and now applyes it to a foole. Vent my fol- | ly:        1930
*Studient: but to be said an honest man and a good hous- | keeper    1993
*goes as fairely, as to say, a carefull man, & a great | scholler. The
Competitors enter.                                                   1994
man? Talkest thou nothing but of Ladies? | *Tob*. Well said M.(aster)
Parson.                                                              2012
*Mal*. Sir *Topas*, neuer was man thus wronged, good                2014
*man thus abus'd, I am no more madde then you are,                   2033
*Mall*. Foole, there was neuer man so notoriouslie a- | bus'd:       2072
*paper, I tell thee I am as well in my wittes, as any man in | Illyria. 2091
Adieu good man diuell. *Exit*                                        2112
Now go with me, and with this holy man                               2138
*Seb*. Ile follow this good man, and go with you,                    2147
*Vio*. Here comes the man sir, that did rescue mee.                  2201
You are betroth'd both to a maid and man.                            2429
*well as a man in his case may do: has heere writ a letter to        2453
(For so you shall be while you are a man:)                           2556
MANAKIN = 1
*Fa*. This is a deere Manakin to you Sir *Toby*.                     1433
MANHOODE = *1
*accent sharpely twang'd off, giues manhoode more                    1697
MANIFESTS = *1
*and in this she manifests her selfe to my loue, &                   1172
MANKINDE = 2
*Ol*. What kinde o'man is he? | *Mal*. Why of mankinde.              445
he's an enemy to mankinde.                                           1621
MANNER = 3*3
*Ol*. What manner of man?                                            447
*Mal*. Of verie ill manner: hee'l speake with you, will | you, or no. 448
*legge, the manner of his gate, the expressure of his eye,           850
But in very strange manner. He is sure possest Madam.                1529
*manner how: as a sad face, a reuerend carriage, a slow              1595
*Vio*. I beseech you what manner of man is he?                       1781
MANNERS = 1*3
*willing to keepe in: therefore it charges me in manners,            624
*am yet so neere the manners of my mother, that vpon the             648
*Haue you no wit, manners, nor honestie, but to gabble               787
Where manners nere were preach'd: out of my sight.                   1966
MANS = 4*2
*Enter Valentine, and Viola in mans attire.*                         250
*Euery wise mans sonne doth know.*                                   745
*An*. 'Twere as good a deede as to drinke when a mans               822
As full of labour as a Wise-mans Art:                                1278
*can more preuaile in mans commendation with woman, | then report
of valour.                                                           1417
*But when I came to mans estate, | with hey ho, &c.*                2564

MANY = 4\*3

| | |
|---|---|
| And speake to him in many sorts of Musicke, | 110 |
| *Clo*. Many a good hanging, preuents a bad marriage: | 314 |
| *me, was yet of many accounted beautiful: but thogh | 635 |
| I haue many enemies in Orsino's Court, | 652 |
| *And*. I knew 'twas I, for many do call mee foole. | 1096 |
| *thou'st him some thrice, it shall not be amisse, and as ma-\|ny | 1424 |
| And heare thou there how many fruitlesse prankes | 1972 |

MAPPE = \*1

| | |
|---|---|
| *then is in the new Mappe, with the augmentation of the | 1458 |

MAR = 10\*23

MARBLE-BRESTED = 1

| | |
|---|---|
| Liue you the Marble-brested Tirant still. | 2280 |

*MARIA see also Ma., Mar.* = 14\*2

| | |
|---|---|
| Enter Sir Toby, and Maria. | 118 |
| I let go your hand, I am barren. *Exit Maria* | 193 |
| *Enter Maria, and Clowne.* | 296 |
| *Enter Maria.* | 391 |
| *Enter Maria.* | 459 |
| *Enter Maria.* | 771 |
| crums. A stope of Wine *Maria*. | 816 |
| *Enter Maria.* | 1029 |
| *Mal*. 'Tis but Fortune, all is fortune. *Maria* once | 1040 |
| *Enter Maria.* | 1189 |
| *Enter Maria.* | 1445 |
| *Enter Oliuia and Maria.* | 1521 |
| *Good *Maria*, let this fellow be look'd too. Where's my | 1583 |
| *Enter Toby, Fabian, and Maria.* | 1606 |
| *Enter Maria and Clowne.* | 1985 |
| We had conceiu'd against him. *Maria* writ | 2533 |

MARIAN = 1

| | |
|---|---|
| *Marian* I say, a stoope of wine. | 714 |

MARIAS = 1

| | |
|---|---|
| But out of question, tis *Marias* hand. | 2517 |

MARK = \*1

| | |
|---|---|
| *Mar*. If you will then see the fruites of the sport, mark | 1201 |

MARKE = 1

| | |
|---|---|
| Marke it Cesario, it is old and plaine; | 933 |

MARKETS = 1

| | |
|---|---|
| I thinke is not for idle Markets, sir. | 1515 |

MARRIAGE = \*1

| | |
|---|---|
| *Clo*. Many a good hanging, preuents a bad marriage: | 314 |

MARRIE = 1\*2

| | |
|---|---|
| *Mar*. Marrie sir, sometimes he is a kinde of Puritane. | 834 |
| *To*. Marrie hang thee brocke. | 1114 |
| *oath sake: marrie hee hath better bethought him of his | 1814 |

MARRIED = 3\*1

| | |
|---|---|
| married the yeoman of the wardrobe. | 1056 |
| *Mal*. Hauing beene three moneths married to her, \| sitting in my state. | 1060 |
| *will keepe no foole sir, till she be married, and fooles are | 1246 |
| In recompence whereof, he hath married her: | 2535 |

MARRY = 4\*7

| | |
|---|---|
| *An*. Marry but you shall haue, and heeres my hand. | 182 |
| *Ma*. I Sir, I haue them at my fingers ends: marry now | 192 |
| *Ol*. I marry, what is he? | 421 |
| *To*. I could marry this wench for this deuice. \| *An*. So could I too. | 1185 |
| *And*. Marry I saw your Neece do more fauours to the | 1386 |

MARRY *cont.*
*\*Mar.* Marry and it shall be done to morrow morning    1626
    marry Ile ride your horse as well as I ride you.    1807
*\*And.* Marry will I sir: and for that I promis'd you Ile    1840
*\*Who* I sir, not I sir. God buy you good sir Topas: Mar-|ry Amen. I
    will sir, I will.    2085
*\*Clo.* Marry sir, they praise me, and make an asse of me,    2170
*\*Clo.* Marry sir, lullaby to your bountie till I come a-|gen.    2195
MARTIAL = *1
*\*To.* Go, write it in a martial hand, be curst and briefe:    1421
MARUELL = *1
*\*Mal.* I maruell your Ladyship takes delight in such    375
MARY = 3*1
*\*Ma.* Good Mistris accost, I desire better acquaintance | *Ma.* My name
    is *Mary* sir.    168
*And.* Good mistris *Mary*, accost.    170
*Clo.* Where good mistris *Mary*?    306
*\*Mal.* Mistris Mary, if you priz'd my Ladies fauour    817
MASCULINE = 1
    But this my masculine vsurp'd attyre:    2416
MASKES = *1
*\*strangest* minde i'th world: I delight in Maskes and Re-|uels
    sometimes altogether.    222
MASTE = 1
    To a strong Maste, that liu'd vpon the sea:    64
MASTER = 10*5
    My Lord, and master loues you: O such loue    544
    My Master, not my selfe, lackes recompence.    581
    Vnlesse the Master were the man. How now?    590
    How will this fadge? My master loues her deerely,    690
*\*Foole* should be as oft with your Master, as with my Mi-|stris:    1253
*\*Vio.* Nothing but this, your true loue for my master.    1730
*\*speake* with her: nor your name is not Master *Cesario*,    1925
*To.* Ioue blesse thee M.(aster) Parson.    1997
*\*of* King *Gorbodacke*, that that is, is: so I being M.(aster) Parson,    2000
*\*am* M.(aster) Parson; for what is that, but that? and is, but is?    2001
    man? Talkest thou nothing but of Ladies? | *Tob.* Well said M.(aster)
    Parson.    2012
*Clo.* M.(aster) *Maluolio*? | *Mal.* I good Foole.    2069
*Clo.* Good M.(aster) *Fabian*, grant me another request. | *Fab.* Any
    thing.    2155
    Your Master quits you: and for your seruice done him,    2487
    And since you call'd me Master, for so long:    2490
MASTERLY = 1
    *Du.* Thou dost speake masterly,    908
MASTERS = 6*1
    *Vio.* If I did loue you in my masters flame,    557
    And let your feruour like my masters be,    583
*\*Mal.* My masters are you mad? Or what are you?    786
    Will I my Masters teares to you deplore.    1378
    Goes on my Masters greefes.    1724
    Where he sits crowned in his masters spight.    2284
    Heere is my hand, you shall from this time bee | Your Masters Mistris.    2491
MATCH = *1
*\*To.* Shee'l none o'th Count, she'l not match aboue hir    218
MATER = 1
    One of thy kin has a most weake *Pia-mater*.    409

MATTER = 9*8

*Ol. Sure you haue some hiddeous matter to deliuer,    501

in my hand: my words are as full of peace, as matter.    505

*your Neece, on a forgotten matter wee can hardly make | distinction of
our hands.    853

*Clo. No such matter sir, I do liue by the Church: For,    1219

*Clo. The matter I hope is not great sir; begging, but a    1267

*Vio. My matter hath no voice Lady, but to your owne | most pregnant
and vouchsafed eare.    1301

*it is no matter how wittie, so it bee eloquent, and full of    1422

*in thy inke, though thou write with a Goose-pen, | no matter: about it.    1428

Ol. Why what's the matter, does he raue?    1530

What is the matter with thee?    1547

Fa. More matter for a May morning.    1664

*thee kindly: but thou lyest in thy throat, that is not the matter    1676

Vio. Pray you sir, do you know of this matter?    1777

*I'de haue challeng'd him. Let him let the matter slip, and    1803

it's no matter for that.    1952

Cride fame and honor on him: What's the matter? | 1.Offi. Orsino, this
is that Anthonio    2210

Ol. What's the matter?    2338

MAUGRE = 1

I loue thee so, that maugre all thy pride,    1367

MAY l.7 *57 109 112 *298 *307 *328 476 *515 591 *618 654 985 994 1006
*1115 *1125 1227 1229 *1589 *1658 *1685 *1690 1729 1731 *2053 2124
2143 2150 *2189 *2193 *2256 2257 2331 *2453 2537 = 19*18, 1

Fa. More matter for a May morning.    1664

MAYST = 2

Ol. Yet come againe: for thou perhaps mayst moue    1379

Mayst smile at this: Thou shalt not choose but goe:    1974

ME see also o'me l.6 25 28 46 105 108 111 116 *197 212 *216 *247 256
270 *297 *300 *326 423 441 460 464 *466 *495 500 522 541 547 562 570
577 578 592 *616 *620 *623 *624 *631 *635 641 642 *643 *649 669 676
677 679 680 692 698 *734 752 *761 768 774 779 *794 *829 870 *871 879
*880 *885 888 901 943 *952 959 990 1020 *1023 *1041 *1043 *1063
1077 1086 1122 *1126 1130 *1161 *1170 1182 1208 *1255 *1292 1293
1306 1316 1325 1328 1336 1341 1346 1353 *1354 1389 *1413 *1414
*1420 *1438 *1448 1471 1492 1507 1511 1544 1576 *1587 *1588 *1590
*1597 *1604 *1612 *1619 1632 *1637 1669 1680 1682 1700 1720 *1725
1728 *1746 *1767 *1772 *1794 *1818 1819 *1824 1830 1845 1852 1859
1865 1868 *1879 1882 1893 *1894 *1919 1922 1928 *1933 *1935 1958
1971 1980 *1981 *2051 *2057 *2066 *2076 *2077 2078 *2090 *2098 2100
2116 2117 2121 2122 2128 2138 2141 2154 2155 *2170 *2171 *2179 2182
2217 2218 2228 2239 2240 2242 2258 2262 2276 2279 2285 2296 2317
2324 2349 2350 2354 *2359 2376 2378 2383 2395 2417 2433 2434 2439
2440 2441 2446 *2469 *2471 *2476 2483 2490 2497 2505 2506 2507 2511
2514 2518 2519 2526 = 143*77

MEANE = 4*2

*meane? Is it a world to hide vertues in? I did thinke by    239

*Vio. I am bound to your Neece sir, I meane she is the | list of my
voyage.    1289

what you meane by bidding me taste my legs.    1293

To. I meane to go sir, to enter.    1294

Ol. Blame not this haste of mine: if you meane well    2137

A solemne Combination shall be made | Of our deere soules. Meane
time sweet sister,    2553

MEANES = *5
*Sir To. What a plague meanes my Neece to take the                        119
*Vio. I left no Ring with her: what meanes this Lady?                     674
*meanes for this vnciuill rule; she shall know of it by this | hand. *Exit*  819
*To. Neuer trust me then: and by all meanes stirre on                   1438
*that meanes to be saued by beleeuing rightly, can euer                 1450
MEANING = 2
company. Is that the meaning of Accost? | *Ma.* Far you well
Gentlemen.                                                               174
(Not meaning to partake with me in danger)                             2239
MEANST = 1
*Ol.* What meanst thou by that *Maluolio?*                               1562
MEANTIME *see* meane
MEASURE = *1
*tripping measure, or the belles of S.(aint) *Bennet* sir, may put | you in
minde, one, two, three.                                                 2189
MEASURES = *1
*To. Then he's a Rogue, and a passy measures pauyn: I | hate a
drunken rogue.                                                          2363
MEDDLE = 1*1
*starke naked: for meddle you must that's certain, or for-|sweare to
weare iron about you.                                                   1769
*And.* Pox on't, Ile not meddle with him.                               1798
MEDITATE = *1
*To. I wil meditate the while vpon some horrid message | for a
Challenge.                                                              1716
MEE *l.*197 *349 355 *469 *474 *508 579 *625 *643 *663 1094 1096 *1147
*1169 *1173 *1305 *1387 *1693 1852 1975 *2015 *2076 *2191 2201 2225
2254 *2470 *2473 = 9*19
MEERE = *1
*Seb.* No sooth sir: my determinate voyage is meere                      621
MEET = 1
Where thou, and I (henceforth) may neuer meet.                          2331
MEETING = 1
*Iourneys end in louers meeting,*                                        744
MELANCHOLLY = 2*2
*Clo.* Now the melancholly God protect thee, and the                     960
And with a greene and yellow melancholly,                               1003
let me be boyl'd to death with Melancholly.                             1020
*being addicted to a melancholly, as shee is, that it                   1206
MELLIFLUOUS = 1
*An.* A mellifluous voyce, as I am true knight.                          754
MELLOW = 1
Till I had made mine owne occasion mellow | What my estate is.           94
MEMORIALS = 1
With the memorials, and the things of fame | That do renowne this
City.                                                                   1490
MEN = 4*4
(They say) she hath abiur'd the sight | And company of men.              90
*a Peg-a-ramsie, and *Three merry men be wee.* Am not I                   776
*minde is a very Opall. I would haue men of such constan-|cie            962
*Vio.* Too well what loue women to men may owe:                          994
We men may say more, sweare more, but indeed                           1006
*To. And they haue beene grand Iurie men, since before | *Noah* was a
Saylor.                                                                 1396
*of some kinde of men, that put quarrells purposely on o-|thers,        1761
*Gainst Knaues and Theeues men shut their gate, | for the raine, &c.*   2566

MEND = 1*3
*not dry: bid the dishonest man mend himself, if he mend,    337
*mend him: any thing that's mended, is but patch'd: vertu    339
*Ol. What thinke you of this foole *Maluolio*, doth he | not mend?    365
MENDED = 1*1
*An*. Why, would that haue mended my haire?    210
*mend him: any thing that's mended, is but patch'd: vertu    339
MERCIE = *2
*Tob. Fartheewell, and God haue mercie vpon one of our*    1684
*soules. He may haue mercie vpon mine, but my hope is better,*    1685
MERCIES = 1
What foolish boldnesse brought thee to their mercies,    2221
MERCURY = *1
*Clo*. Now Mercury indue thee with leasing, for thou | speak'st well of
fooles.    389
MERCY = *1
*pastime tyred out of breath, prompt vs to haue mercy    1660
MERMIDONS = 1
*is no Whip-stocke. My Lady has a white hand, and the | Mermidons
are no bottle-ale houses.    728
MERRY = 2*2
*a Peg-a-ramsie, and *Three merry men be wee*. Am not I    776
*Vio*. I warrant thou art a merry fellow, and car'st for | nothing.    1239
*Ol*. My seruant sir? 'Twas neuer merry world,    1310
I am as madde as hee, | If sad and merry madnesse equall bee.    1536
MESSAGE = 1*1
*my speech in your praise, and then shew you the heart of | my
message.    485
*To*. I wil meditate the while vpon some horrid message | for a
Challenge.    1716
MESSALINE = 1*1
*my father was that *Sebastian* of *Messaline*, whom I    627
What Countreyman? What name? What Parentage? | *Vio*. Of *Messaline*:
*Sebastian* was my Father,    2396
MESSENGER = 3
tell me your minde, I am a messenger.    500
*Ol*. Run after that same peeuish Messenger    598
Inuites me in this churlish messenger:    680
MET = *1
*And*. Now sir, haue I met you again: ther's for you.    1942
METAPHOR = *1
*An*. Wherefore (sweet-heart?) What's your Meta-|phor?    185
METHINKES *see* thinkes
METHOD = *1
*Vio*. To answer by the method, in the first of his hart.    519
METHOUGHT *see* thought
METTLE = 3
*To*. Heere comes the little villaine: How now my | Mettle of India?    1030
not who knowes so much of my mettle. *Exeunt*.    1790
So much against the mettle of your sex,    2488
MIDNIGHT = *3
*midnight, is to be vp betimes, and *Deliculo surgere*, thou | know'st.    702
*To be vp after midnight, and to go to bed then is early:    707
*so that to go to bed after midnight, is to goe to bed be-|times.    708
MIDSOMMER = 1
*Ol*. Why this is verie Midsommer madnesse.    1577

MIDWIFE = 1
*Ma.* Nay but say true, do's it worke vpon him? | *To.* Like Aqua vite
with a Midwife.                                                                1199
MIGHT *l.*30 93 *178 556 571 *616 *662 *963 997 *1143 *1233 *1270
    *1331 1360 1473 1474 1500 1501 1735 *1768 *2037 2122 = 12*10
MIGHTST *l.*177 *2049 = 1*1
MILKE = 1
mothers milke were scarse out of him.                                         456
MIND = *1
*Ol.* Your Lord does know my mind, I cannot loue him                          550
MINDE = 5*5
I will beleeue thou hast a minde that suites                                  102
*strangest minde i'th world: I delight in Maskes and Re-|uels
sometimes altogether.                                                         222
tell me your minde, I am a messenger.                                         500
Mine eye too great a flatterer for my minde:                                  607
*bore a minde that enuy could not but call faire: Shee is                     638
*minde is a very Opall. I would haue men of such constan-|cie                 962
*Mal.* Not blacke in my minde, though yellow in my                           1548
*To.* Wonder not, nor admire not in thy minde why I doe call                 1672
In Nature, there's no blemish but the minde:                                 1887
*tripping measure, or the belles of S.(aint) *Bennet* sir, may put | you in
minde, one, two, three.                                                      2189
MINE *see also* o'mine *l.*24 69 94 115 *410 594 607 *649 740 988 1332
    *1446 *1685 1719 1731 1976 2127 2137 2150 2242 2264 2409
    2449 = 19*4
MINION = 1
But this your Minion, whom I know you loue,                                  2281
MINISTER = 1*1
*laugh and minister occasion to him, he is gag'd. I protest                   379
*Clo.* Aduise you what you say: the Minister is heere.                       2079
MINISTERS = *1
*darkenesse, send Ministers to me, Asses, and doe all they                  2077
MINT = *1
*iests, fire-new from the mint, you should haue bangd                       1402
MINUTE = 1
Euen in a minute; so full of shapes is fancie,                               18
MINUTES = 1
No *intrim*, not a minutes vacancie,                                        2248
MINX = 1
*Mal.* My prayers Minx.                                                     1642
MIRACLE = 1
But 'tis that miracle, and Queene of Iems                                    972
MIRTH = 1
*Present mirth, hath present laughter:*                                      749
MISCARRIE = *1
*of him, I would not haue him miscarrie for the halfe of | my Dowry.
*Exit*                                                                      1585
MISCHIEFE = 1
Come boy with me, my thoughts are ripe in mischiefe:                        2285
MISDEMEANORS = *1
*separate your selfe and your misdemeanors, you are wel-|come               796
MISERY = 1
Ist possible that my deserts to you | Can lacke perswasion. Do not
tempt my misery,                                                            1866
MISPRISION = *1
*Clo.* Misprision in the highest degree. Lady, *Cucullus*                    347

MISTAKE = 1*2
   *To, You mistake knight: Accost, is front her, boord | her, woe her,
   assayle her.    171
   *Vio. You mistake sir I am sure, no man hath any quar-|rell    1745
   An. You do mistake me sir.    1845
MISTAKEN = 1
   And she (mistaken) seemes to dote on me:    692
MISTOOKE = 1
   Seb. So comes it Lady, you haue beene mistooke:    2425
MISTRIS = 7*5
   *Ma. Good Mistris accost, I desire better acquaintance | Ma. My name
   is Mary sir.    168
   And. Good mistris Mary, accost.    170
   *And. And you part so mistris, I would I might neuer    178
   *dust, like mistris Mals picture? Why dost thou not goe    235
   Clo. Where good mistris Mary?    306
   Clowne sings. | O Mistris mine where are you roming?    739
   *Mal. Mistris Mary, if you priz'd my Ladies fauour    817
   *Foole should be as oft with your Master, as with my Mi-|stris:    1253
   Shall mistris be of it, saue I alone.    1376
   Mal. How now mistris? | Mar. Oh Lord.    1629
   Heere is my hand, you shall from this time bee | Your Masters Mistris.    2491
   Orsino's Mistris, and his fancies Queene. Exeunt    2558
MITIGATION = *1
   *Catches without any mitigation or remorse of voice?    790
MOAI = 1*3
   *With bloodlesse stroke my heart doth gore, M.O.A.I. doth | sway my
   life.    1117
   *Mal. M.O.A.I. doth sway my life. Nay but first    1121
   *portend, if I could make that resemble something | in me? Softly,
   M.O.A.I.    1129
   *Mal. M, O, A, I. This simulation is not as the former:    1146
MOALE = 1
   Vio. My father had a moale vpon his brow. | Seb. And so had mine.    2408
MOCKERIE = *1
   *houre: obserue him for the loue of Mockerie: for I know    1035
MOCKES = 1
   That it but mockes reproofe.    1722
MODERATE = *1
   *Vio. Euen now sir, on a moderate pace, I haue since a-|riu'd but
   hither.    660
MODEST = 1*2
   Ma. I, but you must confine your selfe within the | modest limits of
   order.    126
   *modest assurance, if you be the Ladie of the house, that | (I    475
   *most modest termes, for I am one of those gentle ones,    2018
MODESTIE = 1*1
   *of modestie, that you will not extort from me, what I am    623
   And tell me in the modestie of honor,    2505
MOLLIFICATION = *1
   *Some mollification for your Giant, sweete Ladie;    499
MOMENT = *1
   *at this moment is so implacable, that satisfaction    1756
MONACHUM = *1
   *Non facit monachum: that's as much to say, as I weare not    348
MONETH = *1
   *And. Ile stay a moneth longer. I am a fellow o'th    221

MONETHS = 1
*Mal.* Hauing beene three moneths married to her, | sitting in my state.  1060
MONEY = 3*5
*To.* Let's to bed knight: Thou hadst neede send for | more money.  874
*To.* Send for money knight, if thou hast her not i'th | end, call me Cut.  878
*Ant.* I must entreat of you some of that money.  1857
*Vio.* What money sir?  1858
*To.* I dare lay any money, twill be nothing yet. *Exit*  1916
*money for thee, if you tarry longer, I shall giue worse | paiment.  1936
*that giue fooles money, get themselues a good re-|port, after
foureteene yeares purchase.  1939
*Du.* You can foole no more money out of mee at this  2191
MONSIEUR = 1*1
*much out of quiet. For Monsieur Maluolio, let me alone  829
*And. Dieu vou guard Monsieur.* | *Vio. Et vouz ousie vostre seruiture.*  1284
MONSTER = 1
And I (poore monster) fond asmuch on him:  691
MONTH = 1
For but a month ago I went from hence,  81
MONTHES = 1
Three monthes this youth hath tended vpon mee,  2254
MONTHS = *1
*Ant.* To day my Lord: and for three months before,  2247
MONUMENT = 1
She sate like Patience on a Monument,  1004
MOOD = 1
He must obserue their mood on whom he iests, | The quality of persons,
and the time:  1274
MOONE = *1
*'tis not that time of Moone with me, to make one in so | skipping a
dialogue.  495
MOOUE = *1
*Mal. Ioue knowes I loue, but who, Lips do not mooue, no*  1110
MORE = 30*29
Stealing, and giuing Odour. Enough, no more,  11
*more wit then a Christian, or an ordinary man ha's: but I  198
Then in a Nuntio's of more graue aspect.  278
Is not more smooth, and rubious: thy small pipe  283
*Ma.* Peace you rogue, no more o'that: here comes my  323
*Ol.* Go too, y'are a dry foole: Ile no more of you: be-|sides you grow
dis-honest.  333
*Clo.* The more foole (Madona) to mourne for your  362
*an ordinary foole, that has no more braine then a stone.  377
Wee'l once more heare *Orsinos* Embassie.  461
*Ol.* Whence came you sir? | *Vio.* I can say little more then I haue
studied, & that  472
*Ol.* It is the more like to be feigned, I pray you keep  491
*Ol.* O, I haue read it: it is heresie. Haue you no more | to say?  520
I cannot loue him: let him send no more,  576
drowne her remembrance againe with more.  640
*least occasion more, mine eyes will tell tales of me: I am  649
*thing more, that you be neuer so hardie to come againe  666
*do I too: he does it with a better grace, but I do it more | naturall.  781
*To.* Out o'tune sir, ye lye: Art any more then a Stew-|ard?  810
Shall be no more Cakes and Ale?  812
*at any thing more then contempt, you would not giue  818
*To.* Let's to bed knight: Thou hadst neede send for | more money.  874

MORE *cont.*

| | |
|---|---|
| More then light ayres, and recollected termes | 889 |
| Our fancies are more giddie and vnfirme, | 921 |
| More longing, wauering, sooner lost and worne, \| Then womens are. | 922 |
| *Du.* Let all the rest giue place: Once more *Cesario*, | 966 |
| Tell her my loue, more noble then the world | 968 |
| We men may say more, sweare more, but indeed | 1006 |
| Our shewes are more then will: for still we proue | 1007 |
| *my complection. Besides she vses me with a more ex- \| alted | 1043 |
| *see more detraction at your heeles, then Fortunes before \| you. | 1144 |
| *champian discouers not more: This is open, I will bee | 1165 |
| *Vio*. Nay, and thou passe vpon me, Ile no more with \| thee. Hold | |
| there's expences for thee. | 1255 |
| A murdrous guilt shewes not it selfe more soone, | 1363 |
| And so adieu good Madam, neuer more, | 1377 |
| *And*. Marry I saw your Neece do more fauours to the | 1386 |
| *can more preuaile in mans commendation with woman, \| then report | |
| of valour. | 1417 |
| *to betray him: He does smile his face into more lynes, | 1457 |
| (More sharpe then filed steele) did spurre me forth, | 1471 |
| *For youth is bought more oft, then begg'd, or borrow'd. | 1524 |
| *if I liue. My Lady would not loose him for more then ile \| say. | 1627 |
| *things, I am not of your element, you shall knowe more \| heereafter. | |
| *Exit* | 1646 |
| *Fa*. More matter for a May morning. | 1664 |
| *accent sharpely twang'd off, giues manhoode more | 1697 |
| *a mortall arbitrement, but nothing of the circumstance \| more. | 1779 |
| *Ant*. One sir, that for his loue dares yet do more | 1833 |
| Much more, for what I cannot do for you, | 1853 |
| I hate ingratitude more in a man, | 1873 |
| *To*. A very dishonest paltry boy, and more a coward | 1906 |
| *but ignorance, in which thou art more puzel'd then the \| Aegyptians in | |
| their fogge. | 2029 |
| *man thus abus'd, I am no more madde then you are, | 2033 |
| *Lady: it shall aduantage thee more, then euer the bea- \|ring of Letter | |
| did. | 2096 |
| *Du*. You can foole no more money out of mee at this | 2191 |
| But more of that anon. Take him aside. | 2255 |
| More then I loue these eyes, more then my life, | 2292 |
| More by all mores, then ere I shall loue wife. | 2293 |
| *Heere comes sir *Toby* halting, you shall heare more: but if | 2355 |
| An apple cleft in two, is not more twin | 2388 |

MOREOUER = *1

| | |
|---|---|
| *selfe. She adds moreouer, that you should put your Lord | 664 |

MOREOUR = *1

| | |
|---|---|
| *Ma*. They that adde moreour, hee's drunke nightly \| in your company. | 152 |

MORES = 1

| | |
|---|---|
| More by all mores, then ere I shall loue wife. | 2293 |

MORNING = 2*2

| | |
|---|---|
| *Mar*. Marry and it shall be done to morrow morning | 1626 |
| *Fa*. More matter for a May morning. | 1664 |
| *Clo*. O he's drunke sir *Toby* an houre agone: his eyes \| were set at eight | |
| i'th morning. | 2361 |
| *you, I should haue giuen't you to day morning. But as a | 2454 |

MOROW = *1

| | |
|---|---|
| *Du*. Giue me some Musick; Now good morow frends. | 885 |

148

MORROW = 4*3
*An. And I thought that, I'de forsweare it. Ile ride | home to morrow sir
Toby.                                                                                           202
*An. Faith Ile home to morrow sir Toby, your niece wil                   215
If that the youth will come this way to morrow,                               603
*Ant. To morrow sir, best first go see your Lodging?                      1487
*Mar. Marry and it shall be done to morrow morning                      1626
And I beseech you come againe to morrow.                                    1727
Ol. Well, come againe to morrow: far-thee-well,                            1734
MORTALL = 1*2
*a mortall arbitrement, but nothing of the circumstance | more.      1779
*and he giues me the stucke in with such a mortall motion             1794
He finished indeed his mortall acte                                               2413
MOST = 23*10
Most prouident in perill, binde himselfe,                                          62
One of thy kin has a most weake Pia-mater.                                    409
*Vio. Most radiant, exquisite, and vnmatchable beau- | tie.            465
*Vio. Most certaine, if you are she, you do vsurp your                   482
*We will heare this diuinitie. Now sir, what is your text? | Vio. Most
sweet Ladie.                                                                                    513
An. Most certaine: Let our Catch be, Thou Knaue.                         764
*forehead, and complection, he shall finde himselfe most              851
Of these most briske and giddy-paced times.                                  890
*To. To the gates of Tartar, thou most excellent diuell | of wit.     1209
*Most excellent accomplish'd Lady, the heauens raine O- | dours on you.   1298
*Vio. My matter hath no voice Lady, but to your owne | most pregnant
and vouchsafed eare.                                                                      1301
Vio. My dutie Madam, and most humble seruice.                          1307
To. And crosse garter'd? | *Mar. Most villanously: like a Pedant that
keepes a                                                                                         1453
Most of our City did. Onely my selfe stood out,                            1503
*into a most hideous opinion of his rage, skill, furie, and             1710
*his valour. He is indeede sir, the most skilfull, bloudy, &            1784
And to his image, which me thought did promise | Most venerable
worth, did I deuotion.                                                                     1882
whisper ore a couplet or two of most sage sawes.                         1899
*Fab. A Coward, a most deuout Coward, religious in | it.              1910
*most modest termes, for I am one of those gentle ones,              2018
Mal. Sir Topas, sir Topas. | Tob. My most exquisite sir Topas.    2046
That my most iealious, and too doubtfull soule                             2142
With the most noble bottome of our Fleete,                                   2208
That most ingratefull boy there by your side,                                 2229
Vio. And I most iocund, apt, and willinglie,                                   2288
Then these two creatures. Which is Sebastian? | Ol. Most wonderfull.   2389
I shall haue share in this most happy wracke,                               2432
A most extracting frensie of mine owne                                         2449
Du. Madam, I am most apt t'embrace your offer:                         2486
And made the most notorious gecke and gull,                               2513
This practice hath most shrewdly past vpon thee:                        2522
Most freely I confesse my selfe, and Toby                                    2530
Ol. He hath bene most notoriously abus'd.                                    2549
MOTHER = *1
*am yet so neere the manners of my mother, that vpon the          648
MOTHERS = 1
mothers milke were scarse out of him.                                          456
MOTION = 2*2
No motion of the Liuer, but the Pallat,                                           986

MOTION *cont.*

*To.* Taste your legges sir, put them to motion. 1291
*and he giues me the stucke in with such a mortall motion 1794
*To.* Ile make the motion: stand heere, make a good 1805
MOTIONS = 1
Vnstaid and skittish in all motions else, 903
MOTLEY = *1
*motley in my braine: good *Madona*, giue mee leaue to | proue you a
foole. 349
MOUE = 3
*Ol.* Yet come againe: for thou perhaps mayst moue 1379
you not see you moue him? Let me alone with him. 1632
*To.* If this Letter moue him not, his legges cannot: | Ile giu't him. 1688
MOUNTAINES = 1
Fit for the Mountaines, and the barbarous Caues, 1965
MOURNE = *1
*Clo.* The more foole (Madona) to mourne for your 362
MOURNST = 1
*Clo.* Good Madona, why mournst thou? | *Ol.* Good foole, for my
brothers death. 358
MOUSE = 1
*Clo.* I must catechize you for it Madona, Good my | Mouse of vertue
answer mee. 354
MOUTH = 3*1
*Clo.* Yes by *S.*(aint) Anne, and Ginger shall bee hotte y'th | mouth
too. 813
deliuer thy indignation to him by word of mouth. 826
*But sir, I will deliuer his Challenge by word of mouth; 1707
From the rude seas enrag'd and foamy mouth 2230
MUCH = 22*14
*My verie walke should be a Iigge: I would not so much 237
*Cesario*, you are like to be much aduanc'd, he hath known 252
*Non facit monachum*: that's as much to say, as I weare not 348
*Mar.* Madam, there is at the gate, a young Gentle-|man, much desires
to speake with you. 392
*him to vnderstand so much, and therefore comes to speak 436
*Ol.* A comfortable doctrine, and much may bee saide 515
*Ol.* You might do much: 571
*Seb.* A Lady sir, though it was said shee much resem-|bled 634
She made good view of me, indeed so much, 676
Wherein the pregnant enemie does much. 685
*Mal.* This is much credit to you. 805
*much out of quiet. For Monsieur Maluolio, let me alone 829
Me thought it did releeue my passion much, 888
*Oliuiaes* Father tooke much delight in. He is about the | house. 896
So bigge, to hold so much, they lacke retention. 984
And can digest as much, make no compare 989
Much in our vowes, but little in our loue. 1008
If one should be a prey, how much the better 1343
*and you finde so much blood in his Liuer, as will clog the 1441
And not all loue to see you (though so much 1472
*Ol.* I haue said too much vnto a hart of stone, 1718
*vndertake that with me, which with as much safetie you 1767
*Vio.* I shall bee much bound to you for't: I am one, 1788
not who knowes so much of my mettle. *Exeunt.* 1790
me tell them how much I lacke of a man. 1819
Much more, for what I cannot do for you, 1853

MUCH *cont.*

Out of my leane and low ability | Ile lend you something: my hauing is
not much, — 1861

*Du.* Well, I will be so much a sinner to be a double | dealer: there's
another. — 2185

Hold little faith, though thou hast too much feare. — 2334

They say poore Gentleman, he's much distract. — 2447

*madmans Epistles are no Gospels, so it skilles not much — 2455

*do my selfe much right, or you much shame: thinke of — 2475

*Du.* This sauours not much of distraction. — 2480

So much against the mettle of your sex, — 2488

Though I confesse much like the Charracter: — 2516

MURDROUS = 1

A murdrous guilt shewes not it selfe more soone, — 1363

MURMURE = 1

And then 'twas fresh in murmure (as you know — 82

MURTHER = *1

*Ant.* If you will not murther me for my loue, let mee | be your seruant. — 643

MURTHERER = *1

*Schoole i'th Church: I haue dogg'd him like his murthe-|rer. — 1455

MUSICK = *2

*Du.* Giue me some Musick; Now good morow frends. — 885

*Vio.* Saue thee Friend and thy Musick: dost thou liue | by thy Tabor? — 1215

MUSICKE = 6

*Duke.* | If Musicke be the food of Loue, play on, — 4

And speake to him in many sorts of Musicke, — 110

*Du.* Seeke him out, and play the tune the while. | *Musicke playes.* — 898

*Clo.* Are you ready Sir? | *Duke.* I prethee sing. *Musicke.* — 939

I had rather heare you, to solicit that, | Then Musicke from the
spheares. — 1322

It is as fat and fulsome to mine eare | As howling after Musicke. — 2264

MUST = 16*13

*Mar.* By my troth sir *Toby*, you must come in earlyer — 122

*Ma.* I, but you must confine your selfe within the | modest limits of
order. — 126

*Clo.* I must catechize you for it Madona, Good my | Mouse of vertue
answer mee. — 354

What is decreed, must be: and be this so. | *Finis, Actus primus.* — 609

*the rather to expresse my selfe: you must know of mee — 625

O time, thou must vntangle this, not I, — 697

*Mal. Sir Toby,* I must be round with you. My Lady — 793

*To.* Farewell deere heart, since I must needs be gone. — 799

*Vio.* Sooth but you must. — 976

You tel her so: Must she not then be answer'd? | *Du.* There is no
womans sides — 980

the Trowt, that must be caught with tickling. *Exit* — 1038

*To.* What, what? | *Mal.* You must amend your drunkennesse. | *To.* Out
scab. — 1087

*man must know.* No man must know. What followes? — 1111

The numbers alter'd: No man must know, — 1112

when the image of it leaues him, he must run mad. — 1198

He must obserue their mood on whom he iests, | The quality of persons,
and the time: — 1274

*Vio.* And he is yours, and his must needs be yours: — 1313

Vnder your hard construction must I sit, — 1329

*Fab.* You must needes yeelde your reason, Sir An-|drew? — 1385

*And.* And't be any way, it must be with Valour, for — 1410

MUST *cont.*

*Mal.* Ah ha, does she so? | *To.* Go too, go too: peace, peace, wee must
deale        1617

*starke naked: for meddle you must that's certain, or for-|sweare to
weare iron about you.        1769

*Ant.* I must obey. This comes with seeking you:        1849

*Ant.* I must entreat of you some of that money.        1857

*To.* What, what? Nay then I must haue an Ounce or | two of this
malapert blood from you.        1959

I must haue done no lesse with wit and safety.        2375

*Ladyship will haue it as it ought to bee, you must allow | *Vox.*        2462

You must not now denie it is your hand,        2501

MUTE = 1

*Cap.* Be you his Eunuch, and your Mute Ile bee,        114

MUTTON = 1

*To.* And I can cut the Mutton too't.        230

MUTUALL = 1

Confirm'd by mutuall ioynder of your hands,        2319

MY *see also* o'my *l.*9 20 27 30 54 *57 69 78 95 105 107 113 115 *119 *122
*123 *128 *133 *154 *155 *157 167 169 *173 182 189 *192 200 204 210
*211 *226 *237 *254 260 263 268 *273 274 275 276 279 288 292 294
*298 299 *323 *349 *354 359 398 457 458 460 *467 *474 476 *478 481
*484 *485 486 *492 505 *509 *524 *537 *538 544 *550 557 563 573 581
583 586 607 *615 *616 *618 *621 *625 *626 *627 *628 632 *643 *647
*648 *663 675 681 690 694 *704 *717 *720 *728 769 *773 *775 *786
*789 *793 *817 *828 832 846 *852 856 *858 860 *864 888 *895 909 916
924 *946 947 949 951 *953 968 973 983 996 1000 1009 1010 1015 1024
1030 *1043 1061 *1063 *1069 *1070 *1074 *1076 *1081 *1085 *1101
*1105 *1107 *1117 1118 *1121 *1126 1134 *1148 *1149 *1168 *1170
*1171 *1172 *1174 *1176 *1178 *1180 *1183 1191 *1194 *1202 *1220
*1230 *1233 *1241 *1253 *1259 *1260 *1268 *1270 *1287 1290 *1292
1293 *1301 1306 1307 1310 1328 1336 1353 1368 1373 1378 *1406 *1415
*1460 1467 1470 1477 1480 1484 1503 1507 1526 *1548 1561 *1583
*1584 1586 *1599 *1604 *1612 *1615 *1627 *1635 1642 *1658 *1675
*1685 *1691 *1704 1720 1724 *1725 *1730 1735 *1746 *1773 1774 1776
1790 1804 1828 *1841 1851 1852 1854 1861 1862 1863 1864 1866 1867
1900 1901 1902 *1924 *1926 *1929 *1930 *1933 *1938 *1946 *1954 1966
1971 1979 *1989 *2009 2047 *2054 2056 2060 *2066 2073 2078 *2091
*2095 2123 2128 2142 2146 2159 2163 *2165 2166 *2171 *2172 *2175
*2177 2178 *2193 *2197 2217 2233 2235 *2247 *2256 2261 2262 2263
2270 *2272 2277 2279 2285 2292 2295 2301 2305 2323 2324 2332 *2339
2345 *2346 2374 2382 2392 2397 2398 2406 2408 2412 2414 2416 2421
2423 2428 2442 2444 2450 *2466 *2472 *2475 *2476 2477 *2482 2485
2491 2496 2515 2530 2572 = 192*164

MYSELFE *see* selfe

NAKED = *1

*starke naked: for meddle you must that's certain, or for-|sweare to
weare iron about you.        1769

NAMD = 1

*Vio.* He nam'd *Sebastian*: I my brother know        1900

NAME = 9*6

*Vio.* Who gouernes heere? | *Cap.* A noble Duke in nature, as in name.        74

*Vio.* What is his name? | *Cap.* Orsino.        76

*Vio.* Orsino: I haue heard my father name him.        78

*Ma.* Good Mistris accost, I desire better acquaintance | *Ma.* My name
is *Mary* sir.        168

Hallow your name to the reuerberate hilles,        566

NAME *cont.*
\*then *Antonio*, my name is *Sebastian* (which I call'd *Rodo-*|*rigo*) 626
\*in the name of ieasting, lye thou there: for heere comes 1037
*Mal. M. Maluolio, M.* why that begins my name. 1134
\*one of these Letters are in my name. Soft, here fol-|lowes 1148
\**Clo.* I would therefore my sister had had no name Sir. 1230
*Ol.* What is your name? 1308
*Vio. Cesario* is your seruants name, faire Princesse. 1309
\**To.* Which way is hee in the name of sanctity. If all 1607
\*speake with her: nor your name is not Master *Cesario*, 1925
What Countreyman? What name? What Parentage? | *Vio.* Of *Messaline*:
*Sebastian* was my Father, 2396
NAMES = 1\*1
*Vio.* Why man? | \**Clo.* Why sir, her names a word, and to dallie with 1231
*Ant. Orsino*: Noble sir, | Be pleas'd that I shake off these names you
giue mee: 2224
NAPPE = \*1
\*you say sir, let your bounty take a nappe, I will awake it | anon. *Exit* 2198
NATURALL = 2\*1
\**Ma.* He hath indeed, almost naturall: for besides that 145
\*do I too: he does it with a better grace, but I do it more | naturall. 781
A naturall Perspectiue, that is, and is not. 2381
NATURE = 10\*1
*Vio.* Who gouernes heere? | *Cap.* A noble Duke in nature, as in name. 74
And though that nature, with a beauteous wall 100
without booke, & hath all the good gifts of nature. 144
\**To.* Past question, for thou seest it will not coole my | (nature 211
And in dimension, and the shape of nature, 554
That nature prankes her in, attracts my soule. 973
*Ant.* Th'offence is not of such a bloody nature, 1498
\*nature the wrongs are thou hast done him, I knowe not: 1740
In Nature, there's no blemish but the minde: 1887
Nor can there be that Deity in my nature 2392
But Nature to her bias drew in that. 2426
NATURES = 1
Natures owne sweet, and cunning hand laid on: 532
NAUGHT *see* nought
NAY = 7\*11
\**Ma.* Nay, either tell me where thou hast bin, or I will 297
\**And.* Nay by my troth I know not: but I know, to | be vp late, is to be
vp late. 704
*Mar.* Nay good Sir *Toby*. 800
*Fab.* Nay Ile come: if I loose a scruple of this sport, 1019
*Fab.* Nay patience, or we breake the sinewes of our | plot? 1090
\**Mal. M.O.A.I.* doth sway my life. Nay but first 1121
*Ma.* Nay but say true, do's it worke vpon him? | *To.* Like Aqua vite
with a Midwife. 1199
\**Vio.* Nay that's certaine: they that dally nicely with 1228
\**Vio.* Nay, and thou passe vpon me, Ile no more with | thee. Hold
there's expences for thee. 1255
\**Mar.* Nay pursue him now, least the deuice take ayre, | and taint. 1653
*And.* Nay let me alone for swearing. *Exit* 1700
*To.* Nay, if you be an vndertaker, I am for you. 1835
\**An.* Nay let him alone, Ile go another way to worke 1949
\**To.* What, what? Nay then I must haue an Ounce or | two of this
malapert blood from you. 1959
\**Ol.* Nay come I prethee, would thoud'st be rul'd by me 1981

NAY *cont.*
  *\*Mar.* Nay, I prethee put on this gown, & this beard,     1986
  *Clo.* Nay I am for all waters.     2048
  *\*Clo.* Nay, Ile nere beleeue a madman till I see his brains     2101
NAYLES = 1
  Like a mad lad, paire thy nayles dad,     2111
NAYWORD = *1
  *with him: If I do not gull him into a nayword, and make     830
NECESSITIE = 1
  What will you do: now my necessitie     1851
NECESSITY = *1
  *heere in necessity, and denying him: and for his coward-|ship aske
  *Fabian.*     1908
NECKE = 1*1
  *with lids to them: Item, one necke, one chin, & so forth.     540
  *To.* Wilt thou set thy foote o'my necke.     1192
NEECE = 1*14
  *\*Sir To.* What a plague meanes my Neece to take the     119
  *\*To.* With drinking healths to my Neece: Ile drinke     154
  *drinke to my Neece, till his braines turne o'th toe, like a     157
  *your Neece, on a forgotten matter wee can hardly make | distinction of
  our hands.     853
  *that they come from my Neece, and that shee's in loue | with him.     858
  *\*An.* If I cannot recouer your Neece, I am a foule way | out.     876
  me on your Neece, giue me this prerogatiue of speech.     1086
  *\*To.* Will you incounter the house, my Neece is desi-|rous     1287
  *\*Vio.* I am bound to your Neece sir, I meane she is the | list of my
  voyage.     1289
  *\*And.* Marry I saw your Neece do more fauours to the     1386
  *hurt him in eleuen places, my Neece shall take note of it,     1415
  *My Neece is already in the beleefe that he's mad: we may     1658
  *Lord and my Neece, confirmes no lesse. Therefore, this     1704
  *\*Fab.* Heere he comes with your Neece, giue them way     1714
  *that neuer saw pen and inke, very wittily sayd to a Neece     1999
NEECES = 1
  *And.* What's that? | *To.* My Neeces Chamber-maid.     166
NEEDE = 1*1
  *\*To.* Let's to bed knight: Thou hadst neede send for | more money.     874
  In a trice, like to the old vice, | your neede to sustaine.     2107
NEEDES = *1
  *\*Fab.* You must needes yeelde your reason, Sir *An-|drew?*     1385
NEEDS = 2*1
  *\*Clo.* Let her hang me: hee that is well hang'de in this | world, needs to
  feare no colours.     300
  *\*To.* Farewell deere heart, since I must needs be gone.     799
  *Vio.* And he is yours, and his must needs be yours:     1313
NEER = *1
  *begger dwell neer him: or the Church stands by thy Ta-|bor,     1223
NEERE = 1*3
  *am yet so neere the manners of my mother, that vpon the     648
  *thus neere, that should shee fancie, it should bee one of     1042
  *Fa.* Now is the Woodcocke neere the gin.     1098
  *\*Mal.* Oh ho, do you come neere me now: no worse     1587
NEGATIUES = *1
  *your foure negatiues make your two affirmatiues, why     2174
NEGLIGENCE = *2
  *\*Vio.* You either feare his humour, or my negligence,     254

NEGLIGENCE *cont.*
 *my offence to him is: it is something of my negligence, | nothing of my
 purpose. 1773
NEGOTIATE = *1
 *negotiate with my face: you are now out of your Text: 524
NEITHER = 1*1
 *degree, neither in estate, yeares, nor wit: I haue heard her 219
 *An.* Nor I neither. 1190
NEPHEW = 1
 When your yong Nephew *Titus* lost his legge; 2214
NERE = 1*1
 Where manners nere were preach'd: out of my sight. 1966
 *Clo.* Nay, Ile nere beleeue a madman till I see his brains 2101
NEUER *see also* nere = 16*13
 *To.* And thou let part so Sir *Andrew*, would thou | mightst neuer draw
 sword agen. 176
 *And.* And you part so mistris, I would I might neuer 178
 *An.* Neuer in your life I thinke, vnlesse you see Ca- | narie 196
 As it is spoke, she neuer will admit me. 270
 *for I neuer saw her. I would bee loath to cast away my 467
 *thing more, that you be neuer so hardie to come againe 666
 *Clo.* How now my harts: Did you neuer see the Pic- | ture of we three? 717
 *Clo.* I shall neuer begin if I hold my peace. 769
 bid him turne you out of doores, neuer trust me. 774
 *To.* But I will neuer dye. 803
 *An.* If I do not, neuer trust me, take it how you will. 880
 *Sad true louer neuer find my graue, to weepe there.* 953
 *Du.* And what's her history? | *Vio.* A blanke my Lord: she neuer told
 her loue, 999
 *Ol.* My seruant sir? 'Twas neuer merry world, 1310
 I bad you neuer speake againe of him; 1320
 And that no woman has, nor neuer none 1375
 And so adieu good Madam, neuer more, 1377
 *To.* Neuer trust me then: and by all meanes stirre on 1438
 *To.* Do, cuffe him soundly, but neuer draw thy sword 1913
 *that neuer saw pen and inke, very wittily sayd to a Neece 1999
 *Mal.* Sir *Topas*, neuer was man thus wronged, good 2014
 *Ignorance were as darke as hell; and I say there was ne- | uer 2032
 *Mall.* Foole, there was neuer man so notoriouslie a- | bus'd: 2072
 *Anthonio* neuer yet was Theefe, or Pyrate, 2226
 Where thou, and I (henceforth) may neuer meet. 2331
 *Vio.* Why do you speake to me, I neuer hurt you: 2349
 *Seb.* Do I stand there? I neuer had a brother: 2391
 Thou neuer should'st loue woman like to me. 2434
 *By swaggering could I neuer thriue, | for the raine, &c.* 2570
NEW = *2
 *iests, fire-new from the mint, you should haue bangd 1402
 *then is in the new Mappe, with the augmentation of the 1458
NEWES = 1
 Ere since pursue me. How now what newes from her? 28
NEWLY = 1
 Hath newly past, betweene this youth, and me. 2317
NEXT = *1
 *Clo.* Now Ioue in his next commodity of hayre, send | thee a beard. 1257
NEYTHER = *2
 *Ma.* You are resolute then? | *Clo.* Not so neyther, but I am resolu'd on
 two points 316

NEYTHER _cont._
*nor this is not my nose neyther: Nothing that is so, is so.     1926
NICELY = *1
*_Vio._ Nay that's certaine: they that dally nicely with     1228
NIECE _see also_ neece = *2
*_An._ Faith Ile home to morrow sir _Toby_, your niece wil     215
*he were, for I am now so farre in offence with my Niece,     2054
NIGGARDLY = *1
*_To._ Wouldst thou not be glad to haue the niggard- | ly     1021
NIGHT = 8*6
*knight that you brought in one night here, to be hir woer     134
And sing them lowd euen in the dead of night:     565
*in very gracious fooling last night, when thou spok'st of     723
*like Tinkers at this time of night? Do yee make an Ale- | house     788
*_Mar._ Sweet Sir Toby be patient for to night: Since     827
*obserue his construction of it: For this night to bed, and     867
_To._ Good night _Penthisilea._     869
That old and Anticke song we heard last night;     887
_Du._ O fellow come, the song we had last night:     932
*Then loue that would seeme hid: Loues night, is noone.     1364
_Seb._ I am not weary, and 'tis long to night     1488
Both day and night did we keepe companie.     2249
As doth that Orbed Continent, the fire, | That seuers day from night.     2437
Twelfe Night, Or what you will.     2581
NIGHTINGALES = 1
Yes Nightingales answere Dawes.     1558
NIGHTLY = *1
*_Ma._ They that adde moreour, hee's drunke nightly | in your company.     152
NIGHTS = *1
*a nights: your Cosin, my Lady, takes great exceptions | to your ill
houres.     123
NIGHT-OWLE = *1
*rowze the night-Owle in a Catch, that will drawe three     759
NO _l._11 97 98 *128 *197 201 *247 253 256 262 301 305 *323 333 *338
*343 *372 373 *377 381 *385 *387 449 *470 *478 *498 *503 *504 *520
535 559 576 580 *613 *615 *621 *674 *728 729 743 751 *787 791 809
812 *838 947 955 981 983 986 989 1015 *1110 *1111 1112 *1127 *1137
*1187 1217 *1219 *1230 *1245 *1246 *1255 *1301 1339 1370 1375 1383
*1416 1419 *1422 1429 *1443 1449 1469 1481 *1531 *1587 *1601 *1602
*1633 *1643 1673 *1704 *1705 1726 *1745 *1760 *1764 *1813 *1821
1846 1847 1850 1887 *1923 1952 *2028 *2033 *2040 2075 2084 2124
2168 *2177 *2191 2248 2305 2375 *2455 *2461 2499 2527 = 62*62
NOAH = 1
*_To._ And they haue beene grand Iurie men, since before | _Noah_ was a
Saylor.     1396
NOB = 1
*can be none, but by pangs of death and sepulcher: Hob, | nob, is his
word: giu't or take't.     1757
NOBLE = 9
_Vio._ Who gouernes heere? | _Cap._ A noble Duke in nature, as in name.     74
_Vio._ Sure my Noble Lord,     268
Yet I suppose him vertuous, know him noble,     551
Tell her my loue, more noble then the world     968
_Fab._ Heere comes my noble gull catcher.     1191
With the most noble bottome of our Fleete,     2208
_Ant._ Orsino: Noble sir, | Be pleas'd that I shake off these names you
giue mee:     2224

NOBLE *cont.*
I was preseru'd to serue this Noble Count: 2422
*Du.* Be not amaz'd, right noble is his blood: 2430
NOBLEST = 1
*Du.* Why so I do, the Noblest that I haue: 23
NOBLY = 1*1
*Mal.* I thinke nobly of the soule, and no way aproue | his opinion. 2040
That sometime sauours nobly) but heare me this: 2276
NON *l.*\*348 = *1
NONE = 9*6
*not be seene, or if she be it's four to one, she'l none of me: 216
*To.* Shee'l none o'th Count, she'l not match aboue hir 218
*Ma.* Make that good. | *Clo.* He shall see none to feare. 302
Would I, or not: tell him, Ile none of it. 600
*into a desperate assurance, she will none of him. And one 665
*Vio.* She tooke the Ring of me, Ile none of it. 669
None of my Lords Ring? Why he sent her none; 681
*Clo.* Troth sir, I can yeeld you none without wordes, 1236
*Which you knew none of yours. What might you think? 1331
And that no woman has, nor neuer none 1375
*can be none, but by pangs of death and sepulcher: Hob, | nob, is his
word: giu't or take't. 1757
*Vio.* I know of none, 1871
None can be call'd deform'd, but the vnkinde. 1888
You can say none of this. Well, grant it then, 2504
NON-PAREIL = 1
Could be but recompenc'd, though you were crown'd | The non-pareil
of beautie. 545
NON-REGARDANCE = 1
Since you to non-regardance cast my faith, 2277
NOONE = *1
*Then loue that would seeme hid: Loues night, is noone. 1364
NOR *l.*\*219 *387 *451 602 *613 *787 791 1190 1368 1375 *1599 *1672
1872 *1924 *1925 *1926 *1992 2392 2428 2527 = 10*11
NORTH = *2
*the North of my Ladies opinion, where you will hang 1406
*and the cleere stores toward the South north, are 2023
NOSE = 2*2
*Clo.* I did impeticos thy gratillity: for *Maluolios* nose 727
*To.* To heare by the nose, it is dulcet in contagion. 757
*To.* Excellent, I smell a deuice. | *An.* I hau't in my nose too. 855
*nor this is not my nose neyther: Nothing that is so, is so. 1926
NOT *l.*12 30 33 *55 73 93 98 115 *130 *156 *173 181 *188 *205 *211 212
*216 *218 *226 *235 *237 *244 265 279 283 *298 *312 *317 *332 *337
*342 *348 366 *372 *396 *402 *422 441 *451 *479 481 *483 *494 *495
*526 *536 560 568 581 589 600 601 602 606 608 *613 *623 *636 *638
*643 *645 *646 *658 *672 675 688 697 *701 *704 *709 738 748 753 767
*773 *776 *777 *797 808 809 *818 *830 *831 862 *878 *880 *892 911
*915 948 950 969 980 1005 1011 *1021 *1026 1028 *1083 *1110 *1135
*1146 *1150 *1161 *1162 *1165 *1168 *1178 *1183 *1241 *1242 1244
*1248 *1260 1262 *1267 *1315 1332 1335 1339 1347 1355 1357 1363
1369 1383 *1424 1437 *1459 1467 1470 1472 1488 1493 1498 1506 1507
1515 *1548 1561 1576 *1585 *1599 1604 *1615 1624 *1627 *1631 1632
1634 *1637 *1643 *1646 *1672 *1676 1688 *1701 1726 *1740 *1766 1790
*1792 1798 1799 1817 *1824 1862 1867 1895 1914 *1919 *1923 *1924
*1925 *1926 1928 *1946 *1954 1967 1969 1974 1975 *1991 *2015 *2026
2050 *2085 *2098 2100 2118 2119 2131 2137 2157 *2179 *2196 2219

NOT *cont.*
2239 2244 2248 *2256 2258 2273 2305 2308 2328 2333 2351 *2356 2381
2388 2417 2430 *2455 *2474 2480 2501 2503 2515 2529 *2544 *2546
2551 2555 = 116*113
NOTABLE = 3*2

| | |
|---|---:|
| my reuenge finde notable cause to worke. | 846 |
| Rascally sheepe-biter, come by some notable shame? | 1022 |
| *cannot but turn him into a notable contempt: if you wil \| see it follow me. | 1207 |
| *set vpon *Ague-cheeke* a notable report of valor, and driue | 1708 |
| *Du*. Notable Pyrate, thou salt-water Theefe, | 2220 |

NOTE = 3*3

| | |
|---|---:|
| *hurt him in eleuen places, my Neece shall take note of it, | 1415 |
| I did some seruice, of such note indeede, | 1495 |
| *tongue, in the habite of some Sir of note, and so foorth. | 1596 |
| *Fa*. A good note, that keepes you from the blow of y \| (Law | 1674 |
| Whiles you are willing it shall come to note, | 2144 |
| That they may fairely note this acte of mine. *Exeunt*. \| *Finis Actus Quartus*. | 2150 |

NOTHING = 8*12

| | |
|---|---:|
| *in an allow'd foole, though he do nothing but rayle; | 386 |
| *nor no rayling, in a knowne discreet man, though hee do \| nothing but reproue. | 387 |
| *Ol*. Fetch him off I pray you, he speakes nothing but | 400 |
| *she's nothing ally'd to your disorders. If you can | 795 |
| makes a good voyage of nothing. Farewell. *Exit* | 965 |
| *Vio*. I warrant thou art a merry fellow, and car'st for \| nothing. | 1239 |
| *sir, I do not care for you: if that be to care for no-\|thing | 1242 |
| You'l nothing Madam to my Lord, by me: | 1353 |
| *Mar*. No Madam, he does nothing but smile: your La-\|dyship | 1531 |
| *can be saide? Nothing that can be, can come betweene | 1603 |
| *Vio*. Nothing but this, your true loue for my master. | 1730 |
| *my offence to him is: it is something of my negligence, \| nothing of my purpose. | 1773 |
| *a mortall arbitrement, but nothing of the circumstance \| more. | 1779 |
| *Fab*. Nothing of that wonderfull promise to read him | 1782 |
| *To*. I dare lay any money, twill be nothing yet. *Exit* | 1916 |
| *nor this is not my nose neyther: Nothing that is so, is so. | 1926 |
| man? Talkest thou nothing but of Ladies? \| *Tob*. Well said M.(aster) Parson. | 2012 |
| *for nothing, and that that I did, I was set on to do't by sir \| *Toby*. | 2347 |
| me: I thinke you set nothing by a bloody Coxecombe. | 2354 |
| *Vio*. If nothing lets to make vs happie both, | 2415 |

NOTORIOUS = 2

| | |
|---|---:|
| *Mal*. Madam, you haue done me wrong, \| Notorious wrong. | 2497 |
| And made the most notorious gecke and gull, | 2513 |

NOTORIOUSLIE = *1

| | |
|---|---:|
| *Mall*. Foole, there was neuer man so notoriouslie a-\|bus'd: | 2072 |

NOTORIOUSLY = 1

| | |
|---|---:|
| *Ol*. He hath bene most notoriously abus'd. | 2549 |

NOTWITHSTANDING = 1

| | |
|---|---:|
| That notwithstanding thy capacitie, | 14 |

NOUGHT = 1

| | |
|---|---:|
| Receiueth as the Sea. Nought enters there, | 15 |

NOW = 39*32

| | |
|---|---:|
| 'Tis not so sweet now, as it was before. | 12 |
| Ere since pursue me. How now what newes from her? | 28 |

NOW *cont.*

| | |
|---|---:|
| He was a Batchellor then. \| *Cap.* And so is now, or was so very late: | 79 |
| *And.* Sir *Toby Belch.* How now sir *Toby Belch?* \| *To.* Sweet sir *Andrew.* | 161 |
| *\*Ma.* Now sir, thought is free: I pray you bring your | 183 |
| *\*Ma.* I Sir, I haue them at my fingers ends: marry now | 192 |
| *\*Looke you now, he's out of his gard already: vnles you | 378 |
| *\*Clo.* Now Mercury indue thee with leasing, for thou \| speak'st well of | |
| fooles. | 389 |
| *\*Now you see sir, how your fooling growes old, & peo-\|ple dislike it. | 404 |
| *\*To.* 'Tis a Gentleman heere. A plague o'these pickle \| herring: How | |
| now Sot. | 414 |
| *\*We will heare this diuinitie. Now sir, what is your text? \| *Vio.* Most | |
| sweet Ladie. | 513 |
| *\*negotiate with my face: you are now out of your Text: | 524 |
| Vnlesse the Master were the man. How now? | 590 |
| *\*Mal.* Were not you eu'n now, with the Countesse *O-*\|*liuia?* | 658 |
| *\*Vio.* Euen now sir, on a moderate pace, I haue since a-\|riu'd but | |
| hither. | 660 |
| As I am woman (now alas the day) | 695 |
| *\*Clo.* How now my harts: Did you neuer see the Pic-\|ture of we three? | 717 |
| *To.* Welcome asse, now let's haue a catch. | 719 |
| *\*An.* Excellent: Why this is the best fooling, when \| all is done. Now a | |
| song. | 730 |
| *An.* And your horse now would make him an Asse. | 861 |
| to go to bed now: Come knight, come knight. *Exeunt* | 882 |
| *\*Du.* Giue me some Musick; Now good morow frends. | 885 |
| Now good *Cesario*, but that peece of song, | 886 |
| *Du.* Giue me now leaue, to leaue thee. | 959 |
| *\*Clo.* Now the melancholly God protect thee, and the | 960 |
| *To.* Heere comes the little villaine: How now my \| Mettle of India? | 1030 |
| *\*Fa.* O peace, now he's deepely in: looke how imagi-\|nation blowes | |
| him. | 1058 |
| *To.* Boltes and shackles. \| *Fa.* Oh peace, peace, peace, now, now. | 1072 |
| *Fa.* Now is the Woodcocke neere the gin. | 1098 |
| *To.* O I, make vp that, he is now at a cold sent. | 1131 |
| *\*deuise, the very man. I do not now foole my selfe, to let | 1168 |
| *\*vpon her, which will now be so vnsuteable to her dispo-\|sition, | 1205 |
| *\*Clo.* Now Ioue in his next commodity of hayre, send \| thee a beard. | 1257 |
| I wish it might, for now I am your foole. | 1360 |
| That heart which now abhorres, to like his loue. *Exeunt* | 1380 |
| *And.* As plaine as I see you now. | 1390 |
| *\*you let time wash off, and you are now sayld into | 1405 |
| How now *Maluolio?* \| *Mal.* Sweet Lady, ho, ho. | 1538 |
| *\*Mal.* Oh ho, do you come neere me now: no worse | 1587 |
| *\*thankefull. And when she went away now, let this Fel-\|low | 1598 |
| *Mal.* How now mistris? \| *Mar.* Oh Lord. | 1629 |
| *\*To.* Why how now my bawcock? how dost y chuck? \| *Mal.* Sir. | 1635 |
| *\*Fa.* If this were plaid vpon a stage now, I could con-\|demne it as an | |
| improbable fiction. | 1649 |
| *\*Mar.* Nay pursue him now, least the deuice take ayre, \| and taint. | 1653 |
| *\*Mar.* You may haue verie fit occasion for't: he is now | 1690 |
| *\*To.* Now will not I deliuer his Letter: for the behaui-\|our | 1701 |
| *To.* I but he will not now be pacified. | 1799 |
| *\*quarrell, and hee findes that now scarse to bee worth tal-\|king | 1815 |
| Though now you haue no sea-cap on your head: | 1847 |
| What will you do: now my necessitie | 1851 |
| *Ant.* Will you deny me now, | 1865 |

NOW *cont.*

| | |
|---|---|
| Proue true imagination, oh proue true, \| That I deere brother, be now tane for you. | 1896 |
| *great man, and now applyes it to a foole. Vent my fol-\|ly: | 1930 |
| *Cockney: I prethee now vngird thy strangenes, and tell | 1932 |
| *And. Now sir, haue I met you again: ther's for you. | 1942 |
| *Seb. I would be free from thee. What wouldst y now? | 1957 |
| *he were, for I am now so farre in offence with my Niece, | 2054 |
| His councell now might do me golden seruice, | 2122 |
| Now go with me, and with this holy man | 2138 |
| Fab. Now as thou lou'st me, let me see his Letter. | 2154 |
| *now my foes tell me plainly, I am an Asse: so that by my | 2171 |
| *Du. Heere comes the Countesse, now heauen walkes \| on earth: | 2251 |
| To keepe in darkenesse, what occasion now | 2315 |
| Du. How now Gentleman? how ist with you? | 2358 |
| Is now in durance, at *Maluolio's* suite, | 2443 |
| and yet alas, now I remember me, | 2446 |
| Ol. How now, art thou mad? \| *Clo. No Madam, I do but reade madnesse: and your | 2460 |
| Du. Is this the Madman? \| Ol. I my Lord, this same: How now *Maluolio*? | 2495 |
| You must not now denie it is your hand, | 2501 |
| And now I do bethinke me, it was shee | 2518 |

NUMBER = 2

| | |
|---|---|
| When you, and those poore number saued with you, | 60 |
| Seb. Belike you slew great number of his people. | 1497 |

NUMBERS = 1

| | |
|---|---|
| The numbers alter'd: No man must know, | 1112 |

NUMBRED = 1

| | |
|---|---|
| Vio. And dide that day when *Viola* from her birth \| Had numbred thirteene yeares. | 2410 |

NUNTIOS = 1

| | |
|---|---|
| Then in a Nuntio's of more graue aspect. | 278 |

O *l.9* 13 24 39 *57 92 *194 *207 274 *382 *520 *536 544 568 642 688 697 740 741 783 809 *835 863 932 *946 *952 *1058 1062 1067 1131 1141 1319 1342 1361 1837 1983 2182 2312 2326 2333 *2361 2382 2412 = 32*11, 3*2

| | |
|---|---|
| Mar. For the loue o'God peace. | 784 |
| *To. Out o'tune sir, ye lye: Art any more then a Stew-\|ard? | 810 |
| o'fauour with my Lady, about a Beare-baiting heere. | 1024 |
| *that suffers vnder probation: A. should follow, but O. \| does. | 1138 |
| Fa. And O shall end, I hope. \| To. I, or Ile cudgell him, and make him cry O. | 1140 |

OATH = 1*2

| | |
|---|---|
| *it comes to passe oft, that a terrible oath, with a swagge-\|ring | 1696 |
| *oath sake: marrie hee hath better bethought him of his | 1814 |
| And. Pray God he keepe his oath. | 1826 |

OATHES = *1

| | |
|---|---|
| *Fab. I will proue it legitimate sir, vpon the Oathes of \| iudgement, and reason. | 1394 |

OBEDIENT = 1*1

| | |
|---|---|
| *Mal. Seauen of my people with an obedient start, | 1074 |
| And acting this in an obedient hope, | 2510 |

OBEY = 2*1

| | |
|---|---|
| *He does obey euery point of the Letter that I dropt, | 1456 |
| Ant. I must obey. This comes with seeking you: | 1849 |
| and let your flesh and blood obey it. | 2184 |

OBSCURE = *1
*To*. What wilt thou do? | *\*Mar*. I will drop in his way some obscure
Epistles of     847
OBSERUE = 1*2
*obserue his construction of it: For this night to bed, and     867
*houre: obserue him for the loue of Mockerie: for I know     1035
He must obserue their mood on whom he iests, | The quality of persons,
and the time:     1274
OBSTACLE = *1
*obstacle, no incredulous or vnsafe circumstance: What     1602
OBSTRUCTION = 1*2
*euident to any formall capacitie. There is no obstruction     1127
This does make some obstruction in the blood:     1542
*as lustrous as Ebony: and yet complainest thou of ob-|struction?     2024
OCCASION = 3*3
Till I had made mine owne occasion mellow | What my estate is.     94
*laugh and minister occasion to him, he is gag'd. I protest     379
*least occasion more, mine eyes will tell tales of me: I am     649
*Ol*. Smil'st thou? I sent for thee vpon a sad occasion.     1540
*\*Mar*. You may haue verie fit occasion for't: he is now     1690
To keepe in darkenesse, what occasion now     2315
OCCURRENCE = 1
All the occurrence of my fortune since     2423
ODDS = *1
*Du*. My Gentleman *Cesario*? | *\*And*. Odd's lifelings heere he is: you
broke my head     2345
ODOUR = 1
Stealing, and giuing Odour. Enough, no more,     11
ODOURS = *3
*Most excellent accomplish'd Lady, the heauens raine O-|dours on you.     1298
*\*And*. That youth's a rare Courtier, raine odours, wel.     1300
*\*And*. Odours, pregnant, and vouchsafed: Ile get 'em | all three already.     1303
OF *see also* a, o'man, o'me, o'mine, o'my, o'that, o'th, o'these, = 228*184
OFF *l*.214 *400 *1167 *1405 1483 *1612 1613 *1697 2225 = 4*5
OFFENCE = 3*2
*Ant*. Th'offence is not of such a bloody nature,     1498
any image of offence done to any man.     1747
*my offence to him is: it is something of my negligence, | nothing of my
purpose.     1773
Haue done offence, I take the fault on me:     1830
*he were, for I am now so farre in offence with my Niece,     2054
OFFEND = 1
If you offend him, I for him defie you.     1831
OFFENDED = 2
Be not offended, deere *Cesario*:     1967
I do perceiue it hath offended you:     2377
OFFENDING = 1
With eye-offending brine: all this to season     36
OFFER = 1
*Du*. Madam, I am most apt t'embrace your offer:     2486
OFFICE = 1*2
*when the curtesie of it is so fearefull. Speake your office.     502
*me this courteous office, as to know of the Knight what     1772
1.*Off*. This is the man, do thy Office.     1843
*OFFICER see* 1.*Off*., 1.*Offi*., 2.*Off*.
OFFICERS = 3*1
*\*Mal*. Calling my Officers about me, in my branch'd     1063

OFFICERS *cont.*

| | |
|---|---|
| *Enter Officers.* | 1836 |
| *Fab.* O good sir *Toby* hold: heere come the Officers. | 1837 |
| *Enter Anthonio and Officers.* | 2200 |

OFFRINGS = 1

| | |
|---|---|
| My soule the faithfull'st offrings haue breath'd out | 2270 |

OFT = 4*4

| | |
|---|---|
| Doth oft close in pollution: yet of thee | 101 |
| *those wits that thinke they haue thee, doe very oft proue | 327 |
| *Foole should be as oft with your Master, as with my Mi- \| stris: | 1253 |
| *Vio.* No not a grize: for tis a vulgar proofe \| That verie oft we pitty enemies. | 1339 |
| And thankes: and euer oft good turnes, | 1482 |
| *For youth is bought more oft, then begg'd, or borrow'd. | 1524 |
| *Ol.* God comfort thee: Why dost thou smile so, and \| kisse thy hand so oft? | 1554 |
| *it comes to passe oft, that a terrible oath, with a swagge- \| ring | 1696 |

OFTEN = 1

| | |
|---|---|
| Vnguided, and vnfriended, often proue \| Rough, and vnhospitable. My willing loue, | 1476 |

OH *see also* O *l.* *1047 1073 *1099 *1587 1630 1877 1885 1896 1904 = 6*3

OL = 94*23

OLD = 8*3

| | |
|---|---|
| *the degree of my betters, & yet I will not compare with \| an old man. | 226 |
| *Now you see sir, how your fooling growes old, & peo- \|ple dislike it. | 404 |
| *Mal.* Not yet old enough for a man, nor yong enough | 451 |
| That old and Anticke song we heard last night; | 887 |
| *Du.* Too old by heauen: Let still the woman take | 917 |
| Marke it Cesario, it is old and plaine; | 933 |
| And dallies with the innocence of loue, \| Like the old age. | 937 |
| *To.* Did she see the while, old boy, tell me that. | 1389 |
| *Clo.* Bonos dies sir *Toby*: for as the old hermit of *Prage* | 1998 |
| In a trice, like to the old vice, \| your neede to sustaine. | 2107 |
| *Ol.* If it be ought to the old tune my Lord, | 2263 |

OLDE = *1

| | |
|---|---|
| *Clo.* Primo, secundo, tertio, is a good play, and the olde | 2187 |

OLIUIA *see also* Ol. = 17*3

| | |
|---|---|
| O when mine eyes did see *Oliuia* first, | 24 |
| That he did seeke the loue of faire *Oliuia*. | 84 |
| *Enter Lady Oliuia, with Maluolio.* | 325 |
| Cry out *Oliuia*: O you should not rest | 568 |
| *Mal.* Were not you eu'n now, with the Countesse O- \|liuia? | 658 |
| What thriftlesse sighes shall poore *Oliuia* breath? | 696 |
| As you haue for *Oliuia*: you cannot loue her: | 979 |
| Betweene that loue a woman can beare me, \| And that I owe *Oliuia*. | 990 |
| *Veluet gowne: hauing come from a day bedde, where I \| haue left *Oliuia* sleeping. | 1064 |
| *Clo.* No indeed sir, the Lady *Oliuia* has no folly, shee | 1245 |
| *Enter Oliuia, and Gentlewoman.* | 1297 |
| *Enter Oliuia and Maria.* | 1521 |
| *To. Thou comst to the Lady Oliuia, and in my sight she vses* | 1675 |
| *Enter Oliuia and Viola.* | 1713 |
| *Enter Oliuia.* | 1961 |
| *Enter Oliuia, and Priest.* | 2136 |
| *Duke.* Belong you to the Lady *Oliuia*, friends? | 2161 |
| *Enter Oliuia and attendants.* | 2250 |
| Wherein *Oliuia* may seeme seruiceable? | 2257 |

*OLIUIA cont.*
 *Vio.* Madam: | *Du.* Gracious *Oliuia.*  2259
OLIUIAES = *1
 **Oliuiaes* Father tooke much delight in. He is about the | house.  896
OLIUIAS = 1
 *Vio.* Art not thou the Lady *Oliuia's* foole?  1244
OLYFFE = *1
 *of warre, no taxation of homage; I hold the Olyffe  504
OMAN = 1
 *Ol.* What kinde o'man is he? | *Mal.* Why of mankinde.  445
OME = 1
 *And.* S'light; will you make an Asse o'me.  1393
OMINE = 1
 *An.* Or o'mine either?  1193
OMNES = 1
 *To.* Come bring vs, bring vs where he is. | *Exeunt Omnes.*  1463
OMY = 1*1
 *o'my Coz: for he's in the third degree of drinke: hee's | drown'd: go
  looke after him.  429
 *To.* Wilt thou set thy foote o'my necke.  1192
ON = 38*28
ONCE = 7*2
 And water once a day her Chamber round  35
 Wee'l once more heare *Orsinos* Embassie.  461
 *ye well at once, my bosome is full of kindnesse, and I  647
 *An.* I was ador'd once too.  873
 Being once displaid, doth fall that verie howre.  928
 *Du.* Let all the rest giue place: Once more *Cesario*,  966
 **Mal.* 'Tis but Fortune, all is fortune. *Maria* once  1040
 Once in a sea-fight 'gainst the Count his gallies,  1494
 *Clo.* Put your grace in your pocket sir, for this once,  2183
ONE *see also* 1. = 27*33
 Her sweete perfections with one selfe king:  45
 *knight that you brought in one night here, to be hir woer  134
 *not be seene, or if she be it's four to one, she'l none of me:  216
 **Ma.* That if one breake, the other will hold: or if both | breake, your
  gaskins fall.  318
 One of thy kin has a most weake *Pia-mater.*  409
 **To.* Letcherie, I defie Letchery: there's one at the | gate.  419
 me faith say I. Well, it's all one. *Exit*  423
 *One draught aboue heate, makes him a foole, the second | maddes
  him, and a third drownes him.  426
 *and he speakes verie shrewishly: One would thinke his  455
 *question's out of my part. Good gentle one, giue mee  474
 *'tis not that time of Moone with me, to make one in so | skipping a
  dialogue.  495
 *Looke you sir, such a one I was this present: Ist not well | done?  526
 *with lids to them: Item, one necke, one chin, & so forth.  540
 Euen so quickly may one catch the plague?  591
 *into a desperate assurance, she will none of him. And one  665
 **An.* There's a testrill of me too: if one knight giue a  734
 soules out of one Weauer? Shall we do that?  760
 *An.* 'Tis not the first time I haue constrained one to  767
 **To.* She's a beagle true bred, and one that adores me: | what o'that?  871
 Come, but one verse.  891
 *My part of death no one so true did share it.*  947
 **Clo.* Truely sir, and pleasure will be paide one time, or | another.  957

ONE *cont.*

| | |
|---|---|
| *thus neere, that should shee fancie, it should bee one of | 1042 |
| *respect, then any one else that followes her. What \| should I thinke on't? | |
| | 1044 |
| *And.* That's mee I warrant you. \| *Mal.* One sir *Andrew.* | 1094 |
| *one of these Letters are in my name. Soft, here fol-\|lowes | 1148 |
| *And.* Ile make one too. *Exeunt.* \| *Finis Actus secundus* | 1211 |
| *one, though I would not haue it grow on my chinne. Is \| thy Lady within? | |
| | 1260 |
| *That tyrannous heart can think? To one of your receiuing | 1334 |
| If one should be a prey, how much the better | 1343 |
| I haue one heart, one bosome, and one truth, | 1374 |
| As might haue drawne one to a longer voyage) | 1473 |
| If it please the eye of one, it is with me as the very true | 1544 |
| Sonnet is: Please one, and please all. | 1545 |
| *Tob. Fartheewell, and God haue mercie vpon one of our* | 1684 |
| kill one another by the looke, like Cockatrices. | 1712 |
| *Vio.* I shall bee much bound to you for't: I am one, | 1788 |
| *will for his honors sake haue one bowt with you: | 1822 |
| *Ant.* One sir, that for his loue dares yet do more | 1833 |
| I snatch'd one halfe out of the iawes of death, | 1880 |
| He started one poore heart of mine, in thee. | 1976 |
| *most modest termes, for I am one of those gentle ones, | 2018 |
| *Clo.* By my troth sir, no: though it please you to be \| one of my friends. | |
| | 2177 |
| *tripping measure, or the belles of S.(aint) *Bennet* sir, may put \| you in minde, one, two, three. | |
| | 2189 |
| While one would winke: denide me mine owne purse, | 2242 |
| *And.* For the loue of God a Surgeon, send one pre-\|sently to sir *Toby.* | 2336 |
| *And.* The Counts Gentleman, one *Cesario*: we tooke | 2343 |
| *To.* That's all one, has hurt me, and there's th'end on't: | 2359 |
| Pardon me (sweet one) euen for the vowes | 2378 |
| *Du.* One face, one voice, one habit, and two persons, | 2380 |
| One day shall crowne th'alliance on't, so please you, | 2484 |
| *was one sir, in this Enterlude, one sir *Topas* sir, but that's | 2543 |
| *all one: By the Lord Foole, I am not mad: but do you re-\|member, | 2544 |
| *But that's all one, our Play is done,* | 2578 |

ONELY = 2*1

| | |
|---|---|
| Onely shape thou thy silence to my wit. | 113 |
| *onely to exasperate you, to awake your dormouse valour, | 1399 |
| Most of our City did. Onely my selfe stood out, | 1503 |

ONES = 1*1

| | |
|---|---|
| What great ones do, the lesse will prattle of, ) | 83 |
| *most modest termes, for I am one of those gentle ones, | 2018 |

ONT = 4*3

| | |
|---|---|
| *respect, then any one else that followes her. What \| should I thinke on't? | |
| | 1044 |
| And laid mine honour too vnchary on't: | 1719 |
| *And.* Pox on't, Ile not meddle with him. | 1798 |
| *An.* Plague on't, and I thought he had beene valiant, | 1801 |
| *shew on't, this shall end without the perdition of soules, | 1806 |
| *To.* That's all one, has hurt me, and there's th'end on't: | 2359 |
| One day shall crowne th'alliance on't, so please you, | 2484 |

OPALL = *1

| | |
|---|---|
| *minde is a very Opall. I would haue men of such constan-\|cie | 962 |

OPEN = 1*4

| | |
|---|---|
| *not open my lippes so wide as a brissle may enter, in way | 298 |

OPEN *cont.*
    *haue greatnesse thrust vppon em. Thy fates open theyr ................ 1152
    *champian discouers not more: This is open, I will bee ................ 1165
    *Seb.* Do not then walke too open. ................ 1506
    *Clo.* By my troth thou hast an open hand: these Wise-|men ................ 1938
OPEND = *1
    *cannot hale them together. For *Andrew*, if he were open'd ................ 1440
OPENT = 1
    When they are deliuer'd. | *Ol.* Open't, and read it. ................ 2456
OPINION = 3*3
    *the North of my Ladies opinion, where you will hang ................ 1406
    *into a most hideous opinion of his rage, skill, furie, and ................ 1710
    *Clo.* What is the opinion of *Pythagoras* concerning | Wilde-fowle? ................ 2035
    ,*Clo.* What thinkst thou of his opinion? ................ 2039
    *Mal.* I thinke nobly of the soule, and no way aproue | his opinion. ................ 2040
    *thou shalt hold th'opinion of *Pythagoras*, ere I will allow ................ 2043
OPPORTUNITIE = *1
    *hand, and this was baulkt: the double gilt of this oppor-|tunitie ................ 1404
OPPOSIT = *1
    *Fab.* And his opposit the youth beares in his visage no | great presage
        of cruelty. ................ 1443
OPPOSITE = *4
    *slough, and appeare fresh. Be opposite with a kinsman, ................ 1155
    *the Letter. Cast thy humble slough sayes she: be oppo-|site ................ 1591
    *for your opposite hath in him what youth, strength, skill, | and wrath,
        can furnish man withall. ................ 1750
    *fatall opposite that you could possibly haue found in anie ................ 1785
OR *l.*80 *143 *198 *205 *216 *254 287 *297 *312 *318 *402 449 *452 600
    *735 *786 *790 *825 *840 926 *957 *1076 1090 1141 1193 1196 *1223
    *1408 1435 *1524 *1602 1758 *1768 *1769 1872 1875 1899 *1945 *1959
    1978 2099 2130 *2189 2226 2233 2328 *2475 2502 2503 2581 = 24*27
ORBE = *1
    *Clo.* Foolery sir, does walke about the Orbe like the ................ 1251
ORBED = 1
    As doth that Orbed Continent, the fire, | That seuers day from night. ................ 2437
ORCHARD = 1*2
    I saw't i'th Orchard. ................ 1388
    *of the Orchard like a bum-Baylie: so soone as euer thou ................ 1694
    *attends thee at the Orchard end: dismount thy tucke, ................ 1742
ORDER = 1
    *Ma.* I, but you must confine your selfe within the | modest limits of
        order. ................ 126
ORDINARY = *2
    *more wit then a Christian, or an ordinary man ha's: but I ................ 198
    *an ordinary foole, that has no more braine then a stone. ................ 377
ORE = 3*1
    O, it came ore my eare, like the sweet sound ................ 9
    *Ol.* Giue me my vaile: come throw it ore my face, ................ 460
    whisper ore a couplet or two of most sage sawes. ................ 1899
    *To.* Hold sir, or Ile throw your dagger ore the house ................ 1945
ORE-FLOURISHD = 1
    Are empty trunkes, ore-flourish'd by the deuill. ................ 1890
ORGAN = 1
    Is as the maidens organ, shrill, and sound, ................ 284
ORION = 1
    Where like *Orion* on the Dolphines backe, ................ 65

ORNAMENT = 1
Still in this fashion, colour, ornament,                                1903
ORSINO = 7*1
*Enter Orsino Duke of Illyria, Curio, and other | Lords.*                  2
*Vio.* What is his name? | *Cap.* Orsino.                                 76
*Vio. Orsino:* I haue heard my father name him.                          78
*Ol.* From the Count *Orsino,* is it?                                     394
Y'are seruant to the Count *Orsino* youth.                               1312
*2.Off.* Anthonio, I arrest thee at the suit of Count *Orsino*           1844
Cride fame and honor on him: What's the matter? | 1.*Offi. Orsino,* this
is that *Anthonio*                                                        2210
*Ant. Orsino:* Noble sir, | Be pleas'd that I shake off these names you
giue mee:                                                                 2224
ORSINOES = 1
of it. Where lies your Text? | *Vio.* In *Orsinoes* bosome.              516
ORSINOS = 6*1
Wee'l once more heare *Orsinos* Embassie.                                461
bound to the Count Orsino's Court, farewell. *Exit*                      650
I haue many enemies in Orsino's Court,                                    652
*Vio.* I saw thee late at the Count *Orsino's.*                          1250
*Orsino's* is return'd, I could hardly entreate him backe: he           1580
*Orsino's* enemie. A witchcraft drew me hither:                          2228
*Orsino's* Mistris, and his fancies Queene. *Exeunt*                     2558
OTH = *6
*To.* Fie, that you'l say so: he playes o'th Viol-de-gam- | boys,        142
*drinke to my Neece, till his braines turne o'th toe, like a            157
*To.* Shee'l none o'th Count, she'l not match aboue hir                 218
*And.* Ile stay a moneth longer. I am a fellow o'th                      221
*To.* And do's not *Toby* take you a blow o'th lippes, | then?          1083
*Fa.* Still you keepe o'th windie side of the Law: good.                1683
OTHAT = 1*1
*Ma.* Peace you rogue, no more o'that: here comes my                    323
*To.* She's a beagle true bred, and one that adores me: | what o'that?   871
OTHER = 6*4
*Enter Orsino Duke of Illyria, Curio, and other | Lords.*                  2
*Ma.* That if one breake, the other will hold: or if both | breake, your
gaskins fall.                                                             318
*Ol.* Well sir, for want of other idlenesse, Ile bide your | proofe.     356
*a barren rascall: I saw him put down the other day, with               376
*To.* And aske no other dowry with her, but such ano- | ther iest.      1187
*Seb.* My kinde *Anthonio,* | I can no other answer make, but thankes,   1480
To any other trust, but that I am mad,                                   2129
*he had not beene in drinke, hee would haue tickel'd you | other gates
then he did.                                                             2356
We made each other, but so late ago.                                     2379
But when in other habites you are seene,                                 2557
OTHERS = 2*1
*would, are as secret as maiden-head: to your eares, Di- | uinity; to any
others, prophanation.                                                    510
*Enter Duke, Viola, Curio, and others.*                                  884
*of some kinde of men, that put quarrells purposely on o- | thers,      1761
OTHERWISE = *1
*To.* You'l finde it otherwise I assure you: therefore, if              1748
OTHESE = *1
*To.* 'Tis a Gentleman heere. A plague o'thesc pickle | herring: How
now Sot.                                                                 414

OUER *see also* ore = 1*2
    \*ouer me; the malignancie of my fate, might perhaps di- | stemper    616
    *Vio*. And all those sayings, will I ouer sweare,    2435
    \*darkenesse, and giuen your drunken Cosine rule ouer me,    2471
OUERTHROW = 1
    That thine owne trip shall be thine ouerthrow:    2329
OUERTURE = *1
    \**Vio*. It alone concernes your eare: I bring no ouer- | ture    503
OUER-FARRE = *1
    \*I could not with such estimable wonder ouer-farre be- | leeue    636
OUER-WEENING = 1
    *To*. Heere's an ouer-weening rogue.    1046
OUER-WORNE = 1
    \*what you would are out of my welkin, I might say Ele- | ment, but the
    word is ouer-worne. *Exit*    1270
OUGHT = 1*1
    *Ol*. If it be ought to the old tune my Lord,    2263
    \*Ladyship will haue it as it ought to bee, you must allow | *Vox*.    2462
OUNCE = *1
    \**To*. What, what? Nay then I must haue an Ounce or | two of this
    malapert blood from you.    1959
OUR *see also* byrlady *l*.59 61 608 *709 764 *792 854 920 921 1007 1008
    1028 *1079 1090 1489 1503 1509 *1659 *1684 1876 *2037 2145 2208
    2554 2578 = 20*7
OURSELUES *see* selues
OUSIE = 1
    *And. Dieu vou guard Monsieur.* | *Vio. Et vouz ousie vostre seruiture.*    1284
OUT *l*.315 *378 456 *474 *524 *537 568 760 774 *789 *810 *829 877 898
    *1023 *1075 1089 *1135 *1270 1503 *1660 *1702 *1764 1861 1880 *1923
    1966 *2011 2078 2121 *2191 2240 2270 2283 2477 2517 = 19*17
OUTWARD = 2
    With this thy faire and outward charracter.    103
    wrong side may be turn'd outward.    1227
OUT-SIDE = 1
    Fortune forbid my out-side haue not charm'd her:    675
OWE = 3
    Fate, shew thy force, our selues we do not owe,    608
    Betweene that loue a woman can beare me, | And that I owe *Oliuia*.    990
    *Vio*. Too well what loue women to men may owe:    994
OWLE = *1
    \*rowze the night-Owle in a Catch, that will drawe three    759
OWN = *1
    \*Sunne practising behauiour to his own shadow this halfe    1034
OWNE = 8*3
    Mine owne escape vnfoldeth to my hope,    69
    Till I had made mine owne occasion mellow | What my estate is.    94
    \*these boots too: and they be not, let them hang them- | selues in their
    owne straps.    130
    Natures owne sweet, and cunning hand laid on:    532
    \**Vio*. My matter hath no voice Lady, but to your owne | most pregnant
    and vouchsafed eare.    1301
    \**To*. To him in thine owne voyce, and bring me word    2051
    While one would winke: denide me mine owne purse,    2242
    That thine owne trip shall be thine ouerthrow:    2329
    A most extracting frensie of mine owne    2449
    \*I haue your owne letter, that induced mee to the    2473
    Thou shalt be both the Plaintiffe and the Iudge | Of thine owne cause.    2524

OXEN = *1
*the youth to an answer. I thinke Oxen and waine-ropes 1439
PACE = *2
*as make water but in a Sinke-a-pace: What dooest thou 238
*Vio. Euen now sir, on a moderate pace, I haue since a-|riu'd but
hither. 660
PACED = 1
Of these most briske and giddy-paced times. 890
PACIFIED = 1
To. I but he will not now be pacified, 1799
PACKE = 1
Mal. Ile be reueng'd on the whole packe of you? 2548
PAID = 1
of thousands to be paid from the Sophy. 1184
PAIDE = *1
*Clo. Truely sir, and pleasure will be paide one time, or | another. 957
PAIMENT = 1
*money for thee, if you tarry longer, I shall giue worse | paiment. 1936
PAINES = 5*3
It may be worth thy paines: for I can sing, 109
*taken great paines to con it. Good Beauties, let mee su-|staine 469
*Vio. Alas, I tooke great paines to studie it, and 'tis | Poeticall. 489
I thanke you for your paines: spend this for mee. 579
*haue saued mee my paines, to haue taken it away your 663
Du. There's for thy paines. 954
Clo. No paines sir, I take pleasure in singing sir. 955
But since you make your pleasure of your paines, 1468
PAIRE = 2
Clo Would not a paire of these haue bred sir? 1262
Like a mad lad, paire thy nayles dad, 2111
PALE = 1
lookes pale, as if a Beare were at his heeles. 1812
PALLAT = 1
No motion of the Liuer, but the Pallat, 986
PALTRY = *1
*To. A very dishonest paltry boy, and more a coward 1906
PANDARUS = *1
*Clo. I would play Lord Pandarus of Phrygia sir, to bring | a Cressida to
this Troylus. 1264
PANG = 1
Hath for your loue as great a pang of heart 978
PANGS = 1*2
*Mal. Yes, and shall do, till the pangs of death shake 367
In the sweet pangs of it, remember me: 901
*can be none, but by pangs of death and sepulcher: Hob, | nob, is his
word: giu't or take't. 1757
PANTS = *1
*Fa. He is as horribly conceited of him: and pants, & 1811
PAPER = 1*4
*Lyes, as will lye in thy sheete of paper, although the 1425
*my hand, helpe me to a Candle, and pen, inke, and paper: 2066
*paper, I tell thee I am as well in my wittes, as any man in | Illyria. 2091
*Mal. By this hand I am: good foole, some inke, pa-|per, 2094
I will fetch you light, and paper, and inke. 2102
PARDON = 3
Ant. Pardon me sir, your bad entertainment. 641
Ant. Would youl'd pardon me: 1492

PARDON *cont.*
Pardon me (sweet one) euen for the vowes · · · · · · · · · · · 2378
PAREIL = 1
Could be but recompenc'd, though you were crown'd | The non-pareil
of beautie. · · · · · · · · · · · · · · · · · · · · · · · · · 545
PARENTAGE = 3
What is your Parentage? | *Vio.* Aboue my fortunes, yet my state is well: · · 572
*Ol.* What is your Parentage? | Aboue my fortunes, yet my state is well; · · 585
What Countreyman? What name? What Parentage? | *Vio.* Of *Messaline:*
*Sebastian* was my Father, · · · · · · · · · · · · · · · · · · · 2396
PARISH = *1
*parish top. What wench? *Castiliano vulgo*: for here coms | Sir *Andrew*
*Agueface.* · · · · · · · · · · · · · · · · · · · · · · · · · · 158
PARSON = 2*2
*To.* Ioue blesse thee M.(aster) Parson. · · · · · · · · · · · · 1997
*of King *Gorbodacke*, that that is, is: so I being M.(aster) Parson, · · 2000
*am M.(aster) Parson; for what is that, but that? and is, but is? · · 2001
man? Talkest thou nothing but of Ladies? | *Tob.* Well said M.(aster)
Parson. · · · · · · · · · · · · · · · · · · · · · · · · · · · · 2012
PART = 5*4
*To.* And thou let part so Sir *Andrew*, would thou | mightst neuer draw
sword agen. · · · · · · · · · · · · · · · · · · · · · · · · · · 176
*And.* And you part so mistris, I would I might neuer · · · · · 178
And all is semblatiue a womans part. · · · · · · · · · · · · · 285
*question's out of my part. Good gentle one, giue mee · · · · · 474
*My part of death no one so true did share it.* · · · · · · · · 947
*Fab.* I will not giue my part of this sport for a pensi-|on · · 1183
*part of Illyria: will you walke towards him, I will make | your peace
with him, if I can. · · · · · · · · · · · · · · · · · · · · · · 1786
And part being prompted by your present trouble, · · · · · · · 1860
We will not part from hence. *Cesario* come · · · · · · · · · · 2555
PARTAKE = 1
(Not meaning to partake with me in danger) · · · · · · · · · · 2239
PARTICIPATE = 1
Which from the wombe I did participate. · · · · · · · · · · · · 2404
PARTICLE = *1
*and euery particle and vtensile labell'd to my will: As, · · · 538
PARTLY = 1
And that I partly know the instrument · · · · · · · · · · · · · 2278
PARTS = 3
The parts that fortune hath bestow'd vpon her: · · · · · · · · 970
Being skillesse in these parts: which to a stranger, · · · · · 1475
Vpon some stubborne and vncourteous parts · · · · · · · · · · · 2532
PASSAGE = *1
*to her as long as there is a passage in my throat, & drinke · · 155
PASSAGES = *1
*beleeue such impossible passages of grossenesse. Hee's in | yellow
stockings. · · · · · · · · · · · · · · · · · · · · · · · · · · 1451
PASSE = *5
*fooles: and I that am sure I lacke thee, may passe for a · · · 328
*I am no Fox, but he wil not passe his word for two pence | that you
are no Foole. · · · · · · · · · · · · · · · · · · · · · · · · · 372
*Vio.* Nay, and thou passe vpon me, Ile no more with | thee. Hold
there's expences for thee. · · · · · · · · · · · · · · · · · · 1255
*it comes to passe oft, that a terrible oath, with a swagge-|ring · · 1696
*a firago: I had a passe with him, rapier, scabberd, and all: · · 1793

PASSING = *1
   *Pigrogromitus*, of the *Vapians* passing the Equinoctial of        724
PASSION = 6*2
   *Vio*. Say I do speake with her (my Lord) what then? | *Du*. O then,
   vnfold the passion of my loue,        273
   She loues me sure, the cunning of her passion        679
   Me thought it did releeue my passion much,        888
   Can bide the beating of so strong a passion,        982
   Nor wit, nor reason, can my passion hide:        1368
   *Vio*. With the same hauiour that your passion beares,        1723
   *Vio*. Me thinkes his words do from such passion flye        1894
   Let thy fayre wisedome, not thy passion sway | In this vnciuill, and
   vniust extent        1969
PASSY = *1
   *To*. Then he's a Rogue, and a passy measures pauyn: I | hate a
   drunken rogue.        2363
PAST = 4*1
   *To*. Past question, for thou seest it will not coole my | (nature        211
   Did I redeeme: a wracke past hope he was:        2231
   Hath newly past, betweene this youth, and me.        2317
   This practice hath most shrewdly past vpon thee:        2522
   If that the iniuries be iustly weigh'd, | That haue on both sides past.        2538
PASTIME = *1
   *pastime tyred out of breath, prompt vs to haue mercy        1660
PATCHD = *1
   *mend him: any thing that's mended, is but patch'd: vertu        339
PATCHT = *2
   *that transgresses, is but patcht with sinne, and sin that a-|mends,        340
   *Is but patcht with vertue. If that this simple        341
PATIENCE = 2*1
   *Seb*. By your patience, no: my starres shine darkely        615
   She sate like Patience on a Monument,        1004
   *Fab*. Nay patience, or we breake the sinewes of our | plot?        1090
PATIENT = *2
   *Mar*. Sweet Sir Toby be patient for to night: Since        827
   *Clo*. Alas sir be patient. What say you sir, I am shent | for speaking to
   you.        2088
PAUYN = *1
   *To*. Then he's a Rogue, and a passy measures pauyn: I | hate a
   drunken rogue.        2363
PAY = 5
   To pay this debt of loue but to a brother,        40
   I prethee (and Ile pay thee bounteously)        104
   *Du*. Ile pay thy pleasure then.        956
   Are shuffel'd off with such vncurrant pay:        1483
   For which if I be lapsed in this place | I shall pay deere.        1504
PAYES = *2
   *that it is ineuitable: and on the answer, he payes you as        1795
   *saying is, the third payes for all: the triplex sir, is a good        2188
PEACE = 18*8
   *Ma*. Peace you rogue, no more o'that: here comes my        323
   in my hand: my words are as full of peace, as matter.        505
   *Clo*. *Hold thy peace, thou Knaue* knight. I shall be con-|strain'd in't, to
   call thee knaue, Knight.        765
   call me knaue. Begin foole: it begins, *Hold thy peace*.        768
   *Clo*. I shall neuer begin if I hold my peace.        769
   *Mar*. For the loue o'God peace.        784

PEACE *cont.*

| | |
|---|---|
| *Fa.* Oh peace: Contemplation makes a rare Turkey | 1047 |
| *And.* Slight I could so beate the Rogue. \| *To.* Peace I say. | 1049 |
| *An.* Pistoll him, pistoll him. \| *To.* Peace, peace. | 1053 |
| *Fa.* O peace, now he's deepely in: looke how imagi-\|nation blowes | |
| him. | 1058 |
| *To.* Fire and Brimstone. \| *Fa.* O peace, peace. | 1066 |
| *To.* Boltes and shackles. \| *Fa.* Oh peace, peace, peace, now, now. | 1072 |
| *Fa.* Though our silence be drawne from vs with cars, \| yet peace. | 1079 |
| *To.* Oh peace, and the spirit of humors intimate rea-\|ding aloud to | |
| him. | 1099 |
| *Mal.* Ah ha, does she so? \| *To.* Go too, go too: peace, peace, wee must | |
| deale | 1617 |
| *To.* Prethee hold thy peace, this is not the way: Doe | 1631 |
| *part of Illyria: will you walke towards him, I will make \| your peace | |
| with him, if I can. | 1786 |
| Against thy peace. Go with me to my house, | 1971 |
| *To.* To him sir *Topas.* \| *Clow.* What hoa, I say, Peace in this prison. | 2002 |
| May liue at peace. He shall conceale it, | 2143 |
| *Du.* Pursue him, and entreate him to a peace: | 2550 |

PEARLE = 1

| | |
|---|---|
| This pearle she gaue me, I do feel't, and see't, | 2116 |

PEDANT = *1

| | |
|---|---|
| *To.* And crosse garter'd? \| *Mar.* Most villanously: like a Pedant that | |
| keepes a | 1453 |

PEECE = 1

| | |
|---|---|
| Now good *Cesario*, but that peece of song, | 886 |

PEEUISH = 1

| | |
|---|---|
| *Ol.* Run after that same peeuish Messenger | 598 |

PEEUISHLY = *1

| | |
|---|---|
| *Mal.* Come sir, you peeuishly threw it to her: and | 670 |

PEG-A-RAMSIE = *1

| | |
|---|---|
| *a Peg-a-ramsie, and *Three merry men be wee.* Am not I | 776 |

PEN = *3

| | |
|---|---|
| *in thy inke, though thou write with a Goose-pen, \| no matter: about it. | 1428 |
| *that neuer saw pen and inke, very wittily sayd to a Neece | 1999 |
| *my hand, helpe me to a Candle, and pen, inke, and paper: | 2066 |

PENCE = 1 *3

| | |
|---|---|
| *I am no Fox, but he wil not passe his word for two pence \| that you | |
| are no Foole. | 372 |
| *Queubus*: 'twas very good yfaith: I sent thee sixe pence | 725 |
| *To.* Come on, there is sixe pence for you. Let's haue \| a song. | 732 |
| in some of your coats for two pence. | 1947 |

PEND = *1

| | |
|---|---|
| *speech: for besides that it is excellently well pend, I haue | 468 |

PENNANCE = *1

| | |
|---|---|
| *carry it thus for our pleasure, and his pennance, til our ve-\|ry | 1659 |

PENSION = *1

| | |
|---|---|
| *Fab.* I will not giue my part of this sport for a pensi-\|on | 1183 |

PENTHISILEA = 1

| | |
|---|---|
| *To.* Good night *Penthisilea.* | 869 |

PEOPLE = 4 *3

| | |
|---|---|
| *Ol.* Who of my people hold him in delay? \| *Ma.* Sir *Toby* Madam, your | |
| kinsman. | 398 |
| *Now you see sir, how your fooling growes old, & peo-\|ple dislike it. | 404 |
| *Mal.* Seauen of my people with an obedient start, | 1074 |
| *Seb.* Belike you slew great number of his people. | 1497 |

PEOPLE *cont*.

| | |
|---|---|
| *Cosine *Toby*, let some of my people haue a speciall care | 1584 |
| Are all the people mad? | 1944 |
| Vpon sir *Toby*, and the lighter people: | 2509 |

PEPPER = 1

| | |
|---|---|
| *An*. Heere's the Challenge, reade it: I warrant there's \| vinegar and pepper in't. | 1665 |

PERCEIUE = 2*1

| | |
|---|---|
| *extrauagancie. But I perceiue in you so excellent a touch | 622 |
| As I perceiue she do's: there's something in't | 2134 |
| I do perceiue it hath offended you: | 2377 |

PERCHANCE = 2*3

| | |
|---|---|
| *Perchance he is not drown'd: What thinke you saylors? | 55 |
| *Cap*. It is perchance that you your selfe were saued. | 56 |
| *Vio*. O my poore brother, and so perchance may he be. | 57 |
| Vnlesse (perchance) you come to me againe, | 577 |
| *make out for him: I frowne the while, and perchance | 1075 |

PERDIE = 1

| | |
|---|---|
| *Clo*. My Lady is vnkind, *perdie*. \| *Mal*. Foole. | 2060 |

PERDITION = *1

| | |
|---|---|
| *shew on't, this shall end without the perdition of soules, | 1806 |

PERFECTION = 1

| | |
|---|---|
| To die, euen when they to perfection grow. | 930 |

PERFECTIONS = 2

| | |
|---|---|
| Her sweete perfections with one selfe king: | 45 |
| Me thinkes I feele this youths perfections | 592 |

PERHAPPES = 1

| | |
|---|---|
| Say that some Lady, as perhappes there is, | 977 |

PERHAPS = 2*1

| | |
|---|---|
| *ouer me; the malignancie of my fate, might perhaps di-\|stemper | 616 |
| As it might be perhaps, were I a woman \| I should your Lordship. | 997 |
| *Ol*. Yet come againe: for thou perhaps mayst moue | 1379 |

PERILL = 1

| | |
|---|---|
| Most prouident in perill, binde himselfe, | 62 |

PERPEND = *1

| | |
|---|---|
| *reade thus: therefore, perpend my Princesse, and giue \| eare. | 2466 |

PERSON = 1

| | |
|---|---|
| A gracious person; But yet I cannot loue him: | 555 |

PERSONAGE = 1

| | |
|---|---|
| *Ol*. Of what personage, and yeeres is he? | 450 |

PERSONATED = *1

| | |
|---|---|
| *feelingly personated. I can write very like my Ladie | 852 |

PERSONS = 2*1

| | |
|---|---|
| Is there no respect of place, persons, nor time in you? | 791 |
| He must obserue their mood on whom he iests, \| The quality of persons, and the time: | 1274 |
| *Du*. One face, one voice, one habit, and two persons, | 2380 |

PERSPECTIUE = 1

| | |
|---|---|
| A naturall Perspectiue, that is, and is not. | 2381 |

PERSWADED = *2

| | |
|---|---|
| *The best perswaded of himselfe: so cram'd (as he thinkes) | 843 |
| *I haue his horse to take vp the quarrell, I haue perswaded \| him the youths a diuell. | 1809 |

PERSWADES = 1

| | |
|---|---|
| And wrangle with my reason that perswades me | 2128 |

PERSWASION = 1
Ist possible that my deserts to you | Can lacke perswasion. Do not
tempt my misery, 1866
PERUERSENESSE = 1
*Du.* What to peruersenesse? you vnciuill Ladie 2268
PERUSE = 1
*Ol.* Haue I *Maluolio*? No. | *Mal.* Lady you haue, pray you peruse that
Letter. 2499
PESCOD = *1
*for a boy: as a squash is before tis a pescod, or a Codling 452
PESTILENCE = 1
Me thought she purg'd the ayre of pestilence; 25
PHANGS = *1
*phangs of malice, I sweare) I am not that I play. Are you | the Ladie
of the house? 479
PHOENIX = 1
That tooke the *Phoenix*, and her fraught from *Candy*, 2212
PHRASE = 1
Write from it if you can, in hand, or phrase, 2502
PHRASES = *1
*Her very Phrases: By your leaue wax. Soft, and the im-|pressure 1106
PHRYGIA = *1
*Clo.* I would play Lord *Pandarus* of *Phrygia* sir, to bring | a *Cressida* to
this *Troylus*. 1264
PHYSICKE = *1
*Mar.* Sport royall I warrant you: I know my Phy-|sicke 864
PIA-MATER = 1
One of thy kin has a most weake *Pia-mater*. 409
PICKLE = *1
*To.* 'Tis a Gentleman heere. A plague o'these pickle | herring: How
now Sot. 414
PICTURE = *4
*dust, like mistris *Mals* picture? Why dost thou not goe 235
*but we will draw the Curtain, and shew you the picture. 525
*Clo.* How now my harts: Did you neuer see the Pic-|ture of we three? 717
*Ol.* Heere, weare this Iewell for me, tis my picture: 1725
PIECE *see also* peece = *1
*sir *Toby* would leaue drinking, thou wert as witty a piece | of *Eues*
flesh, as any in Illyria. 321
PIGROGROMITUS = *1
*Pigrogromitus*, of the *Vapians* passing the Equinoctial of 724
PILCHERS = *1
*as like husbands, as Pilchers are to Herrings, the Hus-|bands 1247
PIND = 1
Feede on her damaske cheeke: she pin'd in thought, 1002
PIPE = 1
Is not more smooth, and rubious: thy small pipe 283
PIRATE *see* pyrate
PISTOLL = 2
*An.* Pistoll him, pistoll him. | *To.* Peace, peace. 1053
PIT = *1
*grauity to play at cherrie-pit with sathan. Hang him foul | Colliar. 1638
PITCH = 1
Of what validity, and pitch so ere, 16
PITTIE = 3
But you should pittie me. 570
*An.* And we do not, it is pittie of our liues. 1028

PITTIE *cont*.
    Hides my heart: so let me heare you speake. | *Vio*. I pittie you.     1336
PITTY = 1
    *Vio*. No not a grize: for tis a vulgar proofe | That verie oft we pitty
    enemies.     1339
PLACD = 1
    Plac'd in contempt: Farwell fayre crueltie. *Exit*     584
PLACE = 8*1
    Not three houres trauaile from this very place.     73
    *Ol*. Giue vs the place alone,     512
    Is there no respect of place, persons, nor time in you?     791
    *Du*. Let all the rest giue place: Once more *Cesario*,     966
    My loue can giue no place, bide no denay. *Exeunt*     1015
    *place, as I would they should doe theirs: to aske for my | kinsman
    *Toby*.     1070
    For which if I be lapsed in this place | I shall pay deere.     1504
    That screwes me from my true place in your fauour:     2279
    Of place, time, fortune, do co-here and iumpe     2418
PLACES = *1
    *hurt him in eleuen places, my Neece shall take note of it,     1415
PLAGUE = 1*3
    *Sir To*. What a plague meanes my Neece to take the     119
    *To*. 'Tis a Gentleman heere. A plague o'these pickle | herring: How
    now Sot.     414
    Euen so quickly may one catch the plague?     591
    *An*. Plague on't, and I thought he had beene valiant,     1801
PLAID = 1*1
    *Fa*. If this were plaid vpon a stage now, I could con- | demne it as an
    improbable fiction.     1649
    That ere inuention plaid on? Tell me why?     2514
PLAINE = 2
    Marke it Cesario, it is old and plaine;     933
    *And*. As plaine as I see you now.     1390
PLAINLY = *1
    *now my foes tell me plainly, I am an Asse: so that by my     2171
PLAINTIFFE = 1
    Thou shalt be both the Plaintiffe and the Iudge | Of thine owne cause.     2524
PLANT = *1
    *will worke with him, I will plant you two, and let     865
PLAY = 4*6
    *Duke*. | If Musicke be the food of Loue, play on,     4
    *phangs of malice, I sweare) I am not that I play. Are you | the Ladie
    of the house?     479
    *Du*. Seeke him out, and play the tune the while. | *Musicke playes*.     898
    *winde vp my watch, or play with my some rich Iewell:     1076
    *To*. Shall I play my freedome at tray-trip, and becom | thy bondslaue?     1194
    *Clo*. I would play Lord *Pandarus* of *Phrygia* sir, to bring | a *Cressida* to
    this *Troylus*.     1264
    *Vio*. This fellow is wise enough to play the foole,     1272
    *grauity to play at cherrie-pit with sathan. Hang him foul | Colliar.     1638
    *Clo*. *Primo*, *secundo*, *tertio*, is a good play, and the olde     2187
    *But that's all one, our Play is done*,     2578
PLAYES = 1*1
    *To*. Fie, that you'l say so: he playes o'th Viol-de-gam- | boys,     142
    *Du*. Seeke him out, and play the tune the while. | *Musicke playes*.     898
PLEASD = 1*1
    *beene pleas'd, would we had so ended. But you sir, al- | ter'd     630

PLEASD cont.
Ant. Orsino; Noble sir, | Be pleas'd that I shake off these names you
giue mee:                                                        2224
PLEASE = 7*6
Val. So please my Lord, I might not be admitted,                 30
*to the house: if not, and it would please you to take           797
*Cur. He is not heere (so please your Lordshippe) that | should sing it?  892
If it please the eye of one, it is with me as the very true      1544
Sonnet is: Please one, and please all.                           1545
Vio. Pray sir, put your sword vp if you please.                  1839
*Clo. By my troth sir, no: though it please you to be | one of my
friends.                                                         2177
*Ol. Euen what it please my Lord, that shal becom him            2272
*me as you please. I leaue my duty a little vnthought of,        2476
*My Lord, so please you, these things further thought on,        2482
One day shall crowne th'alliance on't, so please you,            2484
and wee'l striue to please you euery day.                        2579
PLEASER = *1
*constantly but a time-pleaser, an affection'd Asse, that        841
PLEASURE = 4*2
Clo. No paines sir, I take pleasure in singing sir.              955
Du. Ile pay thy pleasure then.                                   956
*Clo. Truely sir, and pleasure will be paide one time, or | another.  957
But since you make your pleasure of your paines,                 1468
attends your Ladyships pleasure. | Ol. Ile come to him.          1581
*carry it thus for our pleasure, and his pennance, til our ve- | ry  1659
PLENTIE = 1
In delay there lies no plentie,                                  751
PLIGHT = 1
Plight me the full assurance of your faith,                      2141
PLOT = 1
Fab. Nay patience, or we breake the sinewes of our | plot?       1090
PLUCKE = 1
May rather plucke on laughter then reuenge,                      2537
PLUMES = 1
Cocke of him, how he iets vnder his aduanc'd plumes.             1048
POAST = 1
Vio. I am no feede poast, Lady; keepe your purse,                580
POCKET = 1
Clo. Put your grace in your pocket sir, for this once,           2183
POETICALL = 1
*Vio. Alas, I tooke great paines to studie it, and 'tis | Poeticall.  489
POINT = 1*2
*Toby, I will wash off grosse acquaintance, I will be point      1167
*He does obey euery point of the Letter that I dropt,            1456
Like to th'Egyptian theefe, at point of death                    2274
POINTS = *1
Ma. You are resolute then? | *Clo. Not so neyther, but I am resolu'd on
two points                                                       316
POLE = *1
*in the youth: he will finde it comes from a Clodde-pole.        1706
POLICIE = 1*1
*it, by some laudable attempt, either of valour or | policie.    1408
*policie I hate: I had as liefe be a Brownist, as a Politi- | cian.  1411
POLITICIAN = *1
*policie I hate: I had as liefe be a Brownist, as a Politi- | cian.  1411

POLITICIANS = *1
   *To.* My Lady's a *Catayan*, we are politicians, *Maluolio*s     775
POLITICKE = *1
   *proud, I will reade politicke Authours, I will baffle Sir     1166
POLLUTION = 1
   Doth oft close in pollution: yet of thee     101
POORE = 9*1
   *Vio.* O my poore brother, and so perchance may he be.     57
   When you, and those poore number saued with you,     60
   Poore Lady, she were better loue a dreame:     683
   And I (poore monster) fond asmuch on him:     691
   What thriftlesse sighes shall poore *Oliuia* breath?     696
   *My poore corpes, where my bones shall be throwne:*     951
   O world, how apt the poore are to be proud?     1342
   He started one poore heart of mine, in thee.     1976
   They say poore Gentleman, he's much distract.     2447
   *Ol.* Alas poore Foole, how haue they baffel'd thee?     2540
PORTEND = *1
   *portend, if I could make that resemble something | in me? Softly,
*M.O.A.I.*     1129
POSITION = *1
   *in this, and the end: What should that Alphabeticall po- |sition     1128
POSSESSE = *2
   *To.* Possesse vs, possesse vs, tell vs something of him.     833
POSSEST = 2
   But in very strange manner. He is sure possest Madam.     1529
   *the diuels of hell be drawne in little, and Legion himselfe | possest
him, yet Ile speake to him.     1608
POSSIBLE = 2
   *To.* Ist possible?     1648
   Ist possible that my deserts to you | Can lacke perswasion. Do not
tempt my misery,     1866
POSSIBLY = *1
   *fatall opposite that you could possibly haue found in anie     1785
POST = *1
   *your doore like a Sheriffes post, and be the supporter to     443
POSTSCRIPT = *1
   *starres be praised. Heere is yet a postscript. *Thou canst*     1177
POTENT = 1
   But such a head-strong potent fault it is,     1721
POUND = 1
   helpe, I had rather then forty pound I were at home.     2341
POX = 1
   *And.* Pox on't, Ile not meddle with him.     1798
POYSON = 1
   *Fab.* What dish a poyson has she drest him?     1123
PRACTICE = 2
   That comes before his eye. This is a practice,     1277
   This practice hath most shrewdly past vpon thee:     2522
PRACTISE = 1
   (Courage and hope both teaching him the practise)     63
PRACTISING = *1
   *Sunne practising behauiour to his own shadow this halfe     1034
PRAGE = *1
   *Clo.* *Bonos dies* sir *Toby*: for as the old hermit of *Prage*     1998

PRAISE = 3*3

  *my speech in your praise, and then shew you the heart of | my
  message.    485
  *Ol.* Come to what is important in't: I forgiue you | the praise.    487
  Were you sent hither to praise me?    541
  For boy, howeuer we do praise our selues,    920
  *stockings of late, shee did praise my legge being crosse- | garter'd,    1171
  *Clo.* Marry sir, they praise me, and make an asse of me,    2170

PRAISED = *1

  *starres be praised. Heere is yet a postscript. *Thou canst*    1177

PRANKES = 2

  That nature prankes her in, attracts my soule.    973
  And heare thou there how many fruitlesse prankes    1972

PRATTLE = 1

  What great ones do, the lesse will prattle of, )    83

PRAY = 10*5

  *Ma.* Now sir, thought is free: I pray you bring your    183
  *Ol.* Fetch him off I pray you, he speakes nothing but    400
  *I pray you tell me if this bee the Lady of the house,    466
  *Ol.* It is the more like to be feigned, I pray you keep    491
  *Ol.* O by your leaue I pray you.    1319
  I pray you let vs satisfie our eyes    1489
  he takes it at heart. Pray God he be not bewitch'd.    1624
  *Mar.* Get him to say his prayers, good sir *Toby*, gette | him to pray.    1640
  *Vio.* I pray you sir what is he?    1752
  *Vio.* Pray you sir, do you know of this matter?    1777
  *Vio.* Pray God defend me: a little thing would make    1818
  *And.* Pray God he keepe his oath.    1826
  *Vio.* Pray sir, put your sword vp if you please.    1839
  *2.Off.* Come sir, I pray you go.    1878
  *Ol.* Haue I *Maluolio?* No. | *Mal.* Lady you haue, pray you peruse that
  Letter.    2499

PRAYERS = 1*1

  *Mar.* Get him to say his prayers, good sir *Toby*, gette | him to pray.    1640
  *Mal.* My prayers Minx.    1642

PRAYES = *1

  *did not I tell you? Sir *Toby*, my Lady prayes you to haue | a care of
  him.    1615

PREACHD = 1

  Where manners nere were preach'd: out of my sight.    1966

PREGNANT = 2*1

  Wherein the pregnant enemie does much.    685
  *Vio.* My matter hath no voice Lady, but to your owne | most pregnant
  and vouchsafed eare.    1301
  *And.* Odours, pregnant, and vouchsafed: Ile get 'em | all three already.    1303

PREPARATION = *1

  *be yare in thy preparation, for thy assaylant is quick, skil- | full, and
  deadly.    1743

PREPARE = *1

  *My shrowd of white, stuck all with Ew, O prepare it.*    946

PREROGATIUE = 1

  me on your Neece, giue me this prerogatiue of speech.    1086

PRESAGE = 1

  *Fab.* And his opposit the youth beares in his visage no | great presage
  of cruelty.    1443

PRESENCE = *1

  *in my presence still smile, deero my sweete, I prethee.* Ioue    1180

PRESENT = 6*1
Thou shalt present me as an Eunuch to him, 108
*Looke you sir, such a one I was this present: Ist not well | done? 526
*Present mirth, hath present laughter:* 749
And part being prompted by your present trouble, 1860
Ile make diuision of my present with you: 1863
Taint the condition of this present houre, 2528
PRESENTLY = 1*1
till he take leaue, and presently after him. 1715
*And*. For the loue of God a Surgeon, send one pre-|sently to sir *Toby*. 2336
PRESERUD = 1
I was preseru'd to serue this Noble Count: 2422
PRESUPPOSD = 1
And in such formes, which heere were presuppos'd 2520
PRETHEE = 6*8
I prethee (and Ile pay thee bounteously) 104
*Clo*. Are you ready Sir? | *Duke*. I prethee sing. *Musicke*. 939
*in my presence still smile, deero my sweete, I prethee*. Ioue 1180
*Ol*. Stay: I prethee tell me what thou thinkst of me? 1354
*To*. Prethee hold thy peace, this is not the way: Doe 1631
*Seb*. I prethee vent thy folly some-where else, thou | know'st not me. 1927
*Cockney: I prethee now vngird thy strangenes, and tell 1932
*Seb*. I prethee foolish greeke depart from me, there's 1935
Rudesbey be gone. I prethee gentle friend, 1968
*Ol*. Nay come I prethee, would thoud'st be rul'd by me 1981
*Mar*. Nay, I prethee put on this gown, & this beard, 1986
*Mal*. Foole, Ile requite it in the highest degree: | I prethee be gone. 2103
*Ol*. Prethee reade i'thy right wits. 2464
Vpon thee in the Letter: prethee be content, 2521
PRETTIE = 1
*Trip no further prettie sweeting*. 743
PREUAILE = *1
*can more preuaile in mans commendation with woman, | then report
of valour. 1417
PREUENTED = 1
*Vio*. I will answer you with gate and entrance, but we | are preuented. 1295
PREUENTS = *1
*Clo*. Many a good hanging, preuents a bad marriage: 314
PREY = 1
If one should be a prey, how much the better 1343
PRICE = 1*1
But falles into abatement, and low price 17
*you hold your life at any price, betake you to your gard: 1749
PRIDE = 1
I loue thee so, that maugre all thy pride, 1367
PRIEST = 3*1
*that had rather go with sir Priest, then sir knight: I care 1789
*Enter Oliuia, and Priest*. 2136
*Enter Priest*. 2311
Kept in a darke house, visited by the Priest, 2512
PRIEST = 1
PRIMA *l*.1  611  1213  1917  2152 = 5
PRIMO = *1
*Clo*. *Primo, secundo, tertio*, is a good play, and the olde 2187
PRIMUS *l*.1  610 = 2
PRINCESSE = 1*1
*Vio*. *Cesario* is your seruants name, faire Princesse. 1309

PRINCESSE *cont.*
*reade thus: therefore, perpend my Princesse, and giue | eare.   2466
PRISON = 1
*To.* To him sir *Topas.* | *Clow.* What hoa, I say, Peace in this prison.   2002
PRIUATE = 1*2
*Mal.* Go off, I discard you: let me enioy my priuate: | go off.   1612
*on carpet consideration, but he is a diuell in priuate brall,   1754
In priuate brabble did we apprehend him.   2216
PRIZD = *1
*Mal.* Mistris Mary, if you priz'd my Ladies fauour   817
PRIZES = 1
Prizes not quantitie of dirtie lands,   969
PROBATION = *1
*that suffers vnder probation: *A.* should follow, but *O.* | does.   1138
PROCEEDE = 1
may proceede in my speech.   476
PRODIGALL = 1
He's a very foole, and a prodigall.   141
PROFIT = *1
*foes sir, I profit in the knowledge of my selfe, and by my   2172
PROFOUND = *1
*Ol.* Are you a Comedian? | *Vio.* No my profound heart: and yet (by
the verie   477
PROMISD = *1
*And.* Marry will I sir: and for that I promis'd you Ile   1840
PROMISE = 3*1
promise with him, and make a foole of him.   824
*Fab.* Nothing of that wonderfull promise to read him   1782
And to his image, which me thought did promise | Most venerable
worth, did I deuotion.   1882
*Cesario,* you do not keepe promise with me.   2258
PROMISED = *1
*he cannot by the Duello auoide it: but hee has promised   1823
PROMPT = *1
*pastime tyred out of breath, prompt vs to haue mercy   1660
PROMPTED = 1
And part being prompted by your present trouble,   1860
PROOFE = 3*2
*Ol.* Make your proofe.   353
*Ol.* Well sir, for want of other idlenesse, Ile bide your | proofe.   356
*Vio.* No not a grize: for tis a vulgar proofe | That verie oft we pitty
enemies.   1339
*approbation, then euer proofe it selfe would haue earn'd | him. Away.   1698
*by his forme, as you are like to finde him in the proofe of   1783
PROPER = 3
How easie is it, for the proper false   686
Your wife is like to reape a proper man:   1349
Heere at my house, and at my proper cost.   2485
PROPERTIED = *1
*Mal.* They haue heere propertied me: keepe mee in   2076
PROPHANATION = 1
*would, are as secret as maiden-head: to your eares, Di- | uinity; to any
others, prophanation.   510
PROPRIETY = 1
That makes thee strangle thy propriety:   2307
PROSE = *1
*prose: *If this fall into thy hand, reuolue.* In my stars   1149

PROSPECT = *1
*me, and the full prospect of my hopes. Well Ioue, not I,                    1604
PROSPER = 1
When least in companie: prosper well in this,                               289
PROTECT = *1
*Clo. Now the melancholly God protect thee, and the                        960
PROTECTION = 1
In the protection of his sonne, her brother,                                88
PROTEST = 1*1
*laugh and minister occasion to him, he is gag'd. I protest                 379
Vio. My Lord, I do protest. | Ol. O do not sweare,                         2332
PROTESTS = 1
he protests he will not hurt you.                                          1817
PROUD = 2*1
   Vio. I see you what you are, you are too proud:                          542
*proud, I will reade politicke Authours, I will baffle Sir                 1166
O world, how apt the poore are to be proud?                                1342
PROUE = 6*4
*those wits that thinke they haue thee, doe very oft proue                  327
*motley in my braine: good *Madona*, giue mee leaue to | proue you a
foole.                                                                      349
Our shewes are more then will: for still we proue                          1007
*and wordes are growne so false, I am loath to proue rea-|son with
them.                                                                       1237
*Fab. I will proue it legitimate sir, vpon the Oathes of | iudgement, and
reason.                                                                     1394
Vnguided, and vnfriended, often proue | Rough, and vnhospitable. My
willing loue,                                                              1476
Proue true imagination, oh proue true, | That I deere brother, be now
tane for you.                                                              1896
For him I imitate: Oh if it proue,                                          1904
*I am affraid this great lubber the World will proue a                     1931
PROUES = 1
   Ant. But oh, how vilde an idoll proues this God:                        1885
PROUIDENT = 1
Most prouident in perill, binde himselfe,                                   62
PRUDENT = *1
*'tis thought among the prudent, he would quickely | haue the gift of a
graue.                                                                     148
PS = 1
great *P's*. It is in contempt of question her hand.                      1103
PUBLISH = *1
*that, yet thus farre I will boldly publish her, shee                      637
PUNISH = 1
If I do feigne, you witnesses aboue | Punish my life, for tainting of my
loue.                                                                     2294
PURCHASE = 2
You haue desire to purchase: and your store                               1514
*that giue fooles money, get themselues a good re-|port, after
foureteene yeares purchase.                                                1939
PURE = 1
Did I expose my selfe (pure for his loue)                                  2235
PURGD = 1
Me thought she purg'd the ayre of pestilence;                               25
PURITAN = *1
*To. What for being a Puritan, thy exquisite reason, | deere knight.       836

PURITANE = *2
*Mar*. Marrie sir, sometimes he is a kinde of Puritane.    834
*Mar*. The diu'll a Puritane that hee is, or any thing    840
PURPOSE = 3*1
Ma. What's that to th'purpose? | To. Why he ha's three thousand
ducates a yeare.    138
Mar. My purpose is indeed a horse of that colour.    860
*with the Letter, she sends him on purpose, that I may    1589
*my offence to him is: it is something of my negligence, | nothing of my
purpose.    1773
PURPOSELY = *1
*of some kinde of men, that put quarrells purposely on o- | thers,    1761
PURQUOY see also pur-quoy = *1
*An. What is purquoy? Do, or not do? I would I had    205
PURSE = 5
Vio. I am no feede poast, Lady; keepe your purse,    580
Ant. It doth not fit me: hold sir, here's my purse,    1507
Seb. Why I your purse? | Ant. Haply your eye shall light vpon some toy    1512
Makes me to aske you for my purse. It greeues mee    1852
While one would winke: denide me mine owne purse,    2242
PURSE-BEARER = 1
Seb. Ile be your purse-bearer, and leaue you | For an houre.    1516
PURSUE = 2*2
Ere since pursue me. How now what newes from her?    28
*Mar. Nay pursue him now, least the deuice take ayre, | and taint.    1653
*that I cannot pursue with any safety this sport the vppe- | shot.    2055
Du. Pursue him, and entreate him to a peace:    2550
PURSUITE = 1
The rather by these arguments of feare | Set forth in your pursuite.    1478
PUR-QUOY = 1
To. Pur-quoy my deere knight?    204
PUT = 8*16
*To. O knight, thou lack'st a cup of Canarie: when did | I see thee so
put downe?    194
*put me downe: mee thinkes sometimes I haue no    197
*Clo. Wit, and't be thy will, put me into good fooling:    326
*a barren rascall: I saw him put down the other day, with    376
*selfe. She adds moreouer, that you should put your Lord    664
*put to Sea, that their businesse might be euery thing,    963
*state; put thy selfe into the tricke of singularitie. Shee    1157
*Tob. Why, thou hast put him in such a dreame, that    1197
Vio. Yes being kept together, and put to vse.    1263
To. Taste your legges sir, put them to motion.    1291
*to put fire in your Heart, and brimstone in your Liuer:    1400
*langer with arguments of state, put thy selfe into the    1593
*of some kinde of men, that put quarrells purposely on o- | thers,    1761
Ant. Put vp your sword: if this yong Gentleman    1829
Vio. Pray sir, put your sword vp if you please.    1839
*souldier put vp your yron: you are well flesh'd: Come | on.    1955
*Mar. Nay, I prethee put on this gown, & this beard,    1986
*Clo. Well, Ile put it on, and I will dissemble my selfe    1989
Clo. Put your grace in your pocket sir, for this once,    2183
*tripping measure, or the belles of S.(aint) Bennet sir, may put | you in
minde, one, two, three.    2189
But in conclusion put strange speech vpon me,    2218
*the world shall know it: Though you haue put mee into    2470
*semblance I put on; with the which I doubt not, but to    2474

PUT *cont*.
To put on yellow stockings, and to frowne                                          2508
PUTTING = *1
*euen with the swiftnesse of putting on. Ioue, and my                              1176
PUZELD = *1
*but ignorance, in which thou art more puzel'd then the | Aegyptians in
their fogge.                                                                        2029
PYRATE = 2
*Du*. Notable Pyrate, thou salt-water Theefe,                                      2220
*Anthonio* neuer yet was Theefe, or Pyrate,                                        2226
PYTHAGORAS = 1*1
*Clo*. What is the opinion of *Pythagoras* concerning | Wilde-fowle?               2035
*thou shalt hold th'opinion of *Pythagoras*, ere I will allow                     2043
QUAFFING = *1
*Ma*. That quaffing and drinking will vndoe you: I                                 132
QUALITY = 2
He must obserue their mood on whom he iests, | The quality of persons,
and the time:                                                                      1274
Albeit the quality of the time, and quarrell                                       1499
QUANTITIE = 1
Prizes not quantitie of dirtie lands,                                              969
QUARRELL = 2*3
Albeit the quality of the time, and quarrell                                       1499
*Vio*. You mistake sir I am sure, no man hath any quar-|rell                       1745
*I haue his horse to take vp the quarrell, I haue perswaded | him the
youths a diuell.                                                                   1809
*quarrell, and hee findes that now scarse to bee worth tal-|king                   1815
And let no quarrell, nor no braule to come,                                        2527
QUARRELLER = *1
*he's a foole, he's a great quarreller: and but that hee hath                      146
QUARRELLING = *1
*the gift of a Coward, to allay the gust hc hath in quarrel-|ling,                 147
QUARRELLS = *1
*of some kinde of men, that put quarrells purposely on o-|thers,                   1761
QUARTA *l*.249 883 1520 = 3
QUARTUS *l*.1917 2151 = 2
QUEENE = 2
But 'tis that miracle, and Queene of Iems                                          972
*Orsino's* Mistris, and his fancies Queene. *Exeunt*                              2558
QUENCHING = *1
*Mal*. I extend my hand to him thus: quenching my                                 1081
QUESTION = 4*2
*To*. No question.                                                                 201
*To*. Past question, for thou seest it will not coole my | (nature                211
*that you call in question the continuance of his loue. Is                        255
great *P's*. It is in contempt of question her hand.                              1103
make the triall of it in any constant question.                                   2034
But out of question, tis *Marias* hand.                                           2517
QUESTIONS = *1
*question's out of my part. Good gentle one, giue mee                             474
QUEUBUS = *1
*Queubus*: 'twas very good yfaith: I sent thee six pence                          725
QUICK = *1
*be yare in thy preparation, for thy assaylant is quick, skil-|full, and
deadly.                                                                            1743
QUICKE = 1
O spirit of Loue, how quicke and fresh art thou,                                   13

QUICKELY = 2*2
   *'tis thought among the prudent, he would quickely | haue the gift of a
   graue.           148
   *but a cheu'rill gloue to a good witte, how quickely the     1226
   words, may quickely make them wanton.     1229
   Or will not else thy craft so quickely grow,     2328
QUICKLY = 2
   Euen so quickly may one catch the plague?     591
   quickly. Ile call sir *Toby* the whilst.     1988
QUIET = *1
   *much out of quiet. For Monsieur Maluolio, let me alone     829
QUIETER = 1
   *Mar.* The house will be the quieter.     1656
QUINAPALUS = *1
   *wise man. For what saies *Quinapalus*, Better a witty foole,     329
QUINTA *l.*295 1016 = 2
QUINTUS *l.*2152 = 1
QUIRKE = 1
   *to taste their valour: belike this is a man of that | quirke.     1762
QUITE = 1
   But wisemens folly falne, quite taint their wit.     1280
QUITS = 1
   Your Master quits you: and for your seruice done him,     2487
RACKD = 1
   How haue the houres rack'd, and tortur'd me, | Since I haue lost thee?     2383
RADIANT = *1
   *Vio.* Most radiant, exquisite, and vnmatchable beau-|tie.     465
RAGE = 1*1
   *into a most hideous opinion of his rage, skill, furie, and     1710
   Who with dagger of lath, in his rage and his wrath,     2109
RAINE = 5*2
   *Most excellent accomplish'd Lady, the heauens raine O-|dours on you.     1298
   *And.* That youth's a rare Courtier, raine odours, wel.     1300
   *with hey, ho, the winde and the raine:*     2561
   *for the raine it raineth euery day.*     2563
   *Gainst Knaues and Theeues men shut their gate,* | *for the raine, &c.*     2566
   *By swaggering could I neuer thriue,* | *for the raine, &c.*     2570
   *With tospottes still had drunken heades,* | *for the raine, &c.*     2574
RAINES = 1
   *be as good as my word. Hee will beare you easily, and | raines well.     1841
RAINETH = 1
   *for the raine it raineth euery day.*     2563
RAMSIE = *1
   *a Peg-a-ramsie, and *Three merry men be wee*. Am not I     776
RANGE = 1
   That he did range the towne to seeke me out,     2121
RANKE = 1
   *Fab.* Sowter will cry vpon't for all this, though it bee | as ranke as a
   Fox.     1132
RAPIER = *2
   *To.* He is knight dubb'd with vnhatch'd Rapier, and     1753
   *a firago: I had a passe with him, rapier, scabberd, and all:     1793
RARE = *3
   *Fa.* Oh peace: Contemplation makes a rare Turkey     1047
   *And.* That youth's a rare Courtier, raine odours, wel.     1300
   *Fa.* We shall haue a rare Letter from him; but you'le | not deliuer't.     1436

RASCALL = *2
    *a barren rascall: I saw him put down the other day, with      376
    *Madam, why laugh you at such a barren rascall,      2545
RASCALLY = 1
    Rascally sheepe-biter, come by some notable shame?      1022
RASCALS = 1
    words are very Rascals, since bonds disgrac'd them. | *Vio.* Thy reason
    man?      1234
RATHER = 7*5
    Rather then make vnprofited returne,      272
    *approach rather to wonder at you, then to heare you. If      493
    *the rather to expresse my selfe: you must know of mee      625
    *And. Faith so they say, but I thinke it rather consists | of eating and
    drinking.      711
    *had rather then forty shillings I had such a legge, and so      721
    Would they were blankes, rather then fill'd with me.      1316
    I had rather heare you, to solicit that, | Then Musicke from the
    spheares.      1322
    But rather reason thus, with reason fetter;      1371
    The rather by these arguments of feare | Set forth in your pursuite.      1478
    *that had rather go with sir Priest, then sir knight: I care      1789
    helpe, I had rather then forty pound I were at home.      2341
    May rather plucke on laughter then reuenge,      2537
RAUE = 1
    *Ol.* Why what's the matter, does he raue?      1530
RAUENS = 1
    To spight a Rauens heart within a Doue.      2287
RAYLE = *1
    *in an allow'd foole, though he do nothing but rayle;      386
RAYLING = *1
    *nor no rayling, in a knowne discreet man, though hee do | nothing but
    reproue.      387
READ = 3*2
    *Ol.* O, I haue read it: it is heresie. Haue you no more | to say?      520
    *And.* I, ist? I warrant him: do but read. | *To.* Giue me.      1668
    *Fab.* Nothing of that wonderfull promise to read him      1782
    When they are deliuer'd. | *Ol.* Open't, and read it.      2456
    *Ol.* Read it you, sirrah.      2468
READE = 1*5
    *proud, I will reade politicke Authours, I will baffle Sir      1166
    *An. Heere's the Challenge, reade it: I warrant there's | vinegar and
    pepper in't.      1665
    *Ol.* How now, art thou mad? | *Clo.* No Madam, I do but reade
    madnesse: and your      2460
    *Ol.* Prethee reade i'thy right wits.      2464
    *Clo.* So I do Madona: but to reade his right wits, is to      2465
    *reade thus: therefore, perpend my Princesse, and giue | eare.      2466
READIE = 1
    That I am readie to distrust mine eyes,      2127
READING = *1
    *To.* Oh peace, and the spirit of humors intimate rea- | ding aloud to
    him.      1099
READS = *1
    *Fab. Reads.* By the Lord Madam, you wrong me, and      2469
READY = 1
    *Clo.* Are you ready Sir? | *Duke.* I prethee sing. *Musicke.*      939

REAPE = 1
Your wife is like to reape a proper man: 1349
REASON = 9*7
*you be not mad, be gone: if you haue reason, be breefe: 494
*To. What for being a Puritan, thy exquisite reason, | deere knight. 836
*An. I haue no exquisite reason for't, but I haue reason | good enough. 838
*imagination iade mee; for euery reason excites to this, 1169
words are very Rascals, since bonds disgrac'd them. | Vio. Thy reason man? 1234
*and wordes are growne so false, I am loath to proue rea-|son with them. 1237
Nor wit, nor reason, can my passion hide: 1368
But rather reason thus, with reason fetter; 1371
To. Thy reason deere venom, giue thy reason. 1384
*Fab. You must needes yeelde your reason, Sir An-|drew? 1385
*Fab. I will proue it legitimate sir, vpon the Oathes of | iudgement, and reason. 1394
*thee so, for I will shew thee no reason for't.* 1673
And wrangle with my reason that perswades me 2128
REASONS = 2
Ile giue him reasons for't: hie thee Maluolio. | Mal. Madam, I will. Exit. 604
Do not extort thy reasons from this clause, 1369
RECEIUE = 1*1
*in his affaires, vnlesse it bee to report your Lords taking | of this: receiue it so. 667
*the Gentleman (as I know his youth will aptly receiue it) 1709
RECEIUETH = 1
Receiueth as the Sea. Nought enters there, 15
RECEIUING = *1
*That tyrannous heart can think? To one of your receiuing 1334
RECOLLECTED = 1
More then light ayres, and recollected termes 889
RECOMMENDED = 1
Which I had recommended to his vse, | Not halfe an houre before. 2243
RECOMPENCD = 1
Could be but recompenc'd, though you were crown'd | The non-pareil of beautie. 545
RECOMPENCE = 2*2
My Master, not my selfe, lackes recompence. 581
*that I may beare my euils alone. It were a bad recom-|pence 618
*Fab. This is to giue a dogge, and in recompence desire | my dogge againe. 2158
In recompence whereof, he hath married her: 2535
RECORD = 1
Seb. O that record is liuely in my soule, 2412
RECOUER = *1
*An. If I cannot recouer your Neece, I am a foule way | out. 876
RECOUERD = *1
*kill him, whom you haue recouer'd, desire it not. Fare 646
RECREATION = *1
*him a common recreation, do not thinke I haue witte e-|nough 831
RED = 1
Vio. Tis beauty truly blent, whose red and white, 531
REDDE = *1
*Item two lippes indifferent redde, Item two grey eyes, 539

REDEEME = 1*1

*like an ysickle on a Dutchmans beard, vnlesse you do re-|deeme                1407
Did I redeeme: a wracke past hope he was:                                       2231
REFUSE = 1

Refuse it not, it hath no tongue, to vex you:                                   1726
REGARD = 2*1

*a demure trauaile of regard: telling them I knowe my                          1069
familiar smile with an austere regard of controll.                             1082
You throw a strange regard vpon me, and by that                                2376
REGARDANCE = 1

Since you to non-regardance cast my faith,                                      2277
REINS *see* rains
RELEEUD = 1

Releeu'd him with such sanctitie of loue;                                       1881
RELEEUE = 1

Me thought it did releeue my passion much,                                     888
RELIGIOUS = *1

*Fab. A Coward, a most deuout Coward, religious in | it.                        1910
RELIQUES = 1

Shall we go see the reliques of this Towne?                                     1486
RELLISH = 1

Seb. What rellish is in this? How runs the streame?                            1977
REMAINE = *1

*Clo. Fare thee well: remaine thou still in darkenesse,                         2042
REMEDIE = 1*2

*To. There's no remedie sir, he will fight with you for's                      1813
*To. Come sir *Andrew*, there's no remedie, the Gen-|tleman                     1821
But there's no remedie, I shall answer it:                                      1850
REMEDY = *1

*Sillogisme will serue, so: if it will not, what remedy?                        342
REMEMBER = 4*4

In the sweet pangs of it, remember me:                                          901
*thus aduises thee, that sighes for thee. Remember who                          1158
*euer crosse garter'd: I say remember, goe too, thou art                        1160
*Ant*. To th'Elephant. | *Seb*. I do remember. *Exeunt*.                        1518
*Mal*. Remember who commended thy yellow stock-|ings.                           1569
*Du*. That face of his I do remember well,                                      2202
and yet alas, now I remember me,                                               2446
*all one: By the Lord Foole, I am not mad: but do you re-|member,               2544
REMEMBRANCE = 3*1

And lasting, in her sad remembrance.                                           38
drowne her remembrance againe with more.                                       640
*to me: my remembrance is very free and cleere from                            1746
From my remembrance, clearly banisht his.                                       2450
REMORSE = *1

*Catches without any mitigation or remorse of voice?                           790
REMOUED = 1

And grew a twentie yeeres remoued thing                                        2241
RENEGATHO = *1

*Heathen, a verie Renegatho; for there is no christian                         1449
RENOWNE = 1

With the memorials, and the things of fame | That do renowne this
City.                                                                          1490
REPAYING = 1

It might haue since bene answer'd in repaying                                  1501

REPORT = 1*3
 *in his affaires, vnlesse it bee to report your Lords taking | of this:
 receiue it so. 667
 *can more preuaile in mans commendation with woman, | then report
 of valour. 1417
 *set vpon *Ague-cheeke* a notable report of valor, and driue 1708
 *that giue fooles money, get themselues a good re- | port, after
 foureteene yeares purchase. 1939
REPROOFE = 1
 That it but mockes reproofe. 1722
REPROUE = 1
 *nor no rayling, in a knowne discreet man, though hee do | nothing but
 reproue. 387
REPROUES = 1
 There's something in me that reproues my fault: 1720
REQUEST = 2
 *Mar.* How do you *Maluolio*? | *Maluo.* At your request: 1556
 *Clo.* Good M.(aster) *Fabian*, grant me another request. | *Fab.* Any
 thing. 2155
REQUITE = 1
 *Mal.* Foole, Ile requite it in the highest degree: | I prethee be gone. 2103
RESCUE = 1
 *Vio.* Here comes the man sir, that did rescue mee. 2201
RESEMBLE = *1
 *portend, if I could make that resemble something | in me? Softly,
 *M.O.A.I.* 1129
RESEMBLED = *1
 *Seb.* A Lady sir, though it was said shee much resem- | bled 634
RESERUE = *1
 *selfe: for what is yours to bestowe, is, not yours to re- | serue. 483
RESOLUD = *1
 *Ma.* You are resolute then? | *Clo.* Not so neyther, but I am resolu'd on
 two points 316
RESOLUTE = 1
 *Ma.* You are resolute then? | *Clo.* Not so neyther, but I am resolu'd on
 two points 316
RESPECT = 1*1
 Is there no respect of place, persons, nor time in you? 791
 *respect, then any one else that followes her. What | should I thinke
 on't? 1044
REST = 5
 Cry out *Oliuia*: O you should not rest 568
 *Du.* Let all the rest giue place: Once more *Cesario*, 966
 foote of a flea, Ile eate the rest of th'anatomy. 1442
 To do you rest, a thousand deaths would dye. 2289
 Were you a woman, as the rest goes euen, 2405
RESTORE = 1*1
 *Mal.* And some haue greatnesse thrust vpon them. | *Ol.* Heauen restore
 thee. 1567
 *Maluolio, Maluolio*, thy wittes the heauens restore: en- | deauour 2080
RESTRAINT = 1
 My loue without retention, or restraint, 2233
RETENTION = 2
 So bigge, to hold so much, they lacke retention. 984
 My loue without retention, or restraint, 2233
RETURND = *2
 *her will is, it should be so return'd: If it bee worth stoo- | ping 671

RETURND *cont.*
*Orsino's* is return'd, I could hardly entreate him backe: he 1580
RETURNE = 3*1
But from her handmaid do returne this answer: 31
Rather then make vnprofited returne, 272
*Vio.* I will returne againe into the house, and desire 1759
*To.* I will doe so. Signiour *Fabian*, stay you by this | Gentleman, till
my returne. *Exit Toby.* 1775
RETURNES = *1
*Mal.* She returnes this Ring to you (sir) you might 662
REUEALES = 1
Reueales before 'tis ripe: what thou dost know 2316
REUELS = *2
*strangest minde i'th world: I delight in Maskes and Re-|uels
sometimes altogether. 222
*dam'd colour'd stocke. Shall we sit about some Reuels? 243
REUENGD = 1
*Mal.* Ile be reueng'd on the whole packe of you? 2548
REUENGE = 2
my reuenge finde notable cause to worke. 846
May rather plucke on laughter then reuenge, 2537
REUENGES = 1
*and you smile not he's gag'd: and thus the whirlegigge | of time, brings
in his reuenges. 2546
REUERBERATE = 1
Hallow your name to the reuerberate hilles, 566
REUERENCE = 1
O welcome Father: | Father, I charge thee by thy reuerence 2312
REUEREND = *1
*manner how: as a sad face, a reuerend carriage, a slow 1595
REUOLT = 1
That suffer surfet, cloyment, and reuolt, 987
REUOLUE = *1
*prose: *If this fall into thy hand, reuolue.* In my stars 1149
RICH = 2*1
How will she loue, when the rich golden shaft 41
Loue-thoughts lye rich, when canopy'd with bowres. | *Exeunt* 47
*winde vp my watch, or play with my some rich Iewell: 1076
RIDDE = *1
*how thou findst him: I would we were well ridde of this 2052
RIDDLE = 1
*Fa.* A fustian riddle. | *To.* Excellent Wench, say I. 1119
RIDE = 2*1
*An.* And I thought that, I'de forsweare it. Ile ride | home to morrow sir
*Toby.* 202
marry Ile ride your horse as well as I ride you. 1807
RIDICULOUS = *1
*Mar.* Why appeare you with this ridiculous bold-|nesse before my
Lady. 1559
RIGHT = 4*3
I know thy constellation is right apt 286
*To.* Th'art i'th right. Goe sir, rub your Chaine with 815
*Vio.* Then thinke you right: I am not what I am. 1357
*Du.* Be not amaz'd, right noble is his blood: 2430
*Ol.* Prethee reade i'thy right wits. 2464
*Clo.* So I do Madona: but to reade his right wits, is to 2465
*do my selfe much right, or you much shame: thinke of 2475

RIGHTLY = *1
*that meanes to be saued by beleeuing rightly, can euer          1450
RING = 4*2
  The Countes man: he left this Ring behinde him          599
  *Mal. She returnes this Ring to you (sir) you might          662
  Vio. She tooke the Ring of me, Ile none of it.          669
  *Vio. I left no Ring with her: what meanes this Lady?          674
  None of my Lords Ring? Why he sent her none;          681
  A Ring in chace of you. So did I abuse | My selfe, my seruant, and I
  feare me you:          1327
RINGS = 1
  Strengthned by enterchangement of your rings,          2321
RIPE = 2
  Come boy with me, my thoughts are ripe in mischiefe:          2285
  Reueales before 'tis ripe: what thou dost know          2316
ROBIN = *2
  *Clo. Hey Robin, iolly Robin, tell me how thy Lady | does. | Mal.
  Foole.          2057
RODORIGO = *1
  *then Antonio, my name is Sebastian (which I call'd Rodo-|rigo)          626
ROGUE = 5*2
  *Ma. Peace you rogue, no more o'that: here comes my          323
  To. Heere's an ouer-weening rogue.          1046
  And. Slight I could so beate the Rogue. | To. Peace I say.          1049
  Mal. To be Count Maluolio. | To. Ah Rogue.          1051
  To. Thou kilst me like a rogue and a villaine.          1682
  *To. Then he's a Rogue, and a passy measures pauyn: I | hate a
  drunken rogue.          2363
ROMANE = *1
  *be executed. I thinke we doe know the sweet Romane | hand.          1550
ROMING = 1
  Clowne sings. | O Mistris mine where are you roming?          739
ROOFE = 1
  And vnderneath that consecrated roofe,          2140
ROOM = *1
  *To. Come, wee'l haue him in a darke room & bound.          1657
ROPES = *1
  *the youth to an answer. I thinke Oxen and waine-ropes          1439
ROSES = 2
  For women are as Roses, whose faire flowre          927
  Cesario, by the Roses of the Spring,          1365
ROUGH = 2
  Vnguided, and vnfriended, often proue | Rough, and vnhospitable. My
  willing loue,          1476
  is rough, and will not be roughly vs'd.          1634
ROUGHLY = 1
  is rough, and will not be roughly vs'd.          1634
ROUND = 1*1
  And water once a day her Chamber round          35
  *Mal. Sir Toby, I must be round with you. My Lady          793
ROWZE = *1
  *rowze the night-Owle in a Catch, that will drawe three          759
ROYALL = *1
  *Mar. Sport royall I warrant you: I know my Phy-|sicke          864
RUB = *1
  *To. Th'art i'th right. Goe sir, rub your Chaine with          815

RUBIOUS = 1
    Is not more smooth, and rubious: thy small pipe         283
RUDE = 1
    From the rude seas enrag'd and foamy mouth       2230
RUDELY = 1
    *Ol.* Yet you began rudely. What are you? | What would you?     506
RUDENESSE = *1
    *Vio.* The rudenesse that hath appear'd in mee, haue I     508
RUDESBEY = 1
    Rudesbey be gone. I prethee gentle friend,       1968
RUFFIAN = 1
    This Ruffian hath botch'd vp, that thou thereby     1973
RULD = *1
    *Ol.* Nay come I prethee, would thoud'st be rul'd by me   1981
RULE = *2
    *meanes for this vnciuill rule; she shall know of it by this | hand. *Exit*   819
    *darkenesse, and giuen your drunken Cosine rule ouer me,   2471
RUN = 2
    *Ol.* Run after that same peeuish Messenger       598
    when the image of it leaues him, he must run mad.     1198
RUNS = 1
    *Seb.* What rellish is in this? How runs the streame?    1977
SACKE = *1
    *To.* Come, come, Ile go burne some Sacke, tis too late   881
SACRIFICE = 1
    Ile sacrifice the Lambe that I do loue,        2286
SAD = 6*3
    And lasting, in her sad remembrance.         38
    *And in sad cypresse let me be laide.*        943
    *\*Sad true louer neuer find my graue, to weepe there.*   953
    *I speake too loud: Where's *Maluolio*, he is sad, and ciuill,  1525
    I am as madde as hee, | If sad and merry madnesse equall bee.  1536
    *Ol.* Smil'st thou? I sent for thee vpon a sad occasion.   1540
    *Mal.* Sad Lady, I could be sad:         1541
    *manner how: as a sad face, a reuerend carriage, a slow  1595
SAFETIE = *1
    *vndertake that with me, which with as much safetie you  1767
SAFETY = 1*1
    *that I cannot pursue with any safety this sport the vppe- | shot.  2055
    I must haue done no lesse with wit and safety.    2375
SAGE = 1
    whisper ore a couplet or two of most sage sawes.    1899
SAID = 2*4
    *speake with you. What is to be said to him Ladie, hee's | fortified
    against any deniall.            439
    *Seb.* A Lady sir, though it was said shee much resem- | bled  634
    *Clo.* You haue said sir: To see this age: A sentence is  1225
    *Ol.* I haue said too much vnto a hart of stone,    1718
    *Studient: but to be said an honest man and a good hous- | keeper  1993
    man? Talkest thou nothing but of Ladies? | *Tob.* Well said M.(aster)
    Parson.               2012
SAIDE = 1*2
    *Ol.* A comfortable doctrine, and much may bee saide  515
    *can be saide? Nothing that can be, can come betweene  1603
    Boy, thou hast saide to me a thousand times,    2433
SAIES = *1
    *wise man. For what saies *Quinapalus*, Better a witty foole,  329

SAINT = *2
   *Clo*. Yes by S.(aint) Anne, and Ginger shall bee hotte y'th | mouth
too.    813
   *tripping measure, or the belles of S.(aint) *Bennet* sir, may put | you in
minde, one, two, three.    2189
SAKE = 2*2
   What we tooke from them, which for Traffiques sake    1502
   *oath sake: marrie hee hath better bethought him of his    1814
   *will for his honors sake haue one bowt with you:    1822
   All his in dedication. For his sake,    2234
SALT = 1*1
   *drown'd already sir with salt water, though I seeme to    639
   Tempests are kinde, and salt waues fresh in loue.    1905
SALT-WATER = 1
   *Du*. Notable Pyrate, thou salt-water Theefe,    2220
SAME = 4*1
   *Ol*. Run after that same peeuish Messenger    598
   Get thee to yond same soueraigne crueltie:    967
   *Ol*. If I thinke so, I thinke the same of you.    1356
   *Vio*. With the same hauiour that your passion beares,    1723
   *Du*. Is this the Madman? | *Ol*. I my Lord, this same: How now
*Maluolio*?    2495
SANCTITIE = 1
   Releeu'd him with such sanctitie of loue;    1881
SANCTITY = *1
   *To*. Which way is hee in the name of sanctity. If all    1607
SATE = 1
   She sate like Patience on a Monument,    1004
SATHAN = *2
   *grauity to play at cherrie-pit with sathan. Hang him foul | Colliar.    1638
   *Clo*. Fye, thou dishonest sathan: I call thee by the    2017
SATISFACTION = *1
   *at this moment is so implacable, that satisfaction    1756
SATISFIE = 1
   I pray you let vs satisfie our eyes    1489
SAUAGE = 1
   Kill what I loue: (a sauage iealousie,    2275
SAUD = 1
   That honour (sau'd) may vpon asking giue.    1729
SAUE = 4*2
   Saue in the constant image of the creature    904
   *A thousand thousand sighes to saue*, lay me o where    952
   *Vio*. Saue thee Friend and thy Musick: dost thou liue | by thy Tabor?    1215
   *To*. Saue you Gentleman. | *Vio*. And you sir.    1282
   Shall mistris be of it, saue I alone.    1376
   *To*. Gentleman, God saue thee.    1737
SAUED = 2*2
   *Cap*. It is perchance that you your selfe were saued.    56
   When you, and those poore number saued with you,    60
   *haue saued mee my paines, to haue taken it away your    663
   *that meanes to be saued by beleeuing rightly, can euer    1450
SAUOURS = 2
   That sometime sauours nobly) but heare me this:    2276
   *Du*. This sauours not much of distraction.    2480
SAW = 6*4
   Hung on our driuing boate: I saw your brother    61
   I saw him hold acquaintance with the waues, | So long as I could see.    66

SAW *cont.*

| | |
|---|---:|
| *Duke.* Who saw *Cesario* hoa? | *Vio.* On your attendance my Lord heere. | 259 |
| *a barren rascall: I saw him put down the other day, with | 376 |
| *for I neuer saw her. I would bee loath to cast away my | 467 |
| *Vio.* I saw thee late at the Count *Orsino's.* | 1250 |
| I thinke I saw your wisedome there. | 1254 |
| *And.* Marry I saw your Neece do more fauours to the | 1386 |
| *that neuer saw pen and inke, very wittily sayd to a Neece | 1999 |
| Yet when I saw it last, it was besmear'd | 2203 |

SAWCY = 1*1

| | |
|---|---:|
| *it in. I heard you were sawcy at my gates, & allowd your | 492 |
| *Fab.* Ist so sawcy? | 1667 |

SAWES = 1

| | |
|---|---:|
| whisper ore a couplet or two of most sage sawes. | 1899 |

SAWT = 1

| | |
|---|---:|
| I saw't i'th Orchard. | 1388 |

SAY = 28*18

| | |
|---|---:|
| (They say) she hath abiur'd the sight | And company of men. | 90 |
| *To.* Fie, that you'l say so: he playes o'th Viol-de-gam- | boys, | 142 |
| that say so of him. Who are they? | 151 |
| *Vio.* Say I do speake with her (my Lord) what then? | *Du.* O then, vnfold the passion of my loue, | 273 |
| That say thou art a man: *Dianas* lip | 282 |
| *Ma.* In the warrs, & that may you be bolde to say in | your foolerie. | 307 |
| *flower; The Lady bad take away the foole, therefore I | say againe, take her away. | 344 |
| *Non facit monachum:* that's as much to say, as I weare not | 348 |
| *Ol.* How say you to that *Maluolio?* | 374 |
| me faith say I. Well, it's all one. *Exit* | 423 |
| *Ol.* Whence came you sir? | *Vio.* I can say little more then I haue studied, & that | 472 |
| *Ol.* O, I haue read it: it is heresie. Haue you no more | to say? | 520 |
| *And.* Faith so they say, but I thinke it rather consists | of eating and drinking. | 711 |
| *Marian* I say, a stoope of wine. | 714 |
| Say that some Lady, as perhappes there is, | 977 |
| We men may say more, sweare more, but indeed | 1006 |
| To her in haste: giue her this Iewell: say, | 1014 |
| *And.* Slight I could so beate the Rogue. | *To.* Peace I say. | 1049 |
| *Fa.* A fustian riddle. | *To.* Excellent Wench, say I. | 1119 |
| *Fab.* Did not I say he would worke it out, the Curre | is excellent at faults. | 1135 |
| *euer crosse garter'd: I say remember, goe too, thou art | 1160 |
| *Ma.* Nay but say true, do's it worke vpon him? | *To.* Like Aqua vite with a Midwife. | 1199 |
| *Vio.* So thou maist say the Kings lyes by a begger, if a | 1222 |
| *what you would are out of my welkin, I might say Ele- | ment, but the word is ouer-worne. *Exit* | 1270 |
| *Mal.* Do you know what you say? | 1622 |
| *if I liue. My Lady would not loose him for more then ile | say. | 1627 |
| *Mar.* Get him to say his prayers, good sir *Toby*, gette | him to pray. | 1640 |
| say, he has bin Fencer to the Sophy. | 1797 |
| *Seb.* Madam, I will. | *Ol.* O say so, and so be. *Exeunt* | 1982 |
| *goes as fairely, as to say, a carefull man, & a great | scholler. The Competitors enter. | 1994 |
| *To.* To him sir *Topas.* | *Clow.* What hoa, I say, Peace in this prison. | 2002 |
| *Mal.* I am not mad sir *Topas*, I say to you this house is | darke. | 2026 |

SAY *cont.*
*Clo.* Madman thou errest: I say there is no darknesse 2028
*Mal.* I say this house is as darke as Ignorance, thogh 2031
*Ignorance were as darke as hell; and I say there was ne-|uer 2032
*Clo.* Alas why is she so? | *Mal.* Foole, I say. 2062
*Clo.* Aduise you what you say: the Minister is heere. 2079
*Mal.* Foole, foole, foole I say. 2087
*Clo.* Alas sir be patient. What say you sir, I am shent | for speaking to
you. 2088
According to my birth, what do you say? 2146
*you say sir, let your bounty take a nappe, I will awake it | anon. *Exit* 2198
*Ol.* What do you say *Cesario*? Good my Lord. 2261
And say, thrice welcome drowned *Viola*. 2407
They say poore Gentleman, he's much distract. 2447
Or say, tis not your seale, not your inuention: 2503
You can say none of this. Well, grant it then, 2504
SAYD = *1
*that neuer saw pen and inke, very wittily sayd to a Neece 1999
SAYES = 1*2
*Mal.* Ha's beene told so: and hee sayes hee'l stand at 442
*Ol.* I haue sent after him, he sayes hee'l come: 1522
*the Letter. Cast thy humble slough sayes she: be oppo-|site 1591
SAYING = 2*2
*Vio.* For saying so, there's Gold: 68
saying was borne, of I feare no colours. 305
*Mal.* Saying, Cosine *Toby*, my Fortunes hauing cast 1085
*saying is, the third payes for all: the triplex sir, is a good 2188
SAYINGS = 1
*Vio.* And all those sayings, will I ouer sweare, 2435
SAYLD = *1
*you let time wash off, and you are now sayld into 1405
SAYLE = 1
*Ma.* Will you hoyst sayle sir, here lies your way. 497
SAYLOR = 1
*To.* And they haue beene grand Iurie men, since before | *Noah* was a
Saylor. 1396
SAYLORS = 1*1
*Enter Viola, a Captaine, and Saylors.* 50
*Perchance he is not drown'd: What thinke you saylors? 55
SAYST = 1*1
*Mal.* Some atcheeue greatnesse. | *Ol.* What sayst thou? 1565
*that will vse the diuell himselfe with curtesie: sayst thou | that house is
darke? 2019
SCAB = 1
*To.* What, what? | *Mal.* You must amend your drunkennesse. | *To.* Out
scab. 1087
SCABBERD = *1
*a firago: I had a passe with him, rapier, scabberd, and all: 1793
SCAENA *l.*1 117 611 656 1213 1465 1917 2113 = 8
SCARSE = 3*1
mothers milke were scarse out of him. 456
That were I tane heere, it would scarse be answer'd. 1496
*Fabian* can scarse hold him yonder. 1800
*quarrell, and hee findes that now scarse to bee worth tal-|king 1815
SCATHFULL = 1
With which such scathfull grapple did he make, 2207

SCEDULES = *1
  *out diuers scedules of my beautie. It shalbe Inuentoried    537
SCENA *l*.49 249 295 883 1016 2152 = 6
SCENT *see* sent
SCHOLLER = 1*1
  *To*. Th'art a scholler; let vs therefore eate and drinke    713
  *goes as fairely, as to say, a carefull man, & a great | scholler. The
  Competitors enter.    1994
SCHOOLE = *1
  *Schoole i'th Church: I haue dogg'd him like his murthe-|rer.    1455
SCOENA *l*.699 1381 1520 1984 = 4
SCORNE = 1*1
  *no scorne; I am very comptible, euen to the least | sinister vsage.    470
  *Ol*. O what a deale of scorne, lookes beautifull?    1361
SCOUNDRELS = 1
  *Tob*. By this hand they are scoundrels and substra-|ctors    150
SCOUT = *1
  *To*. Go sir *Andrew*: scout mee for him at the corner    1693
SCREWES = 1
  That screwes me from my true place in your fauour:    2279
SCRUPLE = 1*3
  *Fab*. Nay Ile come: if I loose a scruple of this sport,    1019
  *that no dramme of a scruple, no scruple of a scruple, no    1601
SCULL = *1
  *sonne should be a foole: whose scull, Ioue cramme with    407
SCURUY = 1
  Youth, *whatsoeuer thou art, thou art but a scuruy fellow*.    1670
SEA = 4*1
  Receiueth as the Sea. Nought enters there,    15
  To a strong Maste, that liu'd vpon the sea:    64
  breach of the sea, was my sister drown'd. | *Ant*. Alas the day.    632
  *put to Sea, that their businesse might be euery thing,    963
  But mine is all as hungry as the Sea,    988
SEALD = 1
  And all the Ceremonie of this compact | Seal'd in my function, by my
  testimony:    2322
SEALE = 1*1
  *her *Lucrece*, with which she vses to seale: tiṣ my | Lady: To whom
  should this be?    1107
  Or say, tis not your seale, not your inuention:    2503
SEAS = 1
  From the rude seas enrag'd and foamy mouth    2230
SEASON = 1
  With eye-offending brine: all this to season    36
SEATE = 1
  *Vio*. It giues a verie eccho to the seate | Where loue is thron'd.    906
SEAUEN = *1
  *Mal*. Seauen of my people with an obedient start,    1074
SEA-CAP = 1
  Though now you haue no sea-cap on your head:    1847
SEA-FIGHT = 1
  Once in a sea-fight 'gainst the Count his gallies,    1494
SEB = 23*7
*SEBASTIAN see also Seb*. = 11*2
  *Enter Antonio & Sebastian*.    612
  *then *Antonio*, my name is *Sebastian* (which I call'd *Rodo-|rigo* )    626
  *my father was that *Sebastian* of *Messaline*, whom I    627

SEBASTIAN cont.

| | |
|---|---|
| Enter Sebastian and Anthonio. | 1466 |
| Thou hast Sebastian done good feature, shame. | 1886 |
| Vio. He nam'd Sebastian: I my brother know | 1900 |
| Enter Sebastian and Clowne. | 1918 |
| Enter Sebastian. | 2114 |
| Enter Sebastian. | 2372 |
| Ant. Sebastian are you? \| Seb. Fear'st thou that Anthonio? | 2385 |
| Then these two creatures. Which is Sebastian? \| Ol. Most wonderfull. | 2389 |
| What Countreyman? What name? What Parentage? \| Vio. Of Messaline: | |
| Sebastian was my Father, | 2396 |
| Such a Sebastian was my brother too: | 2398 |

SECOND = *1

| | |
|---|---|
| *One draught aboue heate, makes him a foole, the second \| maddes | |
| him, and a third drownes him. | 426 |

SECRET = 1*1

| | |
|---|---|
| To thee the booke euen of my secret soule. | 263 |
| *would, are as secret as maiden-head: to your eares, Di- \| uinity; to any | |
| others, prophanation. | 510 |

SECUNDA l.49 656 1381 1984 = 4

SECUNDO = *1

| | |
|---|---|
| *Clo. Primo, secundo, tertio, is a good play, and the olde | 2187 |

SECUNDUS l.611 1212 = 2

SEE = 28*14

| | |
|---|---|
| O when mine eyes did see Oliuia first, | 24 |
| I saw him hold acquaintance with the waues, \| So long as I could see. | 66 |
| When my tongue blabs, then let mine eyes not see. | 115 |
| *To. O knight, thou lack'st a cup of Canarie: when did \| I see thee so | |
| put downe? | 194 |
| *An. Neuer in your life I thinke, vnlesse you see Ca- \| narie | 196 |
| to see a huswife take thee between her legs, & spin it off. | 214 |
| *To. No sir, it is leggs and thighes: let me see thee ca- \| per. Ha, higher: | |
| ha, ha, excellent. Exeunt | 247 |
| Ma. Make that good. \| Clo. He shall see none to feare. | 302 |
| *Now you see sir, how your fooling growes old, & peo- \| ple dislike it. | 404 |
| Vio. Good Madam, let me see your face. | 522 |
| Vio. I see you what you are, you are too proud: | 542 |
| Else would I very shortly see thee there: | 653 |
| Disguise, I see thou art a wickednesse, | 684 |
| *Clo. How now my harts: Did you neuer see the Pic- \| ture of we three? | 717 |
| let me see, let me see, let me see. | 1122 |
| *see more detraction at your heeles, then Fortunes before \| you. | 1144 |
| *commended thy yellow stockings, and wish'd to see thee | 1159 |
| *made if thou desir'st to be so: If not, let me see thee a ste- \| ward | 1161 |
| *Mar. If you will then see the fruites of the sport, mark | 1201 |
| *cannot but turn him into a notable contempt: if you wil \| see it follow | |
| me. | 1207 |
| *Clo. You haue said sir: To see this age: A sentence is | 1225 |
| To. Did she see the while, old boy, tell me that. | 1389 |
| And. As plaine as I see you now. | 1390 |
| And not all loue to see you (though so much | 1472 |
| Shall we go see the reliques of this Towne? | 1486 |
| *Ant. To morrow sir, best first go see your Lodging? | 1487 |
| Mal. And wish'd to see thee crosse garter'd. \| Ol. Crosse garter'd? | 1572 |
| Mal. If not, let me see thee a seruant still. | 1576 |
| you not see you moue him? Let me alone with him. | 1632 |
| *and crowne thee for a finder of madmen: but see, but see. | 1662 |

195

SEE *cont.*

| | |
|---|---|
| *Fab.* Giue ground if you see him furious. | 1820 |
| *Ant.* Let me speake a little. This youth that you see \| (heere, | 1879 |
| *And.* And I do not. \| *Fab.* Come, let's see the euent. | 1914 |
| *Clo.* Nay, Ile nere beleeue a madman till I see his brains | 2101 |
| *Fab.* Now as thou lou'st me, let me see his Letter. | 2154 |
| *Clo.* Do not desire to see this Letter. | 2157 |
| Sot, didst see Dicke Surgeon, sot? | 2360 |
| *Du.* Giue me thy hand, \| And let me see thee in thy womans weedes. | 2439 |
| *Ol.* See him deliuer'd *Fabian*, bring him hither: | 2481 |

SEEKE = 3*1

| | |
|---|---|
| That he did seeke the loue of faire *Oliuia*. | 84 |
| *Ol.* Go thou and seeke the Crowner, and let him sitte | 428 |
| *Du.* Seeke him out, and play the tune the while. \| *Musicke playes.* | 898 |
| That he did range the towne to seeke me out, | 2121 |

SEEKING = 1

| | |
|---|---|
| *Ant.* I must obey. This comes with seeking you: | 1849 |

SEEME = 2*2

| | |
|---|---|
| *drown'd already sir with salt water, though I seeme to | 639 |
| That danger shall seeme sport, and I will go. *Exit.* | 655 |
| *Then loue that would seeme hid: Loues night, is noone. | 1364 |
| Wherein *Oliuia* may seeme seruiceable? | 2257 |

SEEMES = 2

| | |
|---|---|
| And she (mistaken) seemes to dote on me: | 692 |
| If this be so, as yet the glasse seemes true, | 2431 |

SEEMS = *1

| | |
|---|---|
| *with you. I told him you were asleepe, he seems to haue | 437 |

SEEN = *1

| | |
|---|---|
| *To.* Why man hee's a verie diuell, I haue not seen such | 1792 |

SEENE = 1*3

| | |
|---|---|
| *not be seene, or if she be it's four to one, she'l none of me: | 216 |
| *Indies: you haue not seene such a thing as tis: I can hard-\|ly | 1459 |
| *and so cunning in Fence, I'de haue seene him damn'd ere | 1802 |
| But when in other habites you are seene, | 2557 |

SEES = 1

| | |
|---|---|
| *Mar.* Thou mightst haue done this without thy berd \| and gowne, he | |
| sees thee not. | 2049 |

SEEST = *2

| | |
|---|---|
| *To.* Past question, for thou seest it will not coole my \| (nature | 211 |
| *seest him, draw, and as thou draw'st, sweare horrible: for | 1695 |

SEET = 1

| | |
|---|---|
| This pearle she gaue me, I do feel't, and see't, | 2116 |

SELF = *1

| | |
|---|---|
| *told me she did affect me, and I haue heard her self come | 1041 |

SELFE = 19*19

| | |
|---|---|
| The Element it selfe, till seuen yeares heate, | 32 |
| Her sweete perfections with one selfe king: | 45 |
| *Cap.* It is perchance that you your selfe were saued. | 56 |
| Assure your selfe, after our ship did split, | 59 |
| *Ma.* I, but you must confine your selfe within the \| modest limits of | |
| order. | 126 |
| *To.* Confine? Ile confine my selfe no finer then I am: | 128 |
| All if you will: for I my selfe am best | 288 |
| Who ere I woe, my selfe would be his wife. *Exeunt.* | 294 |
| *Ol.* If I do not vsurpe my selfe, I am. | 481 |
| *selfe: for what is yours to bestowe, is, not yours to re-\|serue. | 483 |
| My Master, not my selfe, lackes recompence. | 581 |

SELFE *cont.*

| | |
|---|---|
| *the rather to expresse my selfe: you must know of mee | 625 |
| *know you haue heard of. He left behinde him, my selfe, | 628 |
| *selfe. She adds moreouer, that you should put your Lord | 664 |
| *separate your selfe and your misdemeanors, you are wel- \| come | 796 |
| An elder then her selfe, so weares she to him; | 918 |
| *Du.* Then let thy Loue be yonger then thy selfe, | 925 |
| *thy selfe to what thou art like to be: cast thy humble | 1154 |
| *state; put thy selfe into the tricke of singularitie. Shee | 1157 |
| *deuise, the very man. I do not now foole my selfe, to let | 1168 |
| *and in this she manifests her selfe to my loue, & | 1172 |
| A Ring in chace of you. So did I abuse \| My selfe, my seruant, and I | |
| feare me you: | 1327 |
| A murdrous guilt shewes not it selfe more soone, | 1363 |
| *and assure thy selfe, there is no loue-Broker in the world, | 1416 |
| Most of our City did. Onely my selfe stood out, | 1503 |
| *langer with arguments of state, put thy selfe into the | 1593 |
| *and so looke to thy selfe. Thy friend as thou vsest him, & thy \| sworne* | |
| *enemie,* Andrew Ague-cheeke. | 1686 |
| *approbation, then euer proofe it selfe would haue earn'd \| him. Away. | 1698 |
| *To.* Sir, no: his indignation deriues it selfe out of a ve- \|ry | 1764 |
| Then what befals my selfe: you stand amaz'd, \| But be of comfort. | 1854 |
| *Clo.* Well, Ile put it on, and I will dissemble my selfe | 1989 |
| *thy selfe to sleepe, and leaue thy vaine bibble \| babble. | 2081 |
| *foes sir, I profit in the knowledge of my selfe, and by my | 2172 |
| Did I expose my selfe (pure for his loue) | 2235 |
| *Ol.* Hast thou forgot thy selfe? Is it so long? | 2298 |
| *Ant.* How haue you made diuision of your selfe, | 2387 |
| *do my selfe much right, or you much shame: thinke of | 2475 |
| Most freely I confesse my selfe, and *Toby* | 2530 |

SELFE-LOUE = *1

| | |
|---|---|
| *Ol.* O you are sicke of selfe-loue *Maluolio,* and taste | 382 |

SELUES = 2*2

| | |
|---|---|
| Fate, shew thy force, our selues we do not owe, | 608 |
| For boy, howeuer we do praise our selues, | 920 |
| *selues into stitches, follow me; yond gull *Maluolio* is tur-\|ned | 1448 |
| *Mal.* Go hang your selues all: you are ydle shallowe | 1645 |

SEMBLANCE = *1

| | |
|---|---|
| *semblance I put on; with the which I doubt not, but to | 2474 |

SEMBLATIUE = 1

| | |
|---|---|
| And all is semblatiue a womans part. | 285 |

SENCE = 2

| | |
|---|---|
| In your deniall, I would finde no sence, | 559 |
| For though my soule disputes well with my sence, | 2123 |

SENCE-LESSE = 1

| | |
|---|---|
| *Fa.* Very breefe, and to exceeding good sence-lesse. | 1678 |

SEND = 2*6

| | |
|---|---|
| *Clow.* God send you sir, a speedie Infirmity, for the | 370 |
| I cannot loue him: let him send no more, | 576 |
| *To.* Let's to bed knight: Thou hadst neede send for \| more money. | 874 |
| *To.* Send for money knight, if thou hast her not i'th \| end, call me Cut. | 878 |
| *Clo.* Now Ioue in his next commodity of hayre, send \| thee a beard. | 1257 |
| *Vio.* Deere Lady. \| *Ol.* Giue me leaue, beseech you: I did send, | 1324 |
| *darkenesse, send Ministers to me, Asses, and doe all they | 2077 |
| *And.* For the loue of God a Surgeon, send one pre-\|sently to sir *Toby.* | 2336 |

SENDS = *1

| | |
|---|---|
| *with the Letter, she sends him on purpose, that I may | 1589 |

SENSE = 1
  Let fancie still my sense in Lethe steepe,            1979
SENSES = *1
  *yet haue I the benefit of my senses as well as your Ladie- |ship.    2472
SENT = 5*3
  Were you sent hither to praise me?        541
  None of my Lords Ring? Why he sent her none;      681
  *Queubus: 'twas very good yfaith: I sent thee sixe pence    725
  To. O I, make vp that, he is now at a cold sent.    1131
  Ol. I haue sent after him, he sayes hee'l come:    1522
  Ol. Smil'st thou? I sent for thee vpon a sad occasion.    1540
  *Clo. Will you make me beleeue, that I am not sent for | you?    1919
  *nor I am not sent to you by my Lady, to bid you come    1924
SENTENCE = *1
  *Clo. You haue said sir: To see this age: A sentence is    1225
SEPARATE = *1
  *separate your selfe and your misdemeanors, you are wel- |come    796
SEPULCHER = *1
  *can be none, but by pangs of death and sepulcher: Hob, | nob, is his
  word: giu't or take't.    1757
SEQUELL = *1
  *Mal. M. But then there is no consonancy in the sequell    1137
SER = *1
SERUANT see also Ser. = 9
  *Ant. If you will not murther me for my loue, let mee | be your seruant.    643
  Ol. My seruant sir? 'Twas neuer merry world,    1310
  Y'are seruant to the Count Orsino youth.    1312
  Your seruants seruant, is your seruant Madam.    1314
  A Ring in chace of you. So did I abuse | My selfe, my seruant, and I
  feare me you:    1327
  And suites well for a seruant with my fortunes,    1526
  Mal. If not, let me see thee a seruant still.    1576
  Enter Seruant.    1578
SERUANTS = 2*3
  *surly with seruants: Let thy tongue tang arguments of    1156
  *still, the fellow of seruants, and not woorthie to    1162
  Vio. Cesario is your seruants name, faire Princesse.    1309
  Your seruants seruant, is your seruant Madam.    1314
  *with a Kinsman, surly with seruants, let thy tongue    1592
SERUD = 1
  Vio. O that I seru'd that Lady,    92
SERUE = 2*2
  The forme of my intent. Ile serue this Duke,    107
  *Sillogisme will serue, so: if it will not, what remedy?    342
  *command me: I serue her, she is my Ladie. Why this is    1126
  I was preseru'd to serue this Noble Count:    2422
SERUES = 1
  Whereto thy speech serues for authoritie    70
SERUICE = 6
  That will allow me very worth his seruice.    111
  Mal. Heere Madam, at your seruice.    597
  Vio. My dutie Madam, and most humble seruice.    1307
  I did some seruice, of such note indeede,    1495
  His councell now might do me golden seruice,    2122
  Your Master quits you: and for your seruice done him,    2487
SERUICEABLE = 1
  Wherein Oliuia may seeme seruiceable?    2257

SERUICES = *1
*seruices with thee, the fortunate vnhappy daylight and     1164
SERUING-MAN = *1
*Counts Seruing-man, then euer she bestow'd vpon mee:     1387
SERUITURE = 1
*And. Dieu vou guard Monsieur. | Vio. Et vouz ousie vostre seruiture.*     1284
SET = 7*5
*I take these Wise͡men, that crow so at these set kinde of     380
In womens waxen hearts to set their formes:     687
*To*. Wilt thou set thy foote o'my necke.     1192
Haue you not set mine Honor at the stake,     1332
*set 'em downe, go about it. Let there bee gaulle e- | nough     1427
The rather by these arguments of feare | Set forth in your pursuite.     1478
*set vpon *Ague-cheeke* a notable report of valor, and driue     1708
*and light: and conuey what I will set downe to my     2095
*for nothing, and that that I did, I was set on to do't by sir | *Toby*.     2347
me: I thinke you set nothing by a bloody Coxecombe.     2354
*Clo*. O he's drunke sir *Toby* an houre agone: his eyes | were set at eight
i'th morning.     2361
Set this deuice against *Maluolio* heere,     2531
SETTS = *1
*tricke of singularity: and consequently setts downe the     1594
SEUEN = 1
The Element it selfe, till seuen yeares heate,     32
SEUERALL = 1
*Enter Viola and Maluolio, at seuerall doores.*     657
SEUERS = 1
As doth that Orbed Continent, the fire, | That seuers day from night.     2437
SEX = 1
So much against the mettle of your sex,     2488
SHACKLES = 1
*To*. Boltes and shackles. | *Fa*. Oh peace, peace, peace, now, now.     1072
SHADOW = *1
*Sunne practising behauiour to his own shadow this halfe     1034
SHAFT = 1
How will she loue, when the rich golden shaft     41
SHAKE = 2*1
*Mal*. Yes, and shall do, till the pangs of death shake     367
*Mar*. Go shake your eares.     821
*Ant. Orsino*: Noble sir, | Be pleas'd that I shake off these names you
giue mee:     2224
SHAL *l*.582 *2272 = 1*1
SHALBE = *1
*out diuers scedules of my beautie. It shalbe Inuentoried     537
SHALL *l*.33 106 182 *243 *244 266 276 281 303 *367 *431 441 464 *617
655 696 *758 760 *765 769 806 808 812 *813 *819 *851 *857 *866 951
1012 *1026 1078 1140 *1194 1376 *1415 *1424 1430 *1436 1486 1505
1511 1513 1523 *1549 *1626 *1646 1655 1728 *1766 *1788 *1806 1850
*1933 *1936 *2096 2143 2144 2271 2293 2329 *2355 2432 2445 *2470
2484 2491 2529 2553 2556 = 42*30
SHALLOW = 1
For shallow draught and bulke vnprizable,     2206
SHALLOWE = *1
*Mal*. Go hang your selues all: you are ydle shallowe     1645
SHALT *l*.108 290 900 1974 *2043 *2179 2524 = 5*2
SHAME = 3*1
Rascally sheepe-biter, come by some notable shame?     1022

SHAME *cont.*

| | |
|---|---|
| Thou hast *Sebastian* done good feature, shame. | 1886 |
| Heere in the streets, desperate of shame and state, | 2215 |
| *do my selfe much right, or you much shame: thinke of | 2475 |

SHAMEFULL = 1

| | |
|---|---|
| To force that on you in a shamefull cunning | 1330 |

SHAPE = 2*1

| | |
|---|---|
| Onely shape thou thy silence to my wit. | 113 |
| And in dimension, and the shape of nature, | 554 |
| *loue, wherein by the colour of his beard, the shape of his | 849 |

SHAPES = 1

| | |
|---|---|
| Euen in a minute; so full of shapes is fancie, | 18 |

SHARE = 2

| | |
|---|---|
| *My part of death no one so true did share it.* | 947 |
| I shall haue share in this most happy wracke, | 2432 |

SHARPE = 1

| | |
|---|---|
| (More sharpe then filed steele) did spurre me forth, | 1471 |

SHARPELY = *1

| | |
|---|---|
| *accent sharpely twang'd off, giues manhoode more | 1697 |

SHE = 33*25

SHEE *l.*85 *634 *637 *638 *1042 *1102 *1125 *1157 *1163 *1171 *1204
*1206 *1245 *1398 *1461 2518 = 2*14, 1

| | |
|---|---|
| Lady, you are the cruell'st shee aliue, | 533 |

SHEEL = *1

| | |
|---|---|
| *To. Shee'l none o'th Count, she'l not match aboue hir | 218 |

SHEEPE-BITER = 1

| | |
|---|---|
| Rascally sheepe-biter, come by some notable shame? | 1022 |

SHEES = *1

| | |
|---|---|
| *that they come from my Neece, and that shee's in loue \| with him. | 858 |

SHEETE = *2

| | |
|---|---|
| *Lyes, as will lye in thy sheete of paper, although the | 1425 |
| *sheete were bigge enough for the bedde of *Ware* in Eng-\|land, | 1426 |

SHEL = *2

| | |
|---|---|
| *not be seene, or if she be it's four to one, she'l none of me: | 216 |
| *To. Shee'l none o'th Count, she'l not match aboue hir | 218 |

SHENT = *1

| | |
|---|---|
| *Clo. Alas sir be patient. What say you sir, I am shent \| for speaking to you. | 2088 |

SHERIFFES = *1

| | |
|---|---|
| *your doore like a Sheriffes post, and be the supporter to | 443 |

SHES = 1*2

| | |
|---|---|
| *she's nothing ally'd to your disorders. If you can | 795 |
| *An*. Before me she's a good wench. | 870 |
| *To. She's a beagle true bred, and one that adores me: \| what o'that? | 871 |

SHEW = 3*4

| | |
|---|---|
| *my speech in your praise, and then shew you the heart of \| my message. | 485 |
| *but we will draw the Curtain, and shew you the picture. | 525 |
| Fate, shew thy force, our selues we do not owe, | 608 |
| *Clo*. His eyes do shew his dayes are almost done. \| *Mal*. Is't euen so? | 801 |
| *Fab. Shee did shew fauour to the youth in your sight, | 1398 |
| *thee so, for I will shew thee no reason for't.* | 1673 |
| *shew on't, this shall end without the perdition of soules, | 1806 |

SHEWD = 1

| | |
|---|---|
| For the fayre kindnesse you haue shew'd me heere, | 1859 |

SHEWES = 3

| | |
|---|---|
| Our shewes are more then will: for still we proue | 1007 |

SHEWES *cont.*
  For folly that he wisely shewes, is fit;               1279
  A murdrous guilt shewes not it selfe more soone,     1363
SHEWNE = 1
  Enough is shewne, a Cipresse, not a bosome,       1335
SHILLINGS = *1
  *had rather then forty shillings I had such a legge, and so  721
SHINE = *2
  *Seb.* By your patience, no: my starres shine darkely    615
  *Ol.* Then lead the way good father, & heauens so shine,  2149
SHINES = *1
  *Sun, it shines euery where. I would be sorry sir, but the  1252
SHIP = 1
  Assure your selfe, after our ship did split,            59
SHORE = 1
  *Vio.* The Captaine that did bring me first on shore    2441
SHORTLY = 2
  Who shortly also dide: for whose deere loue          89
  Else would I very shortly see thee there:            653
SHOULD *l.*53 *237 *407 568 570 *664 *671 893 998 *1042 1045 *1070
  1108 1113 *1128 *1138 *1253 1288 1343 *1401 *1402 1485 2273 2406
  *2454 = 13*13
SHOULDST *l.*2434 = 1
SHOW *see* shew
SHOWD *see* shew'd
SHOWES *see* shewes
SHOWNE *see* shewne
SHREW = 1
  *And.* Blesse you faire Shrew. | *Mar.* And you too sir.    163
SHREWDLY = 1
  This practice hath most shrewdly past vpon thee:      2522
SHREWISHLY = *1
  *and he speakes verie shrewishly: One would thinke his   455
SHRILL = 1
  Is as the maidens organ, shrill, and sound,           284
SHROWD = *1
  *My shrowd of white, stuck all with Ew, O prepare it.*   946
SHUFFELD = 1
  Are shuffel'd off with such vncurrant pay:           1483
SHUT = 1*1
  *Ol.* Let the Garden doore be shut, and leaue mee to | my hearing.
  Giue me your hand sir.                    1305
  *Gainst Knaues and Theeues men shut their gate, | for the raine, &c.*  2566
SICKE = *4
  *Ol.* O you are sicke of selfe-loue *Maluolio*, and taste   382
  *from the Count, I am sicke, or not at home. What you | will, to
  dismisse it. *Exit Maluo.*                 402
  *speake with you. I told him you were sicke, he takes on   435
  *Vio.* By my troth Ile tell thee, I am almost sicke for    1259
SICKEN = 1
  The appetite may sicken, and so dye.               7
SIDE = 4*1
  Fortune forbid my out-side haue not charm'd her:      675
  wrong side may be turn'd outward.               1227
  *Fa.* Still you keepe o'th windie side of the Law: good.   1683
  *Vio.* He did me kindnesse sir, drew on my side,      2217
  That most ingratefull boy there by your side,       2229

SIDES = 3
   *And*. Taurus? That sides and heart.    246
   You tel her so: Must she not then be answer'd? | *Du*. There is no
   womans sides    980
   If that the iniuries be iustly weigh'd, | That haue on both sides past.    2538
SIGHES = 2*2
   With groanes that thunder loue, with sighes of fire.    549
   What thriftlesse sighes shall poore *Oliuia* breath?    696
   *A thousand thousand sighes to saue, lay me o where*    952
   *thus aduises thee, that sighes for thee. Remember who    1158
SIGHT = 2*2
   (They say) she hath abiur'd the sight | And company of men.    90
   *Fab*. Shee did shew fauour to the youth in your sight,    1398
   *To. Thou comst to the Lady Oliuia, and in my sight she vses*    1675
   Where manners nere were preach'd: out of my sight.    1966
SIGNIOR = 1
   *To*. Come thy wayes Signior *Fabian*.    1018
SIGNIOUR = *1
   *To*. I will doe so. Signiour *Fabian*, stay you by this | Gentleman, till
   my returne. *Exit Toby*.    1775
SILENCE = 1*2
   Onely shape thou thy silence to my wit.    113
   *Fa*. Though our silence be drawne from vs with cars, | yet peace.    1079
   *Mal. I may command where I adore, but silence like a Lu-|cresse knife:*    1115
SILLOGISME = *1
   *Sillogisme will scrue, so: if it will not, what remedy?    342
SILLY = 1
   Do vse to chaunt it: it is silly sooth,    936
SIMPLE = *1
   *Is but patcht with vertue. If that this simple    341
SIMPLY = *1
   *And*. And I thinke I haue the backe-tricke, simply as | strong as any
   man in Illyria.    231
SIMULATION = *1
   *Mal. M, O, A, I.* This simulation is not as the former:    1146
SIN = *1
   *that transgresses, is but patcht with sinne, and sin that a-|mends,    340
SINCE = 11*4
   Ere since pursue me. How now what newes from her?    28
   That dide some tweluemonth since, then leauing her    87
   *Vio*. Euen now sir, on a moderate pace, I haue since a-|riu'd but
   hither.    660
   *To*. Farewell deere heart, since I must needs be gone.    799
   *Mar*. Sweet Sir Toby be patient for to night: Since    827
   words are very Rascals, since bonds disgrac'd them. | *Vio*. Thy reason
   man?    1234
   Since lowly feigning was call'd complement:    1311
   *To*. And they haue beene grand Iurie men, since before | *Noah* was a
   Saylor.    1396
   But since you make your pleasure of your paines,    1468
   It might haue since bene answer'd in repaying    1501
   Since you to non-regardance cast my faith,    2277
   Since when, my watch hath told me, toward my graue    2324
   How haue the houres rack'd, and tortur'd me, | Since I haue lost thee?    2383
   All the occurrence of my fortune since    2423
   And since you call'd me Master, for so long:    2490

SINEWES = 1
    *Fab.* Nay patience, or we breake the sinewes of our | plot?                                    1090
SING = 5*1
    It may be worth thy paines: for I can sing,                                                     109
    And sing them lowd euen in the dead of night:                                                   565
    *sweet a breath to sing, as the foole has. Insooth thou wast                                    722
    *That can sing both high and low.*                                                              742
    *Cur.* He is not heere (so please your Lordshippe) that | should sing it?                        892
    *Clo.* Are you ready Sir? | *Duke.* I prethee sing. *Musicke.*                                   939
SINGING = 1
    *Clo.* No paines sir, I take pleasure in singing sir.                                            955
SINGS = 2
    *Clowne sings.* | *O Mistris mine where are you roming?*                                         739
    *Clowne sings.* | *When that I was and a little tine boy,*                                       2559
SINGULARITIE = *1
    *state; put thy selfe into the tricke of singularitie. Shee                                      1157
SINGULARITY = *1
    *tricke of singularity: and consequently setts downe the                                        1594
SINISTER = 1
    *no scorne; I am very comptible, euen to the least | sinister vsage.                             470
SINKE-A-PACE = *1
    *as make water but in a Sinke-a-pace: What dooest thou                                           238
SINNE = *2
    *that transgresses, is but patcht with sinne, and sin that a-|mends,                             340
    *my desire of hauing is the sinne of couetousnesse: but as                                       2197
SINNER = 1
    *Du.* Well, I will be so much a sinner to be a double | dealer: there's
    another.                                                                                         2185
SIR *l.*118 *122 135 159 160 161 162 164 165 169 176 181 *183 187 190
    *192 203 *215 *247 256 *321 346 *356 *370 *371 399 *404 408 416 472
    497 *513 *526 *529 *536 *621 *630 *634 *639 641 *660 *662 *670 700
    *701 763 *792 *793 800 804 *810 *815 *827 *834 939 955 *957 974 1012
    1017 *1026 1095 *1166 1217 *1219 *1225 *1230 *1232 *1236 *1241
    *1242 1243 *1245 *1246 *1251 *1252 1262 *1264 1266 *1267 *1268 1281
    1283 1286 *1289 1291 *1292 1294 1306 1310 1382 *1385 *1394 1419
    1432 1433 *1487 1507 1515 *1588 1610 *1615 1636 *1640 1663 *1693
    *1707 1738 *1745 1752 *1764 1777 *1784 *1789 *1813 *1821 1832 1833
    1837 1839 *1840 1845 1846 1856 1858 1878 1892 *1942 *1945 1948
    *1954 *1987 1988 *1998 2002 *2007 *2009 *2014 *2015 2021 *2026 2046
    2047 2071 2083 *2085 2087 *2088 2093 2105 2162 *2165 2168 *2170
    *2172 *2177 *2180 2183 *2188 *2189 *2195 *2196 *2198 2201 2217 2224
    2335 2338 *2339 2342 *2347 *2355 *2361 *2367 2509 2534 *2543 =
    94*98, *1
    *tongue, in the habite of some Sir of note, and so foorth.                                       1596
SIR = *1
SIRRAH = 3
    *Du.* Her husband, sirrah? | *Vio.* No my Lord, not I.                                           2304
    How does he sirrah? | *Cl.* Truely Madam, he holds *Belzebub* at the
    staues end as                                                                                    2451
    *Ol.* Read it you, sirrah.                                                                       2468
SISTER = 7*3
    *and a sister, both borne in an houre: if the Heauens had                                        629
    breach of the sea, was my sister drown'd. | *Ant.* Alas the day.                                 632
    *Du.* But di'de thy sister of her loue my Boy?                                                   1009
    *Clo.* I would therefore my sister had had no name Sir.                                          1230
    *that word, might make my sister wanton: But indeede,                                            1233
    Of heere, and euery where. I had a sister,                                                       2393

SISTER *cont*.

| | |
|---|---|
| That day that made my sister thirteene yeares. | 2414 |
| To thinke me as well a sister, as a wife, | 2483 |
| *Ol*. A sister, you are she. | 2493 |
| A solemne Combination shall be made \| Of our deere soules. Meane time sweet sister, | 2553 |

SIT = 1 *1

| | |
|---|---|
| *dam'd colour'd stocke. Shall we sit about some Reuels? | 243 |
| Vnder your hard construction must I sit, | 1329 |

SITS = 1

| | |
|---|---|
| Where he sits crowned in his masters spight. | 2284 |

SITTE = *1

| | |
|---|---|
| *Ol*. Go thou and seeke the Crowner, and let him sitte | 428 |

SITTING = 1

| | |
|---|---|
| *Mal*. Hauing beene three moneths married to her, \| sitting in my state. | 1060 |

SIXE = *2

| | |
|---|---|
| *Queubus*: 'twas very good yfaith: I sent thee sixe pence | 725 |
| *To*. Come on, there is sixe pence for you. Let's haue \| a song. | 732 |

SKILFULL = *2

| | |
|---|---|
| *be yare in thy preparation, for thy assaylant is quick, skil-\|full, and deadly. | 1743 |
| *his valour. He is indeede sir, the most skilfull, bloudy, & | 1784 |

SKILL = *2

| | |
|---|---|
| *into a most hideous opinion of his rage, skill, furie, and | 1710 |
| *for your opposite hath in him what youth, strength, skill, \| and wrath, can furnish man withall. | 1750 |

SKILLES = *1

| | |
|---|---|
| *madmans Epistles are no Gospels, so it skilles not much | 2455 |

SKILLESSE = 1

| | |
|---|---|
| Being skillesse in these parts: which to a stranger, | 1475 |

SKIPPING = 1

| | |
|---|---|
| *'tis not that time of Moone with me, to make one in so \| skipping a dialogue. | 495 |

SKITTISH = 1

| | |
|---|---|
| Vnstaid and skittish in all motions else, | 903 |

SKULL *see* scull

SLAINE = 1

| | |
|---|---|
| *I am slaine by a faire cruell maide:* | 945 |

SLANDER = *1

| | |
|---|---|
| *that you deeme Cannon bullets: There is no slan-\|der | 385 |

SLEEPE = 1 *1

| | |
|---|---|
| If it be thus to dreame, still let me sleepe. | 1980 |
| *thy selfe to sleepe, and leaue thy vaine bibble \| babble. | 2081 |

SLEEPING = 1

| | |
|---|---|
| *Veluet gowne: hauing come from a day bedde, where I \| haue left *Oliuia* sleeping. | 1064 |

SLEW = 1

| | |
|---|---|
| *Seb*. Belike you slew great number of his people. | 1497 |

SLID = 1

| | |
|---|---|
| *And*. Slid Ile after him againe, and beate him. | 1912 |

SLIGHT = 2

| | |
|---|---|
| *And*. Slight I could so beate the Rogue. \| *To*. Peace I say. | 1049 |
| *And*. S'light; will you make an Asse o'me. | 1393 |

SLIP = *1

| | |
|---|---|
| *I'de haue challeng'd him. Let him let the matter slip, and | 1803 |

SLOUGH = *2

| | |
|---|---|
| *slough, and appeare fresh. Be opposite with a kinsman, | 1155 |

SLOUGH *cont.*
*the Letter. Cast thy humble slough sayes she: be oppo-|site 1591
SLOW = *1
*manner how: as a sad face, a reuerend carriage, a slow 1595
SMALL = 1
Is not more smooth, and rubious: thy small pipe 283
SMELL = 1
*To.* Excellent, I smell a deuice. | *An.* I hau't in my nose too. 855
SMILE = 3*8
familiar smile with an austere regard of controll. 1082
*in my presence still smile, deero my sweete, I prethee.* Ioue 1180
*I thanke thee, I will smile, I wil do euery thing that thou | wilt haue
me. *Exit* 1181
*crosse garter'd, a fashion shee detests: and hee will smile 1204
*Ol.* Why then me thinkes 'tis time to smile agen: 1341
*to betray him: He does smile his face into more lynes, 1457
*strike him: if shee doe, hee'l smile, and take't for a great | fauour. 1461
**Mar.* No Madam, he does nothing but smile: your La-|dyship 1531
**Ol.* God comfort thee: Why dost thou smile so, and | kisse thy hand so
oft? 1554
Mayst smile at this: Thou shalt not choose but goe: 1974
*and you smile not he's gag'd: and thus the whirlegigge | of time, brings
in his reuenges. 2546
SMILES = *1
*it appeare in thy smiling, thy smiles become thee well. There-|fore* 1179
SMILING = 3*1
Smiling at greefe. Was not this loue indeede? 1005
*it appeare in thy smiling, thy smiles become thee well. There-|fore* 1179
Bad me come smiling, and crosse-garter'd to you, 2507
First told me thou wast mad; then cam'st in smiling, 2519
SMILST = 1
*Ol.* Smil'st thou? I sent for thee vpon a sad occasion. 1540
SMOAKE = 1
As blacke as Vulcan, in the smoake of warre: 2204
SMOOTH = 2
Is not more smooth, and rubious: thy small pipe 283
With such a smooth, discreet, and stable bearing 2133
SNATCHD = 1
I snatch'd one halfe out of the iawes of death, ·1880
SNECKE = *1
**To.* We did keepe time sir in our Catches. Snecke vp. 792
SO *l.*7 12 16 18 23 30 *57 67 68 80 *129 *142 151 176 *178 *188 195 *237
269 279 *298 *311 *317 *342 *343 *380 417 *436 *442 *495 *502 *536
*540 591 609 *622 *630 *648 654 *666 668 *671 676 682 *708 *711 *721
*780 802 *843 *892 918 919 929 947 975 980 982 984 1049 *1161 1186
*1205 *1222 *1237 *1241 1327 1336 1356 1367 1377 *1422 1435 *1441
1472 *1554 1555 *1574 *1596 1617 1667 1673 *1686 *1694 *1705 *1711
*1756 *1775 1790 *1802 1868 1895 1901 *1926 1983 *2000 *2054 2062
*2072 2126 2130 *2149 *2171 *2173 2185 2222 2266 2267 2298 2328
2379 2399 2409 2425 2431 *2455 *2465 *2482 2484 2488 2489 2490
2556 = 72*57
SOFT = 3*2
Do giue thee fiue-fold blazon: not too fast: soft, soft, 589
*Her very Phrases: By your leaue wax. Soft, and the im-|pressure 1106
*one of these Letters are in my name. Soft, here fol-|lowes 1148
So farre beneath your soft and tender breeding, 2489

SOFTLY = 1
*portend, if I could make that resemble something | in me? Softly,
*M.O.A.I.* 1129
SOLDIOUR = *1
*me, as he is a Gentleman and a Soldiour, he will not hurt | you. Come
on, too't. 1824
SOLEMNE = 1
A solemne Combination shall be made | Of our deere soules. Meane
time sweet sister, 2553
SOLICIT = 1
I had rather heare you, to solicit that, | Then Musicke from the
spheares. 1322
SOME = 18*29
That dide some tweluemonth since, then leauing her 87
*dam'd colour'd stocke. Shall we sit about some Reuels? 243
For this affayre: some foure or fiue attend him, 287
*Some mollification for your Giant, sweete Ladie; 499
*Ol. Sure you haue some hiddeous matter to deliuer, 501
*that, for some houre before you tooke me from the 631
*Clo.* Byrlady sir, and some dogs will catch well. 763
*To.* What wilt thou do? | *Mar.* I will drop in his way some obscure
Epistles of 847
*To.* Come, come, Ile go burne some Sacke, tis too late 881
*Du.* Giue me some Musick; Now good morow frends. 885
Hath staid vpon some fauour that it loues: 910
Say that some Lady, as perhappes there is, 977
Rascally sheepe-biter, come by some notable shame? 1022
*winde vp my watch, or play with my some rich Iewell: 1076
*I am aboue thee, but be not affraid of greatnesse: Some 1150
*are become great, some atcheeues greatnesse, and some 1151
*you should then haue accosted her, and with some excel- | lent 1401
*it, by some laudable attempt, either of valour or | policie. 1408
*thou'st him some thrice, it shall not be amisse, and as ma- | ny 1424
*To.* I haue beene deere to him lad, some two thousand | strong, or so. 1434
I did some seruice, of such note indeede, 1495
*Seb.* Why I your purse? | *Ant.* Haply your eye shall light vpon some toy 1512
*were best to haue some guard about you, if hee 1532
This does make some obstruction in the blood: 1542
*Mal.* Some are borne great. | *Ol.* Ha? 1563
*Mal.* Some atcheeue greatnesse. | *Ol.* What sayst thou? 1565
*Mal.* And some haue greatnesse thrust vpon them. | *Ol.* Heauen restore
thee. 1567
*Cosine *Toby*, let some of my people haue a speciall care 1584
*tongue, in the habite of some Sir of note, and so foorth. 1596
*in some commerce with my Ladie, and will by and by | depart. 1691
*To.* I wil meditate the while vpon some horrid message | for a
Challenge. 1716
*some conduct of the Lady. I am no fighter, I haue heard 1760
*of some kinde of men, that put quarrells purposely on o- | thers, 1761
*Ant.* I must entreat of you some of that money. 1857
*Clo.* Vent my folly: He has heard that word of some 1929
in some of your coats for two pence. 1947
*Mal.* Good foole, helpe me to some light, and some 2090
*Mal.* By this hand I am: good foole, some inke, pa- | per, 2094
That this may be some error, but no madnesse, 2124
*Clo.* I sir, we are some of her trappings. 2162
Hath my Maides garments: he vpon some Action 2442

SOME *cont.*
Vpon some stubborne and vncourteous parts 2532
*Clo.* Why some are borne great, some atchieue great-|nesse, 2541
*and some haue greatnesse throwne vpon them. I 2542
SOMETHING = 3*4
*To.* Possesse vs, possesse vs, tell vs something of him. 833
*portend, if I could make that resemble something | in me? Softly,
*M.O.A.I.* 1129
*Clo.* Not so sir, I do care for something: but in my con-|science 1241
There's something in me that reproues my fault: 1720
*my offence to him is: it is something of my negligence, | nothing of my
purpose. 1773
Out of my leane and low ability | Ile lend you something: my hauing is
not much, 1861
As I perceiue she do's: there's something in't 2134
SOMETIME = 1
That sometime sauours nobly) but heare me this: 2276
SOMETIMES = 1*2
*put me downe: mee thinkes sometimes I haue no 197
*strangest minde i'th world: I delight in Maskes and Re-|uels
sometimes altogether. 222
*Mar.* Marrie sir, sometimes he is a kinde of Puritane. 834
SOME-WHERE = *1
*Seb.* I prethee vent thy folly some-where else, thou | know'st not me. 1927
SONG = 8*2
*An.* Excellent: Why this is the best fooling, when | all is done. Now a
song. 730
*To.* Come on, there is sixe pence for you. Let's haue | a song. 732
*Clo.* Would you haue a loue-song, or a song of good | life? 735
*To.* A loue song, a loue song. 737
Now good *Cesario*, but that peece of song, 886
That old and Anticke song we heard last night; 887
*Du.* O fellow come, the song we had last night: 932
*The Song.* | *Come away, come away death,* 941
SONNE = 2*1
In the protection of his sonne, her brother, 88
*sonne should be a foole: whose scull, Ioue cramme with 407
*Euery wise mans sonne doth know.* 745
SONNET = 1
Sonnet is: Please one, and please all. 1545
SOONE = 1*1
A murdrous guilt shewes not it selfe more soone, 1363
*of the Orchard like a bum-Baylie: so soone as euer thou 1694
SOONER = 1
More longing, wauering, sooner lost and worne, | Then womens are. 922
SOOTH = 2*1
*Seb.* No sooth sir: my determinate voyage is meere 621
Do vse to chaunt it: it is silly sooth, 936
*Vio.* Sooth but you must. 976
SOPHY = 2
of thousands to be paid from the Sophy. 1184
say, he has bin Fencer to the Sophy. 1797
SORROW = 1
If she be so abandon'd to her sorrow 269
SORRY = 1*1
*Sun, it shines euery where. I would be sorry sir, but the 1252
*Seb.* I am sorry Madam I haue hurt your kinsman: 2373

SORTS = 1
And speake to him in many sorts of Musicke,                                    110
SOT = 3
*To. 'Tis a Gentleman heere. A plague o'these pickle | herring: How
now Sot.                                                                        414
Sot, didst see Dicke Surgeon, sot?                                            2360
SOUERAIGNE = 2
These soueraigne thrones, are all supply'd and fill'd                           44
Get thee to yond same soueraigne crueltie:                                     967
SOUGHT = 1
Loue sought, is good: but giuen vnsought is better.                          1372
SOULDIER = *1
*souldier put vp your yron: you are well flesh'd: Come | on.                  1955
SOULE = 13*3
To thee the booke euen of my secret soule.                                    263
Clo. I thinke his soule is in hell, Madona.                                    360
Ol. I know his soule is in heauen, foole.                                      361
*Brothers soule, being in heauen. Take away the Foole, | Gentlemen.           363
And call vpon my soule within the house,                                       563
That nature prankes her in, attracts my soule.                                 973
A Fiend like thee might beare my soule to hell.                               1735
Do not denie, beshrew his soule for mee,                                      1975
*Mal. That the soule of our grandam, might happily | inhabite a bird.         2037
*Mal. I thinke nobly of the soule, and no way aproue | his opinion.           2040
the soule of thy grandam. Fare thee well.                                     2045
For though my soule disputes well with my sence,                             2123
That my most iealious, and too doubtfull soule                               2142
My soule the faithfull'st offrings haue breath'd out                         2270
Seb. O that record is liuely in my soule,                                     2412
And all those swearings keepe as true in soule,                              2436
SOULES = 2*3
soules out of one Weauer? Shall we do that?                                    760
*soules. He may haue mercie vpon mine, but my hope is better,                1685
*soules and bodies hath he diuorc'd three, and his incense- | ment           1755
*shew on't, this shall end without the perdition of soules,                  1806
A solemne Combination shall be made | Of our deere soules. Meane
time sweet sister,                                                            2553
SOUND = 2
O, it came ore my eare, like the sweet sound                                    9
Is as the maidens organ, shrill, and sound,                                    284
SOUNDLY = *1
*To. Do, cuffe him soundly, but neuer draw thy sword                         1913
SOUTH = 1*1
In the South Suburbes at the Elephant | Is best to lodge: I will bespeake
our dyet,                                                                     1508
*and the cleere stores toward the South north, are                           2023
SOWD = 1
When time hath sow'd a grizzle on thy case?                                   2327
SOWTER = *1
*Fab. Sowter will cry vpon't for all this, though it bee | as ranke as a
Fox.                                                                          1132
SPARE = 1
To. Shall I bid him go, and spare not? | Clo. O no, no, no, no, you dare
not.                                                                          808
SPEAK = *2
*him to vnderstand so much, and therefore comes to speak                      436
*throw: if you will let your Lady know I am here to speak                     2192

SPEAKE = 14*9
| | |
|---|---|
| And speake to him in many sorts of Musicke, | 110 |
| *Vio. Say I do speake with her (my Lord) what then? \| Du. O then, vnfold the passion of my loue, | 273 |
| *Mar. Madam, there is at the gate, a young Gentle-\|man, much desires to speake with you. | 392 |
| *speake with you. I told him you were sicke, he takes on | 435 |
| *speake with you. What is to be said to him Ladie, hee's \| fortified against any deniall. | 439 |
| Ol. Tell him, he shall not speake with me. | 441 |
| a bench, but hee'l speake with you. | 444 |
| *Mal. Of verie ill manner: hee'l speake with you, will \| you, or no. | 448 |
| Ol. Speake to me, I shall answer for her: your will. | 464 |
| *when the curtesie of it is so fearefull. Speake your office. | 502 |
| For she did speake in starts distractedly. | 678 |
| Du. Thou dost speake masterly, | 908 |
| I bad you neuer speake againe of him; | 1320 |
| Hides my heart: so let me heare you speake. \| Vio. I pittie you. | 1336 |
| *I speake too loud: Where's Maluolio, he is sad, and ciuill, | 1525 |
| *the diuels of hell be drawne in little, and Legion himselfe \| possest him, yet Ile speake to him. | 1608 |
| *Mar. La you, and you speake ill of the diuell, how | 1623 |
| *Ant. Let me speake a little. This youth that you see \| (heere, | 1879 |
| *speake with her: nor your name is not Master Cesario, | 1925 |
| Vio. My Lord would speake, my dutie hushes me. | 2262 |
| Vio. Why do you speake to me, I neuer hurt you: | 2349 |
| and speake out of my iniury. The madly vs'd Maluolio. | 2477 |
| Fab. Good Madam heare me speake, | 2526 |

SPEAKES = *3
| | |
|---|---|
| *Ol. Fetch him off I pray you, he speakes nothing but | 400 |
| *and he speakes verie shrewishly: One would thinke his | 455 |
| *Mar. Lo, how hollow the fiend speakes within him; | 1614 |

SPEAKING = 1
| | |
|---|---|
| *Clo. Alas sir be patient. What say you sir, I am shent \| for speaking to you. | 2088 |

SPEAKS = *1
| | |
|---|---|
| *and speaks three or four languages word for word | 143 |

SPEAKST = 1
| | |
|---|---|
| *Clo. Now Mercury indue thee with leasing, for thou \| speak'st well of fooles. | 389 |

SPECIALL = *1
| | |
|---|---|
| *Cosine Toby, let some of my people haue a speciall care | 1584 |

SPEECH = 4*2
| | |
|---|---|
| Whereto thy speech serues for authoritie | 70 |
| *speech: for besides that it is excellently well pend, I haue | 468 |
| may proceede in my speech. | 476 |
| *my speech in your praise, and then shew you the heart of \| my message. | 485 |
| me on your Neece, giue me this prerogatiue of speech. | 1086 |
| But in conclusion put strange speech vpon me, | 2218 |

SPEEDIE = *1
| | |
|---|---|
| *Clow. God send you sir, a speedie Infirmity, for the | 370 |

SPEND = 1
| | |
|---|---|
| I thanke you for your paines: spend this for mee. | 579 |

SPHEARES = 1
| | |
|---|---|
| I had rather heare you, to solicit that, \| Then Musicke from the spheares. | 1322 |

SPIGHT = 2
  Where he sits crowned in his masters spight.          2284
  To spight a Rauens heart within a Doue.           2287
SPIN = 1
  to see a huswife take thee between her legs, & spin it off.    214
SPINSTERS = 1
  The Spinsters and the Knitters in the Sun,         934
SPIRIT = 3*2
  O spirit of Loue, how quicke and fresh art thou,      13
  Thy tongue, thy face, thy limbes, actions, and spirit,    588
  *To. Oh peace, and the spirit of humors intimate rea-|ding aloud to
  him.           1099
  *hands, let thy blood and spirit embrace them, and to in-|vre  1153
  Seb. A spirit I am indeed,          2402
SPIRITS = 1
  If spirits can assume both forme and suite, | You come to fright vs.  2400
SPLEENE = *1
  *Mar. If you desire the spleene, and will laughe your    1447
SPLIT = 1
  Assure your selfe, after our ship did split,        59
SPOKE = 1*1
  As it is spoke, she neuer will admit me.         270
  *Clo. Thou hast spoke for vs (Madona) as if thy eldest   406
SPOKST = *1
  *in very gracious fooling last night, when thou spok'st of   723
SPORT = 2*4
  That danger shall seeme sport, and I will go. Exit.     655
  *Mar. Sport royall I warrant you: I know my Phy-|sicke   864
  Fab. Nay Ile come: if I loose a scruple of this sport,    1019
  *Fab. I will not giue my part of this sport for a pensi-|on   1183
  *Mar. If you will then see the fruites of the sport, mark   1201
  *that I cannot pursue with any safety this sport the vppe-|shot.  2055
SPORTFULL = 1
  How with a sportfull malice it was follow'd,       2536
SPRING = 1
  Cesario, by the Roses of the Spring,          1365
SPURRE = 1
  (More sharpe then filed steele) did spurre me forth,    1471
SQUASH = *1
  *for a boy: as a squash is before tis a pescod, or a Codling  452
SQUEAK = *1
  *of my Ladies house, that ye squeak out your Cozi-|ers   789
STABLE = 1
  With such a smooth, discreet, and stable bearing    2133
STAGE = *1
  *Fa. If this were plaid vpon a stage now, I could con-|demne it as an
  improbable fiction.           1649
STAID = 1
  Hath staid vpon some fauour that it loues:       910
STAINLESSE = 1
  Of great estate, of fresh and stainlesse youth;     552
STAKE = 1
  Haue you not set mine Honor at the stake,       1332
STALLION = 1
  To. And with what wing the stallion checkes at it?    1124
STAND = 5*3
  Du. Stand you a-while aloofe. Cesario,        261

STAND *cont.*
Be not deni'de accesse, stand at her doores,    265
*Mal.* Ha's beene told so: and hee sayes hee'l stand at    442
*I do liue at my house, and my house dooth stand by the | Church.    1220
if thy Tabor stand by the Church.    1224
*To.* Ile make the motion: stand heere, make a good    1805
Then what befals my selfe: you stand amaz'd, | But be of comfort.    1854
*Seb.* Do I stand there? I neuer had a brother:    2391
STANDING = *1
*when tis almost an Apple: Tis with him in standing wa- | ter,    453
STANDS = *1
*begger dwell neer him: or the Church stands by thy Ta- | bor,    1223
STARKE = *1
*starke naked: for meddle you must that's certain, or for- | sweare to
weare iron about you.    1769
STARRE = 1
*the excellent constitution of thy legge, it was form'd vn- | der the starre
of a Galliard.    240
STARRES = *3
*Seb.* By your patience, no: my starres shine darkely    615
*her liking. I thanke my starres, I am happy: I will bee    1174
*starres be praised. Heere is yet a postscript. *Thou canst*    1177
STARS = *1
*prose: *If this fall into thy hand, reuolue.* In my stars    1149
START = *1
*Mal.* Seauen of my people with an obedient start,    1074
STARTED = 1
He started one poore heart of mine, in thee.    1976
STARTS = 1
For she did speake in starts distractedly.    678
STATE = 5*4
What is your Parentage? | *Vio.* Aboue my fortunes, yet my state is well:    572
*Ol.* What is your Parentage? | Aboue my fortunes, yet my state is well;    585
My state is desperate for my maisters loue:    694
*cons State without booke, and vtters it by great swarths.    842
*Mal.* Hauing beene three moneths married to her, | sitting in my state.    1060
*Mal.* And then to haue the humor of state: and after    1068
*state; put thy selfe into the tricke of singularitie. Shee    1157
*langer with arguments of state, put thy selfe into the    1593
Heere in the streets, desperate of shame and state,    2215
STAUES = *1
How does he sirrah? | *Cl.* Truely Madam, he holds *Belzebub* at the
staues end as    2451
STAY = 4*4
*And.* Ile stay a moneth longer. I am a fellow o'th    221
*Ant.* Will you stay no longer: nor will you not that | I go with you.    613
*O stay and heare, your true loues coming,*    741
*Ol.* Stay: I prethee tell me what thou thinkst of me?    1354
*And.* No faith, Ile not stay a iot longer:    1383
*Ant.* I could not stay behinde you: my desire    1470
*To.* I will doe so. Signiour *Fabian,* stay you by this | Gentleman, till
my returne. *Exit Toby.*    1775
*Ol.* Whether my Lord? *Cesario,* Husband, stay.    2301
STEALING = 1
Stealing, and giuing Odour. Enough, no more,    11
STEALTH = 1
With an inuisible, and subtle stealth    593

STEELE = 1
(More sharpe then filed steele) did spurre me forth,                    1471
STEEPE = 1
Let fancie still my sense in Lethe steepe,                              1979
STEP = *1
*surely, as your feete hits the ground they step on. They              1796
STEWARD = *3
*my Ladie haue not call'd vp her Steward *Maluolio*, and               773
*To*. Out o'tune sir, ye lye: Art any more then a Stew- |ard?           810
*made if thou desir'st to be so: If not, let me see thee a ste- |ward  1161
STILL = 11*4
*What's to come, is still vnsure.*                                      750
*Du*. Too old by heauen: Let still the woman take                       917
Our shewes are more then will: for still we proue                       1007
*still, the fellow of seruants, and not woorthie to                    1162
*in my presence still smile, deero my sweete, I prethee.* Ioue         1180
*Mal*. If not, let me see thee a seruant still.                         1576
*Fa*. Still you keepe o'th windie side of the Law: good.               1683
Still in this fashion, colour, ornament,                               1903
Let fancie still my sense in Lethe steepe,                             1979
If it be thus to dreame, still let me sleepe.                          1980
*Clo*. Fare thee well: remaine thou still in darkenesse,               2042
*Du*. Still so cruell? | *Ol*. Still so constant Lord.                 2266
Liue you the Marble-brested Tirant still.                              2280
*With tospottes still had drunken heades, | for the raine, &c.*        2574
STIRRE = *1
*To*. Neuer trust me then: and by all meanes stirre on                 1438
STITCHES = *1
*selues into stitches, follow me; yond gull *Maluolio* is tur- |ned    1448
STOCKE = *2
*dam'd colour'd stocke. Shall we sit about some Reuels?                 243
*is no Whip-stocke. My Lady has a white hand, and the | Mermidons
are no bottle-ale houses.                                               728
STOCKINGS = 3*5
*commended thy yellow stockings, and wish'd to see thee                1159
*stockings of late, shee did praise my legge being crosse- |garter'd,  1171
*strange, stout, in yellow stockings, and crosse Garter'd,             1175
*in yellow stockings, and 'tis a colour she abhorres, and  •          1203
*beleeue such impossible passages of grossenesse. Hee's in | yellow
stockings.                                                              1451
*Mal*. Remember who commended thy yellow stock- |ings.                 1569
*Ol*. Thy yellow stockings?                                            1571
To put on yellow stockings, and to frowne                              2508
STONE = 1*1
*an ordinary foole, that has no more braine then a stone.              377
*Ol*. I haue said too much vnto a hart of stone,                       1718
STONE-BOW = 1
*To*. O for a stone-bow to hit him in the eye.                         1062
STOOD = 1
Most of our City did. Onely my selfe stood out,                        1503
STOOPE = 1
*Marian* I say, a stoope of wine.                                       714
STOOPING = *1
*her will is, it should be so return'd: If it bee worth stoo- |ping    671
STOPE = 1
crums. A stope of Wine *Maria*.                                         816

STORE = 1
You haue desire to purchase: and your store      1514
STORES = *1
*and the cleere stores toward the South north, are      2023
STOUT = *1
*strange, stout, in yellow stockings, and crosse Garter'd,      1175
STRACHY = *1
*Mal. There is example for't: The Lady of the *Stra-|chy*,      1055
STRAIGHT = 1*1
to lye straight in my bed: I know I can do it.      832
*Clo. This will I tell my Lady straight, I would not be      1946
STRAINE = 1
That straine agen, it had a dying fall:      8
STRANGE = 3*2
*strange, stout, in yellow stockings, and crosse Garter'd,      1175
But in very strange manner. He is sure possest Madam.      1529
*Vio. This is as vnciuill as strange. I beseech you doe      1771
But in conclusion put strange speech vpon me,      2218
You throw a strange regard vpon me, and by that      2376
STRANGENES = *1
*Cockney: I prethee now vngird thy strangenes, and tell      1932
STRANGER = 2
you but three dayes, and already you are no stranger.      253
Being skillesse in these parts: which to a stranger,      1475
STRANGEST = *1
*strangest minde i'th world: I delight in Maskes and Re-|uels
sometimes altogether.      222
STRANGLE = 1
That makes thee strangle thy propriety:      2307
STRAPS = 1
*these boots too: and they be not, let them hang them-|selues in their
owne straps.      130
STREAME = 1
*Seb.* What rellish is in this? How runs the streame?      1977
STREETES = 1
I do not without danger walke these streetes.      1493
STREETS = 1
Heere in the streets, desperate of shame and state,      2215
STRENGTH = *1
*for your opposite hath in him what youth, strength, skill, | and wrath,
can furnish man withall.      1750
STRENGTHNED = 1
Strengthned by enterchangement of your rings,      2321
STREWNE = 1
*On my blacke coffin, let there be strewne:*      949
STRIFE = 1
*Vio.* Ile do my best | To woe your Lady: yet a barrefull strife,      292
STRIKE = *1
*strike him: if shee doe, hee'l smile, and take't for a great | fauour.      1461
STRIKES = 1
*Clocke strikes.*      1345
STRIPPE = *1
*might answer him: therefore on, or strippe your sword      1768
STRIUE = 1
*and wee'l striue to please you euery day.*      2579

STROKE = *2
*With bloodlesse stroke my heart doth gore, M.O.A.I. doth | sway my
life.                                                                      1117
*there be any law in Illyria: though I stroke him first, yet               1951
STRONG = 6*1
To a strong Maste, that liu'd vpon the sea:                                 64
*And. And I thinke I haue the backe-tricke, simply as | strong as any
man in Illyria.                                                            231
*And. I, 'tis strong, and it does indifferent well in a        °          242
Can bide the beating of so strong a passion,                               982
*To. I haue beene deere to him lad, some two thousand | strong, or so.    1434
But such a head-strong potent fault it is,                                1721
Or any taint of vice, whose strong corruption | Inhabites our fraile
blood.                                                                    1875
STUBBORNE = 1*1
*appeare stubborne to him: for she incites me to that in                  1590
Vpon some stubborne and vncourteous parts                                 2532
STUCK = *1
*My shrowd of white, stuck all with Ew, O prepare it.                     946
STUCKE = *1
*and he giues me the stucke in with such a mortall motion                 1794
STUDIE = *1
*Vio. Alas, I tooke great paines to studie it, and 'tis | Poeticall.      489
STUDIED = *1
Ol. Whence came you sir? | *Vio. I can say little more then I haue
studied, & that                                                           472
STUDIENT = *1
*Studient: but to be said an honest man and a good hous- | keeper         1993
STUFFE = 1
Youths a stuffe will not endure.                                          753
SUBSTRACTORS = 1
Tob. By this hand they are scoundrels and substra- | ctors                150
SUBTLE = 1
With an inuisible, and subtle stealth                                     593
SUBURBES = 1
In the South Suburbes at the Elephant | Is best to lodge: I will bespeake
our dyet,                                                                 1508
SUCH = 18*16
For such disguise as haply shall become                                   106
*And. Why I thinke so: I am not such an asse, but I                       188
*Mal. I maruell your Ladyship takes delight in such                       375
*Looke you sir, such a one I was this present: Ist not well | done?       526
My Lord, and master loues you: O such loue                                544
With such a suffring, such a deadly life:                                  558
*I could not with such estimable wonder ouer-farre be- | leeue            636
For such as we are made, if such we bee:                                   689
*had rather then forty shillings I had such a legge, and so                721
For such as I am, all true Louers are,                                     902
*minde is a very Opall. I would haue men of such constan- | cie           962
*To. And aske no other dowry with her, but such ano- | ther iest.        1187
*Tob. Why, thou hast put him in such a dreame, that                      1197
*Clo. No such matter sir, I do liue by the Church: For,                  1219
*beleeue such impossible passages of grossenesse. Hee's in | yellow
stockings.                                                               1451
*Indies: you haue not seene such a thing as tis: I can hard- | ly        1459
Are shuffel'd off with such vncurrant pay:                               1483
I did some seruice, of such note indeede,                                1495

214

SUCH *cont.*

| | |
|---|---|
| *Ant.* Th'offence is not of such a bloody nature, | 1498 |
| But such a head-strong potent fault it is, | 1721 |
| *To.* Why man hee's a verie diuell, I haue not seen such | 1792 |
| *and he giues me the stucke in with such a mortall motion | 1794 |
| Releeu'd him with such sanctitie of loue; | 1881 |
| *Vio.* Me thinkes his words do from such passion flye | 1894 |
| Yet liuing in my glasse: euen such, and so | 1901 |
| *in such a gowne. I am not tall enough to become the | 1991 |
| With such a smooth, discreet, and stable bearing | 2133 |
| With which such scathfull grapple did he make, | 2207 |
| Such a *Sebastian* was my brother too: | 2398 |
| Why you haue giuen me such cleare lights of fauour, | 2506 |
| And in such formes, which heere were presuppos'd | 2520 |
| *Madam, why laugh you at such a barren rascall, | 2545 |

SUFFER = 1

| | |
|---|---|
| That suffer surfet, cloyment, and reuolt, | 987 |

SUFFERD = 1

| | |
|---|---|
| Why haue you suffer'd me to be imprison'd, | 2511 |

SUFFERS = *1

| | |
|---|---|
| *that suffers vnder probation: *A.* should follow, but *O.* \| does. | 1138 |

SUFFRING = 1

| | |
|---|---|
| With such a suffring, such a deadly life: | 558 |

SUIT = *2

| | |
|---|---|
| *madman: Fie on him. Go you *Maluolio*; If it be a suit | 401 |
| *2.*Off. Anthonio*, I arrest thee at the suit of Count *Orsino* | 1844 |

SUITE = 4

| | |
|---|---|
| Because she will admit no kinde of suite, \| No, not the Dukes. | 97 |
| But would you vndertake another suite | 1321 |
| If spirits can assume both forme and suite, \| You come to fright vs. | 2400 |
| Is now in durance, at *Maluolio's* suite, | 2443 |

SUITED = 1

| | |
|---|---|
| So went he suited to his watery tombe: | 2399 |

SUITES = 2

| | |
|---|---|
| I will beleeue thou hast a minde that suites | 102 |
| And suites well for a seruant with my fortunes, | 1526 |

SUMMER = 1

| | |
|---|---|
| and for turning away, let summer beare it out. | 315 |

SUN = 1*1

| | |
|---|---|
| The Spinsters and the Knitters in the Sun, | 934 |
| *Sun, it shines euery where. I would be sorry sir, but the | 1252 |

SUNG = 1

| | |
|---|---|
| *An.* Good ifaith: Come begin. *Catch sung* | 770 |

SUNNE = 1*1

| | |
|---|---|
| *Sunne practising behauiour to his own shadow this halfe | 1034 |
| This is the ayre, that is the glorious Sunne, | 2115 |

SUPPLYD = 1

| | |
|---|---|
| These soueraigne thrones, are all supply'd and fill'd | 44 |

SUPPORTANCE = *1

| | |
|---|---|
| *of: therefore draw for the supportance of his vowe, | 1816 |

SUPPORTER = *1

| | |
|---|---|
| *your doore like a Sheriffes post, and be the supporter to | 443 |

SUPPOSE = 1

| | |
|---|---|
| Yet I suppose him vertuous, know him noble, | 551 |

SURE = 4*4

| | |
|---|---|
| *death of her brother thus? I am sure care's an enemie to \| life. | 120 |
| *Vio.* Sure my Noble Lord, | 268 |

SWEARINGS = 1
And all those swearings keepe as true in soule,                                    2436
SWEART = 1
swear't. Tut there's life in't man.                                                220
SWEET = 13*3
O, it came ore my eare, like the sweet sound                                         9
'Tis not so sweet now, as it was before.                                            12
Away before me, to sweet beds of Flowres,                                           46
*And*. Sir *Toby Belch*. How now sir *Toby Belch*? | *To*. Sweet sir *Andrew*.     161
*We will heare this diuinitie. Now sir, what is your text? | *Vio*. Most
sweet Ladie.                                                                        513
Natures owne sweet, and cunning hand laid on:                                      532
*sweet a breath to sing, as the foole has. Insooth thou wast                       722
*Then come kisse me sweet and twentie:*                                            752
*An*. Very sweet, and contagious ifaith.                                           756
*Mar*. Sweet Sir Toby be patient for to night: Since                               827
In the sweet pangs of it, remember me:                                             901
How now *Maluolio*? | *Mal*. Sweet Lady, ho, ho.                                   1538
*be executed. I thinke we doe know the sweet Romane | hand.                        1550
*Mal*. To bed? I sweet heart, and Ile come to thee.                                1553
Pardon me (sweet one) euen for the vowes                                           2378
A solemne Combination shall be made | Of our deere soules. Meane
time sweet sister,                                                                 2553
SWEETE = 2*2
Her sweete perfections with one selfe king:                                         45
*Some mollification for your Giant, sweete Ladie;                                  499
*Not a flower, not a flower sweete*                                                948
*in my presence still smile, deero my sweete, I prethee*. Ioue                    1180
SWEETING = 1
*Trip no further prettie sweeting*.                                                743
SWEET-HEART = *1
*An*. Wherefore (sweet-heart?) What's your Meta-|phor?                             185
SWIFTNESSE = *1
*euen with the swiftnesse of putting on. Ioue, and my                             1176
SWORD = 5*3
*To*. And thou let part so Sir *Andrew*, would thou | mightst neuer draw
sword agen.                                                                        176
*draw sword agen: Faire Lady, doe you thinke you haue | fooles in
hand?                                                                              179
*might answer him: therefore on, or strippe your sword                            1768
*Ant*. Put vp your sword: if this yong Gentleman                                   1829
*Vio*. Pray sir, put your sword vp if you please.                                 1839
*To*. Do, cuffe him soundly, but neuer draw thy sword                             1913
If thou dar'st tempt me further, draw thy sword.                                  1958
You drew your sword vpon me without cause,                                         2350
SWORN = *1
*better increasing your folly: Sir *Toby* will be sworn that                       371
SWORNE = 3
I am a Gentleman. Ile be sworne thou art,                                          587
*and so looke to thy selfe. Thy friend as thou vsest him, & thy | sworne
enemie*, Andrew Ague-cheeke.                                                       1686
And hauing sworne truth, euer will be true.                                        2148
SYLLOGISME *see* sillogisme
T = 2
It is too hard a knot for me t'vnty.                                               698
*Du*. Madam, I am most apt t'embrace your offer:                                  2486

217

TABOR = 2*1
   *Vio. Saue thee Friend and thy Musick: dost thou liue | by thy Tabor?   1215
   *begger dwell neer him: or the Church stands by thy Ta-|bor,   1223
   if thy Tabor stand by the Church.   1224
TAFFATA = *1
   *Tailor make thy doublet of changeable Taffata, for thy   961
TAILOR = *1
   *Tailor make thy doublet of changeable Taffata, for thy   961
TAINT = 4
   But wisemens folly falne, quite taint their wit.   1280
   *Mar. Nay pursue him now, least the deuice take ayre, | and taint.   1653
   Or any taint of vice, whose strong corruption | Inhabites our fraile
   blood.   1875
   Taint the condition of this present houre,   2528
TAINTED = 1
   come, for sure the man is tainted in's wits.   1533
TAINTING = 1
   If I do feigne, you witnesses aboue | Punish my life, for tainting of my
   loue.   2294
TAKE = 13*14
   *Sir To. What a plague meanes my Neece to take the   119
   to see a huswife take thee between her legs, & spin it off.   214
   *these gifts a Curtaine before 'em? Are they like to take   234
   Ol. Take the foole away.   331
   *Clo. Do you not heare fellowes, take away the Ladie.   332
   *flower; The Lady bad take away the foole, therefore I | say againe,
   take her away.   344
   Ol. Sir, I bad them take away you.   346
   *Brothers soule, being in heauen. Take away the Foole, | Gentlemen.   363
   *I take these Wisemen, that crow so at these set kinde of   380
   *and of free disposition, is to take those things for Bird-|bolts,   384
   *to the house: if not, and it would please you to take   797
   *An. If I do not, neuer trust me, take it how you will.   880
   Du. Too old by heauen: Let still the woman take   917
   Clo. No paines sir, I take pleasure in singing sir.   955
   *To. And do's not Toby take you a blow o'th lippes, | then?   1083
   *hurt him in eleuen places, my Neece shall take note of it,   1415
   *Mar. Nay pursue him now, least the deuice take ayre, | and taint.   1653
   till he take leaue, and presently after him.   1715
   *I haue his horse to take vp the quarrell, I haue perswaded | him the
   youths a diuell.   1809
   Haue done offence, I take the fault on me:   1830
   Take him away, he knowes I know him well.   1848
   Take, and giue backe affayres, and their dispatch,   2132
   *you say sir, let your bounty take a nappe, I will awake it | anon. Exit   2198
   But more of that anon. Take him aside.   2255
   Feare not Cesario, take thy fortunes vp,   2308
   Farewell, and take her, but direct thy feete,   2330
TAKEN see also tane = *3
   *taken great paines to con it. Good Beauties, let mee su-|staine   469
   *haue saued mee my paines, to haue taken it away your   663
   *To. His very genius hath taken the infection of the | deuice man.   1651
TAKES = 2*3
   *a nights: your Cosin, my Lady, takes great exceptions | to your ill
   houres.   123
   *Mal. I maruell your Ladyship takes delight in such   375
   *speake with you. I told him you were sicke, he takes on   435

TAKES *cont.*
    To tell me how he takes it: Fare you well:     578
    he takes it at heart. Pray God he be not bewitch'd.     1624
TAKET = 1*1
    *strike him: if shee doe, hee'l smile, and take't for a great | fauour.     1461
    *can be none, but by pangs of death and sepulcher: Hob, | nob, is his
    word: giu't or take't.     1757
TAKING = *1
    *in his affaires, vnlesse it bee to report your Lords taking | of this:
    receiue it so.     667
TALENTS = 1
    those that are fooles, let them vse their talents.     310
TALES = *1
    *least occasion more, mine eyes will tell tales of me: I am     649
TALKE = *1
    *heard my Lady talke of it yesterday: and of a foolish     133
TALKEST = 1
    man? Talkest thou nothing but of Ladies? | *Tob.* Well said M.(aster)
    Parson.     2012
TALKING = *1
    *quarrell, and hee finds that now scarse to bee worth tal- | king     1815
TALL = 1*1
    *To.* He's as tall a man as any's in Illyria.     137
    *in such a gowne. I am not tall enough to become the     1991
TANE = 2
    That were I tane heere, it would scarse be answer'd.     1496
    Proue true imagination, oh proue true, | That I deere brother, be now
    tane for you.     1896
TANG = *1
    *surly with seruants: Let thy tongue tang arguments of     1156
TARRY = *1
    *money for thee, if you tarry longer, I shall giue worse | paiment.     1936
TARTAR = *1
    *To.* To the gates of Tartar, thou most excellent diuell | of wit.     1209
TASTE = 2*2
    *Ol.* O you are sicke of selfe-loue *Maluolio*, and taste     382
    *To.* Taste your legges sir, put them to motion.     1291
    what you meane by bidding me taste my legs.     1293
    *to taste their valour: belike this is a man of that | quirke.     1762
TAUGHT = 1
    Taught him to face me out of his acquaintance,     2240
TAUNT = *1
    *inuention: taunt him with the license of Inke: if thou     1423
TAURUS = 2
    *To.* What shall we do else: were we not borne vnder | Taurus?     244
    *And.* Taurus? That sides and heart.     246
TAXATION = *1
    *of warre, no taxation of homage; I hold the Olyffe     504
TEACHING = 1
    (Courage and hope both teaching him the practise)     63
TEARE = 1
    Him will I teare out of that cruell eye,     2283
TEARES = 3
    *Ol.* How does he loue me? | *Vio.* With adorations, fertill teares,     547
    Will I my Masters teares to you deplore.     1378
    I should my teares let fall vpon your cheeke,     2406

TEL = 1*1
You tel her so: Must she not then be answer'd? | *Du*. There is no
womans sides                                                                          980
*Clo*. I will help you too't. But tel me true, are you not                           2098
TELL = 12*14
And tell them, there thy fixed foot shall grow | Till thou haue audience.             266
*Ma*. Nay, either tell me where thou hast bin, or I will                             297
*Ma*. A good lenton answer: I can tell thee where y                                 304
*Ol*. Tell him, he shall not speake with me.                                         441
*I pray you tell me if this bee the Lady of the house,                               466
tell me your minde, I am a messenger.                                                 500
To tell me how he takes it: Fare you well:                                           578
Would I, or not: tell him, Ile none of it.                                            600
*least occasion more, mine eyes will tell tales of me: I am                           649
*bad me tell you, that though she harbors you as her kins-|man,                      794
*To*. Possesse vs, possesse vs, tell vs something of him.                            833
Tell her my loue, more noble then the world                                          968
Tell her I hold as giddily as Fortune:                                               971
*Vio*. By my troth Ile tell thee, I am almost sicke for                             1259
*Ol*. Stay: I prethee tell me what thou thinkst of me?                              1354
*To*. Did she see the while, old boy, tell me that.                                  1389
*did not I tell you? Sir *Toby*, my Lady prayes you to haue | a care of
him.                                                                                  1615
me tell them how much I lacke of a man.                                               1819
*Cockney: I prethee now vngird thy strangenes, and tell                             1932
*Clo*. This will I tell my Lady straight, I would not be                            1946
*Clo*. Hey Robin, iolly Robin, tell me how thy Lady | does. | *Mal*.
Foole.                                                                               2057
*paper, I tell thee I am as well in my wittes, as any man in | Illyria.             2091
*Mal*. Beleeue me I am not, I tell thee true.                                       2100
*now my foes tell me plainly, I am an Asse: so that by my                            2171
And tell me in the modestie of honor,                                                2505
That ere inuention plaid on? Tell me why?                                            2514
TELLING = *1
*a demure trauaile of regard: telling them I knowe my                               1069
TEMPESTS = 1
Tempests are kinde, and salt waues fresh in loue.                                    1905
TEMPT = 2
Ist possible that my deserts to you | Can lacke perswasion. Do not
tempt my misery,                                                                     1866
If thou dar'st tempt me further, draw thy sword.                                     1958
TENDED = 1
Three monthes this youth hath tended vpon mee,                                       2254
TENDER = 2
And whom, by heauen I sweare, I tender deerely,                                      2282
So farre beneath your soft and tender breeding,                                      2489
TENDERD = 1
That ere deuotion tender'd. What shall I do?                                         2271
TERMES = 2*1
More then light ayres, and recollected termes                                        889
*most modest termes, for I am one of those gentle ones,                             2018
Whom thou in termes so bloudie, and so deere | Hast made thine
enemies?                                                                             2222
TERRIBLE = *1
*it comes to passe oft, that a terrible oath, with a swagge-|ring                   1696
TERROR = *1
*Letter being so excellently ignorant, will breed no terror                         1705

TERTIA *l.*117 699 1465 2113 = 4
TERTIO = *1
    *Clo. Primo, secundo, tertio*, is a good play, and the olde        2187
TERTIUS *l.*1213 = 1
TESTIMONY = 1
    And all the Ceremonie of this compact | Seal'd in my function, by my
    testimony:        2322
TESTRILL = *1
    *An.* There's a testrill of me too: if one knight giue a        734
TEXT = 1 *2
    *We will heare this diuinitie. Now sir, what is your text? | *Vio.* Most
    sweet Ladie.        513
    of it. Where lies your Text? | *Vio.* In *Orsinoes* bosome.        516
    *negotiate with my face: you are now out of your Text:        524
TH *see also* by'th, i'th, o'th, to'th, y'th = 8 *2
    *Ma.* What's that to th'purpose? | *To.* Why he ha's three thousand
    ducates a yeare.        138
    And baited it with all th'vnmuzled thoughts        1333
    foote of a flea, Ile eate the rest of th'anatomy.        1442
    *Ant.* Th'offence is not of such a bloody nature,        1498
    *Ant.* To th'Elephant. | *Seb.* I do remember. *Exeunt.*        1518
    *Fab.* Carry his water to th'wise woman.        1625
    *thou shalt hold th'opinion of *Pythagoras*, ere I will allow        2043
    Like to th'Egyptian theefe, at point of death        2274
    *To.* That's all one, has hurt me, and there's th'end on't:        2359
    One day shall crowne th'alliance on't, so please you,        2484
THAN *see* then
THANKE = 3 *2
    *Vio.* I thanke thee: Lead me on. *Exeunt*        116
    *Vio.* I thanke you: heere comes the Count.        258
    I thanke you for your paines: spend this for mee.        579
    *her liking. I thanke my starres, I am happy: I will bee        1174
    *I thanke thee, I will smile, I wil do euery thing that thou | wilt haue
    me. *Exit*        1181
THANKED = 1
    is the doer of this, and he is to be thanked.        1605
THANKEFULL = *2
    *thankefull. And when she went away now, let this Fel- | low        1598
    *as I am a Gentleman, I will liue to bee thankefull to thee | for't.        2067
THANKES = 2
    *Seb.* My kinde *Anthonio*, | I can no other answer make, but thankes,        1480
    And thankes: and euer oft good turnes,        1482
THART = *2
    *To.* Th'art a scholler; let vs therefore eate and drinke        713
    *To.* Th'art i'th right. Goe sir, rub your Chaine with        815
THAT *see also* o'that, y *l.*6 8 10 14 19 23 26 39 43 56 64 84 87 92 96 100
    102 111 *132 *134 138 *142 *145 *146 151 *152 *156 166 174 *199 *202
    *206 210 246 *255 282 *300 302 *307 *309 310 *312 *318 *327 *328
    *335 *340 *341 *368 *371 373 374 *377 *380 *385 *438 *468 *473 *475
    *479 *495 *508 549 582 598 603 *613 *618 *623 *627 *631 *637 *638
    *645 *648 655 *664 *666 *672 677 *708 742 *759 760 *789 *794 *835
    *840 *841 *844 *845 *857 *858 860 *871 886 887 *892 *895 905 910 928
    929 935 *963 *964 970 972 973 977 987 990 991 1038 *1042 *1044 1104
    *1128 *1129 1131 1134 *1138 *1158 *1163 *1170 *1181 *1197 *1206
    *1228 *1233 *1242 1273 1277 1279 *1300 1322 1330 *1334 1340 1355
    *1364 1367 1370 1375 1380 1389 *1450 *1454 *1456 1491 1496 1543
    1562 *1589 *1590 *1601 *1603 *1658 *1674 *1676 *1696 *1711 1720

THAT *cont.*
 1722 *1723 1728 1729 1731 *1739 *1756 *1761 *1762 *1767 *1782 *1785
*1789 *1795 *1815 1833 *1840 1857 1866 1868 1870 *1879 1884 1895
1897 *1919 *1926 *1929 *1933 *1939 1952 1973 *1990 *1999 *2000
*2001 *2019 2020 *2037 *2055 2093 2115 2117 2121 2124 2127 2128
2129 2135 2140 2142 2150 2169 *2171 *2173 *2180 *2196 2201 2202
2209 2211 2212 2213 2225 2229 2255 *2256 2271 *2272 2276 2278 2279
2283 2286 2303 2307 2309 2310 2329 *2347 2376 2381 2386 2392 2403
2410 2412 2414 2419 2426 2437 2438 2441 *2473 2500 2514 2538 2539
2552 2560 = 143*130, *1

*am M.(aster) Parson; for what is that, but that? and is, but is?          2001
THATS = 4*7
*mend him: any thing that's mended, is but patch'd: vertu          339
*Non facit monachum*: that's as much to say, as I weare not          348
*and their intent euerie where, for that's it, that alwayes          964
Sir, shall I to this Lady? | *Du.* I that's the Theame,          1012
*And.* That's mee I warrant you. | *Mal.* One sir *Andrew*.          1094
*Vio.* Nay that's certaine: they that dally nicely with          1228
*Ol.* That's a degree to loue.          1338
*starke naked: for meddle you must that's certain, or for-|sweare to
weare iron about you.          1769
*To.* That's all one, has hurt me, and there's th'end on't:          2359
*was one sir, in this Enterlude, one sir *Topas* sir, but that's          2543
*But that's all one*, *our Play is done*,          2578
THE *see also* i'the, o'the, th', y = 262*253, 1*1
*To.* Did she see the while, old boy, tell me that.          1389
*To.* That defence thou hast, betake the too't: of what          1739
THEAME = 1
Sir, shall I to this Lady? | *Du.* I that's the Theame,          1012
THEE *see also* the *l.*99 101 104 116 195 214 *247 263 276 299 *304 *327
*328 330 *389 589 604 651 653 654 *725 767 *825 *915 959 *960 967
1113 1114 *1150 *1158 *1159 *1161 *1164 *1179 *1181 *1215 1250 1256
1258 *1259 1367 1431 1540 1547 1553 *1554 1568 1572 1576 *1662 1673
*1676 1677 *1679 1734 1735 1737 *1742 *1844 1922 *1936 1943 *1957
1962 1976 1997 *2017 *2042 2045 2050 *2067 *2091 *2096 2100 2163
2221 2253 2307 2313 2384 2440 2521 2522 2540 = 56*32
THEEFE = 3
*Du.* Notable Pyrate, thou salt-water Theefe,          2220
*Anthonio* neuer yet was Theefe, or Pyrate,          2226
Like to th'Egyptian theefe, at point of death          2274
THEEUES = 1
*Gainst Knaues and Theeues men shut their gate*, | *for the raine*, *&c.*          2566
THEIR *l.*132 310 687 935 *963 *964 985 1274 1280 *1762 2030 2132 2221
2566 = 11*3
THEIRS = *1
*place, as I would they should doe theirs: to aske for my | kinsman
*Toby*.          1070
THEM *see also* 'em *l.*130 191 *192 266 *309 310 346 *540 565 619 *1069
*1153 1229 1234 1239 *1269 1291 *1440 1502 1567 *1711 *1714 1819
2366 *2542 = 14*11
THEMSELUES = 1*2
*these boots too: and they be not, let them hang them-|selues in their
owne straps.          130
*Ant.* Oh heauens themselues.          1877
*that giue fooles money, get themselues a good re-|port, after
fourteene yeares purchase.          1939

THEN *l.*79 82 87 115 *128 *198 209 272 *273 274 278 316 330 *336 *377
381 *473 *485 *493 *626 *707 *721 752 *810 *818 *823 889 *915 918
923 925 956 968 980 1007 *1044 *1068 1084 *1137 1142 *1144 *1201
*1292 1316 1323 1341 1344 1351 1357 1359 *1364 *1387 *1401 *1413
1418 *1438 *1458 1471 1506 *1524 *1588 *1627 *1698 *1789 1834 1854
1874 *1907 *1959 *2029 *2033 *2074 2075 *2096 2118 *2149 *2175 2292
2293 2309 2341 2357 *2363 2389 2458 2504 2519 2537 = 49*41
THERE *l.*15 99 *155 266 *343 *385 *392 653 *672 *732 751 778 791 804
*811 949 *953 977 981 *1037 *1055 1077 *1127 *1137 1254 1350 *1416
1419 *1427 *1449 1511 1943 *1951 1972 2006 *2028 *2032 *2072 2120
2139 2229 2391 2392 = 26*19

THEREBY = 1
    This Ruffian hath botch'd vp, that thou thereby        1973
THEREFORE = 2*14
    Therefore good youth, addresse thy gate vnto her,    264
    *flower; The Lady bad take away the foole, therefore I | say againe,
    take her away.    344
    *him to vnderstand so much, and therefore comes to speak    436
    *a fore knowledge of that too, and therefore comes to    438
    *yours; therefore I shall craue of you your leaue,    617
    *willing to keepe in: therefore it charges me in manners,    624
    *To. Th'art a scholler; let vs therefore eate and drinke    713
    *it appeare in thy smiling, thy smiles become thee well. There- |fore    1179
    *Clo. I would therefore my sister had had no name Sir.    1230
    For that I woo, thou therefore hast no cause:    1370
    *Lord and my Neece, confirmes no lesse. Therefore, this    1704
    *To. You'l finde it otherwise I assure you: therefore, if    1748
    *computent iniurie, therefore get you on, and giue him    1765
    *might answer him: therefore on, or strippe your sword    1768
    *of: therefore draw for the supportance of his vowe,    1816
    *reade thus: therefore, perpend my Princesse, and giue | eare.    2466
THEREIN = 1
    Nor are you therein (by my life) deceiu'd,    2428
THERES = 11*8
    Vio. For saying so, there's Gold:    68
    swear't. Tut there's life in't man.    220
    *To. Letcherie, I defie Letchery: there's one at the | gate.    419
    *An. There's a testrill of me too: if one knight giue a    734
    Du. There's for thy paines.    954
    *Vio. Nay, and thou passe vpon me, Ile no more with | thee. Hold
    there's expences for thee.    1255
    *An. Heere's the Challenge, reade it: I warrant there's | vinegar and
    pepper in't.    1665
    There's something in me that reproues my fault:    1720
    *To. There's no remedie sir, he will fight with you for's    1813
    *To. Come sir Andrew, there's no remedie, the Gen- |tleman    1821
    But there's no remedie, I shall answer it:    1850
    Hold, there's halfe my Coffer.    1864
    In Nature, there's no blemish but the minde:    1887
    *Seb. I prethee foolish greeke depart from me, there's    1935
    Seb. Why there's for thee, and there, and there,    1943
    As I perceiue she do's: there's something in't    2134
    *Du. Thou shalt not be the worse for me, there's gold.    2179
    Du. Well, I will be so much a sinner to be a double | dealer: there's
    another.    2185
    *To. That's all one, has hurt me, and there's th'end on't:    2359

THERETO = 1
His life I gaue him, and did thereto adde  2232
THERS = *1
*And. Now sir, haue I met you again: ther's for you.  1942
THESE see also o'these l.44 *129 *130 *140 224 *233 *234 *251 *380 534
890 *1101 *1148 *1173 1262 1475 1478 1493 *1938 2225 2292 2389
*2482 = 11*13
THEY = 14*16
THEYR l.*1152 = *1
THIGHES = *1
*To. No sir, it is leggs and thighes: let me see thee ca- | per. Ha, higher:
ha, ha, excellent. Exeunt  247
THIN = 1
a knaue: a thin fac'd knaue, a gull?  2370
THINE = 6*1
And thou shalt liue as freely as thy Lord, | To call his fortunes thine.  290
My life vpon't, yong though thou art, thine eye  909
*To. To him in thine owne voyce, and bring me word  2051
Whom thou in termes so bloudie, and so deere | Hast made thine
enemies?  2222
That thine owne trip shall be thine ouerthrow:  2329
Thou shalt be both the Plaintiffe and the Iudge | Of thine owne cause.  2524
THING = 4*9
*mend him: any thing that's mended, is but patch'd: vertu  339
*thing more, that you be neuer so hardie to come againe  666
*at any thing more then contempt, you would not giue  818
*Mar. The diu'll a Puritane that hee is, or any thing  840
*put to Sea, that their businesse might be euery thing,  963
*I thanke thee, I will smile, I wil do euery thing that thou | wilt haue
me. Exit  1181
By maid-hood, honor, truth, and euery thing,  1366
*Indies: you haue not seene such a thing as tis: I can hard- | ly  1459
*degree, but Fellow. Why euery thing adheres togither,  1600
*Vio. Pray God defend me: a little thing would make  1818
Clo. Good M.(aster) Fabian, grant me another request. | Fab. Any
thing.  2155
And grew a twentie yeeres remoued thing  2241
A foolish thing was but a toy,  2562
THINGS = 1*5
*To. Wherefore are these things hid? Wherefore haue  233
*and of free disposition, is to take those things for Bird- | bolts,  384
*forbeare hurling things at him, I know my Ladie will  1460
With the memorials, and the things of fame | That do renowne this
City.  1490
*things, I am not of your element, you shall knowe more | heereafter.
Exit  1646
*My Lord, so please you, these things further thought on,  2482
THINK = *2
*Which you knew none of yours. What might you think?  1331
*That tyrannous heart can think? To one of your receiuing  1334
THINKE = 12*20
*Perchance he is not drown'd: What thinke you saylors?  55
*draw sword agen: Faire Lady, doe you thinke you haue | fooles in
hand?  179
*And. Why I thinke so: I am not such an asse, but I  188
*An. Neuer in your life I thinke, vnlesse you see Ca- | narie  196

THINKE *cont.*

*\*And.* And I thinke I haue the backe-tricke, simply as | strong as any man in Illyria. 231
*\*meane?* Is it a world to hide vertues in? I did thinke by 239
*Vio.* I thinke not so, my Lord. | *Du.* Deere Lad, beleeue it; 279
*\*those* wits that thinke they haue thee, doe very oft proue 327
*Clo.* I thinke his soule is in hell, Madona. 360
*\*Ol.* What thinke you of this foole *Maluolio*, doth he | not mend? 365
*\*and* he speakes verie shrewishly: One would thinke his 455
*\*And.* Faith so they say, but I thinke it rather consists | of eating and drinking. 711
*\*Dost* thou thinke because thou art vertuous, there 811
*\*him* a common recreation, do not thinke I haue witte e- | nough 831
*\*To.* He shall thinke by the Letters that thou wilt drop 857
*Vio.* I thinke it well my Lord. 924
*\*respect,* then any one else that followes her. What | should I thinke on 't? 1044
I thinke I saw your wisedome there. 1254
*\*Ol.* For him, I thinke not on him: for his thoughts, 1315
*Vio.* That you do thinke you are not what you are. 1355
*Ol.* If I thinke so, I thinke the same of you. 1356
*Vio.* Then thinke you right: I am not what I am. 1357
*\*the* youth to an answer. I thinke Oxen and waine-ropes 1439
I thinke is not for idle Markets, sir. 1515
*\*be* executed. I thinke we doe know the sweet Romane | hand. 1550
*\*sir* *Topas* do not thinke I am mad: they haue layde mee | heere in hideous darknesse. 2015
*\*Mal.* I thinke nobly of the soule, and no way aproue | his opinion. 2040
*\*I* go sir, but I would not haue you to thinke, that 2196
me: I thinke you set nothing by a bloody Coxecombe. 2354
*\*do* my selfe much right, or you much shame: thinke of 2475
To thinke me as well a sister, as a wife, 2483

THINKES = 2\*3

*\*put* me downe: mee thinkes sometimes I haue no 197
Me thinkes I feele this youths perfections 592
*\*The* best perswaded of himselfe: so cram'd (as he thinkes) 843
*Ol.* Why then me thinkes 'tis time to smile agen: 1341
*\*Vio.* Me thinkes his words do from such passion flye 1894

THINKST = 1\*1

*\*Ol.* Stay: I prethee tell me what thou thinkst of me? 1354
*Clo.* What thinkst thou of his opinion? 2039

THIRD = 1\*3

*\*One* draught aboue heate, makes him a foole, the second | maddes him, and a third drownes him. 426
*\*o'my* Coz: for he's in the third degree of drinke: hee's | drown'd: go looke after him. 429
*\*the* Foole make a third, where he shall finde the Letter: 866
*\*saying* is, the third payes for all: the triplex sir, is a good 2188

THIRTEENE = 2

*Vio.* And dide that day when *Viola* from her birth | Had numbred thirteene yeares. 2410
That day that made my sister thirteene yeares. 2414

THIS *l.*31 36 40 51 52 71 73 103 107 150 \*173 287 289 \*300 \*341 \*365 418 \*466 \*484 \*513 \*526 579 592 599 603 609 \*662 668 \*674 680 690 693 697 \*730 \*788 805 \*819 \*867 905 1005 1012 1014 1019 \*1033 \*1034 \*1036 1078 1086 \*1101 \*1105 1108 1109 1113 \*1126 \*1128 \*1132 \*1146 \*1147 \*1149 \*1165 \*1169 \*1172 \*1183 1185 \*1225 1265 1272 1277 1369

THIS *cont.*
   *1391 *1403 *1404 1419 1433 1486 1491 1504 1542 1543 *1559 1577
   *1583 *1588 *1598 1605 *1631 *1649 1688 *1704 *1711 *1725 *1730
   *1756 *1762 *1771 *1772 *1775 1777 *1806 1829 1843 1849 *1879 1885
   1903 *1926 *1931 *1946 1960 1970 1973 1974 1977 1978 *1986 2003
   *2011 *2026 *2031 *2049 *2052 *2055 *2094 2115 2116 2120 2124 2125
   2137 2138 2147 2150 2157 *2158 2176 2183 *2191 2211 2213 2236 2245
   2246 2254 2276 2281 2317 2322 2342 2365 2416 2420 2422 2424 2431
   2432 2478 2480 2491 2495 2496 2504 2510 2515 2522 2528 2531
   *2543 = 105*67

THOGH = *2

| | |
|---|---|
| *me, was yet of many accounted beautiful: but thogh | 635 |
| *Mal*. I say this house is as darke as Ignorance, thogh | 2031 |

THOSE *l*.60 310 *327 *384 1869 *2018 2435 2436 = 5*3

THOU *see also* y *l*.13 71 102 108 113 176 *194 209 *211 224 *235 *238
   262 267 282 290 *297 *321 358 *389 *406 *428 587 684 697 *702 *722
   *723 764 *765 *811 847 *857 *874 *878 900 905 908 909 993 *1021
   *1037 *1154 *1160 *1161 *1177 *1178 *1181 1192 *1197 *1209 *1215
   1218 *1222 *1239 1244 *1255 *1354 1370 1379 *1423 *1428 1540 1546
   1552 *1554 1562 1566 *1574 1670 *1675 *1676 1682 *1686 *1694 *1695
   *1739 *1740 1886 1921 *1927 1934 *1938 1958 1972 1973 1974 *1987
   *2011 2012 *2017 *2019 *2024 *2028 *2029 2039 *2042 *2043 *2044
   *2049 *2052 *2065 2073 2154 2163 *2179 2220 2222 2298 2309 2310
   2316 2326 2331 2334 2386 2433 2434 2460 2519 2524 = 67*61

THOUDST = *1

| | |
|---|---|
| *Ol*. Nay come I prethee, would thoud'st be rul'd by me | 1981 |

THOUGH = 11*13

| | |
|---|---|
| And though that nature, with a beauteous wall | 100 |
| *in an allow'd foole, though he do nothing but rayle; | 386 |
| *nor no rayling, in a knowne discreet man, though hee do \| nothing but reproue. | 387 |
| Could be but recompenc'd, though you were crown'd \| The non-pareil of beautie. | 545 |
| *Seb*. A Lady sir, though it was said shee much resem-\|bled | 634 |
| *drown'd already sir with salt water, though I seeme to | 639 |
| *bad me tell you, that though she harbors you as her kins-\|man, | 794 |
| My life vpon't, yong though thou art, thine eye | 909 |
| *Fa*. Though our silence be drawne from vs with cars, \| yet peace. | 1079 |
| *Fab*. Sowter will cry vpon't for all this, though it bee \| as ranke as a Fox. | 1132 |
| *one, though I would not haue it grow on my chinne. Is \| thy Lady within? | 1260 |
| *in thy inke, though thou write with a Goose-pen, \| no matter: about it. | 1428 |
| And not all loue to see you (though so much | 1472 |
| *Mal*. Not blacke in my minde, though yellow in my | 1548 |
| Though now you haue no sea-cap on your head: | 1847 |
| *there be any law in Illyria: though I stroke him first, yet | 1951 |
| And though tis wonder that enwraps me thus, | 2117 |
| For though my soule disputes well with my sence, | 2123 |
| *Clo*. By my troth sir, no: though it please you to be \| one of my friends. | 2177 |
| Though I confesse, on base and ground enough | 2227 |
| Heere to vnfold, though lately we intended | 2314 |
| Hold little faith, though thou hast too much feare. | 2334 |
| *the world shall know it: Though you haue put mee into | 2470 |
| Though I confesse much like the Charracter: | 2516 |

THOUGHT = 5*7

| | |
|---|---:|
| Me thought she purg'd the ayre of pestilence; | 25 |
| *'tis thought among the prudent, he would quickely \| haue the gift of a graue. | 148 |
| *Ma. Now sir, thought is free: I pray you bring your | 183 |
| *An. And I thought that, I'de forsweare it. Ile ride \| home to morrow sir Toby. | 202 |
| That me thought her eyes had lost her tongue, | 677 |
| *An. O, if I thought that, Ide beate him like a dogge. | 835 |
| Me thought it did releeue my passion much, | 888 |
| Feede on her damaske cheeke: she pin'd in thought, | 1002 |
| *An. Plague on't, and I thought he had beene valiant, | 1801 |
| And to his image, which me thought did promise \| Most venerable worth, did I deuotion. | 1882 |
| *function well, nor leane enough to bee thought a good | 1992 |
| *My Lord, so please you, these things further thought on, | 2482 |

THOUGHTS = 3*2

| | |
|---|---:|
| Loue-thoughts lye rich, when canopy'd with bowres. \| *Exeunt* | 47 |
| *Ol. For him, I thinke not on him: for his thoughts, | 1315 |
| *Vio. Madam, I come to whet your gentle thoughts \| On his behalfe. | 1317 |
| And baited it with all th'vnmuzled thoughts | 1333 |
| Come boy with me, my thoughts are ripe in mischiefe: | 2285 |

THOUSAND = 3*3

| | |
|---|---:|
| Ma. What's that to th'purpose? \| To. Why he ha's three thousand ducates a yeare. | 138 |
| *A thousand thousand sighes to saue, lay me o where | 952 |
| *To. I haue beene deere to him lad, some two thousand \| strong, or so. | 1434 |
| To do you rest, a thousand deaths would dye. | 2289 |
| Boy, thou hast saide to me a thousand times, | 2433 |

THOUSANDS = 1

| | |
|---|---:|
| of thousands to be paid from the Sophy. | 1184 |

THOUST = *1

| | |
|---|---:|
| *thou'st him some thrice, it shall not be amisse, and as ma-\|ny | 1424 |

THRED = 1

| | |
|---|---:|
| And the free maides that weaue their thred with bones, | 935 |

THREE = 8*6

| | |
|---|---:|
| Not three houres trauaile from this very place. | 73 |
| Ma. What's that to th'purpose? \| To. Why he ha's three thousand ducates a yeare. | 138 |
| *and speaks three or four languages word for word | 143 |
| you but three dayes, and already you are no stranger. | 253 |
| *Clo. How now my harts: Did you neuer see the Pic-\|ture of we three? | 717 |
| *rowze the night-Owle in a Catch, that will drawe three | 759 |
| *a Peg-a-ramsie, and Three merry men be wee. Am not I | 776 |
| *Mar. Get ye all three into the box tree: Maluolio's | 1032 |
| Mal. Hauing beene three moneths married to her, \| sitting in my state. | 1060 |
| *And. Odours, pregnant, and vouchsafed: Ile get 'em \| all three already. | 1303 |
| *soules and bodies hath he diuorc'd three, and his incense-\|ment | 1755 |
| *tripping measure, or the belles of S.(aint) Bennet sir, may put \| you in minde, one, two, three. | 2189 |
| *Ant. To day my Lord: and for three months before, | 2247 |
| Three monthes this youth hath tended vpon mee, | 2254 |

THREW = *1

| | |
|---|---:|
| *Mal. Come sir, you peeuishly threw it to her: and | 670 |

THRICE = 1*1

| | |
|---|---:|
| *thou'st him some thrice, it shall not be amisse, and as ma-\|ny | 1424 |
| And say, thrice welcome drowned Viola. | 2407 |

THRIFTLESSE = 1
What thriftlesse sighes shall poore *Oliuia* breath?    696
THRIUE = 1
*By swaggering could I neuer thriue*, | *for the raine*, &c.    2570
THROAT = *2
*to her as long as there is a passage in my throat, & drinke    155
*thee kindly: but thou lyest in thy throat, that is not the matter*    1676
THROND = 1
*Vio*. It giues a verie eccho to the seate | Where loue is thron'd.    906
THRONES = 1
These soueraigne thrones, are all supply'd and fill'd    44
THROW = 2*2
*Ol*. Giue me my vaile: come throw it ore my face,    460
*To*. Hold sir, or Ile throw your dagger ore the house    1945
*throw: if you will let your Lady know I am here to speak    2192
You throw a strange regard vpon me, and by that    2376
THROWNE = 1*1
*My poore corpes, where my bones shall be throwne:*    951
*and some haue greatnesse throwne vpon them. I    2542
THRUST = 1*1
*haue greatnesse thrust vppon em. Thy fates open theyr    1152
*Mal*. And some haue greatnesse thrust vpon them. | *Ol*. Heauen restore
thee.    1567
THUNDER = 1
With groanes that thunder loue, with sighes of fire.    549
THUS = 4*11
*death of her brother thus? I am sure care's an enemie to | life.    120
*that, yet thus farre I will boldly publish her, shee    637
*thus neere, that should shee fancie, it should bee one of    1042
*Mal*. I extend my hand to him thus: quenching my    1081
*very *C's*, her *V's*, and her *T's*, and thus makes shee her    1102
*thus aduises thee, that sighes for thee. Remember who    1158
But rather reason thus, with reason fetter;    1371
*carry it thus for our pleasure, and his pennance, til our ve- | ry    1659
*Ol*. Will it be euer thus? Vngracious wretch,    1964
If it be thus to dreame, still let me sleepe.    1980
*Mal*. Sir *Topas*, neuer was man thus wronged, good    2014
*man thus abus'd, I am no more madde then you are,    2033
And though tis wonder that enwraps me thus,    2117
*reade thus: therefore, perpend my Princesse, and giue | eare.    2466
*and you smile not he's gag'd: and thus the whirlegigge | of time, brings
in his reuenges.    2546
THY *see also* i'thy *l*.14 70 103 109 113 228 *240 264 266 277 281 283 286
290 299 *320 *326 *406 409 588 608 726 *727 *765 768 826 *836 925
926 954 956 *961 1009 1018 *1149 *1152 *1153 *1154 *1156 *1157
*1159 *1179 1192 1195 *1215 1216 *1223 1224 1235 1261 1367 1369
1384 *1413 *1416 *1425 *1428 1555 *1569 1571 *1591 *1592 *1593
*1631 *1672 *1676 *1679 *1686 *1741 *1742 *1743 1843 *1913 *1927
*1932 1953 1958 1962 1969 1971 *2044 2045 *2049 *2057 *2080 *2081
2111 2167 2253 2298 2306 2307 2308 2313 2327 2328 2330 2439
2440 = 63*49
THYSELFE *see* selfe
TICKELD = *1
*he had not beene in drinke, hee would haue tickel'd you | other gates
then he did.    2356
TICKLING = 1
the Trowt, that must be caught with tickling. *Exit*    1038

TIGER = 1
And this is he that did the *Tiger* boord, 2213
TIL = *1
\*carry it thus for our pleasure, and his pennance, til our ve-|ry 1659
TILL = 6*5
The Element it selfe, till seuen yeares heate, 32
Till I had made mine owne occasion mellow | What my estate is. 94
\*drinke to my Neece, till his braines turne o'th toe, like a 157
And tell them, there thy fixed foot shall grow | Till thou haue audience. 266
\**Mal.* Yes, and shall do, till the pangs of death shake 367
\*will keepe no foole sir, till she be married, and fooles are 1246
till he take leaue, and presently after him. 1715
\**To.* I will doe so. Signiour *Fabian*, stay you by this | Gentleman, till
my returne. *Exit Toby.* 1775
\**Clo.* Nay, Ile nere beleeue a madman till I see his brains 2101
\**Clo.* Marry sir, lullaby to your bountie till I come a-|gen. 2195
Do not embrace me, till each circumstance, 2417
TILLY = *1
\*consanguinious? Am I not of her blood: tilly vally. La-|die, 777
TIME = 17*8
What else may hap, to time I will commit, 112
\*bestowed that time in the tongues, that I haue in fencing 206
\*'tis not that time of Moone with me, to make one in so | skipping a
dialogue. 495
O time, thou must vntangle this, not I, 697
*An.* 'Tis not the first time I haue constrained one to 767
\*like Tinkers at this time of night? Do yee make an Ale-|house 788
Is there no respect of place, persons, nor time in you? 791
\**To.* We did keepe time sir in our Catches. Snecke vp. 792
\**Clo.* Truely sir, and pleasure will be paide one time, or | another. 957
*Mal.* Besides you waste the treasure of your time, | with a foolish
knight. 1092
He must obserue their mood on whom he iests, | The quality of persons,
and the time: 1274
*Ol.* Why then me thinkes 'tis time to smile agen: 1341
The clocke vpbraides me with the waste of time: 1346
\*you let time wash off, and you are now sayld into 1405
Albeit the quality of the time, and quarrell 1499
\*Whiles you beguile the time, and feed your knowledge 1510
\*on him: at which time, we wil bring the deuice to the bar 1661
1.*Off.* What's that to vs, the time goes by: Away. 1884
What time we will our celebration keepe 2145
When time hath sow'd a grizzle on thy case? 2327
Of place, time, fortune, do co-here and iumpe 2418
Heere is my hand, you shall from this time bee | Your Masters Mistris. 2491
\*and you smile not he's gag'd: and thus the whirlegigge | of time, brings
in his reuenges. 2546
When that is knowne, and golden time conuents 2552
A solemne Combination shall be made | Of our deere soules. Meane
time sweet sister, 2553
TIMES = 2
Of these most briske and giddy-paced times. 890
Boy, thou hast saide to me a thousand times, 2433
TIME-PLEASER = *1
\*constantly but a time-pleaser, an affection'd Asse, that 841
TINE = 1
*Clowne sings. | When that I was and a little tine boy,* 2559

TINKERS = *1
  *like Tinkers at this time of night? Do yee make an Ale- | house     788
TIRANT = 1
  Liue you the Marble-brested Tirant still.     2280
TIRED *see* tyred
TIS *l*.12 *148 *242 *396 *414 *452 *453 *489 *495 *529 531 682 748 767
  *881 972 *1040 *1107 *1203 1266 1339 1341 *1459 1488 *1637 *1725
  1828 2117 2118 2316 2503 2517 = 16*17
TITUS = 1
  When your yong Nephew *Titus* lost his legge;     2214
TO *see also* t', too = 193*197
TO = 68*79
TOB = 4*2
*TOBY see also To., Tob.* = 30*18
  *Enter Sir Toby, and Maria.*     118
  *Mar.* By my troth sir *Toby*, you must come in earlyer     122
  *And.* Sir *Toby Belch.* How now sir *Toby Belch*? | *To.* Sweet sir *Andrew.*     161
  *An.* And I thought that, I'de forsweare it. Ile ride | home to morrow sir
  *Toby.*     202
  *An.* Faith Ile home to morrow sir *Toby*, your niece wil     215
  *sir *Toby* would leaue drinking, thou wert as witty a piece | of *Eues*
  flesh, as any in Illyria.     321
  *better increasing of your folly: Sir *Toby* will be sworn that     371
  *Ol.* Who of my people hold him in delay? | *Ma.* Sir *Toby* Madam, your
  kinsman.     398
  braines, for heere he comes. *Enter Sir Toby.*     408
  *Clo.* Good Sir *Toby.*     416
  *Enter Sir Toby, and Sir Andrew.*     700
  *Mal.* Sir *Toby*, I must be round with you. My Lady     793
  *Mar.* Nay good Sir *Toby.*     800
  *Clo.* Sir *Toby* there you lye.     804
  *Mar.* Sweet Sir Toby be patient for to night: Since     827
  *Enter Sir Toby, Sir Andrew, and Fabian.*     1017
  *place, as I would they should doe theirs: to aske for my | kinsman
  *Toby.*     1070
  *Toby* approaches; curtsies there to me. | *To.* Shall this fellow liue?     1077
  *To.* And do's not *Toby* take you a blow o'th lippes, | then?     1083
  *Mal.* Saying, Cosine *Toby*, my Fortunes hauing cast     1085
  *Toby*, I will wash off grosse acquaintance, I will be point     1167
  *Enter Sir Toby and Andrew.*     1281
  *Enter Sir Toby, Sir Andrew, and Fabian.*     1382
  *Fa.* This is a deere Manakin to you Sir *Toby.*     1433
  *Cosine *Toby*, let some of my people haue a speciall care     1584
  *man then sir *Toby* to looke to me. This concurres direct- | ly     1588
  *Enter Toby, Fabian, and Maria.*     1606
  *did not I tell you? Sir *Toby*, my Lady prayes you to haue | a care of
  him.     1615
  *Mar.* Get him to say his prayers, good sir *Toby*, gette | him to pray.     1640
  *Enter Toby and Fabian.*     1736
  *To.* I will doe so. Signiour *Fabian*, stay you by this | Gentleman, till
  my returne. *Exit Toby.*     1775
  *Enter Toby and Andrew.*     1791
  *Fab.* O good sir *Toby* hold: heere come the Officers.     1837
  *Enter Andrew, Toby, and Fabian.*     1941
  *Ol.* Hold *Toby*, on thy life I charge thee hold. | *To.* Madam.     1962
  quickly. Ile call sir *Toby* the whilst.     1988
  *Enter Toby.*     1996

*TOBY cont.*
   *\*Clo. Bonos dies* sir *Toby*: for as the old hermit of *Prage*    1998
   *\*And.* For the loue of God a Surgeon, send one pre- | sently to sir *Toby*.    2336
   *\*Toby* a bloody Coxcombe too: for the loue of God your    2340
   *\*for nothing, and that that I did, I was set on to do't by sir | *Toby*.    2347
   *Enter Toby and Clowne.*    2352
   *\*Heere comes sir *Toby* halting, you shall heare more: but if    2355
   *\*Clo.* O he's drunke sir *Toby* an houre agone: his eyes | were set at eight
   i'th morning.    2361
   *\*And.* Ile helpe you sir *Toby*, because we'll be drest to- | gether.    2367
   Vpon sir *Toby*, and the lighter people:    2509
   Most freely I confesse my selfe, and *Toby*    2530
TOBYES = 1
   The Letter, at sir *Tobyes* great importance,    2534
TODAY *see* day
TOE = *1
   *\*drinke to my Neece, till his braines turne o'th toe, like a    157
TOGETHER = 1*2
   *Vio.* Yes being kept together, and put to vse.    1263
   *\*cannot hale them together. For *Andrew*, if he were open'd    1440
   *\*And.* Ile helpe you sir *Toby*, because we'll be drest to- | gether.    2367
TOGITHER = *1
   *\*degree, but Fellow. Why euery thing adheres togither,    1600
TOLD = 4*4
   *\*speake with you. I told him you were sicke, he takes on    435
   *\*with you. I told him you were asleepe, he seems to haue    437
   *\*Mal.* Ha's beene told so: and hee sayes hee'l stand at    442
   *Du.* And what's her history? | *Vio.* A blanke my Lord: she neuer told
   her loue,    999
   *\*told me she did affect me, and I haue heard her self come    1041
   Since when, my watch hath told me, toward my graue    2324
   First told me thou wast mad; then cam'st in smiling,    2519
   He hath not told vs of the Captaine yet,    2551
TOMBE = 1
   So went he suited to his watery tombe:    2399
TOMORROW *see* morrow
TONGUE = 5*3
   When my tongue blabs, then let mine eyes not see.    115
   Thy tongue, thy face, thy limbes, actions, and spirit,    588
   That me thought her eyes had lost her tongue,    677
   *\*surly with seruants: Let thy tongue tang arguments of    1156
   *\*with a Kinsman, surly with seruants, let thy tongue    1592
   *\*tongue, in the habite of some Sir of note, and so foorth.    1596
   Refuse it not, it hath no tongue, to vex you:    1726
   That very enuy, and the tongue of losse    2209
TONGUES = *1
   *\*bestowed that time in the tongues, that I haue in fencing    206
TONIGHT *see* night
TOO = 23*13
   *\*these boots too: and they be not, let them hang them- | selues in their
   owne straps.    130
   *And.* Blesse you faire Shrew. | *Mar.* And you too sir.    163
   *Ol.* Go too, y'are a dry foole: Ile no more of you: be- | sides you grow
   dis-honest.    333
   *\*a fore knowledge of that too, and therefore comes to    438
   *Vio.* I see you what you are, you are too proud:    542
   Do giue thee fiue-fold blazon: not too fast: soft, soft,    589

TOO *cont.*

| | |
|---|---|
| Mine eye too great a flatterer for my minde: | 607 |
| It is too hard a knot for me t'vnty. | 698 |
| *\*An.* There's a testrill of me too: if one knight giue a | 734 |
| \*do I too: he does it with a better grace, but I do it more \| naturall. | 781 |
| *\*Clo.* Yes by *S.*(aint) Anne, and Ginger shall bee hotte y'th \| mouth | |
| too. | 813 |
| *To.* Excellent, I smell a deuice. \| *An.* I hau't in my nose too. | 855 |
| *An.* I was ador'd once too. | 873 |
| *\*To.* Come, come, Ile go burne some Sacke, tis too late | 881 |
| *Du.* Too old by heauen: Let still the woman take | 917 |
| *Vio.* Too well what loue women to men may owe: | 994 |
| And all the brothers too: and yet I know not. | 1011 |
| \*euer crosse garter'd: I say remember, goe too, thou art | 1160 |
| *To.* I could marry this wench for this deuice. \| *An.* So could I too. | 1185 |
| *And.* Ile make one too. *Exeunt.* \| *Finis Actus secundus* | 1211 |
| *Seb.* Do not then walke too open. | 1506 |
| \*I speake too loud: Where's *Maluolio*, he is sad, and ciuill, | 1525 |
| *\*Mal.* Go too, thou art made, if thou desir'st to be so. | 1574 |
| \*Good *Maria*, let this fellow be look'd too. Where's my | 1583 |
| \*be look'd too: Fellow? not *Maluolio*, nor after my | 1599 |
| *Mal.* Ah ha, does she so? \| *\*To.* Go too, go too: peace, peace, wee must | |
| deale | 1617 |
| *Ol.* I haue said too much vnto a hart of stone, | 1718 |
| And laid mine honour too vnchary on't: | 1719 |
| *Seb.* Go too, go too, thou art a foolish fellow, | 1921 |
| That my most iealious, and too doubtfull soule | 2142 |
| Hold little faith, though thou hast too much feare. | 2334 |
| *\*Toby* a bloody Coxcombe too: for the loue of God your | 2340 |
| *Ol.* Get him to bed, and let his hurt be look'd too. | 2371 |
| Such a *Sebastian* was my brother too: | 2398 |

TOOKE = 4\*4

| | |
|---|---|
| *\*Vio.* Alas, I tooke great paines to studie it, and 'tis \| Poeticall. | 489 |
| He might haue tooke his answer long ago. | 556 |
| \*that, for some houre before you tooke me from the | 631 |
| *Vio.* She tooke the Ring of me, Ile none of it. | 669 |
| *\*Oliuiaes* Father tooke much delight in. He is about the \| house. | 896 |
| What we tooke from them, which for Traffiques sake | 1502 |
| That tooke the *Phoenix*, and her fraught from *Candy*, | 2212 |
| *\*And.* The Counts Gentleman, one *Cesario*: we tooke | 2343 |

TOOT = 2\*2

| | |
|---|---|
| *To.* And I can cut the Mutton too't. | 230 |
| *\*To.* That defence thou hast, betake the too't: of what | 1739 |
| \*me, as he is a Gentleman and a Soldiour, he will not hurt \| you. Come | |
| on, too't. | 1824 |
| *\*Clo.* I will help you too't. But tel me true, are you not | 2098 |

TOP = \*1

| | |
|---|---|
| \*parish top. What wench? *Castiliano vulgo*: for here coms \| Sir *Andrew* | |
| *Agueface.* | 158 |

TOPAS = 6\*10

| | |
|---|---|
| \*make him beleeue thou art sir *Topas* the Curate, doe it | 1987 |
| *To.* To him sir *Topas.* \| *Clow.* What hoa, I say, Peace in this prison. | 2002 |
| *\*Clo.* Sir *Topas* the Curate, who comes to visit *Maluo-*\|*lio* the | |
| Lunaticke. | 2007 |
| *\*Mal.* Sir *Topas*, sir *Topas*, good sir *Topas* goe to my \| Ladie. | 2009 |
| *\*Mal.* Sir *Topas*, neuer was man thus wronged, good | 2014 |

TOPAS *cont.*
*sir *Topas* do not thinke I am mad: they haue layde mee | heere in
hideous darknesse. 2015
*Mal.* As hell sir *Topas*. 2021
*Mal.* I am not mad sir *Topas*, I say to you this house is | darke. 2026
*Mal.* Sir *Topas*, sir *Topas*. | *Tob.* My most exquisite sir *Topas*. 2046
*Mal.* Sir *Topas*. | *Clo.* Maintaine no words with him good fellow. 2083
*Who I sir, not I sir. God buy you good sir Topas: Mar-|ry Amen. I
will sir, I will. 2085
*was one sir, in this Enterlude, one sir *Topas* sir, but that's 2543
TORTURD = 1
How haue the houres rack'd, and tortur'd me, | Since I haue lost thee? 2383
TOSPOTTES = 1
*With tospottes still had drunken heades*, | *for the raine*, &c. 2574
TOTH = 1
hand to'th Buttry barre, and let it drinke. 184
TOUCH = *2
*extrauagancie. But I perceiue in you so excellent a touch 622
*touch Fortunes fingers. Farewell, Shee that would alter 1163
TOWARD = 1*2
*Fab.* This was a great argument of loue in her toward | you. 1391
*and the cleere stores toward the South north, are 2023
Since when, my watch hath told me, toward my graue 2324
TOWARDS = *2
*Val.* If the Duke continue these fauours towards you 251
*part of Illyria: will you walke towards him, I will make | your peace
with him, if I can. 1786
TOWNE = 6
Shall we go see the reliques of this Towne? 1486
With viewing of the Towne, there shall you haue me. 1511
That he did range the towne to seeke me out, 2121
Into the danger of this aduerse Towne, 2236
*Vio.* How can this be? | *Du.* When came he to this Towne? 2245
Ile bring you to a Captaine in this Towne, 2420
TOY = 2
*Seb.* Why I your purse? | *Ant.* Haply your eye shall light vpon some toy 1512
*A foolish thing was but a toy*, 2562
TRADE = 1
you should enter, if your trade be to her. 1288
TRAFFIQUES = 1
What we tooke from them, which for Traffiques sake 1502
TRANSGRESSES = *1
*that transgresses, is but patcht with sinne, and sin that a-|mends, 340
TRANSPARANT = *1
*Clo.* Why it hath bay Windowes transparant as bari-|cadoes, 2022
TRAPPINGS = 1
*Clo.* I sir, we are some of her trappings. 2162
TRAUAILD = 1
I haue trauail'd but two houres. 2325
TRAUAILE = 1*1
Not three houres trauaile from this very place. 73
*a demure trauaile of regard: telling them I knowe my 1069
TRAUELL = 1
But iealousie, what might befall your trauell, 1474
TRAY-TRIP = *1
*To.* Shall I play my freedome at tray-trip, and becom | thy bondslaue? 1194

TREASURE = 1
*Mal.* Besides you waste the treasure of your time, | with a foolish
  knight.                                     1092
TREE = *1
*Mar.* Get ye all three into the box tree: *Maluolio*'s      1032
TRIALL = 1
make the triall of it in any constant question.         2034
TRICE = 1
In a trice, like to the old vice, | your neede to sustaine.   2107
TRICKE = *3
*And.* And I thinke I haue the backe-tricke, simply as | strong as any
  man in Illyria.                                  231
*state; put thy selfe into the tricke of singularitie. Shee   1157
*tricke of singularity: and consequently setts downe the   1594
TRIP = 2*1
*Trip no further prettie sweeting.*                  743
*To.* Shall I play my freedome at tray-trip, and becom | thy bondslaue?   1194
That thine owne trip shall be thine ouerthrow:      2329
TRIPLEX = *1
*saying is, the third payes for all: the triplex sir, is a good   2188
TRIPPING = *1
*tripping measure, or the belles of S.(aint) *Bennet* sir, may put | you in
  minde, one, two, three.                              2189
TROTH = *8
*Mar.* By my troth sir *Toby*, you must come in earlyer     122
*And.* By my troth I would not vndertake her in this     173
*And.* Nay by my troth I know not: but I know, to | be vp late, is to be
  vp late.                                        704
*And.* By my troth the foole has an excellent breast. I   720
*Clo.* Troth sir, I can yeeld you none without wordes,   1236
*Vio.* By my troth Ile tell thee, I am almost sicke for   1259
*Clo.* By my troth thou hast an open hand: these Wise-|men   1938
*Clo.* By my troth sir, no: though it please you to be | one of my
  friends.                                      2177
TROUBLE = 2
*Seb.* O good *Antonio*, forgiue me your trouble.     642
And part being prompted by your present trouble,   1860
TROUBLED = 1
*Seb.* I would not by my will haue troubled you,   1467
TROWT = 1
the Trowt, that must be caught with tickling. *Exit*   1038
TROYLUS = 1
*Clo.* I would play Lord *Pandarus* of *Phrygia* sir, to bring | a *Cressida* to
  this *Troylus*.                                 1264
TRUE = 15*5
*Cap.* True Madam, and to comfort you with chance,     58
*As there is no true Cuckold but calamity, so beauties a   343
*O stay and heare, your true loues coming,*         741
*An.* A mellifluous voyce, as I am true knight.     754
*To.* She's a beagle true bred, and one that adores me: | what o'that?   871
For such as I am, all true Louers are,          902
*My part of death no one so true did share it.*     947
*Sad true louer neuer find my graue, to weepe there.*   953
In faith they are as true of heart, as we.       995
*Ma.* Nay but say true, do's it worke vpon him? | *To.* Like Aqua vite
  with a Midwife.                              1199
If it please the eye of one, it is with me as the very true   1544

TRUE *cont*.

*Vio*. Nothing but this, your true loue for my master. 1730

Proue true imagination, oh proue true, | That I deere brother, be now

tane for you. 1896

*Clo*. I will help you too't. But tel me true, are you not 2098

*Mal*. Beleeue me I am not, I tell thee true. 2100

And hauing sworne truth, euer will be true. 2148

That screwes me from my true place in your fauour: 2279

If this be so, as yet the glasse seemes true, 2431

And all those swearings keepe as true in soule, 2436

TRUELY = *3

*Clo*. Truely sir, and pleasure will be paide one time, or | another. 957

*Clo*. Truely sir, the better for my foes, and the worse | for my friends. 2165

How does he sirrah? | *Cl*. Truely Madam, he holds *Belzebub* at the

staues end as 2451

TRULY = 1

*Vio*. Tis beauty truly blent, whose red and white, 531

TRUNKES = 1

Are empty trunkes, ore-flourish'd by the deuill. 1890

TRUST = 2*2

bid him turne you out of doores, neuer trust me. 774

*An*. If I do not, neuer trust me, take it how you will. 880

*To*. Neuer trust me then: and by all meanes stirre on 1438

To any other trust, but that I am mad, 2129

TRUTH = 3

By maid-hood, honor, truth, and euery thing, 1366

I haue one heart, one bosome, and one truth, 1374

And hauing sworne truth, euer will be true. 2148

TS = 1*1

*very *C's*, her *V's*, and her *T's*, and thus makes shee her 1102

*An*. Her *C's*, her *V's*, and her *T's*: why that? 1104

TUCKE = *1

*attends thee at the Orchard end: dismount thy tucke, 1742

TUNE = 3*1

*To*. Out o'tune sir, ye lye: Art any more then a Stew-|ard? 810

*Du*. Seeke him out, and play the tune the while. | *Musicke playes*. 898

That is belou'd. How dost thou like this tune? 905

*Ol*. If it be ought to the old tune my Lord, 2263

TURKEY = *1

*Fa*. Oh peace: Contemplation makes a rare Turkey 1047

TURN = *1

*cannot but turn him into a notable contempt: if you wil | see it follow

me. 1207

TURND = 2*1

That instant was I turn'd into a Hart, 26

*or to be turn'd away: is not that as good as a hanging to | you? 312

wrong side may be turn'd outward. 1227

TURNE = 1*1

*drinke to my Neece, till his braines turne o'th toe, like a 157

bid him turne you out of doores, neuer trust me. 774

TURNED = *1

*selues into stitches, follow me; yond gull *Maluolio* is tur-|ned 1448

TURNES = 1

And thankes: and euer oft good turnes, 1482

TURNING = 1

and for turning away, let summer beare it out. 315

TUT = 1
 swear't. Tut there's life in't man.       220
TWANGD = *1
 *accent sharpely twang'd off, giues manhoode more   1697
TWAS = 5*1
 And then 'twas fresh in murmure (as you know    82
 *Queubus: 'twas very good yfaith: I sent thee sixe pence   725
 And. I knew 'twas I, for many do call mee foole.   1096
 Ol. My seruant sir? 'Twas neuer merry world,   1310
 Mal. Be not afraid of greatnesse: 'twas well writ.   1561
 I know not what 'twas, but distraction.   2219
TWELFE = 2
 To. O the twelfe day of December.    783
 Twelfe Night, Or what you will.    2581
TWELUEMONTH = 1
 That dide some tweluemonth since, then leauing her   87
TWENTIE = 2
 Then come kisse me sweet and twentie:    752
 And grew a twentie yeeres remoued thing   2241
TWERE = 1*1
 *An. 'Twere as good a deede as to drink when a mans   822
 Or else the Ladies mad; yet if 'twere so,   2130
TWILL = 1*2
 *Ol. 'Tis in graine sir, 'twill endure winde and wea- | ther.   529
 An. O twill be admirable.    863
 *To. I dare lay any money, twill be nothing yet. Exit   1916
TWIN = 1
 An apple cleft in two, is not more twin   2388
TWO see also 2. = 7*9
 Ma. You are resolute then? | *Clo. Not so neyther, but I am resolu'd on
 two points    316
 *Clo. Two faults Madona, that drinke & good counsell   335
 *I am no Fox, but he wil not passe his word for two pence | that you
 are no Foole.    372
 *Item two lippes indifferent redde, Item two grey eyes,   539
 *will worke with him, I will plant you two, and let   865
 *To. I haue beene deere to him lad, some two thousand | strong, or so.   1434
 whisper ore a couplet or two of most sage sawes.   1899
 in some of your coats for two pence.   1947
 *To. What, what? Nay then I must haue an Ounce or | two of this
 malapert blood from you.    1959
 *your foure negatiues make your two affirmatiues, why   2174
 *tripping measure, or the belles of S.(aint) Bennet sir, may put | you in
 minde, one, two, three.    2189
 I haue trauail'd but two houres.   2325
 *Du. One face, one voice, one habit, and two persons,   2380
 An apple cleft in two, is not more twin   2388
 Then these two creatures. Which is Sebastian? | Ol. Most wonderfull.   2389
TYRANNOUS = *1
 *That tyrannous heart can think? To one of your receiuing   1334
TYRANT see tirant
TYRED = *1
 *pastime tyred out of breath, prompt vs to haue mercy   1660
VACANCIE = 1
 No intrim, not a minutes vacancie,   2248
VAILE = 1
 Ol. Giue me my vaile: come throw it ore my face,   460

VAILED = 1
  But like a Cloystresse she will vailed walke,                                    34
VAINE = *1
  *thy selfe to sleepe, and leaue thy vaine bibble | babble.                     2081
VAINNESSE = 1
  Then lying, vainnesse, babling drunkennesse,                                   1874
VAL = 2*1
*VALENTINE see also Val.* = 2
  *Enter Valentine.*                                                                29
  *Enter Valentine, and Viola in mans attire.*                                     250
VALIANT = 2*1
  In voyces well divulg'd, free, learn'd, and valiant,                            553
  *Fa.* Good, and valiant.                                                        1671
  *An.* Plague on't, and I thought he had beene valiant,                         1801
VALIDITY = 1
  Of what validity, and pitch so ere,                                              16
VALLY = *1
  *consanguinious? Am I not of her blood: tilly vally. La-|die,                    777
VALOR = *1
  *set vpon *Ague-cheeke* a notable report of valor, and driue                   1708
VALOUR = 1*6
  *onely to exasperate you, to awake your dormouse valour,                       1399
  *it, by some laudable attempt, either of valour or | policie.                  1408
  *And.* And't be any way, it must be with Valour, for                          1410
  *valour. Challenge me the Counts youth to fight with him                      1414
  *can more preuaile in mans commendation with woman, | then report
  of valour.                                                                    1417
  *to taste their valour: belike this is a man of that | quirke.                1762
  *his valour. He is indeede sir, the most skilfull, bloudy, &                  1784
VAPIANS = *1
  *Pigrogromitus*, of the *Vapians* passing the Equinoctial of                   724
VEILE *see* vaile
VEILED *see* vailed
VELUET = *1
  *Veluet gowne: hauing come from a day bedde, where I | haue left
  *Oliuia* sleeping.                                                             1064
VENERABLE = 1
  And to his image, which me thought did promise | Most venerable
  worth, did I deuotion.                                                        1882
VENOM = 1
  *To.* Thy reason deere venom, giue thy reason.                                1384
VENT = *5
  *Seb.* I prethee vent thy folly some-where else, thou | know'st not me.       1927
  *Clo.* Vent my folly: He has heard that word of some                          1929
  *great man, and now applyes it to a foole. Vent my fol-|ly:                   1930
  *me what I shall vent to my Lady? Shall I vent to hir that | thou art
  comming?                                                                      1933
VERIE = 4*9
  *My verie walke should be a Iigge: I would not so much                         237
  *Mal.* Of verie ill manner: hee'l speake with you, will | you, or no.          448
  *betweene boy and man. He is verie well-fauour'd,                              454
  *and he speakes verie shrewishly: One would thinke his                         455
  *Ol.* Are you a Comedian? | *Vio.* No my profound heart: and yet (by
  the verie                                                                      477
  *Vio.* It giues a verie eccho to the seate | Where loue is thron'd.            906
  Being once displaid, doth fall that verie howre.                               928

VERIE *cont.*

*Vio.* No not a grize: for tis a vulgar proofe | That verie oft we pitty
enemies.                                                                1339
*Heathen, a verie Renegatho; for there is no christian                  1449
*Ol.* Why this is verie Midsommer madnesse.                             1577
*Mar.* You may haue verie fit occasion for't: he is now                 1690
*To.* Why man hee's a verie diuell, I haue not seen such                1792
*him for a Coward, but hee's the verie diuell, incardinate.             2344

VERSE = 1

Come, but one verse.                                                    891

VERTU = *1

*mend him: any thing that's mended, is but patch'd: vertu              339

VERTUE = 2*1

*Is but patcht with vertue. If that this simple                         341
*Clo.* I must catechize you for it Madona, Good my | Mouse of vertue
answer mee.                                                             354
Vertue is beauty, but the beauteous euill                              1889

VERTUES = *1

*meane? Is it a world to hide vertues in? I did thinke by              239

VERTUOUS = 2*1

*Vio.* What's shee? | *Cap.* A vertuous maid, the daughter of a Count   85
Yet I suppose him vertuous, know him noble,                            551
*Dost thou thinke because thou art vertuous, there                     811

VERY = 12*16

Not three houres trauaile from this very place.                        73
He was a Batchellor then. | *Cap.* And so is now, or was so very late:  79
That will allow me very worth his seruice.                             111
He's a very foole, and a prodigall.                                    141
*Clo.* Apt in good faith, very apt: well go thy way, if                320
*those wits that thinke they haue thee, doe very oft proue             327
*no scorne; I am very comptible, euen to the least | sinister vsage.   470
Else would I very shortly see thee there:                              653
*in very gracious fooling last night, when thou spok'st of            723
*Queubus*: 'twas very good yfaith: I sent thee sixe pence             725
*An.* Very sweet, and contagious ifaith.                               756
leaue of her, she is very willing to bid you farewell.                 798
*feelingly personated. I can write very like my Ladie                 852
*minde is a very Opall. I would haue men of such constan- | cie       962
*very *C's*, her *V's*, and her *T's*, and thus makes shee her        1102
*Her very Phrases: By your leaue wax. Soft, and the im- | pressure    1106
*deuise, the very man. I do not now foole my selfe, to let            1168
words are very Rascals, since bonds disgrac'd them. | *Vio.* Thy reason
man?                                                                    1234
But in very strange manner. He is sure possest Madam.                  1529
If it please the eye of one, it is with me as the very true            1544
*To.* His very genius hath taken the infection of the | deuice man.    1651
*carry it thus for our pleasure, and his pennance, til our ve- | ry    1659
*Fa.* Very breefe, and to exceeding good sence-lesse.                  1678
*to me: my remembrance is very free and cleere from                   1746
*To.* Sir, no: his indignation deriues it selfe out of a ve- | ry      1764
*To.* A very dishonest paltry boy, and more a coward                  1906
*that neuer saw pen and inke, very wittily sayd to a Neece            1999
That very enuy, and the tongue of losse                               2209

VESSELL = 1

A bawbling Vessell was he Captaine of,                                 2205

VEX = 1

Refuse it not, it hath no tongue, to vex you:                         1726

VNCHARY = 1
And laid mine honour too vnchary on't:     1719
VNCIUILL = 2*2
  *meanes for this vnciuill rule; she shall know of it by this | hand. *Exit*   819
  *Vio*. This is as vnciuill as strange. I beseech you doe   1771
  Let thy fayre wisedome, not thy passion sway | In this vnciuill, and
  vniust extent   1969
  *Du*. What to peruersenesse? you vnciuill Ladie   2268
VNCLASPD = 1
  Thou knowst no lesse, but all: I haue vnclasp'd   262
VNCOURTEOUS = 1
  Vpon some stubborne and vncourteous parts   2532
VNCURRANT = 1
  Are shuffel'd off with such vncurrant pay:   1483
VNDER = 2*4
  *And*. As any man in Illyria, whatsoeuer he be, vnder   225
  *the excellent constitution of thy legge, it was form'd vn- | der the starre
  of a Galliard.   240
  *To*. What shall we do else: were we not borne vnder | Taurus?   244
  Cocke of him, how he iets vnder his aduanc'd plumes.   1048
  *that suffers vnder probation: *A*. should follow, but *O*. | does.   1138
  Vnder your hard construction must I sit,   1329
VNDERNEATH = 1
  And vnderneath that consecrated roofe,   2140
VNDERSTAND = 2*3
  *him to vnderstand so much, and therefore comes to speak   436
  I would not vnderstand it.   560
  *Vio*. I vnderstand you sir, tis well begg'd.   1266
  *Vio*. My legges do better vnderstand me sir, then I vn- | derstand   1292
VNDERTAKE = 1*2
  *And*. By my troth I would not vndertake her in this   173
  But would you vndertake another suite   1321
  *vndertake that with me, which with as much safetie you   1767
VNDERTAKER = 1
  *To*. Nay, if you be an vndertaker, I am for you.   1835
VNDO = *1
  *Seb*. If you will not vndo what you haue done, that is   645
VNDOE = *1
  *Ma*. That quaffing and drinking will vndoe you: I   132
VNFILLD = *1
  *To*. A false conclusion: I hate it as an vnfill'd Canne.   706
VNFIRME = 1
  Our fancies are more giddie and vnfirme,   921
VNFOLD = 2
  *Vio*. Say I do speake with her (my Lord) what then? | *Du*. O then,
  vnfold the passion of my loue,   273
  Heere to vnfold, though lately we intended   2314
VNFOLDETH = 1
  Mine owne escape vnfoldeth to my hope,   69
VNFRIENDED = 1
  Vnguided, and vnfriended, often proue | Rough, and vnhospitable. My
  willing loue,   1476
VNGIRD = *1
  *Cockney: I prethee now vngird thy strangenes, and tell   1932
VNGRACIOUS = 1
  *Ol*. Will it be euer thus? Vngracious wretch,   1964

VNGRATEFULL *see* ingratefull
VNGUIDED = 1
   Vnguided, and vnfriended, often proue | Rough, and vnhospitable. My
   willing loue,          1476
VNHAPPY = *1
   *seruices with thee, the fortunate vnhappy daylight and      1164
VNHATCHD = *1
   *To. He is knight dubb'd with vnhatch'd Rapier, and      1753
VNHOSPITABLE = 1
   Vnguided, and vnfriended, often proue | Rough, and vnhospitable. My
   willing loue,          1476
VNIUST = 1
   Let thy fayre wisedome, not thy passion sway | In this vnciuill, and
   vniust extent          1969
VNKIND = 1
   *Clo.* My Lady is vnkind, *perdie.* | *Mal.* Foole.      2060
VNKINDE = 1
   None can be call'd deform'd, but the vnkinde.      1888
VNKNOWNE = *1
   *Mal. To the vnknowne belou'd, this, and my good Wishes*:      1105
VNLES = *1
   *Looke you now, he's out of his gard already: vnles you      378
VNLESSE = 2*4
   *An.* Neuer in your life I thinke, vnlesse you see Ca- | narie      196
   Vnlesse (perchance) you come to me againe,      577
   Vnlesse the Master were the man. How now?      590
   *in his affaires, vnlesse it bee to report your Lords taking | of this:
   receiue it so.          667
   *like an ysickle on a Dutchmans beard, vnlesse you do re- | deeme      1407
   *his desire. Backe you shall not to the house, vnlesse you      1766
VNMATCHABLE = *1
   *Vio.* Most radiant, exquisite, and vnmatchable beau- | tie.      465
VNMUZLED = 1
   And baited it with all th'vnmuzled thoughts      1333
VNPRIZABLE = 1
   For shallow draught and bulke vnprizable,      2206
VNPROFITED = 1
   Rather then make vnprofited returne,      272
VNSAFE = *1
   *obstacle, no incredulous or vnsafe circumstance: What      1602
VNSOUGHT = 1
   Loue sought, is good: but giuen vnsought is better.      1372
VNSOUND = 1
   Least that it make me so vnsound a man      1868
VNSTAID = 1
   Vnstaid and skittish in all motions else,      903
VNSURE = 1
   *What's to come, is still vnsure.*      750
VNSUTEABLE = *1
   *vpon her, which will now be so vnsuteable to her dispo- | sition,      1205
VNTANGLE = 1
   O time, thou must vntangle this, not I,      697
VNTHOUGHT = *1
   *me as you please. I leaue my duty a little vnthought of,      2476
VNTO = 3
   Therefore good youth, addresse thy gate vnto her,      264
   *Ol.* I haue said too much vnto a hart of stone,      1718

VNTO  *cont.*
    *But when I came vnto my beds, | with hey ho, &c.*    2572
VNTY = 1
    It is too hard a knot for me t'vnty.    698
VOICE = *3
    *Catches without any mitigation or remorse of voice?    790
    *Vio.* My matter hath no voice Lady, but to your owne | most pregnant
    and vouchsafed eare.    1301
    *Du.* One face, one voice, one habit, and two persons,    2380
VOSTRE *l.*1285 = 1
VOU = 1
    *And. Dieu vou guard Monsieur. | Vio. Et vouz ousie vostre seruiture.*    1284
VOUCHSAFED = 1*1
    *Vio.* My matter hath no voice Lady, but to your owne | most pregnant
    and vouchsafed eare.    1301
    *And.* Odours, pregnant, and vouchsafed: Ile get 'em | all three already.    1303
VOUZ = 1
    *And. Dieu vou guard Monsieur. | Vio. Et vouz ousie vostre seruiture.*    1284
VOWE = *1
    *of: therefore draw for the supportance of his vowe,    1816
VOWES = 2
    Much in our vowes, but little in our loue.    1008
    Pardon me (sweet one) euen for the vowes    2378
VOX = 1
    *Ladyship will haue it as it ought to bee, you must allow | *Vox.*    2462
VOYAGE = 3*1
    *Seb.* No sooth sir: my determinate voyage is meere    621
    makes a good voyage of nothing. Farewell. *Exit*    965
    *Vio.* I am bound to your Neece sir, I meane she is the | list of my
    voyage.    1289
    As might haue drawne one to a longer voyage)    1473
VOYCE = 2*1
    *An.* A mellifluous voyce, as I am true knight.    754
    Nor know I you by voyce, or any feature:    1872
    *To.* To him in thine owne voyce, and bring me word    2051
VOYCES = 1
    In voyces well divulg'd, free, learn'd, and valiant,    553
VP = 8*7
    Nor hold him vp with hopes, I am not for him:    602
    *midnight, is to be vp betimes, and *Deliculo surgere,.*thou | know'st.    702
    *And.* Nay by my troth I know not: but I know, to | be vp late, is to be
    vp late.    704
    *To be vp after midnight, and to go to bed then is early:    707
    *my Ladie haue not call'd vp her Steward *Maluolio,* and    773
    *To.* We did keepe time sir in our Catches. Snecke vp.    792
    *winde vp my watch, or play with my some rich Iewell:    1076
    *To.* O I, make vp that, he is now at a cold sent.    1131
    *I haue his horse to take vp the quarrell, I haue perswaded | him the
    youths a diuell.    1809
    *Ant.* Put vp your sword: if this yong Gentleman    1829
    *Vio.* Pray sir, put your sword vp if you please.    1839
    *souldier put vp your yron: you are well flesh'd: Come | on.    1955
    This Ruffian hath botch'd vp, that thou thereby    1973
    Feare not *Cesario,* take thy fortunes vp,    2308
VPBRAID = 1
    As to vpbraid you with those kindnesses    1869

VPBRAIDES = 1
The clocke vpbraides me with the waste of time:                          1346
VPON = 21*12
    That breathes vpon a banke of Violets;                             10
    To a strong Maste, that liu'd vpon the sea:                        64
    And call vpon my soule within the house,                          563
    *am yet so neere the manners of my mother, that vpon the         648
    Hath staid vpon some fauour that it loues:                        910
    The parts that fortune hath bestow'd vpon her:                    970
    *Ma*. Nay but say true, do's it worke vpon him? | *To*. Like Aqua vite
    with a Midwife.                                                  1199
    *vpon her, which will now be so vnsuteable to her dispo-|sition,  1205
    *Vio*. Nay, and thou passe vpon me, Ile no more with | thee. Hold
    there's expences for thee.                                       1255
    *Counts Seruing-man, then euer she bestow'd vpon mee:            1387
    *Fab*. I will proue it legitimate sir, vpon the Oathes of | iudgement, and
    reason.                                                          1394
    *To*. Why then build me thy fortunes vpon the basis of           1413
    *Seb*. Why I your purse? | *Ant*. Haply your eye shall light vpon some toy  1512
    *Ol*. Smil'st thou? I sent for thee vpon a sad occasion.         1540
    *Mal*. And some haue greatnesse thrust vpon them. | *Ol*. Heauen restore
    thee.                                                            1567
    *Fa*. If this were plaid vpon a stage now, I could con-|demne it as an
    improbable fiction.                                              1649
    *Tob. Fartheewell, and God haue mercie vpon one of our*          1684
    *soules. He may haue mercie vpon mine, but my hope is better*,   1685
    *set vpon Ague-cheeke* a notable report of valor, and driue      1708
    *To*. I wil meditate the while vpon some horrid message | for a
    Challenge.                                                       1716
    That honour (sau'd) may vpon asking giue.                        1729
    But in conclusion put strange speech vpon me,                    2218
    Three monthes this youth hath tended vpon mee,                   2254
    You drew your sword vpon me without cause,                       2350
    You throw a strange regard vpon me, and by that                  2376
    I should my teares let fall vpon your cheeke,                    2406
    *Vio*. My father had a moale vpon his brow. | *Seb*. And so had mine.  2408
    Hath my Maides garments: he vpon some Action                     2442
    Vpon sir *Toby*, and the lighter people:                         2509
    Vpon thee in the Letter: prethee be content,                     2521
    This practice hath most shrewdly past vpon thee:                 2522
    Vpon some stubborne and vncourteous parts                        2532
    *and some haue greatnesse throwne vpon them. I                   2542
VPONT = 1*1
    My life vpon't, yong though thou art, thine eye                  909
    *Fab*. Sowter will cry vpon't for all this, though it bee | as ranke as a
    Fox.                                                             1132
VPPESHOT = *1
    *that I cannot pursue with any safety this sport the vppe-|shot. 2055
VPPON = *1
    *haue greatnesse thrust vppon em. Thy fates open theyr           1152
VS *see also* let's *l*.*406 512 *713 *833 *1079 1463 1489 1500 *1660 1884
    2401 2415 2551 = 9*7, 1*1
    *very *C*'s, her *V*'s, and her *T*'s, and thus makes shee her   1102
    *An*. Her *C*'s, her *V*'s, and her *T*'s: why that?             1104
VSAGE = 1
    *no scorne; I am very comptible, euen to the least | sinister vsage.  470

VSD = 2
  is rough, and will not be roughly vs'd.                 1634
  and speake out of my iniury. *The madly vs'd Maluolio.*     2477
VSE = 4*1
  those that are fooles, let them vse their talents.           310
  Do vse to chaunt it: it is silly sooth,               936
  *Vio.* Yes being kept together, and put to vse.        1263
  *that will vse the diuell himselfe with curtesie: sayst thou | that house is
  darke?                          2019
  Which I had recommended to his vse, | Not halfe an houre before.  2243
VSES = *3
  *my complection. Besides she vses me with a more ex- |alted    1043
  *her *Lucrece*, with which she vses to seale: tis my | Lady: To whom
  should this be?                     1107
  *To. Thou comst to the Lady Oliuia, and in my sight she vses*  1675
VSEST = *1
  *and so looke to thy selfe. Thy friend as thou vsest him, & thy | sworne
  enemie*, Andrew Ague-cheeke.              1686
VSURP = *1
  *Vio.* Most certaine, if you are she, you do vsurp your     482
VSURPD = 1
  But this my masculine vsurp'd attyre:            2416
VSURPE = 1
  *Ol.* If I do not vsurpe my selfe, I am.            481
VTENSILE = *1
  *and euery particle and vtensile labell'd to my will: As,    538
VTTERS = *1
  *cons State without booke, and vtters it by great swarths.   842
VULCAN = 1
  As blacke as Vulcan, in the smoake of warre:        2204
VULGAR = 1
  *Vio.* No not a grize: for tis a vulgar proofe | That verie oft we pitty
  enemies.                          1339
VULGO = *1
  *parish top. What wench? *Castiliano vulgo*: for here coms | Sir *Andrew
  Agueface*.                       158
WAINE-ROPES = *1
  *the youth to an answer. I thinke Oxen and waine-ropes   1439
WALKE = 3*4
  But like a Cloystresse she will vailed walke,         34
  *My verie walke should be a Iigge: I would not so much   237
  *comming downe this walke, he has beene yonder i'the    1033
  *Clo.* Foolery sir, does walke about the Orbe like the    1251
  I do not without danger walke these streetes.        1493
  *Seb.* Do not then walke too open.            1506
  *part of Illyria: will you walke towards him, I will make | your peace
  with him, if I can.                   1786
WALKES = *1
  *Du.* Heere comes the Countesse, now heauen walkes | on earth:  2251
WALL = 1
  And though that nature, with a beauteous wall       100
WANT = *1
  *Ol.* Well sir, for want of other idlenesse, Ile bide your | proofe.  356
WANTON = 1*1
  words, may quickely make them wanton.          1229
  *that word, might make my sister wanton: But indeede,   1233

WARDROBE = 1
   married the yeoman of the wardrobe.                   1056
WARE = *1
   *sheete were bigge enough for the bedde of *Ware* in Eng-|land,    1426
WARRANT = 2*4
   *Mar.* Sport royall I warrant you: I know my Phy-|sicke        864
   *And.* That's mee I warrant you. | *Mal.* One sir *Andrew.*     1094
   *Vio.* I warrant thou art a merry fellow, and car'st for | nothing.   1239
   *Mar.* No I warrant you, he will not heare of godly-|nesse.    1643
   *An.* Heere's the Challenge, reade it: I warrant there's | vinegar and
   pepper in't.                                   1665
   *And.* I, ist? I warrant him: do but read. | *To.* Giue me.    1668
WARRE = 1*1
   *of warre, no taxation of homage; I hold the Olyffe        504
   As blacke as Vulcan, in the smoake of warre:         2204
WARRS = *1
   *Ma.* In the warrs, & that may you be bolde to say in | your foolerie.  307
WAS *see also* 'twas = 26*15
WASH = *2
   *Toby,* I will wash off grosse acquaintance, I will be point   1167
   *you let time wash off, and you are now sayld into       1405
WAST *l.*722 2519 = 1*1
WASTE = 2
   *Mal.* Besides you waste the treasure of your time, | with a foolish
   knight.                                       1092
   The clocke vpbraides me with the waste of time:       1346
WATCH = 1*1
   *winde vp my watch, or play with my some rich Iewell:    1076
   Since when, my watch hath told me, toward my graue     2324
WATER = 3*3
   And water once a day her Chamber round           35
   *as make water but in a Sinke-a-pace: What dooest thou     238
   *when tis almost an Apple: Tis with him in standing wa-|ter,    453
   *drown'd already sir with salt water, though I seeme to     639
   *Fab.* Carry his water to th'wise woman.          1625
   *Du.* Notable Pyrate, thou salt-water Theefe,        2220
WATERS = 1
   *Clo.* Nay I am for all waters.              2048
WATERY = 1
   So went he suited to his watery tombe:           2399
WAUERING = 1
   More longing, wauering, sooner lost and worne, | Then womens are.  922
WAUES = 3
   I saw him hold acquaintance with the waues, | So long as I could see.  66
   Tempests are kinde, and salt waues fresh in loue.      1905
   Whom the blinde waues and surges haue deuour'd:     2394
WAX = *1
   *Her very Phrases: By your leaue wax. Soft, and the im-|pressure  1106
WAXEN = 1
   In womens waxen hearts to set their formes:        687
WAY = 4*12
   *not open my lippes so wide as a brissle may enter, in way   298
   *Clo.* Apt in good faith, very apt: well go thy way, if     320
   *Ma.* Will you hoyst sayle sir, here lies your way.     497
   If that the youth will come this way to morrow,      603
   *To.* What wilt thou do? | *Mar.* I will drop in his way some obscure
   Epistles of                                    847

WAY *cont*.

| | |
|---|---|
| *An*. If I cannot recouer your Neece, I am a foule way \| out. | 876 |
| There lies your way, due West. \| *Vio*. Then Westward hoe: | 1350 |
| *And*. And't be any way, it must be with Valour, for | 1410 |
| *Fab*. There is no way but this sir *Andrew*. | 1419 |
| *To*. Which way is hee in the name of sanctity. If all | 1607 |
| *To*. Prethee hold thy peace, this is not the way: Doe | 1631 |
| *Fa*. No way but gentlenesse, gently, gently: the Fiend | 1633 |
| *Fab*. Heere he comes with your Neece, giue them way | 1714 |
| *An*. Nay let him alone, Ile go another way to worke | 1949 |
| *Mal*. I thinke nobly of the soule, and no way aproue \| his opinion. | 2040 |
| *Ol*. Then lead the way good father, & heauens so shine, | 2149 |

WAYES = 1

| | |
|---|---|
| *To*. Come thy wayes Signior *Fabian*. | 1018 |

WAY-LAY = *1

| | |
|---|---|
| *To*. *I will way-lay thee going home, where if it be thy chance \| to kill* | |
| *me*. \| *Fa*. Good. | 1679 |

WE = 27*18

WEAKE = 1

| | |
|---|---|
| One of thy kin has a most weake *Pia-mater*. | 409 |

WEARE = 1*2

| | |
|---|---|
| *Non facit monachum*: that's as much to say, as I weare not | 348 |
| *Ol*. Heere, weare this Iewell for me, tis my picture: | 1725 |
| *starke naked: for meddle you must that's certain, or for-\|sweare to | |
| weare iron about you. | 1769 |

WEARES = 1

| | |
|---|---|
| An elder then her selfe, so weares she to him; | 918 |

WEARY = 1

| | |
|---|---|
| *Seb*. I am not weary, and 'tis long to night | 1488 |

WEATHER = *1

| | |
|---|---|
| *Ol*. 'Tis in graine sir, 'twill endure winde and wea-\|ther. | 529 |

WEAUE = 1

| | |
|---|---|
| And the free maides that weaue their thred with bones, | 935 |

WEAUER = 1

| | |
|---|---|
| soules out of one Weauer? Shall we do that? | 760 |

WEE *l*.688 *758 *776 *853 *1618 = 1*4

WEEDES = 1

| | |
|---|---|
| *Du*. Giue me thy hand, \| And let me see thee in thy womans weedes. | 2439 |

WEEDS = 1

| | |
|---|---|
| Where lye my maiden weeds: by whose gentle helpe, | 2421 |

WEEL = 3*3

| | |
|---|---|
| Wee'l once more heare *Orsinos* Embassie. | 461 |
| *To*. To anger him wee'l haue the Beare againe, and | 1025 |
| *To*. Wee'l call thee at the Cubiculo: Go. \| *Exit Sir Andrew*. | 1431 |
| *To*. Come, wee'l haue him in a darke room & bound. | 1657 |
| *To*. Come hither Knight, come hither *Fabian*: Weel | 1898 |
| *and wee'l striue to please you euery day*. | 2579 |

WEENING = 1

| | |
|---|---|
| *To*. Heere's an ouer-weening rogue. | 1046 |

WEEPE = *1

| | |
|---|---|
| *Sad true louer neuer find my graue, to weepe there*. | 953 |

WEIGHD = 1

| | |
|---|---|
| If that the iniuries be iustly weigh'd, \| That haue on both sides past. | 2538 |

WEL = 1*1

| | |
|---|---|
| *An*. But it becoms me wel enough, dost not? | 212 |
| *And*. That youth's a rare Courtier, raine odours, wel. | 1300 |

WELCOME = 3*1
*To*. Welcome asse, now let's haue a catch.                               719
*separate your selfe and your misdemeanors, you are wel-|come           796
O welcome Father: | Father, I charge thee by thy reuerence            2312
And say, thrice welcome drowned *Viola*.                             2407
WELKIN = *2
*But shall we make the Welkin dance indeed? Shall wee                 758
*what you would are out of my welkin, I might say Ele-|ment, but the
word is ouer-worne. *Exit*                                           1270
WELL = 38*23
The like of him. Know'st thou this Countrey? | *Cap*. I Madam well, for
I was bred and borne                                                    71
company. Is that the meaning of Accost? | *Ma*. Far you well
Gentlemen.                                                            174
*And*. I, 'tis strong, and it does indifferent well in a             242
It shall become thee well to act my woes:                            276
When least in companie: prosper well in this,                        289
*Clo*. Let her hang me: hee that is well hang'de in this | world, needs to
feare no colours.                                                    300
*Clo*. Well, God giue them wisedome that haue it: &                  309
*Clo*. Apt in good faith, very apt: well go thy way, if              320
*Ol*. Well sir, for want of other idlenesse, Ile bide your | proofe. 356
*Clo*. Now Mercury indue thee with leasing, for thou | speak'st well of
fooles.                                                              389
*Ma* I know not (Madam) 'tis a faire young man, and | well attended. 396
me faith say I. Well, it's all one. *Exit*                           423
*speech: for besides that it is excellently well pend, I haue        468
*Looke you sir, such a one I was this present: Ist not well | done?  526
In voyces well divulg'd, free, learn'd, and valiant,                 553
What is your Parentage? | *Vio*. Aboue my fortunes, yet my state is well: 572
To tell me how he takes it: Fare you well:                           578
*Ol*. What is your Parentage? | Aboue my fortunes, yet my state is well; 585
To creepe in at mine eyes. Well, let it be.                          594
*ye well at once, my bosome is full of kindnesse, and I             647
*Clo*. Byrlady sir, and some dogs will catch well.                   763
*An*. I, he do's well enough if he be dispos'd, and so               780
*Vio*. I thinke it well my Lord.                                      924
*Vio*. Too well what loue women to men may owe:                      994
*it appeare in thy smiling, thy smiles become thee well. There-|fore* 1179
*Vio*. I vnderstand you, tis well begg'd.                            1266
And to do that well, craues a kinde of wit:                         1273
Might well haue giuen vs bloody argument:                            1500
And suites well for a seruant with my fortunes,                      1526
*Mal*. Be not afraid of greatnesse: 'twas well writ.                 1561
*me, and the full prospect of my hopes. Well Ioue, not I,           1604
*Ol*. Well, come againe to morrow: far-thee-well,                    1734
marry Ile ride your horse as well as I ride you.                     1807
*be as good as my word. Hee will beare you easily, and | raines well. 1841
1.*Off*. No sir, no iot: I know your fauour well:                    1846
Take him away, he knowes I know him well.                            1848
*Clo*. Well held out yfaith: No, I do not know you,                  1923
*souldier put vp your yron: you are well flesh'd: Come | on.        1955
*Clo*. Well, Ile put it on, and I will dissemble my selfe            1989
*function well, nor leane enough to bee thought a good               1992
*To*. The knaue counterfets well: a good knaue. | *Maluolio within*. 2004
man? Talkest thou nothing but of Ladies? | *Tob*. Well said M.(aster)
Parson.                                                              2012

WELL *cont.*
*\*Clo.* Fare thee well: remaine thou still in darkenesse,   2042
the soule of thy grandam. Fare thee well.   2045
*\*how thou findst him: I would we were well ridde of this   2052
*\*Mal.* Good foole, as euer thou wilt deserue well at   2065
I am as well in my wits (foole) as thou art.   2073
*\*Clo.* But as well: then you are mad indeede, if you be   2074
*\*paper,* I tell thee I am as well in my wittes, as any man in | Illyria.   2091
For though my soule disputes well with my sence,   2123
*Ol.* Blame not this haste of mine: if you meane well   2137
*Duke.* I know thee well: how doest thou my good | Fellow?   2163
*Du.* Well, I will be so much a sinner to be a double | dealer: there's
another.   2185
*Du.* That face of his I do remember well,   2202
*\*And.* Ile helpe you sir *Toby,* because we'll be drest to- | gether.   2367
*\*well as a man in his case may do: has heere writ a letter to   2453
*Clo.* Looke then to be well edified, when the Foole   2458
*\*yet haue I the benefit of my senses as well as your Ladie- | ship.   2472
To thinke me as well a sister, as a wife,   2483
You can say none of this. Well, grant it then,   2504
WELL-A-DAY = 1
*Clo.* Well-a-day, that you were sir.   2093
WELL-FAUOURD = \*1
*\*betweene boy and man. He is verie well-fauour'd,   454
WENCH = 3\*1
*\*parish top. What wench? *Castiliano vulgo:* for here coms | Sir *Andrew
Agueface.*   158
*An.* Before me she's a good wench.   870
*Fa.* A fustian riddle. | *To.* Excellent Wench, say I.   1119
*To.* I could marry this wench for this deuice. | *An.* So could I too.   1185
WENT = 3\*1
For but a month ago I went from hence,   81
*\*thankefull. And when she went away now, let this Fel- | low   1598
In fauour was my Brother, and he went   1902
So went he suited to his watery tombe:   2399
WERE *see also* 'twere *l.*56 96 \*244 324 \*435 \*437 456 \*492 541 543 545
590 \*618 \*658 683 997 1316 1358 \*1426 \*1440 1484 1496 \*1532 \*1649
1812 1966 \*1990 \*2032 \*2052 \*2054 2093 2341 2362 2405 2520 = 21\*14
WERT *l.*\*321 = \*1
WEST = 1
There lies your way, due West. | *Vio.* Then Westward hoe:   1350
WESTWARD = 1
There lies your way, due West. | *Vio.* Then Westward hoe:   1350
WHAT *l.*16 21 28 51 53 \*55 76 83 95 105 112 \*119 \*158 \*205 228 \*238
\*244 \*273 \*329 \*342 \*365 \*402 \*410 413 421 \*439 445 447 450 \*483 487
506 507 \*509 \*513 518 542 561 572 585 595 606 609 \*623 \*645 654 \*674
693 696 748 \*772 \*786 807 \*836 847 872 913 \*915 993 994 \*1044 1087
1097 \*1111 1123 1124 \*1128 \*1154 \*1270 1293 1308 \*1331 \*1354 1355
1357 1361 1474 1502 1523 1543 1547 1562 1566 \*1602 \*1620 1622 \*1637
1728 \*1739 \*1750 1752 \*1772 1781 1832 1851 1853 1854 1858 \*1933
\*1957 \*1959 1977 \*2001 2003 2035 2039 2079 \*2088 \*2095 2145 2146
2219 2221 \*2256 2261 2268 2271 \*2272 2275 2315 2316 2326 2395 2396
2581 = 84\*46
WHATS = 12\*1
*Vio.* What's shee? | *Cap.* A vertuous maid, the daughter of a Count   85
*Ma.* What's that to th'purpose? | *To.* Why he ha's three thousand
ducates a yeare.   138

WHATS *cont.*
*And.* What's that? | *To.* My Neeces Chamber-maid.  166
*\*An.* Wherefore (sweet-heart?) What's your Meta-|phor?  185
can keepe my hand dry. But what's your iest?  189
*Ol.* What's a drunken man like, foole?  424
*What's to come, is still vnsure.*  750
*Du.* And what's her history? | *Vio.* A blanke my Lord: she neuer told
her loue,  999
You should finde better dealing: what's to do?  1485
*Ol.* Why what's the matter, does he raue?  1530
*1.Off.* What's that to vs, the time goes by: Away.  1884
Cride fame and honor on him: What's the matter? | *1.Offi.* Orsino, this
is that *Anthonio*  2210
*Ol.* What's the matter?  2338
WHATSOEUER = 1*1
*\*And.* As any man in Illyria, whatsoeuer he be, vnder  225
*Youth, whatsoeuer thou art, thou art but a scuruy fellow.*  1670
WHEN *l.*24 41 43 47 60 115 *194 289 *453 *502 *723 *730 *822 930 1198
1348 *1598 2203 2214 2237 2246 2324 2327 2410 2456 2458 2523 2552
2557 2560 2564 2568 2572 = 26*7
WHENCE = 1*1
*Ol.* Whence came you sir? | *\*Vio.* I can say little more then I haue
studied, & that  472
*\*will conster to them whence you come, who you are, and  1269
WHERE *l.*65 *297 *304 306 516 740 *866 907 951 *952 *964 *1064 *1115
*1125 *1252 *1406 1430 *1446 1463 1527 *1679 *1927 1966 2238 2284
2290 2331 2393 2421 = 16*13
WHEREFORE = *3
*\*An.* Wherefore (sweet-heart?) What's your Meta-|phor?  185
*\*To.* Wherefore are these things hid? Wherefore haue  233
WHEREIN = 2*1
Wherein the pregnant enemie does much.  685
*\*loue, wherein by the colour of his beard, the shape of his  849
Wherein *Oliuia* may seeme seruiceable?  2257
WHEREOF = 1
In recompence whereof, he hath married her:  2535
WHERES = 1*2
*\*I speake too loud: Where's *Maluolio*, he is sad, and ciuill,  1525
*\*Good *Maria*, let this fellow be look'd too. Where's my  1583
Yet 'tis not madnesse. Where's *Anthonio* then,  2118
WHERETO = 1
Whereto thy speech serues for authoritie  70
WHET = *1
*\*Vio.* Madam, I come to whet your gentle thoughts | On his behalfe.  1317
WHETHER = 1
*Ol.* Whether my Lord? *Cesario*, Husband, stay.  2301
WHICH *l.*37 *463 *626 *1107 *1205 *1331 1380 1475 1502 1504 *1607
*1661 1732 *1767 1882 *2029 2207 2243 2389 2404 2419 *2474 2520
2529 = 14*10
WHILE = 6*2
*Du.* Stand you a-while aloofe. *Cesario,*  261
*Du.* Seeke him out, and play the tune the while. | *Musicke playes.*  898
*\*make out for him: I frowne the while, and perchance  1075
*To.* Did she see the while, old boy, tell me that.  1389
*\*To.* I wil meditate the while vpon some horrid message | for a
Challenge.  1716
While one would winke: denide me mine owne purse,  2242

WHILE *cont*.

(For so you shall be while you are a man:) 2556

*A great while ago the world begon*, | *hey ho*, *&c*. 2576

WHILES = 1*1

*Whiles you beguile the time, and feed your knowledge 1510

Whiles you are willing it shall come to note, 2144

WHILST = 1

quickly. Ile call sir *Toby* the whilst. 1988

WHIP-STOCKE = *1

*is no Whip-stocke. My Lady has a white hand, and the | Mermidons

are no bottle-ale houses. 728

WHIRLEGIGGE = *1

*and you smile not he's gag'd: and thus the whirlegigge | of time, brings

in his reuenges. 2546

WHISPER = 1

whisper ore a couplet or two of most sage sawes. 1899

WHITE = 1*2

*Vio*. Tis beauty truly blent, whose red and white, 531

*is no Whip-stocke. My Lady has a white hand, and the | Mermidons

are no bottle-ale houses. 728

*My shrowd of white, stuck all with Ew, O prepare it*. 946

WHITHER *see also* whether = *1

*An*. Let me yet know of you, whither you are bound. 620

WHO *l*.74 89 135 151 259 294 398 894 *1110 *1158 *1178 *1269 *1569

1790 2006 *2007 2064 *2085 2109 *2297 2342 2365 = 14*9

WHOERE *see* ere

WHOLE = 1

*Mal*. Ile be reueng'd on the whole packe of you? 2548

WHOM *l*.*627 *646 1108 1274 2222 2281 2282 2394 = 6*2

WHOSE = 6*1

Who shortly also dide: for whose deere loue 89

*sonne should be a foole: whose scull, Ioue cramme with 407

*Vio*. Tis beauty truly blent, whose red and white, 531

For women are as Roses, whose faire flowre 927

Or any taint of vice, whose strong corruption | Inhabites our fraile

blood. 1875

To whose ingrate, and vnauspicious Altars 2269

Where lye my maiden weeds: by whose gentle helpe, 2421

WHY *l*.23 125 139 *188 210 *235 358 446 561 681 *730 1104 *1125 *1126

1134 *1197 1231 *1232 1341 *1413 1512 1530 1546 *1554 *1559 1577

*1600 *1635 1655 *1672 *1792 1832 1943 *2022 2062 *2174 2176 2273

2349 2506 2511 2514 *2541 *2545 = 26*18

WICKEDNESSE = 1

Disguise, I see thou art a wickednesse, 684

WIDE = *1

*not open my lippes so wide as a brissle may enter, in way 298

WIFE = 4

Who ere I woe, my selfe would be his wife. *Exeunt*. 294

Your wife is like to reape a proper man: 1349

More by all mores, then ere I shall loue wife. 2293

To thinke me as well a sister, as a wife, 2483

WIL *l*.*215 *336 *372 *1036 *1181 *1207 *1661 *1711 *1716 = *9

WILDE-FOWLE = 1

*Clo*. What is the opinion of *Pythagoras* concerning | Wilde-fowle? 2035

WILL *see also* hee'l, Ile, shee'l, she'l, twill, wee'l, we'll, you'l, you'le *l*.20

34 41 83 97 102 111 112 *132 *156 *211 *226 270 277 288 *297 299

*311 *318 *342 *371 403 *422 *434 *448 *484 497 *513 *525 534 *536

WILL *cont.*

603 605 *613 *623 *637 *643 *645 *649 655 *665 690 693 753 *759 763
803 *845 *848 *865 *880 *957 *1026 *1132 *1165 *1166 *1167 *1174
*1181 *1183 *1201 *1202 *1204 *1205 *1246 *1269 *1287 *1295 1347
1378 1393 *1394 *1406 *1420 *1425 *1441 *1447 *1460 1469 1509 1634
*1643 1656 1673 *1679 *1691 *1701 *1705 *1706 *1707 *1709 *1711
1733 *1759 *1775 *1786 1799 *1813 1817 *1822 *1824 1834 *1840 *1841
1851 1865 *1919 *1931 *1946 *1954 1964 1982 *1989 *2019 *2043 *2067
2087 *2095 *2098 2102 2145 2148 2185 *2192 *2198 2283 2328 *2369
2435 *2462 2555 2581 = 50*90, 4*3

| | |
|---|---:|
| *Clo. Wit, and't be thy will, put me into good fooling: | 326 |
| Ol. Speake to me, I shall answer for her: your will. | 464 |
| *and euery particle and vtensile labell'd to my will: As, | 538 |
| *her will is, it should be so return'd: If it bee worth stoo- \| ping | 671 |
| Our shewes are more then will: for still we proue | 1007 |
| Seb. I would not by my will haue troubled you, | 1467 |
| Vio. I do assure you tis against my will. | 1828 |

WILLING = 3*1

| | |
|---|---:|
| *willing to keepe in: therefore it charges me in manners, | 624 |
| leaue of her, she is very willing to bid you farewell. | 798 |
| Vnguided, and vnfriended, often proue \| Rough, and vnhospitable. My willing loue, | 1476 |
| Whiles you are willing it shall come to note, | 2144 |

WILLINGLIE = 1

| | |
|---|---:|
| Vio. And I most iocund, apt, and willinglie, | 2288 |

WILLOW = 1

| | |
|---|---:|
| Ol. Why, what would you? \| Vio. Make me a willow Cabine at your gate, | 561 |

WILT *l.*847 *857 1182 1192 1552 *2065 2326 = 5*2

WINDE = 1*2

| | |
|---|---:|
| *Ol. 'Tis in graine sir, 'twill endure winde and wea- \| ther. | 529 |
| *winde vp my watch, or play with my some rich Iewell: | 1076 |
| with hey, ho, the winde and the raine: | 2561 |

WINDIE = *1

| | |
|---|---:|
| *Fa. Still you keepe o'th windie side of the Law: good. | 1683 |

WINDOWES = *1

| | |
|---|---:|
| *Clo. Why it hath bay Windowes transparant as bari- \| cadoes, | 2022 |

WINE = 3

| | |
|---|---:|
| Marian I say, a stoope of wine. | 714 |
| crums. A stope of Wine Maria. | 816 |
| But when I came alas to wine, \| with hey ho, &c. | 2568 |

WING = 1

| | |
|---|---:|
| To. And with what wing the stallion checkes at it? | 1124 |

WINKE = 1

| | |
|---|---:|
| While one would winke: denide me mine owne purse, | 2242 |

WINNES = 1

| | |
|---|---:|
| Fab. This winnes him, Liuer and all. | 1109 |

WISE = 3*2

| | |
|---|---:|
| *wise man. For what saies Quinapalus, Better a witty foole, | 329 |
| *him: Infirmity that decaies the wise, doth euer make the \| better foole. | 368 |
| Euery wise mans sonne doth know. | 745 |
| Vio. This fellow is wise enough to play the foole, | 1272 |
| Fab. Carry his water to th'wise woman. | 1625 |

WISEDOME = 2*1

| | |
|---|---:|
| *Clo. Well, God giue them wisedome that haue it: & | 309 |
| I thinke I saw your wisedome there. | 1254 |

WISEDOME *cont.*

Let thy fayre wisedome, not thy passion sway | In this vnciuill, and
vniust extent                                                                                          1969
WISELY = 2

Lady: make your excuse wisely, you were best.                                      324
For folly that he wisely shewes, is fit;                                                 1279
WISEMEN = *2

*I take these Wisemen, that crow so at these set kinde of                        380
*Clo*. By my troth thou hast an open hand: these Wise-|men             1938
WISEMENS = 1

But wisemens folly falne, quite taint their wit.                                    1280
WISE-MANS = 1

As full of labour as a Wise-mans Art:                                                 1278
WISH = 1

I wish it might, for now I am your foole.                                            1360
WISHD = 1*1

*commended thy yellow stockings, and wish'd to see thee                   1159
*Mal*. And wish'd to see thee crosse garter'd. | *Ol*. Crosse garter'd?   1572
WISHES = *1

*Mal. To the vnknowne belou'd, this, and my good Wishes*:             1105
WIT = 9*4

Onely shape thou thy silence to my wit.                                               113
*more wit then a Christian, or an ordinary man ha's: but I                198
*am a great eater of beefe, and I beleeue that does harme | to my wit.   199
*degree, neither in estate, yeares, nor wit: I haue heard her              219
*Clo*. Wit, and't be thy will, put me into good fooling:                    326
then a foolish wit. God blesse thee Lady.                                           330
*Haue you no wit, manners, nor honestie, but to gabble                   787
*To*. To the gates of Tartar, thou most excellent diuell | of wit.        1209
And to do that well, craues a kinde of wit:                                      1273
But wisemens folly falne, quite taint their wit.                                   1280
And yet when wit and youth is come to haruest,                               1348
Nor wit, nor reason, can my passion hide:                                        1368
I must haue done no lesse with wit and safety.                                   2375
WITCHCRAFT = 1

*Orsino's* enemie. A witchcraft drew me hither:                              2228
WITH = 84*84
WITHALL – 1

*for your opposite hath in him what youth, strength, skill, | and wrath,
can furnish man withall.                                                                  1750
WITHIN = 5*2

*Ma*. I, but you must confine your selfe within the | modest limits of
order.                                                                                             126
And call vpon my soule within the house,                                        563
*one, though I would not haue it grow on my chinne. Is | thy Lady
within?                                                                                            1260
*begger: *Cressida* was a begger. My Lady is within sir. I                 1268
*Mar*. Lo, how hollow the fiend speakes within him;                      1614
*To*. The knaue counterfets well: a good knaue. | *Maluolio within*.   2004
To spight a Rauens heart within a Doue.                                          2287
WITHOUT = 4*5

without booke, & hath all the good gifts of nature.                           144
*Catches without any mitigation or remorse of voice?                      790
*cons State without booke, and vtters it by great swarths.                842
*Clo*. Troth sir, I can yeeld you none without wordes,                    1236
I do not without danger walke these streetes.                                    1493
*shew on't, this shall end without the perdition of soules,                 1806

WITHOUT *cont.*
*Mar.* Thou mightst haue done this without thy berd | and gowne, he
sees thee not.                                                    2049
My loue without retention, or restraint,                         2233
You drew your sword vpon me without cause,                       2350
WITNESSES = 1
If I do feigne, you witnesses aboue | Punish my life, for tainting of my
loue.                                                            2294
WITS = 5*3
*those wits that thinke they haue thee, doe very oft proue        327
come, for sure the man is tainted in's wits.                    1533
*of thy wits, and feare to kill a Woodcocke, lest thou dis-|possesse  2044
I am as well in my wits (foole) as thou art.                    2073
no better in your wits then a foole.                             2075
can to face me out of my wits.                                  2078
*Ol.* Prethee reade i'thy right wits.                           2464
*Clo.* So I do Madona: but to reade his right wits, is to       2465
WITTE = *2
*him a common recreation, do not thinke I haue witte e-|nough     831
*but a cheu'rill gloue to a good witte, how quickely the        1226
WITTES = *2
*Maluolio, Maluolio,* thy wittes the heauens restore: en-|deauour  2080
*paper, I tell thee I am as well in my wittes, as any man in | Illyria.  2091
WITTIE = *1
*it is no matter how wittie, so it bee eloquent, and full of    1422
WITTILY = *1
*that neuer saw pen and inke, very wittily sayd to a Neece      1999
WITTS = 1
*Clo.* Alas sir, how fell you besides your fiue witts?          2071
WITTY = *2
*sir *Toby* would leaue drinking, thou wert as witty a piece | of *Eues*
flesh, as any in Illyria.                                        321
*wise man. For what saies *Quinapalus,* Better a witty foole,    329
WOE = 3
*To, You mistake knight: Accost, is front her, boord | her, woe her,
assayle her.                                                     171
*Vio.* Ile do my best | To woe your Lady: yet a barrefull strife,  292
Who ere I woe, my selfe would be his wife. *Exeunt.*            294
WOER = *1
*knight that you brought in one night here, to be hir woer      134
WOES = 1
It shall become thee well to act my woes:                       276
WOLFE = 1
To fall before the Lion, then the Wolfe?                       1344
WOMAN = 9*1
As I am woman (now alas the day)                                 695
*Du.* What kinde of woman ist? | *Vio.* Of your complection.    913
*Du.* Too old by heauen: Let still the woman take               917
Betweene that loue a woman can beare me, | And that I owe *Oliuia.*  990
As it might be perhaps, were I a woman | I should your Lordship.  997
And that no woman has, nor neuer none                           1375
*can more preuaile in mans commendation with woman, | then report
of valour.                                                      1417
*Fab.* Carry his water to th'wise woman.                        1625
Were you a woman, as the rest goes euen,                        2405
Thou neuer should'st loue woman like to me.                     2434

WOMANS = 4
And all is semblatiue a womans part. 285
You tel her so: Must she not then be answer'd? | *Du.* There is no
womans sides 980
As loue doth giue my heart: no womans heart 983
*Du.* Giue me thy hand, | And let me see thee in thy womans weedes. 2439
WOMBE = 1
Which from the wombe I did participate. 2404
WOMEN = 2
For women are as Roses, whose faire flowre 927
*Vio.* Too well what loue women to men may owe: 994
WOMENS = 2
In womens waxen hearts to set their formes: 687
More longing, wauering, sooner lost and worne, | Then womens are. 922
WONDER = 1 *3
*approach rather to wonder at you, then to heare you. If 493
*I could not with such estimable wonder ouer-farre be- | leeue 636
*To.* *Wonder not, nor admire not in thy minde why I doe call* 1672
And though tis wonder that enwraps me thus, 2117
WONDERFULL = 1 *1
*Fab.* Nothing of that wonderfull promise to read him 1782
Then these two creatures. Which is *Sebastian*? | *Ol.* Most wonderfull. 2389
WONDRED = 1
Which I haue wondred at. In hope it shall not, 2529
WOO *see also* woe = 1
For that I woo, thou therefore hast no cause: 1370
WOODCOCKE = 1 *1
*Fa.* Now is the Woodcocke neere the gin. 1098
*of thy wits, and feare to kill a Woodcocke, lest thou dis- | possesse 2044
WOOES = 1
the Count himselfe here hard by, wooes her. 217
WOORTHIE = *1
*still, the fellow of seruants, and not woorthie to 1162
WORD = 3 *9
*and speaks three or four languages word for word 143
*I am no Fox, but he wil not passe his word for two pence | that you
are no Foole. 372
deliuer thy indignation to him by word of mouth. 826
*Vio.* Why man? | *Clo.* Why sir, her names a word, and to dallie with 1231
*that word, might make my sister wanton: But indeede, 1233
*what you would are out of my welkin, I might say Ele- | ment, but the
word is ouer-worne. *Exit* 1270
*But sir, I will deliuer his Challenge by word of mouth; 1707
*can be none, but by pangs of death and sepulcher: Hob, | nob, is his
word: giu't or take't. 1757
*be as good as my word. Hee will beare you easily, and | raines well. 1841
*Clo.* Vent my folly: He has heard that word of some 1929
*To.* To him in thine owne voyce, and bring me word 2051
WORDES = *2
*Clo.* Troth sir, I can yeeld you none without wordes, 1236
*and wordes are growne so false, I am loath to proue rea- | son with
them. 1237
WORDS = 6 *1
in my hand: my words are as full of peace, as matter. 505
words, may quickely make them wanton. 1229
words are very Rascals, since bonds disgrac'd them. | *Vio.* Thy reason
man? 1234

WORDS *cont.*
\*the bigger, I am indeede not her foole, but hir cor-|rupter of words. 1248
\*Vio. Me thinkes his words do from such passion flye 1894
*Mal.* Sir *Topas.* | *Clo.* Maintaine no words with him good fellow. 2083
But for thee fellow, fellow thy words are madnesse, 2253
WORKE = 2\*3
my reuenge finde notable cause to worke. 846
\*will worke with him, I will plant you two, and let 865
\*Fab. Did not I say he would worke it out, the Curre | is excellent at
faults. 1135
*Ma.* Nay but say true, do's it worke vpon him? | *To.* Like Aqua vite
with a Midwife. 1199
\*An. Nay let him alone, Ile go another way to worke 1949
WORLD = 7\*5
And might not be deliuered to the world 93
\*strangest minde i'th world: I delight in Maskes and Re-|uels
sometimes altogether. 222
\*meane? Is it a world to hide vertues in? I did thinke by 239
\*Clo. Let her hang me: hee that is well hang'de in this | world, needs to
feare no colours. 300
If you will leade these graces to the graue, | And leaue the world no
copie. 534
Tell her my loue, more noble then the world 968
*Ol.* My seruant sir? 'Twas neuer merry world, 1310
O world, how apt the poore are to be proud? 1342
\*and assure thy selfe, there is no loue-Broker in the world, 1416
\*I am affraid this great lubber the World will proue a 1931
\*the world shall know it: Though you haue put mee into 2470
*A great while ago the world begon,* | *hey ho, &c.* 2576
WORME = 1
But let concealment like a worme i'th budde 1001
WORNE = 2
More longing, wauering, sooner lost and worne, | Then womens are. 922
\*what you would are out of my welkin, I might say Ele-|ment, but the
word is ouer-worne. *Exit* 1270
WORSE = 1\*5
\*Mal. Oh ho, do you come neere me now: no worse 1587
\*money for thee, if you tarry longer, I shall giue worse | paiment. 1936
\*Clo. Truely sir, the better for my foes, and the worse | for my friends. 2165
*Clo.* No sir, the worse. | *Du.* How can that be? 2168
\*then the worse for my friends, and the better for my foes. 2175
\*Du. Thou shalt not be the worse for me, there's gold. 2179
WORTH = 4\*3
It may be worth thy paines: for I can sing, 109
That will allow me very worth his seruice. 111
\*her will is, it should be so return'd: If it bee worth stoo-|ping 671
\*Du. She is not worth thee then. What yeares ifaith? 915
But were my worth, as is my conscience firme, 1484
\*quarrell, and hee findes that now scarse to bee worth tal-|king 1815
And to his image, which me thought did promise | Most venerable
worth, did I deuotion. 1882
WOULD *see also* I'de, youl'd, *l.*37 \*148 \*173 176 \*178 \*205 210 \*237 294
\*321 \*455 \*467 507 \*510 559 560 561 600 \*630 653 \*735 \*797 \*818 861
\*962 \*1023 \*1070 \*1135 \*1147 \*1163 \*1230 1243 \*1252 \*1260 1262
\*1264 \*1270 1316 1321 1358 1359 \*1364 1467 1492 1496 \*1585 \*1627
\*1698 \*1818 \*1946 \*1957 \*1981 \*1990 \*2052 \*2053 \*2180 \*2196 2242
\*2256 2262 2289 \*2356 2427 = 26\*40

WOULDST *see also* thoud'st *l.* \*1021 \*1957 = \*2
WRACKE = 2
    Did I redeeme: a wracke past hope he was:     2231
    I shall haue share in this most happy wracke,     2432
WRANGLE = 1
    And wrangle with my reason that perswades me     2128
WRATH = 2
    \*for your opposite hath in him what youth, strength, skill, | and wrath,
    can furnish man withall.     1750
    Who with dagger of lath, in his rage and his wrath,     2109
WREN = \*1
    \*To. Looke where the youngest Wren of mine comes.     1446
WRETCH = 1
    Ol. Will it be euer thus? Vngracious wretch,     1964
WRIT = 2\*1
    Mal. Be not afraid of greatnesse: 'twas well writ.     1561
    \*well as a man in his case may do: has heere writ a letter to     2453
    We had conceiu'd against him. *Maria* writ     2533
WRITE = 3\*4
    Write loyall Cantons of contemned loue,     564
    \*To. Doo't knight, Ile write thee a Challenge: or Ile     825
    \*feelingly personated. I can write very like my Ladie     852
    \*To. Go, write it in a martial hand, be curst and briefe:     1421
    \*in thy inke, though thou write with a Goose-pen, | no matter: about it.     1428
    Ol. Did he write this? | Clo. I Madame.     2478
    Write from it if you can, in hand, or phrase,     2502
WRITING = 1
    Ol. Alas *Maluolio*, this is not my writing,     2515
WRONG = 3\*2
    wrong side may be turn'd outward.     1227
    \*Vio. Who does beguile you? who does do you wrong?     2297
    \*Fab. Reads. By the Lord Madam, you wrong me, and     2469
    Mal. Madam, you haue done me wrong, | Notorious wrong.     2497
WRONGED = \*1
    \*Mal. Sir *Topas*, neuer was man thus wronged, good     2014
WRONGS = \*1
    \*nature the wrongs are thou hast done him, I knowe not:     1740
Y = \*4
    \*Ma. A good lenton answer: I can tell thee where y     304
    \*To. Why how now my bawcock? how dost y chuck? | Mal. Sir.     1635
    \*Fa. A good note, that keepes you from the blow of y | (Law     1674
    \*Seb. I would be free from thee. What wouldst y now?     1957
YARE = 2\*1
    Ol. Go too, y'are a dry foole: Ile no more of you: be-|sides you grow
    dis-honest.     333
    Y'are seruant to the Count *Orsino* youth.     1312
    \*be yare in thy preparation, for thy assaylant is quick, skil-|full, and
    deadly.     1743
YDLE = \*1
    \*Mal. Go hang your selues all: you are ydle shallowe     1645
YE *l.* \*647 \*789 \*810 \*1032 = \*4
YEARE = 1\*1
    Ma. What's that to th'purpose? | To. Why he ha's three thousand
    ducates a yeare.     138
    \*Ma. I, but hee'l haue but a yeare in all these ducates:     140
YEARES = 4\*2
    The Element it selfe, till seuen yeares heate,     32

TWELFTH NIGHT

YEARES *cont.*
*degree, neither in estate, yeares, nor wit: I haue heard her          219
*Du.* She is not worth thee then. What yeares ifaith?                  915
*that giue fooles money, get themselues a good re-|port, after
foureteene yeares purchase.                                           1939
*Vio.* And dide that day when *Viola* from her birth | Had numbred
thirteene yeares.                                                     2410
That day that made my sister thirteene yeares.                       2414
YEE *l.*788 = *1
YEELD = *1
*Clo.* Troth sir, I can yeeld you none without wordes,               1236
YEELDE = *1
*Fab.* You must needes yeelde your reason, Sir An-|drew?             1385
YEERES = 4
For they shall yet belye thy happy yeeres,                           281
*Ol.* Of what personage, and yeeres is he?                           450
*Vio.* About your yeeres my Lord.                                    916
And grew a twentie yeeres remoued thing                             2241
YELLOW = 4*6
And with a greene and yellow melancholly,                           1003
*commended thy yellow stockings, and wish'd to see thee             1159
*that my Lady loues me. She did commend my yellow                   1170
*strange, stout, in yellow stockings, and crosse Garter'd,          1175
*in yellow stockings, and 'tis a colour she abhorres, and           1203
*beleeue such impossible passages of grossenesse. Hee's in | yellow
stockings.                                                          1451
*Mal.* Not blacke in my minde, though yellow in my                  1548
*Mal.* Remember who commended thy yellow stock-|ings.               1569
*Ol.* Thy yellow stockings?                                         1571
To put on yellow stockings, and to frowne                           2508
YEOMAN = 1
married the yeoman of the wardrobe.                                 1056
YES = 2*2
*Mal.* Yes, and shall do, till the pangs of death shake             367
*Clo.* Yes by *S.*(aint) Anne, and Ginger shall bee hotte y'th | mouth
too.                                                                813
*Vio.* Yes being kept together, and put to vse.                    1263
Yes Nightingales answere Dawes.                                    1558
YESTERDAY = *1
*heard my Lady talke of it yesterday: and of a foolish             133
YET = 24*15
Doth oft close in pollution: yet of thee                           101
*the degree of my betters, & yet I will not compare with | an old man. 226
For they shall yet belye thy happy yeeres,                         281
*Vio.* Ile do my best | To woe your Lady: yet a barrefull strife,  292
*Ma.* Yet you will be hang'd for being so long absent,             311
*Clo.* He is but mad yet Madona, and the foole shall | looke to the
madman.                                                            431
*Mal.* Not yet old enough for a man, nor yong enough               451
*Ol.* Are you a Comedian? | *Vio.* No my profound heart: and yet (by
the verie                                                          477
*Ol.* Yet you began rudely. What are you? | What would you?        506
Yet I suppose him vertuous, know him noble,                        551
A gracious person; But yet I cannot loue him:                      555
What is your Parentage? | *Vio.* Aboue my fortunes, yet my state is well: 572
*Ol.* What is your Parentage? | Aboue my fortunes, yet my state is well; 585
*An.* Let me yet know of you, whither you are bound.               620

257

YET *cont.*

| | |
|---|---|
| *me, was yet of many accounted beautiful: but thogh | 635 |
| *that, yet thus farre I will boldly publish her, shee | 637 |
| *am yet so neere the manners of my mother, that vpon the | 648 |
| And all the brothers too: and yet I know not. | 1011 |
| *Fa. Though our silence be drawne from vs with cars, \| yet peace. | 1079 |
| *and yet to crush this a little, it would bow to mee, for e-\|uery | 1147 |
| *starres be praised. Heere is yet a postscript. *Thou canst* | 1177 |
| And yet when wit and youth is come to haruest, | 1348 |
| *Ol.* Yet come againe: for thou perhaps mayst moue | 1379 |
| *the diuels of hell be drawne in little, and Legion himselfe \| possest | |
| him, yet Ile speake to him. | 1608 |
| *Ant.* One sir, that for his loue dares yet do more | 1833 |
| Yet liuing in my glasse: euen such, and so | 1901 |
| *To.* I dare lay any money, twill be nothing yet. *Exit* | 1916 |
| *there be any law in Illyria: though I stroke him first, yet | 1951 |
| *as lustrous as Ebony: and yet complainest thou of ob-\|struction? | 2024 |
| Yet 'tis not madnesse. Where's *Anthonio* then, | 2118 |
| Yet there he was, and there I found this credite, | 2120 |
| Yet doth this accident and flood of Fortune, | 2125 |
| Or else the Ladies mad; yet if 'twere so, | 2130 |
| Yet when I saw it last, it was besmear'd | 2203 |
| *Anthonio* neuer yet was Theefe, or Pyrate, | 2226 |
| If this be so, as yet the glasse seemes true, | 2431 |
| and yet alas, now I remember me, | 2446 |
| *yet haue I the benefit of my senses as well as your Ladie-\|ship. | 2472 |
| He hath not told vs of the Captaine yet, | 2551 |

YEW *see* ew

YFAITH = 1*2

| | |
|---|---|
| *And.* Heere comes the foole yfaith. | 716 |
| *Queubus:* 'twas very good yfaith: I sent thee sixe pence | 725 |
| *Clo.* Well held out yfaith: No, I do not know you, | 1923 |

YIELD *see* yeeld, yeelde

YOND = 1*2

| | |
|---|---|
| *Mal.* Madam, yond young fellow sweares hee will | 434 |
| Get thee to yond same soueraigne crueltie: | 967 |
| *selues into stitches, follow me; yond gull *Maluolio* is tur-\|ned | 1448 |

YONDER = 1*1

| | |
|---|---|
| *comming downe this walke, he has beene yonder i'the | 1033 |
| *Fabian* can scarse hold him yonder. | 1800 |

YONG = 3*3

| | |
|---|---|
| *Mal.* Not yet old enough for a man, nor yong enough | 451 |
| My life vpon't, yong though thou art, thine eye | 909 |
| *of the yong Gentleman, giues him out to be of good | 1702 |
| *Ant.* Put vp your sword: if this yong Gentleman | 1829 |
| *To.* Come sir, I will not let you go. Come my yong | 1954 |
| When your yong Nephew *Titus* lost his legge; | 2214 |

YONGER = 1

| | |
|---|---|
| *Du.* Then let thy Loue be yonger then thy selfe, | 925 |

YOU *see also* y'are = 243*203

YOUL = 1*2

| | |
|---|---|
| *To.* Fie, that you'l say so: he playes o'th Viol-de-gam-\|boys, | 142 |
| You'l nothing Madam to my Lord, by me: | 1353 |
| *To.* You'l finde it otherwise I assure you: therefore, if | 1748 |

YOULD = 1

| | |
|---|---|
| *Ant.* Would youl'd pardon me: | 1492 |

YOULE = *1
*Fa. We shall haue a rare Letter from him; but you'le | not deliuer't.                     1436
YOUNG = *4
*Mar. Madam, there is at the gate, a young Gentle- | man, much desires
to speake with you.                                                                        392
*Ma I know not (Madam) 'tis a faire young man, and | well attended.                        396
*Mal. Madam, yond young fellow sweares hee will                                            434
*Ser. Madame, the young Gentleman of the Count                                             1579
YOUNGEST = *1
*To. Looke where the youngest Wren of mine comes.                                          1446
YOUR l.56 59 61 114 *123 124 126 153 *183 *185 189 193 *196 *215 260
293 308 319 324 353 *356 *362 *371 *375 399 *404 *443 464 *482 *485
*492 497 *499 500 *502 *503 *510 *513 516 522 *523 *524 *550 559 562
566 572 575 579 580 583 585 597 *615 *617 619 641 642 644 *663 *664
*667 *672 741 *789 *795 *796 *815 821 *853 861 *876 *892 912 914 916
978 998 1086 1088 1092 *1106 *1144 *1253 1254 1288 *1289 1291 *1301
1306 1308 1309 1314 *1317 1319 1329 *1334 1349 1350 1352 1360 *1385
*1386 *1398 *1399 *1400 *1403 *1447 1468 1474 1479 *1487 *1510 1512
1513 1514 1516 *1531 1557 1581 *1645 *1646 *1714 *1723 *1730 *1749
*1750 *1768 1787 *1796 1807 1829 1846 1847 1860 *1925 *1945
1947 *1955 2071 2075 2108 2141 *2174 2183 2184 *2192 *2195 *2198
2214 2229 2279 2281 2319 2321 *2340 2350 2373 2387 2406 *2461 *2471
*2472 *2473 2486 2487 2488 2489 2492 2501 2503 = 104*77
YOURS = 3*4
*selfe: for what is yours to bestowe, is, not yours to re- | serue.                        483
*yours; therefore I shall craue of you your leaue,                                         617
An. I hope sir, you are, and I am yours.                                                   1286
Vio. And he is yours, and his must needs be yours:                                         1313
*Which you knew none of yours. What might you think?                                       1331
YOURSELFE see selfe
YOURSELUES see selues
YOUTH = 11*11
Therefore good youth, addresse thy gate vnto her,                                          264
She will attend it better in thy youth,                                                    277
Of great estate, of fresh and stainlesse youth;                                            552
If that the youth will come this way to morrow,                                            603
*the youth of the Counts was to day with my Lady, she is                                   828
Y'are seruant to the Count Orsino youth.                                                   1312
Be not affraid good youth, I will not haue you,                                            1347
And yet when wit and youth is come to haruest,                                             1348
Vio. By innocence I sweare, and by my youth,                                               1373
*Fab. Shee did shew fauour to the youth in your sight,                                     1398
*the youth into dumbenesse: this was look'd for at your                                    1403
*valour. Challenge me the Counts youth to fight with him                                   1414
*the youth to an answer. I thinke Oxen and waine-ropes                                     1439
*Fab. And his opposit the youth beares in his visage no | great presage
of cruelty.                                                                                1443
*For youth is bought more oft, then begg'd, or borrow'd.                                   1524
Youth, whatsoeuer thou art, thou art but a scuruy fellow.                                  1670
*in the youth: he will finde it comes from a Clodde-pole.                                  1706
*the Gentleman (as I know his youth will aptly receiue it)                                  1709
*for your opposite hath in him what youth, strength, skill, | and wrath,
can furnish man withall.                                                                   1750
*Ant. Let me speake a little. This youth that you see | (heere,                            1879
Three monthes this youth hath tended vpon mee,                                             2254
Hath newly past, betweene this youth, and me.                                              2317

YOUTHS = 3*1
   Me thinkes I feele this youths perfections     592
   *Youths a stuffe will not endure.*     753
   *And.* That youth's a rare Courtier, raine odours, wel.     1300
   *I haue his horse to take vp the quarrell, I haue perswaded | him the
   youths a diuell.     1809
YRON = *1
   *souldier put vp your yron: you are well flesh'd: Come | on.     1955
YSICKLE = *1
   *like an ysickle on a Dutchmans beard, vnlesse you do re- | deeme     1407
YTH = *1
   *Clo.* Yes by *S.*(aint) Anne, and Ginger shall bee hotte y'th | mouth
   too.     813
ZANIES = 1
   fooles, no better then the fooles Zanies.     381
    & *l.*144 *155 *213 214 *226 *307 *309 *335 *404 *473 *492 *540 612
   931 *1172 *1657 *1686 *1784 *1811 *1986 *1994 *2149 *2369 = 4*19
&C *l.*2565 2567 2569 2571 2573 2575 2577 = 7
1OFF = 4
1OFFI = 1
2OFF = 2*1